M. C.

200 YEARS OF
SPORT
IN AMERICA

CREATIVE DIRECTOR
David Boss

EDITORS
Jeremy Friedlander
John Wiebusch

DESIGNER
Amy Yutani

ART RESEARCH CONSULTANT
Enid Klass

200 YEARS OF SPORT IN AMERICA

A PAGEANT OF A NATION AT PLAY

BY WELLS TWOMBLY

A RUTLEDGE BOOK

McGRAW-HILL BOOK COMPANY
New York   St. Louis   San Francisco   London
Dusseldorf   Mexico   Toronto

Publisher: Fred R. Sammis
Creative Director: David Boss
Editors: Jeremy Friedlander,
    John Wiebusch
Contributing Editors: Dwight Chapin,
    Fred Gregory, John Sammis,
    Stanley Saplin, Adolph Suehsdorf
Editorial Consultants: Larry Bruser,
    Juliana Goldman, Harley Tinkham
Editorial Staff: Tom Bennett,
    Patricia Cross, Earlene Doran,
    Tom Patty, Rick Smith

Designer: Amy Yutani
Art Research Consultant: Enid Klass
Production Staff: Patrick McKee,
    Rob Meneilly, Kathleen Oldenburg

Prepared by National Football
League Properties, Inc. Produced by
Rutledge Books, a division of Arcata
Consumer Products Corp. Published 1976
by McGraw-Hill Book Company.

Library of Congress Cataloging in Publication Data

Twombly, Wells.
    200 years of sport in America.

    1. Sports—United States—History.   I. Title.
GV583.T84   796'.0973   76-14973
ISBN 0-07-065640-1

Printed in Italy by Mondadori, Verona.

Dedicated with love and appreciation
To Peggy Zera Twombly
The freshman girl who married the sports
editor of the campus daily, who bore
four children in different parts of the
nation and who endured the cross-country
journey like pioneer women of the
nineteenth century—with tears,
but not complaints.
And to Wes, Scott, Jason, and Dale
Twombly, who joined her along the way.

CONTENTS

Picture Credits

ond Charles Fight, by Fletcher Martin. Oil on canvas. Courtesy *Sports Illustrated,* © Time, Inc., New York.

224   *Roger Bannister, ca.1954,* by Howard Brodie, 1966. Pencil drawing. From the collection of David Boss, Los Angeles.

225   *Indoor Games,* by John Groth. Pen and wash sketch. Courtesy the artist.

226-227   *The Milers,* by Jim Jonson. Watercolor and pastel. Courtesy the artist.

229   *Ice Boating at Red Bank, New Jersey,* by Stanley Meltzoff. Oil on canvas. Courtesy the artist.

230   *Bernie Parent, Philadelphia Flyers.* Institutional newspaper advertisement. Courtesy John Wanamaker, Inc., Philadelphia.

231   *Gordie Howe, Detroit Red Wings,* by Harvey Schmidt, 1964. Acrylics illustration. Courtesy Timkin Roller Bearing Corporation, Canton, Ohio.

233   *Ebbetts Field Being Demolished, May 5, 1960.* Photograph courtesy Paul Stillwell.

234   *Willie Mays,* by Fred Kaplan, 1964. Courtesy the photographer.

235   *Casey Stengel,* by Rhoda Sherbell. Resin sculpture. Courtesy the artist.

237   *Casey Stengel,* by Paul Conrad, 1975. Editorial cartoon. Copyright, Los Angeles Times. Reprinted with permission.

238   *Fate Takes a Hand,* by Seymour Leichman. Lithograph. Courtesy the artist.

239   *Cover of Jock Magazine, Vol. 1, No. 1.* Courtesy of Mickey Herskowitz, Houston.

240   *Ben Hogan, 1940.* Photograph courtesy World Golf Hall of Fame, Pinehurst, North Carolina.

241   *The Fifteenth at Cypress, Monterey, California,* by Donald Moss. Oil and acrylic on canvas. Courtesy *Sports Illustrated,* © Time, Inc., New York.

243   *Arnold Palmer,* by Fred Kaplan. Courtesy the photographer.

244   *Jack Nicklaus, the Deadly Stroke,* by Donald Moss. Acrylic and oil on canvas. Courtesy *Sports Illustrated,* © Time, Inc., New York.

245   *The Fifteenth at Oakmont Country Club,* by Donald Moss. Acrylic on canvas. Courtesy *Sports Illustrated,* © Time, Inc., New York.

246   *Colts Versus Giants, NFL Championship, 1958,* by Robert Riger. Courtesy Pro Football Hall of Fame, Canton, Ohio.

248   *Big Daddy,* by Daniel Schwartz. Oil on canvas. Courtesy the artist.

249   *Johnny Unitas,* by Merv Corning, 1975. Watercolor. Courtesy the artist.

250   *Lamar Hunt Inducted Into the Pro Football Hall of Fame,* by Rod Hanna, 1972. Courtesy Kansas City Chiefs.

252   *Paul Hornung, ca. 1964,* by Merv Corning, 1969. Watercolor. Courtesy National Football League Properties, Inc., Los Angeles.

253   *Vince Lombardi,* by David A. Leffel, 1973. Oil on masonite. Courtesy the artist.

254   *Jim Brown Versus the Giants,* by Daniel Rubin, 1964. Courtesy the photographer.

256   *Joe Namath,* by LeRoy Neiman, 1968. Oil and acrylic on canvas. Courtesy the artist.

258   *Lakers Versus Celtics,* by James F. Flores. Courtesy the photographer.

259   *Basketball Players,* by Elaine deKooning. Oil on canvas. Courtesy the artist.

262-263   *Thoroughbred and Jockey,* by Bob Peak, 1974. Acrylic and oil on canvas. Courtesy the artist.

264   *Billie Jean King.* Photograph courtesy NBC Television Sports, New York.

266   *Hang Gliders over Torrance Beach, California,* by W. A. Allen, 1974. Courtesy Aerial Underground News Service, Culver City, California.

267   A. *William B. Nash Memorial Medal,* by Joe Brown, 1953. Silver. Courtesy the artist.

     B. *Hawaii Pop Rock Festival Poster,* by Victor Moscoso. Photographic montage and hand lettering. Courtesy the artist.

269   *UCLA Basketball Coach John Wooden.* Photograph courtesy UCLA Athletic Department, Los Angeles.

270   *Pasadena Rose Bowl.* Photograph courtesy Tournament of Roses Committee, Pasadena, California.

271   *O. J. Simpson,* by James F. Flores, 1968. Courtesy the photographer.

273   *Peanuts,* by Charles Schulz, 1974. Copyright United Feature Syndicate, Inc., New York. Reprinted with permission.

274-275   *Forest Hills,* by Donald Moss. Oil on canvas. Courtesy the artist and Ferons, New York.

277   *Controversial Cassius, May 25, 1965.* Photograph courtesy Wide World Photos, New York.

278   *The Passion of Muhammad Ali,* by Carl Fischer, 1968, based on a concept by George Lois. Courtesy the photographer.

279   *George Foreman, 1968 Olympics Heavyweight Champion,* by Robert Gunn, 1975. Acrylic on gesso. Courtesy Sears, Roebuck and Co., Chicago.

280   *Hank Aaron's 715th Home Run,* April 8, 1974. Photograph courtesy United Press International, New York.

282   *The Way It's Spozed To Be, 11:30 A.M.,* by Ron Kleenmann, 1972. Acrylics and oil on canvas. Courtesy Louis K. Meisel Gallery, New York.

283   *Motocross* by J. Richard Forbes. Courtesy the photographer.

285   Mark Spitz photograph courtesy Citizens Athletic Foundation, Los Angeles.

286   *Fisheye View of the Astrodome,* by Ed Mahan, 1973. Courtesy the Philadelphia Eagles.

287   *Louisiana Superdome.* Photograph courtesy the New Orleans Saints.

Excerpt from *Mr. Lincoln's Army* by Bruce Catton. Copyright 1951 by Bruce Catton. Reprinted by permission of Doubleday & Company, Inc.

Excerpts from *Baseball* by Robert Smith. Copyright 1947 by Robert Smith. Reprinted by permission of Harold Matson Co., Inc.

Excerpt from *Collected Poems* by Vachel Lindsay, "John L Sullivan, The Boston Strong Boy" (21 line selection). Reprinted with permission of Macmillan Publishing Co. Inc. Copyright 1920 by Macmillan Publishing Co., Inc renewed 1948 by Elizabeth C. Lindsay.

Shield of Athletes, by R. Tait McKenzie, 1928.

PREFACE

"When I was a small boy in Kansas,
a friend of mine and I went fishing
and as we sat there in the warmth
of a summer afternoon on a river bank
we talked about what we wanted
to do when we grew up. I told him that
I wanted to be a real major
league baseball player, a genuine
professional like Honus Wagner. My
friend said that he'd like to be
president of the United States.
Neither of us got our wish."

—Dwight D. Eisenhower, the thirty-fourth
president of the United States

This volume is an impressionistic look at sports in America. It makes no claim to being a definitive history; it does seek to capture the spirit of American sport and begin to define its importance in American life.

Of course, the spirit of American sport won't be found in an historical vacuum. Those who have tried such an approach have given us pomp and pretension rather than insight—the "World Serious" and Roman numeral designations for Super Bowls. (What else is the latter but an anachronism used to suggest timelessness, history's stamp of approval for a spectacle that is, whatever its roots, essentially of our time?)

More than a window to history, sport, like other diversions, has been a shade obscuring it. Sports fans have tended to stay in their houses of the present and not only draw the blinds but in that dark and dangerous atmosphere subject themselves to the glare of today through television. It's bad for the vision, and we're in danger of becoming a nation of sports myopics.

Woody Hayes, the Ohio State football coach and extemporaneous lecturer on military history, sees the battles of Ancient Greece re-enacted on the playing field at Columbus, Ohio, on autumn Saturday afternoons. He may have a point. But most fans watch football to escape history rather than to relive it. Sports as escapism: the case has been made often enough not to require reiteration here. And yet even there lies one very real if obvious historical lesson about us. We have been escaping to sport, probably more vigorously than many peoples, for over 200 years. The pleasure of watching the sports spectacle has become more and more desirable and attainable, until today it is considered almost a necessity. Some Americans get their television sets even before a telephone, and not only for Star Trek and the soaps.

So there are historical insights to be found in even a casual perusal of our sports past. The trick is to be careful, to see sports not as a short-cut but an interesting, diversionary, and pretty—if not panoramic—route through history. The prospector through sports history will find his share of little treasures; he need not dabble with the fool's gold of great historical truths. Those are not for sportsmen anyway. Our purpose is to look back on some of the ways we as a nation enjoyed ourselves, and it would be contradictory and self-defeating not to enjoy such a retrospective.

The broad historical contexts the author adopts to facilitate this little tour of our sporting past—the Pastoral, Passionate, Golden, and Electronic ages—should not be mistaken for sweeping historical theses. They are merely sets for recreating a series of dramatic episodes. They seem to work well for those episodes presented here; they may not for other equally entertaining and historically significant episodes of the same ages that are not reported here.

One might, for example, find more lead than gold in that era (roughly between the two world wars) here characterized as the Golden Age. With the Depression this period became a time of desperation, for which there were more unhappy outlets than the hero worship covered in this book's rendering of the age. Six-day bicycle races were one; grimly slashed salaries another. There were false idols as well as faithful ones—Primo Carnera as well as Joe Louis. And it was not just an age of culmination, as "Golden" implies, but of tentative beginnings. The National Football League was just starting to glimpse the glitter of its golden future. And not until the end of the Second World War did the National Hockey League take the steps to encourage its potentially free-flowing game to begin to realize its potential.

This book's episodic restaging of the melodramas of the Ruths, Rocknes, et al., de-emphasizes the other aspects of the age, at least partly because the Golden heroes did just that themselves. As herein presented, the Golden Age, like the other sections, is less historical hypothesis than dramatic interpretation, a style for the time.

There is no pretense here at creating an encyclopedic history. You will read about Babe Ruth but you will not read about Ty Cobb. You will read about Vince Lombardi but you will not read about Jim Brown. You will read about Bill Tilden but not about Jimmy Connors. You will read about Hank Aaron but not Willie Mays. You will read about Man o' War but not Secretariat. You will read about Johnny Weissmuller but not Mark Spitz. And so on. Choices were made not for arbitrary reasons but because particular individuals (or events) best symbolized their sport, because some achievements have made more indelible impressions than others. You may not always agree with the choices that were made—or even with the reasons why people are written about in this book—but the editors believe the colors of the book make a complete canvas.

Perhaps it is now becoming clear that this sports history book attempts to succeed in a way similar to that of the theater of sport itself—as dramatic spectacle as well as factual exhibit. Re-creating the spectacle is one way of beginning to pose the most historically pertinent sports question of all—what is the appeal of these games? There is a multitude of marvelous answers to that timeless question. It would do justice neither to sports nor to history to suggest that there are any fewer. This book seeks to provide a few of them, and thereby capture its share of that elusive treasure, the spirit of sports in America.

A Note from the Designers

It is not surprising that the artist has been attracted to sport. The color and action—the spectacle—presents an attractive challenge to the creative personality. Some of the nation's most notable talents have concentrated their skill and mastery on capturing the fleeting precision of the human form engaged in sports. Artists such as Eakins, Homer, Remington, Bellows, and Sheeler have used sports to create masterpieces of American art.

In the commercial area of magazine and book illustration, N. C. Wyeth, Rockwell, Riggs, Helck, Schwartz, Peak, and Moss are but a few of the many people who have interpreted sport with the brilliance of the legitimate painter. The commercial print area is, in fact, the most imaginative and profuse producer of sports art. Over the decades there has been a multitude of publications, both crude and sophisticated in their design and execution, that have succeeded in portraying the vitality of games. Tobacco and, later, chewing gum cards rank as the most banal and disposable form of sports art, yet they tell us quite a bit about our sports culture. Today, they are the object of countless collectors, and many period pieces command staggering prices in the market.

Sports photography has traditionally been utilized as a complement to the written word. Then, following World War II, the great technological advances in the sciences of film and camera manufacture gave the photographer the tools that allowed him greater interpretive freedom. The 35 mm. camera, with its vast selection of lenses, and the availability of economical rolls of fast film allowed photographers to see their subjects in a fresher, more creative manner. The result was photographs that capture the color of sport.

In designing this book the editors consciously avoided creating just another picture book of sports history. Instead, they attempted to display the pageantry of American sport over the last two centuries, as captured by the great artists and photographers and all the creators, many of them anonymous, of folk art and commercial graphics. Yet in the final analysis more deserving graphics have been omitted than included in these pages. This book contains only a sample of the artwork inspired by America's favorite pastime.

The talented few who managed to solidify temporal events through art saw not only pageantry and pleasure in sport but the beauty of people alive with activity. Their work shows that when man achieves his greatest athletic moment, he creates art.

THE PASTORAL AGE
1776-1865

"... And down the stretch came the mighty American Eclipse, as close to living flame as a horse can be, throwing great clods of dirt in his beaten rival's face."

—Darcy's American Sporting Journal, 1823

After the Hunt, by William M. Harnett, 1885.

1 Impure Passions

In his holy zeal to refashion society to be as stern, joyless, and far removed from Anglo-Catholic splendor as possible, the Puritan came to the New World with little revealed love for sport and recreation. Such nonsense as card playing, hawking, hunting, boating, racing, and racquet games were the frivolous playthings of royalty, the loathed establishment, which had strayed far from God by indulging in such pastimes. There would be none of this in Puritan New England.

Try as he might, the Puritan could not suppress man's sporting urge. In his attempts he became a devout practitioner of the double standard. The Puritan kept a copy of the King James version of the Bible under his pillow, but he banned the King James Book of Sport, which openly encouraged an afternoon of recreation following divine services on Sunday. That was the hated, oppressive Anglican way, which the Puritan had sworn to destroy. And so Cotton Mather condemned "the most abominable Impieties of Uncleanness, Drunkenness, and a Lewd, Rude Extravagant sort of Behaviour" as found in the pursuit of sport and pleasure, and then slipped away to go fishing.

Tavern games and card playing were forbidden in some places. In Connecticut it also was against the law to kiss one's wife in public. The records for 1693 of Windham Borough in eastern Connecticut show that Nathaniel Reed was fined twelve shillings and sentenced to six hours in the stocks for "playing ball on the Sabbath after being thrice warned against such an abomination." Apparently, either he was playing alone or his teammates were let go with a warning, since he was the only man convicted. Despite such deterrents, there is evidence that wayward Puritans engaged in some hell-raising at least on Sunday, their only day of rest in an otherwise drab week.

Besides, foreign elements, namely the Scotch-Irish,

were moving into the area, and they were not governed by the all-encompassing restrictions of the Puritan ethic. By enjoying themselves on the Sabbath, they did not feel that they were profaning but on the contrary only following God's commandment. They ignored Governor William Bradford when he exhorted the citizens of Massachusetts to avoid pitching and batting in the streets, "wasting time at stooleball and other such sports."

Although the Puritan had support from the Quaker, who disliked "needless vain sports and pastimes" and the Dutch Reformed Church in New York, which abhorred "bowling and kolf," the Theocrats were fighting a losing battle. They continued to rail about the stupidity of wasting one's time at play when there were such serious tasks to be accomplished as serving God, clearing land, and routing Indians. Sport permeated every level of American society in the colonies and, later, the states. The settlers had to work to survive, but they soon discovered that psychologically they had to play in order to accept the drudgery of the work. The American rationale that sport was a necessary steam valve began long before the first carton of tea struck the surface of Boston harbor.

The Middle Atlantic colonies were more tolerant of recreation than New England, though here, as in the South, lower classes were not to engage in sports favored by the gentry and the aristocracy. All groups adored cockfighting and bullbaiting, but only gentlemen were expected to race horses. One James Bullock, a tailor, was fined one hundred pounds of tobacco and a cask of wine by a Virginia judge in the early 1700s because he had raced a horse.

In the South, black slaves boxed bare knuckled against men from other plantations. And there was a growing class of poor whites who would engage in almost any activity in the hope of earning even a small amount of money.

The common man also hunted and fished, sometimes even when he didn't have to. Long Island was a paradise for game. Wealthy men staged regular expeditions from

New York City, one of which resulted in the death of a local woman in 1734. She was wearing an orange-brown waistcoat and she was mistaken for a fox. The gentleman who shot her dead was described as being in a "melancholy condition." He advised other men of his class who were looking for sport to go farther west, where their mistakes might not be so costly.

The pre-Revolutionary tavern was the rustic version of the community center and the sport arena, complete with a foul "rhum" the natives called "Kill-Devil." Shooting matches, a favorite amusement of the agricultural set in both the North and the South, were held outside the local tavern among contestants from all over the region. As long as wild birds were plentiful, hunters used live birds in their turkey shoots. The riflemen would attempt to sever a bird's head from its neck. These were grim and bloody times and the sports reflected the participants' insensitive attitude toward pain and suffering.

At five A. M. farmers would gather at the tavern, and after fortifying themselves against the rigors of the hunt, they would spread out in a wide ring over the countryside. Then they would close in, driving ahead of them whatever game was trapped in their midst. They would converge around noon on a green behind the tavern and engage in an orgy of slaughter. "Every critter would be driven down and killed . . . bears, deer, beavers, foxes, hares, wild cats, squirrels, wolves, and sometimes pigges gone to the wild state," said one source. "The idea was to rid the countryside of vermin and to provide sport for the farmers. So hated was the wolf that nothing diminished his torture before his death. Often wolves were captured and thrown into pens where they would be baited by large and surly dogs."

Safe in the knowledge that a great deal of food and drink would be vended over their bars on hot and busy afternoons, the tavern owners were generous with their prizes, offering a new rifle to the winner of a bear shoot. There usually was a billiard table in the tavern and a cocking pit in the door yard. Cockfighting was more

popular in the South than in the North, where the climate was less suited to the breeding of hardy fighting stock.

A traveler through Virginia discovered that both planters and common laborers were engaged in backgammon or ninepins in the early morning hours and that the noise did not abate until very late in the evening, when wrestling matches—freestyle, of course—would break out on the great floor in front of the fireplace. Occasionally, skulls would be splintered and blood would gush. "During the course of one full day of sport," wrote the traveler, "the tavern-keeper served seventy-four bowls of rhum punch, one hundred and thirty-two bottles of wine and eight bowls of a suspicious liquid he said was brandy."

The Dutch taverns of what had once been New Amsterdam had their own exuberant style. In the yards adjoining the bars, the patrons played at *kaetzen,* a rude form of handball in which a horsehair-filled ball was bounced against a post or a specially erected board fence. On certain days women would play the game, using racquets and playing by rules vaguely similar to the modern sport of squash. There was no tavern in all of New York that did not have a wooden or stone surface for the playing of skittles, the Dutch passion for bowling having been passed to the English. Here, too, sadism toward animals had its part. A cat would be suspended in a fragile cage above the bowling lane, and for a small entry fee each contestant took a turn at hurling a king pin. The winning blow broke the barrel and sent a psychotic cat skittering across the grass of lower Manhattan.

The Dutch celebrated their holidays loudly and with far less reverence than their Anglo-Saxon neighbors. On Shrovetide, during holy week, they stretched a goose or a hare on a rope across a road. The creature's neck was smeared with grease, making it a slippery prize for the young men of the villages who sprinted by on horseback trying to pull it down. If a contestant slipped and missed, he was doused with buckets of water from townspeople lining the course. Sometimes the riders came away with the animal's bloody head in their hands and nothing

The native American Indians enjoyed games of competition that tested their skill and courage. A mid-nineteenth century Canadian artist, Paul Kane, painted a spirited horse race on the high plains. E. C. Coates's interesting study of a primitive hockey game suggests a winter version of lacrosse modified to fit the boundaries of a frozen pond.

more. In later years the event was transferred to narrow streams and the goose or hare suspended over the water. If the sportsman missed the prize, he took a dunking.

In his final hours as governor of New Amsterdam, Peter Stuyvesant signed a bill prohibiting the game. It did no good. After the English converted New Amsterdam into New York, the Dutch citizens continued to "pull the goose and grab the hare." The new government passed legislation against it only to see Anglo-Saxons join the Dutch at their Shrovetide ritual.

This may have been a debasement of sport, but the English settlers accepted it well. They were less pleased by New Amsterdam's winter sports. In the old country the Briton tended to stay inside during the colder months. Across the channel in Holland his robust continental neighbors were skating on ice-locked canals and sleigh riding on frozen plains. Such vigor in the face of winter's harshness puzzled the British.

"The Dutch are a most unusual breed," wrote Alexander Newbridge in 1748. "They construct sleighs in the most fanciful fashion, some of them in the shape of swans and other water birds. They race them on the frozen ponds and they pretend that winter is not a season of cold and death. They also erect booths on the ice and spend endless hours skating and quaffing warm liquor out of pewter cups. Their penchant for racing on even the most fragile of ice quickens the blood. They fly with great swiftness, mindless of the dangers to themselves and their horses."

Moreover, the Dutch had stolen a game from the Scottish called kolf. It was played with crooked sticks in all sorts of weather. Dutch settlers laid out obstacle courses on Manhattan ponds and the games continued through the worst of weather. Some sources even suggest that the game of hockey began when a kolf ball took an amazing skip off a Dutch colonist's crook. Kolf being thirsty work, the Dutch settlers never played any game too far from a tavern.

"The Dutch are robust in their sports and reflective in

their drinking," wrote one observer. "The English are just the opposite, reflective in their sports and robust in their drinking."

Despite his enthusiasm and his love of games, the commoner at the time of the American Revolution had precious little time to play. Workers in Boston during George Washington's second term demanded a work day limited to ten hours and were refused on the grounds that too much idleness would lead them to trouble. The heavy hand of the Puritan still lingered.

However, his influence was beginning to fade. Ultimately, it would be dissipated by industrialization, urbanization, immigration, increased leisure, and commercial promotion. Yet as late as the Second World War there were still vestiges of the Puritan influence, in the complaints about Sunday baseball. The movement to guard against society enjoying itself died hard.

2   The Cocking Pit

Elkanah Watson, a gentleman and prosperous merchant of Boston, had been traveling for many weeks through the Shenandoah Valley, stopping to visit acquaintances he had made as an officer in the recently completed war. He was, like most New Englanders, a practical man. He had thought about expanding his business interests through the Middle Atlantic and Southern states by visiting the men whom he had come to know and trust while serving under George Washington's command. In the summer of 1787, there were few roads and transportation was still haphazard. Watson arrived by carriage in Philadelphia, where he purchased a horse of unknown breed for the rest of the journey. He set out to find his former friends, carefully plotting his route so as to be near either a reputable inn or a hospitable home each day. The forests were filled with brigands, freed blacks, and formerly indentured white servants who had not learned a trade nor showed an interest in one.

Watson was a guest at the home of Jeremiah Dunn in Hampton County, Virginia, on a fine summer's day when the host mentioned that a cocking main would be held in a shed near the Boar's Head Tavern. Not wishing to let a potential business associate know that he disliked blood sports, Watson agreed to go. However, in his journal he noted that he did not necessarily condone such pursuits.

As they approached the site of the event, Watson was amazed to discover that he was passing through a genteel area of the nearby community. The highway was alive with pedestrians, both black and white, and dozens of carriages were parked along the way. The Boar's Head was a whitewashed inn and not a provincial saloon as he had feared. "We passed through a spacious square formed by a number of grand houses," he reported in his journal. "There were many genteel people, promiscuously mingled with the vulgar and the debased, a most disconcerting mixture."

Inside the wooden shed the temperature was unbearable. The ladies sat on chairs outside, fanning themselves and making small talk while their menfolk gambled. There were shouts in the background, "I'll go thirty-five to fifty on the gray!" and "Give one hundred to seventy on the dungie!"

A preliminary event was in progress inside when Watson arrived. A couple of handlers had moved into the ring, cuddling their roosters to their chests. A referee in hunting breeches preceded them. One rooster was red and runty. The other was brownish-gray with speckles and mean looking. The red was called "Bugle," the grayish one "Worker." Somehow these names didn't seem right to Watson. "No one gives a damn about their names, just how they fight," explained one foul-smelling spectator.

The betting grew more noisy. The handlers left the pit and the ritual started on the sides of the ring wall. The referee kept up a fine patter about the contesting birds. He also remembered to interject reminders about the

Cockfighting is regarded as one of the cruelest of sports, and, despite laws that prohibit it, remains popular even in some places today. Cockfighting was a passion among early Americans, and unaccountable sums of money exchanged hands over the pits. Some birds were famous among the bettors, becoming celebrities of sorts. At left is a famous portrait, titled *War*. On this page is a cock immortalized as a weathervane.

fine, strong drinks being served in the tavern nearby. The handler whose gamecock put on the best show in the main event would win a cask of whiskey from the owner of the Boar's Head.

Although the handlers held the birds firmly so that their spurred legs could not get loose, the cocks were permitted to engage in some preliminary fencing with each other. But no real contact was permitted yet. Then the referee decided that the cocks were ready. He summoned the handlers toward a square chalked on the dirt floor in the middle of the pit.

As soon as the birds were released the mood of the audience became murderous. The collision of feathers, beaks, and claws was a wild, pecking assault on supposedly civilized sensibilities. The gamecocks were a tangled mass, spraying blood in a thin red mist.

Watson was disgusted. "The birds were armed with long steel-pointed gaffs which were firmly attached to their natural spurs," he wrote. "The moment the birds were dropped, bets ran high. Emotions were untrammeled. The little feathered heroes seemed trained to the business and were not the least bit disconcerted by the impassioned shouting of the crowd. Advancing nearer and nearer, they flew upon each other at the same instant with a rude shock, the gaffs often piercing their heads before they were separated."

Someone shouted, "One hundred to seventy on the red!" and the betting began again. "This is going to be an endurance contest," someone told Watson, who felt the need for fresh air. Finally the red landed an uppercut with his spur as he turned away from his adversary. Blood trickled down the gray's beak and his head canted off to the left. He tipped over in the loose sand, flapping his wings and kicking out wildly with his legs. "Been brained," said a man. "Don't really matter. Can't kill a cock by hitting his brain. Liable not to feel it for hours. That gray might be back on his feet yet."

A lady sitting near Watson buried her face in her hands and tried to contain herself. Another man tried to reassure her that fighting cocks were bred to be killed in the pit. "It is their fate," he said. "Nothing can stop it. The birds themselves want it; otherwise they would not attack each other so furiously. They would not even have been permitted to live in the first place if it weren't for the cockfights. Only a few roosters are needed on any farm."

Despite his disability, the gray fought on. Between rounds his handler tried to revitalize the injured cock by pouring beer on its head. The man even blew air down the bird's throat.

"The match is over when you get three shorts and a long," somebody told Watson. "That's three counts of ten and one of twenty over a bird that's down."

With great courage, the gray fought back, driving the three-inch gaff fastened to the back of his left heel straight into the red's stomach. Most matches ended in seconds because both contestants died from the first blows. However, this one dragged on. At last, smeared with blood, the two cocks were carried outside. Watson concluded that they had fought well and would be allowed to live. He was wrong.

"Naw! They'll finish it up out in the 'drag pit' behind here," he was told. "One of them is going to have to die. Too much money been bet. One of 'em gotta die. T'other won't be worth much, so like as not they'll just wring his neck. Can't call anything 'round here a draw. Gotta have a winner."

Elkanah Watson pushed his way through the atmosphere, which was oppressive with smoke and sweat. He pardoned himself as he stepped on the skirts and hems of ladies who did not seem to be offended by the sights within the cocking shed. He found his way to the Boar's Head Tavern and ordered a medicinal shot of rhum. Then he stumbled away in the twilight.

"I was sickened by this barbarous sport, yet I hated to say so, they being so popular at the time," he recorded in his book *Men and Times of the Revolution*, written nearly a half century after his experience at the Boar's Head Tavern in Hampton County. "These contests were

not of my making so it was not up to me to criticize their practice. I retired under the shade of a spread willow and waited for my hosts to come and find me. I could hear the shrieks and yelps of the cocking pit well into the night. On the way home, I said nothing."

It may have been the wise thing to do. Despite attempts to prohibit it, cockfighting continued into the twentieth century.

3   A Fight to the Finish

If Elkanah Watson was distressed by the sight of the Virginia gentry's cruelty toward fowl, he was at least spared the experience of Irish novelist Thomas Ashe, who was traveling through the woods of eastern Kentucky in 1806. At that time wrestling was the favorite sport of the hill people, who went at it with the brutality of the Romans. In some sections of Kentucky it was considered proper for the winner to slit the nostrils of a beaten opponent. In other rural areas almost any form of mutilation of a loser was allowed. A law passed in 1754 by the colonial legislature in North Carolina forbade the biting or cutting off of noses, lips, or limbs in a sporting event. Eye-gouging was a high crime, punishable by death. But police records indicate that wrestling matches ending in gouging persisted in North Carolina and northern Georgia until at least 1899.

In the match witnessed by Ashe, the champion of a county in Virginia was pitted against the champion of a county in Kentucky. This was a no-holds-barred match. There was no referee, only a man who announced the two contestants and rang a bell to let them know when to attack. Ashe wrote:

It was a strong indication that the rural American did not shun bodily contact. Very few rounds had taken place before the Virginian contracted his whole form, drew up his arms to his face, with his hands nearly closed in a concave, by the fingers being bent to the full extension of

the flexors . . . the shock received by the Kentuckian, and the want of breath brought him instantly to the ground. The Virginian had summoned up his energy for one final act of desperation and had pitched himself, full force, at the bosom of his opponent.

The Virginian, a cruel-acting man with a stubbled chin and a foul breath, never lost his hold. He fixed his blood-scuffed fingers in the Kentuckian's hair and he placed his thumbs at the bottom of the beaten man's sockets. The crowd roared in anticipation of what it was about to witness. Many of them had been present before at such sporting events. The Virginian did not let them wait. Placing his thumbs in the proper place, he gave his opponent's eyeballs an instantaneous start from their sockets. The sufferer roared aloud, but offered no complaint at his sudden blindness. The people cheered, their minds being hardened in advance as to the mercilessness of the event. The gouged man was simply an animal, like the bear chained to a tavern wall and set upon by baiting dogs. He was there for their amusement.

The Kentuckian, not being able to disentangle his adversary from his face even after his mutilation, adopted a new mode of warfare. Fighting off both the pain and the darkness, he extended his arms around the Virginian and hugged him into closer contact with his huge body. Making one further effort, he fastened on to the upper lip of his mutilator and tore it down over the chin, blood flying in every direction. At length the Kentuckian gave out, rolling over on the grass where he bled profusely, his face a mass of red organs. Whereupon, the people carried off the victor. Despite his torn lip he preferred a triumphal march to seeing a doctor. He was chaired round the grounds as the first of all the rough and

The early citizens had a special fascination for bloody violence in their sport.
Gouging, a form of wrestling in which men
plucked out the eyeballs of their opponent,
was one of the most brutal sports. Ratting,
shown at left in an early lithograph, was
another blood letting. The caption reads:
"The celebrated terrier dog Major
performing his wonderful feat of killing
100 rats in 8 minutes, 58 seconds," an
endeavor that apparently fascinated the
well-dressed gentlemen in attendance.

tumblers in the region. His beaten foe simply
laid there, a discarded hulk. The blow of the fist
and the spurt of blood, so distasteful to some
races, is part of the exhilarating sport of the
American frontier.

4 From Messenger to Hambletonian

Unaware that he was on his way to becoming a famous father, the large gray stallion
clopped along the cobblestones of Philadelphia's busy Market Street. He paused
at an intersection to steal a wisp of hay
from a passing wagon. This was Messenger, big for a
thoroughbred and a trifle heavy in the hindquarters but
of royal blood.

Earlier that morning in 1788, Messenger had been
removed from Maguire's livery stable by a lean black
groom named King Henry and walked through the center
of America's largest city to a stable called the "Sign of
the Black Horse." The mares were brought here, too.
There were no means to transport horses then. Often
a mare would be ridden thirty miles the day before, left
overnight at a stable, and ridden back home on the day
that she was to be impregnated, assuming all went well.
The breeding cost fifteen dollars plus a dollar for the
stallion's groom and a dollar for the mare's groom, both
of whom watched to ensure that the proper stallion was
covering the proper mare.

Some breeders stood around in the bar at the front of
the Sign of the Black Horse, swilling punch laced with
rhum on this warm May morning, debating whether the
horse coming to service their mares was the famed English racehorse Messenger or some impostor. "There has
been no word of Messenger since he ran at Newmarket
in November, 1785," said one man, who received the
racing journals sent by boat from England. "This might
easily be a fraud. There's much of that, you know."

But this was Messenger, bred by the Earl of Grosvenor

at his Yorkshire farm. Messenger's father was Manbrino,
a descendant of one of the three Arabian horses that
founded the thoroughbred line. While in Allepo, Syria,
Thomas Darley of Yorkshire had purchased a stallion
for his father, but he had no idea that he was about to
found a royal line of horses. Messenger had acquired not
only the blood of the Darley Arabian through his sire but
also the blood of the Byerley Turk and the Dodolphin
Arabian through his mother. As a competitor, Messenger
won one thousand four hundred seventy-three guineas
(about nine thousand dollars) with eight victories, four
seconds, and three thirds in fifteen starts. Then, like many
a celebrity after him, he came to America.

It happened this way. A few years after the Revolution,
Thomas Benger, a prosperous importer from Pennsylvania, visited the English countryside in search of a stud
he could bring back to improve America's racing stock.
Benger discovered that the American rebels were folk
heroes in the old country for having successfully challenged the crown. Those former colonists who visited
England were much sought-after dinner guests, and
Benger found it difficult to get down to the matter of
business. "All things having to do with America were
greatly popular at the time," he told friends upon his
return to Pennsylvania in 1786. "They seemed to admire
us. They thought of us not as a new people but as Englishmen who had stood up to the crown. They seemed
exhilarated, as if another England had been born in the
wilderness. I was amazed at how many members of the
nobility had been sympathetic to our late cause. The
war to suppress the revolution, it seems, had been most
unpopular through large segments of the population.
They seemed overly anxious to help in any way they
could. They knew our racing stock to be rather weak, so
I was able to purchase the great Messenger for the equiva-
lent of two hundred dollars in our money. It was a great
bargain, I thought."

After being tossed about in the hold of an American
merchant schooner during a violent North Atlantic cross-

Alfred Jacob Miller, a deft draftsman of human figures and animals, spent the summer of 1837 among the Indians of the Far West and created an important catalog of notes, in addition to watercolors showing people at work and play. In this painting, two young girls race their horses across a landscape seemingly aglow with eternal sunlight.

ing, Messenger was kept in seclusion on a Pennsylvania farm. He had taken the journey poorly. For months afterward he sulked. He did not take to Benger or to any of Benger's employees. He might have perished if it had not been for a small pony that was his constant companion on the farm. Eventually, the great horse, whose ancestors had been owned by the Bey of Tunis and the Sultan of Morocco, regained his spirits. Two years after bringing the horse to America, Benger brought him to the Black Horse.

"Is that really Messenger?" asked the disbelieving owner of a mare who was to be bred at Black Horse stable.

"Aye, I imported him myself," said Benger.

"That's his name is it?" said the cynic. "Then we shall call him 'Imported Messenger.' That's what he is. I hope that he is as good as they say his bloodlines should be. If not, I'll be wanting my money back."

For the next two decades, Messenger stood at various points in Pennsylvania, New Jersey, and New York. But he aroused little excitement in Philadelphia because the law prohibited horse racing. Even at the bargain breeding rates offered at the Black Horse, Messenger could not attract enough business to keep his owner solvent, and so the horse was sold to the Astor family. He was, perhaps, the first stud to be syndicated; Henry Astor sold half of him to his brother, John Jacob Astor, who split the shares further. Few studs have been asked to be as amorous as often as Messenger. He never raced again.

While horse racing was becoming the new nation's first organized sport, this tall (fifteen and two-thirds hands) stallion with the high flank was siring many fine colts. His finest offspring was Miller's Damsel, who produced American Eclipse in 1814. This strong offspring participated in the country's first intersectional sporting event, a match that convinced promoters everywhere that America was willing to pay to see spectator sports. Messenger's bloodlines were carried on by Whirlaway, Man o' War, Swaps, and Secretariat.

Marksmanship was a prized skill along the frontier and target shooting, on which bets were made and prizes won, was a popular sport. In 1850, George Caleb Bingham painted this study of an intense but friendly competition between riflemen called *Shooting for the Beef*.

Even though Messenger never had to pull a surrey, it was obvious that he was a born trotter. Before his sale to the Astors, he was taken for a ride by Benger, who suddenly had a giddy urge to race the horse he had brought from thousands of miles away. The owner imagined it was Newmarket, and that he was in the irons. When Benger struck him on the withers, Messenger gave the owner more than a vicarious thrill. He broke into a natural trot instead of sprinting. He did not have to learn to trot, and he passed on this innate talent to his children. His great-grandson would become an immortalized harness horse.

This descendant was named after a village in Yorkshire called Hambleton, where the oldest race in England was held. The colt's mother was an extraordinarily ugly beast, Abdullah. But the colt was Messenger's child. He was called Hambletonian and he turned harness racing into a national mania.

In the 1850s, the nation worshiped Hambletonian. It bought commemorative plates on which his likeness was inscribed. Children talked about him as if he were human.

The tenth child by Abdullah was born under a pear tree on a Sunday morning and discovered by a hired hand named Wilhelm Rysdyck, a stolid man with a white beard that reached to the first button of his coat. Rysdyck sensed that the only chance he had to make good in life was somehow to own this mare and her foal. It was a rare piece of extrasensory perception.

Several hours later the owner, Jonas Seeley, returned home from church with his family. They had barely entered the house when Rysdyck made an offer. He wanted the colt more than anything else in the world. He was willing to pay up to one hundred and twenty-five dollars, which was close to five months of his salary.

Seeley looked at the mare and was filled with the urge to be rid of her. This was her tenth foal and few brood mares have more than that. He would make the deal, he told Rysdyck, only if the colt's mother were included.

Rysdyck enthusiastically agreed, and the deal was closed. Off walked the Dutchman, leading the unsightly mare and her infant floundering in the dust. He brought them both to his tiny farm and spent the night trying to figure out how he would pay for this exorbitant purchase.

Several years later he realized that he had indeed found the way to get rich. Like Messenger, Hambletonian was two inches higher in the rump than most horses. He was so magnificent, in fact, that Rysdyck could not resist racing him early. It was unorthodox, at the very least, in an age when no animal raced before maturity, but Hambletonian was permitted to pull a sulky around the Orange County Fair track at Goshen, New York, when he was about six months old. Led out in a white bridle, martingale, and girth, he ran one-third of a mile against a local champion. His manners were perfect and he was invited back the following year to compete against another veteran runner, whereupon he caused a sensation by winning easily. So precocious was Hambletonian that Rysdyck, illiterate and with little knowledge of racing, let him cover four mares when he was only two years old. The innocent Rysdyck did not accept a stud fee; he simply wanted his animal to exercise his natural instincts.

Meanwhile, another son of Abdullah, foaled in 1848, was making a name for himself in upstate New York tracks. He was named Abdullah Chief, owned by a man named Seeley Roe. Both Hambletonian and Abdullah Chief were placed in stud service with a two hundred fifty dollar fee, almost unheard of in those days.

At first, Hambletonian was not permitted to run against Abdullah Chief because Roe was a wealthy man from New York City and Rysdyck was an illiterate from upstate. Moreover, Roe showed a deep contempt for Hambletonian, condemning him as an exhibition horse that had never shown any capability as a trotter. After much talk, the two horses were permitted to meet at the Union Course on Long Island. The owners drove their own horses. "If we do not win," said the Dutchman, "neither

Hambletonian nor I have any future. He is a powerful horse . . . the greatest horse who ever lived. I can win. I *must* win."

Just three minutes and three seconds after the starting signal, Hambletonian crossed the finish line. His opponent was somewhere down the track. Roe did not accept defeat easily and demanded a second heat. This time the margin was even greater. Abdullah Chief covered the mile in two minutes, fifty-five and one-half seconds, considered brilliant in those days. But there was Hambletonian with 2:48.5 clocking. Now every racetrack wanted Hambletonian. Rysdyck became wealthy because Hambletonian now could command five hundred dollars stud fees. In his lifetime, Hambletonian covered at least one thousand nine-hundred mares and produced one thousand three hundred thirty-one foals.

Hambletonian raced for eight years and when his career was finished, Rysdyck owned most of the pear trees in the valley where the champion racer was born. When the horse died, he rated a granite tombstone.

While baseball was little more than a collection of unstructured town games waiting to be brought together under a single set of rules, while football was still an English sport called rugby, and while basketball was nearly a century away from being invented, horse racing was the great American pastime. In 1811, an early advertising campaign with a sports tie-in was made by a Philadelphia tobacco concern, McNulty and Son's. In every pouch of tobacco, the company offered coupons bearing the likeness of famous racehorses. America was becoming a nation of horsemen. It was characteristic of Americans to justify pleasure in terms of utility. A growing nation needed good horses to help tame the Western lands. Racing horses made good sense as well as good sport because it helped improve the breed. Strong and sturdy runners made good sires; weak and beaten horses did not. In the burst of Western expansion, the horse became a patriotic symbol.

The new government was building roads to connect the former colonies as one cohesive, if not large nation. If there was no racetrack in the area—and nearly every county had a racing field—youngbloods harnessed the swiftest runners on their fathers' farms and raced them down long, dusty thoroughfares. Breeding stock was imported from England, France, and Spain. Race courses were laid out. In 1788, Colonel William Whitley had constructed the first circular track west of the Alleghenies near Louisville, Kentucky. It was called Sportsman's Hill, and had seats for eleven thousand spectators.

During the War of 1812, Andrew Jackson asked for and received race results. His own horses ran in Memphis, Louisville, and Cincinnati. Before the first stadium or arena was built in America, there were grandstands seating thousands of spectators at tracks such as Newmarket, Washington Race Course, Union Course, and Fashion Race Course.

Cities competed to build larger and more elaborate tracks. Wealthy Louisiana planters, who kept strings of thoroughbreds on their estates, opened the Metairie Course, which matched any course in the North. The National Course outside Washington opened in 1802. "Many scores of American legislators went on foot from the Capitol, above four English miles where they found not only grog but 'sharks' [bookmakers] at the races," wrote John Quincy Adams. During his own administration Adams rose early on summer mornings to swim in the Potomac and spend an hour or so talking about the races with Colonel Richard Tayloe.

During Andrew Jackson's administration it was obvious to the world that America had a fixation with sport and with horse racing, in particular. Publications appeared devoted entirely to the turf. The first was *Skinner's American Turf Register and Sporting Magazine*. In one of the early editions a nobleman from France—aristocratic visitors were always the most welcome and the most quoted in democratic America—said that the country seemed to reek of horse liniment and that the people, from poorest to wealthiest talked of nothing but racing.

The Morgan was a horse of uncommon stamina and racing characteristics, legendary for its prowess as a competitor and a stud. Black Hawk, the reported grandson of Justin Morgan, was one of the most famous Morgans and his likeness was celebrated in all forms of art for decades after his death. Reproduced here are a flat iron weathervane made in approximately 1850 and a detail of a steel engraving from a hardware catalog published in 1883.

When the Fashion Park course at Newton, Long Island, opened, the citizenry was feverish with delight. It flocked to a white stone stadium, ornate with Greek pillars on its facade, and with seats for twenty-five thousand spectators. For members of the Jockey Club and their associates, there was a restaurant that was similar in luxury and concept to modern stadium clubs. The grounds were lavishly landscaped. There were dozens of bars where the common workingman could drink beer for a nickel and eat thick ham sandwiches and oysters plucked from the shores of the Sound. There were nearly fifty thousand present on opening day, this at a time when the population of the United States had barely reached ten million. There was no Thoroughbred Racing Protective Bureau to root out scoundrels, as the following article from *Frank Leslie's Illustrated Newspaper* clearly indicates:

> The announcement of the first race meeting drew out a large representation from the sporting fraternity. Commencing at noon, Flushing Avenue was thronged with vehicles of all shapes and sizes, leading toward Newton. Fancy men drove fast horses and advanced juveniles belabored wretched and unwilling hacks. There was noise, shouting, and sometimes quarreling, as excited 'sports' met at the drinking houses on the road. It had come out in its strength, this racing world—the huge agglomeration of gambling and fraud, of weakness and wickedness. This 'fancy' profession is surrounded by an atmosphere of immorality almost as fatal as fascinating; and although, undoubtedly, many of our most honorable men interest themselves in such sporting events, what are their numbers compared with those we meet on the road— men whose interest in them is the interest of sharps and gamblers? But moralizing is not the vein for Flushing Avenue on a race day.

As they worshiped the horse, Americans succeeded in establishing their first native breed. The famous ancestral beast still seems more legendary than real because of the numerous stories about his origin. There are at least six versions and many variations.

This mysterious horse was probably born in West Springfield, Massachusetts, perhaps in 1787 or 1791 or 1795. Or perhaps it was 1797. He was sold to a man in Randolph, Vermont, named Justin Morgan, who was a singing master, or a farmer, or a saloon owner, or all three. Some say that Morgan was a saloon keeper who taught singing as an avocation and owned a farm, an unlikely combination of careers. Some say that Morgan bought the horse in West Springfield and rode him back to Randolph. Others say that his breeder, hard-pressed for money, sold him to a farmer near Randolph from whom Morgan purchased him. There are those who say his horse's name was always "Justin Morgan's horse" and others who insist that he was named "Figure" and was renamed "Justin Morgan" after Morgan died.

Historians argue endlessly over Figure's sire. It was probably Beautiful Bay but might have been True Briton. Ah, the tales they told about Figure's father! He was supposed to have been (1) captured from a high-ranking British officer, surely a general, (2) the last blooded stallion smuggled into America before the Revolution, (3) a horse that was taken from an American Tory before he could cross the border into Canada to escape to Halifax, (4) a present from Cornwallis to Washington, (5) a stray rounded up in the streets of Yorktown after the siege, or (6) a splendid English thoroughbred who had been rescued from a sinking British frigate. Some said he was of Dutch origin; others said he was Spanish.

No matter who the father was, and whatever his name, he sired a remarkable colt, an offspring who had the strength of a beer-wagon brute and the style and speed of a thoroughbred. Figure weighed nine hundred fifty pounds and he could draw a one thousand two hundred-pound log. He was a pony-sized bay of fourteen hands, round-barreled, pouter-chested, with fancily fringed fetlocks and small delicate feet. He raced in Vermont

and western Massachusetts and cleaned out the county fair competition. In short he could do anything he was asked. What's more, he passed on to his children his remarkable attributes.

The little animal's strength was supposedly first discovered when Justin Morgan leased him to a farmer named Robert Evans. One afternoon several men chortled at the lilliputian size of the horse Evans was using to draw timber along the graded Vermont terrain to the sawmill. They challenged the horse's ability, of course, but Figure hauled an enormous log—later estimated at one thousand two hundred pounds—all the way to the mill. The story spread. "Say, there's this here horse up in V'amont, so they say, that can draw off a twelve-hundred-pound log and he ain't but a mite over nine-hundred pounds or such hisself. E-magine that!"

It has been written but never proved that Figure passed to sheriff Ephriam Rice of Woodstock on March 22, 1798, when Justin Morgan died of consumption in the sheriff's bedroom. In return for expenses Morgan incurred during his lengthy illness, Figure changed hands, but the deceased former owner retained a spiritual lien on the horse when it was renamed Justin Morgan. Since the sheriff had no use for him, Justin Morgan was put up for sale and purchased by Robert Evans.

Surely no horse was asked to do more in his lifetime. He worked the hillsides during the week and raced over rough country courses on the weekends. The farmers brought all breeds of mares and he covered them. And every offspring looked and acted like their famed progenitor; they were compact and agreeable with an unmistakable gait. His descendants not only raced but worked hard as well. They were tireless and gentle. They helped to win the West, and they carried Phil Sheridan and Stonewall Jackson in the War Between the States.

The confusion over ancestry rendered most American stud books useless. The alleged grandson of Justin Morgan was a superb stallion named Black Hawk. The owner, unaware that Black Hawk would develop into a cham-

pion, took the issue to court in a vain attempt to prove that the animal had been sired by another horse. Here's the story:

The best known son of Justin Morgan was a chestnut named Sherman Morgan, who shared a barn with a black of unknown breed named Paddy. In the spring of 1833 a mare named Old Narragansett, which was in foal to Sherman Morgan, passed from the ownership of a Portsmouth, New Hampshire, saloon keeper named Benjamin Kelly to Shade Twombly, a self-styled horseman of dubious distinction. Twombly agreed to pay a fourteen dollar stud fee if the mare delivered a live foal.

When Old Narragansett did indeed drop a fine colt, the baby was black just like Paddy; he wasn't chestnut like Sherman Morgan. A grim-faced Shade Twombly harnessed another horse and went searching for an attorney. Twombly claimed that the colt was worth only seven dollars, which was Paddy's fee, since it was obvious that Old Narragansett had preferred Paddy over Morgan. The case dragged on until somebody brought in proof that Old Narragansett's mother was black. The judge ordered Shade Twombly to get up the remaining seven dollars, which he did with a blazing fury that almost stood him in contempt of court. "I shall never accept this decision," he shouted as he stomped out of the Portsmouth courtroom. "That colt is not Sherman Morgan's get."

In spite of his questionable heritage, Black Hawk was beloved by the crowds and by the breeders, who commanded a one hundred dollar stud fee for him. In a barn on the shores of Lake Champlain, near Fort Ticonderoga, Black Hawk coupled with a nameless small gray mare and produced an exceptionally strong colt named Ethan Allen.

From that point on, the Morgan began to dominate harness racing through much of the nineteenth century. In time, even Shade Twombly came to admit that paying those extra seven dollars had been an extraordinary bargain, although he still continued to suspect that Paddy was the true sire.

Stickball, an Indian game that is occasionally played today, is similar to lacrosse, although rules vary from tribe to tribe. The sticks are smaller than lacrosse sticks and a player scores by hitting the small rawhide ball directly over a tall pole. Pictured here are Oklahoma Choctaw sticks, made of hickory wood.

5 The Native American Sport

"Hail, O North! Thy wind send
To blow care away,
To bring joy today;
Make Eyes keen,
Make Hands swift for play."

—a Seneca pregame prayer

The early shafts of sunlight were already beginning to make eerie patterns behind the tall pine forests of upstate New York when the two judges, stripped to the waist to show the clan tattoos on their chests, rose from their sitting positions to address the Wind of the North. Holding four tally sticks in their hands, they bowed first to the tribal standards and then led the chant. Several hundred players seated in a circle around them joined in at the close of the stanza to the North. They repeated the act, this time beseeching the Wind of the East.

When the four winds had been appealed to, the two judges lowered their tally sticks and walked to a blanket placed in the center of the circle. The players lifted their racquets in salute. The instruments looked so much like a Christian bishop's crozier that the French were later to call the game "lacrosse." After the salute the athletes remained in a meditative pose until the sun was well over the tops of the nearest trees. The only sounds were the winds responding to the judges' pleas and the frogs chugging in a stream beyond the meadow.

Then, at a signal, a drummer began a slow, steady beat. He broke into song. From beyond the circle the women moved up in gentle, graceful movements. Picking up the words of the drummer, they chanted of past games and great glories. The drummer who carried the beat had been selected by the Seneca nation with care and he was held in high esteem in every community. He changed to a song of the matches to be played that day. His voice grew stronger. The women joined him. From the distant woods came the spectators, some of whom had traveled for a hundred miles. Many of them brought wares and goods to be offered as prizes for exceptional sportsmanship.

White people liked to describe these Indian sporting tournaments, despite the spiritual overtones, as ruthlessly brutal games without rules, the only object being to kill or maim. Whole tribes were said to participate with five thousand players on a team. Some matches, described in detail by settlers who claimed to have been present, were supposed to have been played either with skulls or freshly severed human heads instead of balls. A writer reported in *Darcy's American Sporting Journal* that some whites had been disgusted when they attempted to learn the secrets of the game from an Onandaga chief.

This phony journalism helped to perpetuate the image of the native Indian as a leering, immoral savage whose insane games were played over four-day periods with no time outs to bury the dead. If it were even vaguely true, it might have been shocking.

In preparation for the game, called *Otada-jish-qua-age* by the Seneca, who were part of the Iroquois confederation, the athlete trained daily throughout the spring, running in all sorts of weather, clothed only in a waist-cloth because he believed that such exposure drew all of the natural elements into his body. He could not touch an infant nor have sexual relations seven days before and seven days after the game. Because four and seven were sacred numbers, a Seneca athelete was required to begin training twenty-eight (four times seven) days before the competition.

The diet was carefully controlled. He could not eat the young of any animal. The herb called "atunka," or lamb's quarter, as the white man called it, was forbidden. Hot food and salt also were denied. Since the Seneca believed that a human could pick up certain attributes from animals, either positive or negative, the eating of frogs or rabbits was prohibited. The frog had brittle bones and the rabbit, of course, was timid. Not partaking of them

was a sacrifice since frog legs and fried rabbit were both Seneca delicacies. Similarly outlawed was the freshwater shad, or sucker, a fish known for its stupidity and sluggishness. However, athletes were advised to observe the habits of the wolf and the catamount, or mountain lion. The playing season began in early summer and lasted until snow made playing impossible.

The Seneca, like many native Americans who loved the racquet and ball sport, practiced daily, stripped to the waist like ancient Greek athletes. They worked out plays and had strategy sessions before sundown with coaches. Their sport was as civilized as any their white counterparts played. If anything, the team sports of the Indians were ahead of the rest of America.

Despite the colorful reports of the white settlers, the ball employed in *Otada-jish-qua-age* was not made from the human skull. The ball was approximately three inches in diameter, stuffed with woven animal hair and covered with finely stitched deerhide. In each community one older woman was entrusted with the task of making the balls. The length and shape of the racquet was strictly regulated by the Seneca; it was thirty-four inches long with a soft webbing of deer thongs in the curve. The Chippewa preferred racquets three inches longer and one-half inch smaller balls. The Indians used saplings of the proper length, cured them in shape, which took up to three years, and, when the racquets were properly strung, rubbed them with animal oil. Some racquets were so sturdy that they survive in museums today.

The Seneca used teams of eight to twenty-two men, depending upon the size of the field. In the game a participant was not allowed to carry the ball in his hand except under special conditions. He could not propel it with his feet. The two teams played on an open field with goals set about four hundred forty yards apart. The goals were eighteen yards wide. The ball had to be hurled through the goal mouth, which was protected by two goalies. Since the sacred numbers were four and seven, team captains had to agree on which would be the winning

score. It was customary to play a best five-out-of-nine series. Play began when a judge dropped the ball in a circle at midfield. If a Seneca athlete became disabled or fatigued, he was permitted to leave, but substitutions were not permitted.

There were coaches, managers, and two judges appointed by both sides. Everybody was obliged to observe the rules or they were banished from play. If a player was disabled, he was immediately removed from the field. When most of the athletes were tired, the judges suspended play for refreshments to be served. The Seneca at play were no more rowdy nor less civil than English schoolboys, wrote Robert Bently Howe in 1830:

> When the designated day arrived, the people gathered from the surrounding country to witness the contest between Seneca parties. About meridian they are at the appointed place, aligning themselves behind the teams they support. As soon as the preliminary ceremonies were adjusted, the ball was dropped between two files of players. After a brief struggle between two athletes at the center of the field, the ball was set in play. Often one player would pass to another, using intricate patterns. When one man would catch the ball in his racquet and carry it toward the other team's gate opening, the most exciting part of the game took place.
>
> If the flight of the ball was arrested on any part of the enemy's end of the field, a spirited and even fierce contest would take place. The players handled their racquets with great dexterity and out-maneuvered their opponents with such art and adroitness that frequently several minutes passed before the ball flew clear. Occasionally, in the heat of controversy, but strictly by accident, a player was struck with such violence that blood trickled down his limbs. In such a case, if disabled, he dropped his racquet and left the field and was attended by a shaman who

knew the ancient secrets of Indian medicine. When one team took the ball from the opposite end of the field and, with many shifts in the tide of success, managed to score the winning goal, the crowd sent up a shout of rejoicing.

It wasn't that much different in other Indian communities. Even as the wagons rolled past them, carrying the white pioneers into other lands originally dominated by native Americans, the Indians were playing this extraordinarily civilized sport, complete with rules, referees, and line judges. They had awards for good sportsmanship. But to the Puritanical horror of the whites, they occasionally played in the nude or with only a deerskin loincloth. They did not play until the death, nor did they use fresh skulls, and in most tribes they were prohibited from striking another player.

"The favored means of taking the ball away from an opponent is to slam your stick against his," wrote Howe. "Frequently there is ill-feeling between players, resulting in an attacking player being hit across the arms or the legs. If this happens once or twice, strictly in the passion of the game, it is forgiven. If it persists, the judge asks the offending player to leave the field. Repeated bad sportsmanship can result in a lifetime banishment. . . ."

After scoring a winning goal, a Seneca player would repair to the river, where he cleansed his body and, in the presence of a judge, confessed his gratitude for having played well—first to the North Wind, then the East Wind, the South Wind, and the West Wind. Such was his concept of sportsmanship.

6   Ben Franklin, Swimmer

Benjamin Franklin was the famous kite flyer who dared lightning and helped to harness electricity. He founded the *Saturday Evening Post*. He was a great wit, a noted historian, and the first Postmaster General.

Few people know that he was also America's first great

One of the most famous North versus South match races was contested on May 13, 1845. Peytona and Fashion, two celebrated champions of the time, were brought together at the Union Course, Long Island, to race for a $20,000 purse. In this famous lithograph by Currier & Ives, Peytona is shown leading by a head. The Alabama champion maintained his lead to win the race in 7:39¾, beating his Northern opponent by 6½ seconds.

swimmer and an advocate of aquatic sports. As a young man his swimming skills almost subverted his other talents. As the nation's first skindiver, he developed and wore a wet suit, which kept him warm in great depths, and a pair of webbed sandals, which was probably a prototype of modern flippers. However, he never designed an effective breathing device. And there were cold evenings near the bottom of Philadelphia's Schuylkill River when his reed sandals came apart in the violent currents.

As a visitor in England later, he recommended two hours of swimming every evening to ensure a good night's sleep. The English took to calling him the "watery American." Few Europeans had much interest in swimming. Bathing was infrequent and swimming through the deep was considered an activity only for fish. There also was a great fear of drowning. As a young man Franklin came across a book called the *Science of Natation* written by Maurice Thevenot, a Frenchman. It was the only book about the sport. At twenty-five, Franklin wrote his book on swimming, which was used as a reference work well into the twentieth century.

The secret in learning to swim, Franklin said, was to have confidence in the ability of the water to support the body. Most people looked at a pond and saw liquid space and felt utterly powerless. The way to overcome this fear was to learn to swim in a place where the bottom sloped down gently. He told students to walk out calmly until the water was up to the widest part of their chests and then turn to face the shore. "Throw an egg in the water where you can see it but can't reach it without diving for it," he wrote. "Then plunge forward after the egg. You really have to work at it to force your way downward. That will convince even the most skeptical that water is buoyant. Without thinking about it, one will stroke."

One afternoon while flying a kite next to a pond, Franklin was seized by a great notion. If a man were to hold one end of a rope with the other attached to a giant kite, he could be pulled across the surface by the wind. He experimented and the idea worked. Franklin's mind delved even further. Suppose he fastened barrel staves to his feet? Might the wind pull him fast enough to permit him to skim across the top of the water? Franklin drew designs and wrote a short essay on the subject. He even brought some specifications to a carpenter. Apparently, more important matters came up, preventing him from becoming history's original water skier.

He was America's first swimming master. At eighteen he went to London for the purpose of buying printing equipment. While there he swam a four-mile course in the Thames from Chelsea to the Blackfriars. So impressed was Sir William Wyndham, the ex-Chancellor of the Exchequer, with Franklin's swimming style and his ability to coach that he offered to set up the young Philadelphian with his own academy in London. For several weeks, right up to the time his boat was due to sail, Franklin pondered the offer. Finally he refused. He admitted later that if he had had more time to consider he would have accepted. If not for the poor timing, English swimming might have flourished.

7   An Intersectional Confrontation

On the sidewalks of a sparsely settled New York City that was still farm land above what is now Times Square, profiteers were peddling porcelain plates bearing the painted likenesses of the two contestants. Reportedly, some five thousand of them were produced, yet not one of them remains today, to the utter distress of collectors.

The plates were made to celebrate the first great national horse racing event. Hotel rooms located within a fifty-mile radius of the track had been booked since the news was announced of the match race between the two great regional champions. The presidents of banks in New York, Philadelphia, Charlotte, Baltimore, Charleston, and Richmond were concerned about their institutional stability because so much of the betting money was deposited in their vaults.

"There is an indication that if the horse from the South were to win," said the owner of one of New York's more elegant lending institutions, "that we would be hard-pressed to continue to serve our patrons. Most gentlemen of any substance have a great deal of their property involved in this horse race."

Sanity had all but departed from the nation's shores in the spring of 1823. Newspapers and periodicals described what might happen when American Eclipse and Sir Henry met to defend the honors of the North and South. Some historians would eventually look back at this confrontation and see the first incident of intersectional rivalry that culminated in the Civil War, although it probably was not the case. Feelings were lukewarm but friendly between Northerners and Southerners. Most citizens regarded this match between the grandsons of the stallion Diomed as a mere horse race, albeit an important one.

This was a race to decide which half of the country had the best horseflesh. It was considered an uneven match because most of the truly great breeding stock had gone south. A Virginia planter named Nathaniel Beddingford Arnold bet his cotton crops for the next five years on Sir Henry. A Yankee industrialist agreed to turn over three years of profit from his cotton mill if American Eclipse were beaten.

Congressman John Randolph, the man who in the Senate later gave Henry Clay of Kentucky immortal hell, put up not only ten thousand dollars, then a sizable fortune, but also his entire wardrobe of London-tailored clothes. Although it is a somewhat implausible explanation, the phrase "betting your shirt" might have originated then.

"I am confident that Sir Henry will emerge victorious," said Randolph standing outside a Manhattan hostelry, "and I fully clothed."

The American of the early nineteenth century was a dues-paying romantic. He had fought in two wars against the greatest imperial power on earth. He had done what his cousins from the British Isles had never done: he had tested the powers of the monarchy. He was heady, giddy, intoxicated with pride. Horse races were far more than contests between dumb beasts: they were affairs of honor. The challenge of a horse race could not be refused unless a gentleman wanted to be forever spurned by his fellow gentry.

American Eclipse belonged to Cornelius Van Ranst, a man who, like other Dutchmen, had come to an accommodation with the ruling Anglo-Saxon establishment. The owner of Sir Henry was Colonel William Ransom Johnson, a fussy but friendly man. He was short and his friends called him the Napoleon of racing because of his remarkable record. In the three years before he sent Sir Henry to challenge American Eclipse, he started sixty-three horses, winning with sixty-one and placing two.

However, Johnson was less than confident in his challenge to Van Ranst. He defied American Eclipse to race a Southern horse, but he reserved the right to choose the challenger. All the blooded stock in Dixie was eligible. Van Ranst was game; he sent back a courier to accept. In May, 1823, at the Union Race Course on Long Island, American Eclipse would meet the horse Colonel Johnson selected. If Van Ranst was to meet a Southern cavalry charge, he would at least do it on his home grounds.

"Let them come," Van Ranst told the Eastern press. "My horse will be ready for them. No Northern horse can be defeated by a Southern horse. I press that charge and I accept it fully. This will settle the argument forever."

The owners of the two horses put up twenty thousand dollars between them as a purse for the winner. The nation talked of little else that spring.

Both American Eclipse and Sir Henry were grandsons of Diomed, winner of the first Epsom Derby in England. American Eclipse was sired by Duroc, and Sir Henry by Diomed's magnificent son Sir Archie.

On the evening before the great race, Colonel John-

Ethan Allen, a champion son of Black Hawk, brings uncommon beauty to a copper with gilt weathervane manufactured about 1860 by Cushing & White of Waltham, Massachusetts. Below, a detail of a post-Civil War racing wagon and driver.

son arrived in New York City and attended a party at the home of his Northern racing companions. The Colonel suffered a bad night. He attributed his difficulties to the rich seafood, namely the lobsters, not to the wine that was served. "It was with great difficulty that I reached the race course at all," he told a representative of *Darcy's American Sporting Journal*. "They had plied me with high wines and red lobster. I felt amuck, the journey being long and arduous. I wished that I had never begun this journey, for it took both me and my horse away from so many things familiar. I did not know who was worse for wear, Sir Henry, who had been in this demon land and practicing for three weeks, or myself, who was newly arrived and not well."

There were fifty thousand people kicking up dust on the roads to the race course. About twenty thousand had come from areas south of Delaware and from New England. The spectators slept in wagons, inns, ditches, woodlands, and skiffs rocking in the waters of Long Island Sound. Congress adjourned so that its representatives could attend this event.

In Niblo's pleasure gardens on the Bowery, a white flag of victory would be raised if the Northern hero won and a black one of mourning if the Southern horse prevailed. A rally of lesser horses would bring the news. When Niblo raised the black flag on the first day, moneymen marched over from Wall Street to ask that the flag be lowered for fear there would be a panic. Their fears were allayed by the second heat in which a different man rode Eclipse to victory. The crowd sensed the superiority of the Northern horse and diminished by twenty-five thousand for the final heat.

In the last furlong of the deciding race, Sir Henry, four years younger than his eight-year-old rival, made a gallant sprint. But American Eclipse simply galloped ahead. "Down the stretch came the mighty American Eclipse, as close to living flame as a horse can be, throwing great clods of dirt in his beaten rival's face," it was recorded in *Darcy's American Sporting Journal*. "Several of the ruined Southerners took their lives in black despair. One plunged a dagger into his vitals when Sir Henry lost."

It was reported that a number of the Southerners walked home, defeatedly trudging along in the dust. However, that is strictly a case of Northern reporters indulging themselves. If Colonel Johnson is to be believed, most of the Southern visitors rode back to the city in carriages. "I accepted defeat as graciously as possible," Johnson wrote in his diary. "I ate the most costly lobster dinner . . . at the expense of the man to whom I had lost as much as two hundred thousand dollars. It seemed the least that he could do. The dinner was excellent. My horse was still young and in excellent shape. I felt no great feeling of defeat. Our stay in New York lasted another week. After which time we went back to my homeland."

It was not the start of the Civil War but rather the beginning of a period of commingling of the peoples of the North and the South. Bloodlines of people as well as horses that had heretofore been restricted were now joined together. And for weeks afterward on the sidewalks of New York peddlers sold commemorative plates, memorializing Sir Henry and American Eclipse.

8 The Great American Baseball Myth

The following myth is warm and comfortable, which is why it will endure as long as America herself. On a warm summer morning a handsome young cadet on furlough from the military academy at West Point called some of his friends to a meadow where they usually played the old English schoolboys' game of rounders. The cadet had worked for several days codifying a set of rules. He had also laid out a perfectly geometric playing field. He observed that because it took about thirty yards for a man to gain momentum as he ran, the bases would have to be ninety feet apart. There would be nine men to a side and the pitcher would stand sixty and one-half feet from home plate. So all the cadets chose up sides,

Early settlers played an English game called rounders, a form of cricket. Eventually, the formal rules were altered to embrace a simpler and faster game called Town Ball. The game of baseball emerged from this adaptation and quickly was accepted as a new sport by urban residents. The engravings on these pages are from an instructional book of games for young boys published in 1864. The prep school beanie worn by the players suggests the source from which the familiar baseball cap was styled.

THE STRIKER.

and baseball, America's first team sport, was invented. The only trouble is it never happened.

There is no doubt that in his time Brigadier General Abner Doubleday was an important man. When the Confederate forces fired on Fort Sumter, he sighted the gun that fired the first shot. He wrote detailed descriptions of the battles at Chancellorsville and Gettysburg. While on duty at the presidio in San Francisco he suggested the first cable-operated streetcar in America and obtained the charter for its construction. He was a man for all seasons, except the baseball season. There is absolutely no evidence that Doubleday invented the game.

On the contrary, an enormous amount of literature shows, rather clearly, that the General had nothing to do with baseball. Surely a man who kept as careful an account of his life as Doubleday did would have recorded his love of baseball, yet of the sixty-seven diaries in the possession of Doubleday's heirs not one volume mentioned the sport. In the post-Civil War era, when baseball was presented to the nation as professional entertainment, the General did not even acknowledge its existence, odd behavior for the man credited with inventing the game.

When General Doubleday died in 1893, baseball was a smash hit across the country. Certainly it was something worth boasting about, but Honest Abner went to his grave without saying a word. Those who credited him with inventing the game overlooked certain facts: (1) The game of baseball (or "base ball") appeared in print as early as 1700, (2) The game of baseball was played in America before and during the Revolutionary War, (3) The rules of baseball attributed to Doubleday in 1839 were identical to those in a rule book for the English game of rounders published in London in 1827, and (4) The Doubleday diaries suggest that instead of going home to Cooperstown, New York, in the summer of 1839, he stayed on duty at West Point.

If rounders was not brought from England by the Mayflower settlers, who belittled time-consuming sports,

THE CATCHER.

THE PITCHER.

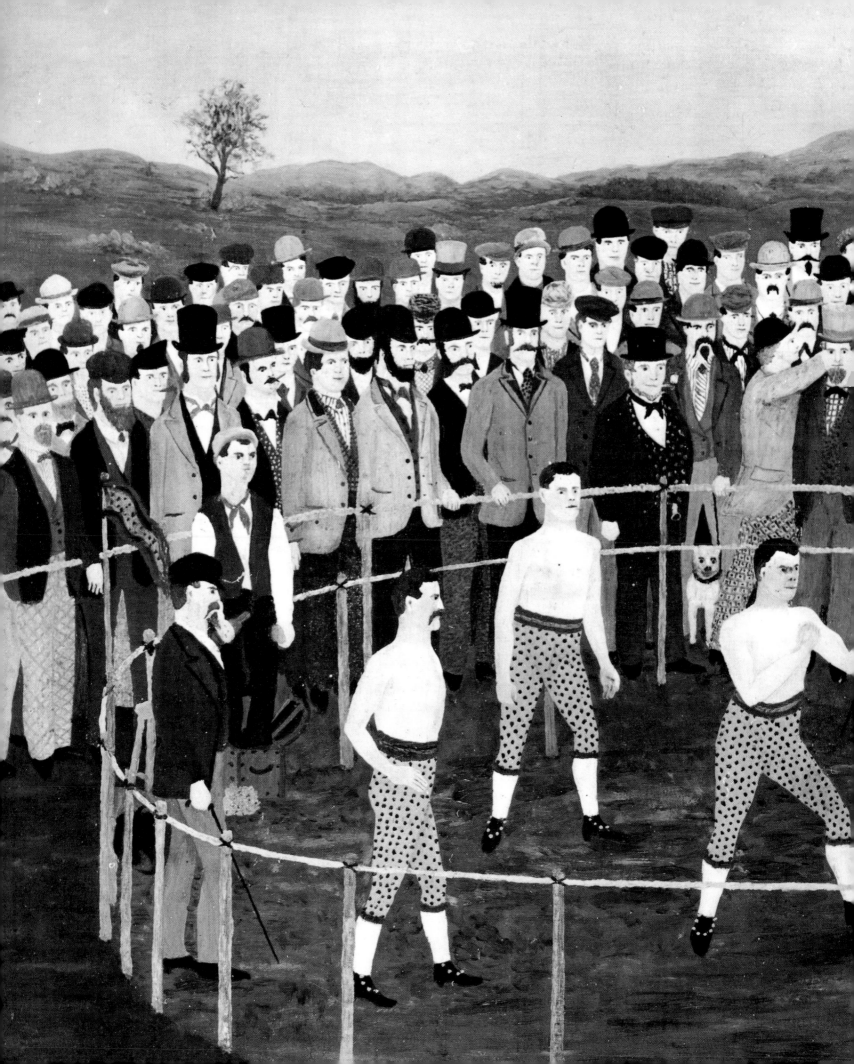

it was not long before it reached America. It became known as Town Ball, from the fact that it was played exclusively on town commons all over New England. It was enormously popular. In 1829, ten years before Abner Doubleday's alleged burst of genius at Cooperstown, Oliver Wendell Holmes spoke of the game being played while he was an undergraduate at Harvard.

According to published descriptions, Town Ball was neither scientifically planned nor skillfully played; it was like a kids sandlot game. Captains, chosen because of their dominant personalities, selected players until everybody was picked. The rules were made up before or even during the game, but different towns had different rules so what was permitted in Irasburg, Vermont, was not necessarily allowed in Craftsbury Common, only six miles away.

The playing field was usually square, roughly sixty feet to a side, with four stone bases at the corners. The pitcher stood in the middle, although in some variations of Town Ball he could throw from any angle inside the square. There were between eight and twenty players on a side, none of them stationed at any particular base since a batter could be put out by catching his hit either on a fly or on one bounce. The catcher was stationed ten yards behind home plate. Everybody on a side had a chance to bat before the game moved into the next inning. Some bats resembled a cricket paddle and others nothing more than a used ax handle. The ball was usually a bullet or a metal slug covered with yards of yarn and pieces of cowhide or deerskin. It was strictly the era of the dead ball.

What made Town Ball thrilling was a quaint but gruesome rule that permitted fielders to "plug" or "soak" the base runner, which was nothing more than hitting him with a throw. The runner had to move fast to reach base lest he be cut down by a defensive player drilling the ball straight into his spine. Some nasty injuries and fascinating fights resulted until the rule was made illegal.

Originally, large wooden stakes were used instead of bases, but after many mishaps of separated shoulders and crushed ribs, the stakes were replaced with flat stones. Still later, these were replaced by flour bags filled with sand, and finally stuffed canvas sacks. By the early 1700s so many games of Town Ball were played with bases instead of stakes that the name "base ball" evolved.

The rules of rounders were codified in *The Book of Sports,* edited by Robin Carver and printed in London in 1827. The author remarked that many people, especially Americans, called rounders by its new name, "base ball." Carver related that many Britons also used that name and that base ball was becoming a distinct threat to cricket.

Carver was not the only writer to make this observation. William Clerke, who had never seen Carver's book, came out with a work called *The Boys' Own Book,* in which he printed the new rounders rules and noted that Americans called the game either "Towne Ball" or "Base Ball." English schoolboys were apparently playing the sport according to the exact rules of the game in Boston, Bridgeport, or New Rochelle.

Many Americans did not want to admit that they had fallen hopelessly in love with the foreign-born game of rounders, especially since it was a game the English regarded as inferior to cricket and less important. But it might not have been necessary for American sportsmen to proclaim baseball an indigenous game had a Britisher not had the effrontery to confront them with the unadorned truth.

In the latter part of the nineteenth century Henry Chadwick, an Englishman who was an old-time baseball player turned sportswriter, wrote a series of columns about his experiences with cricket and rounders in England. He talked so long and loud about the games of his youth that he offended one of his dearest friends, Albert G. Spalding, a man of great power. Some people insist that Chadwick was the father of baseball, and there is a plaque on a Brooklyn street corner today that perpetuates the legend. Whatever, he did institutionalize baseball reporting as a mainstay of the modern newspaper. He also first used a box score, which today is a staple of every newspaper's summer sports section.

Spalding was a man accustomed to having his own way. He was a great pitcher, manager, and club owner. He opened the nation's first sporting goods house. Only twice was he disappointed in his life: when he ran for the United States Senate and lost and when he failed to persuade Henry Chadwick that baseball should be considered a native American sport. Chadwick insisted the game had distant foreign ancestry. Why, the French played a game in the twelfth-century church courtyards with four milking stools for bases. And Ancient Egyptians had a sacred bat-and-ball game. It was too much for Spalding to bear.

"I claim baseball owes its prestige as our National Game to the fact that no other form of sport is such an exponent of American courage, confidence, combativeness, dash, discipline, determination, energy, eagerness, pluck, persistency, performance, spirit, sagacity, success, vim, vigor, and virility," he said. And not content with celebrating America, he began to attack the mother country: "It would be impossible for a Briton, who had not breathed the air of this free land as a naturalized American citizen; for one who had not part or heritage in the hopes and achievements of our country, to play baseball, as it would for an American, free from the trammels of English traditions, customs and conventionalities, to play the national games of Great Britain."

By 1905 Spalding formed a distinguished committee to scotch reports that baseball was a foreigner. His group included Morgan Gardner Bulkeley, Nicholas Young, A. G. Mills, Alfred Reach, George Wright, and the president of the Amateur Athletic Union, James Sullivan, who served as secretary. They were all the surviving members of professional baseball's founding brotherhood. They would as soon have called baseball an English game as predict that Imperial Russia was ready for communism.

It was Mills who in 1880 created the reserve clause, which bound a player for life to the first team that signed

him to a contract. Morgan Gardner Bulkeley, later to become a United States Senator, founded and served as first president of the National League. And Young, Reach, and Wright were among the first great professional baseball players to move effortlessly into influential businesses. These pillars of the baseball establishment were busy men and it seems that none of them helped Sullivan in researching the question. All of Sullivan's information was forwarded to Mills, who knew exactly what Albert G. Spalding was looking for.

Unfortunately for Spalding, there was little evidence to support his thesis and a lot to contradict it. A note from a Connecticut state court justice stated that he participated in nine-man rounders (or "base ball") for a team in Wethersfield in 1830. The judge said he and his colleagues played by the rules they had seen in *Darcy's American Sporting Journal;* these had been reprinted from a London magazine published months earlier. No matter where Sullivan poked and prodded, the evidence came back to the inevitable: baseball came from Town Ball, Town Ball came from rounders, and rounders was an English game. Therefore, baseball was an English game with American improvements.

What saved the situation for Spalding and company was a letter from Abner Graves, an eighty-nine-year-old retired mining engineer from Denver. He claimed he was there the day that Abner Doubleday invented the game. His memory had not dulled in nearly sixty-nine years, he said; he could recall every incident.

"Doubleday laid down the baseball rules, much as they are today, in the spring just prior or following the William Henry Harrison hard cider campaign for the presidency," Graves wrote. "The game has not changed much since that time."

The Graves letter pleased A. G. Mills, who had known Doubleday quite well. Now, he could do exactly what Spalding wanted and at the same time honor an old friend, dead only a few years. Doubleday had played an important part in the battle at Gettysburg, in which Mills

47

When Stephen Foster composed "Camp-town Races" before the Civil War, he struck a musical note ("doo-dah") that affected the nation's popular music. Baseball's emergence in the 1860s led to many musical creations, among them "Home Run Quick Step." Albert G. Spalding, who would become wealthy as a manufacturer of sports equipment, sponsored Brigadier General Abner Doubleday as the inventor of the American game of baseball.

HOME RUN QUICK STEP.

RESPECTFULLY DEDICATED

MEMBERS OF THE

MERCANTILE BASE BALL CLUB

OF

PHILAD.ª

JOHN ZEBLEY, JR.

had also fought. But since Doubleday had sought no publicity and received none, he already was being forgotten. Here was a means of making Abner Doubleday immortal. With obvious delight, Mills penned his report.

"In the days when Abner Doubleday attended school in Cooperstown, it was common for two dozen or more schoolboys to join him in a game of ball," Mills began. "It is easy to understand how this West Point graduate would devise a scheme for limiting the contestants on each side and allotting them to field positions each with a certain amount of territory, also substituting the existing method of putting out the base runner for the old one of plugging him with the ball."

Arbitrarily, Mills set the year as 1839, though Harrison's campaign for the presidency did not start until the late summer of 1840 and ended with his inauguration in April, 1841. One historian said it would not have made any difference to Spalding if Mills told him that Old Tippecanoe himself had invented baseball. In fact, that might have delighted him. He needed a genuine, red-blooded, All-American folk hero. When he discovered that Doubleday had been a general, just like Harrison, he anointed him. Posthumously the Brigadier General became the father of a game for which he had not had even a passing interest.

It took an enormous amount of persuasion by Spalding to put the idea across, since he could not substantiate Abner Graves's story. Eventually, he became quite defensive about the matter. In 1911 he wrote a history of the game that thundered, "Cricket is a genteel pastime [as if anyone had confused cricket with rounders]. Baseball is war! Cricket is an athletic sociable, played and applauded in a conventional, decorous English manner. Baseball is an athletic turmoil, played and applauded in an unconventional, enthusiastic, and American manner. The founder of our national game became a major general in the United States Army. It is quite enough here to say that our commission, after a long, thorough and painstaking investigation of all obtainable facts, unanimously

declared that baseball had its origins in the United States and that the first scheme for playing it, according to the best evidence obtainable to date, was devised by Abner Doubleday at Cooperstown in 1839. Accepting the decision of the commission appointed to consider the subject of the origin of baseball, I have absolutely nothing to add."

Spalding guaranteed that Abner Graves's claim was absolutely correct. Moreover, he claimed that Doubleday had outlined the first diamond with a stick in the dirt, invented the modern players' positions, drew a diagram of the field, and coined the name "baseball." That is not exactly what Graves said in his letter, but for obvious reasons Spalding could hardly confine himself to the facts.

The tale might have survived as history had not Robert W. Henderson, a New York librarian, started searching for the records at West Point. Sure enough, the records showed that Cadet Doubleday, class of 1842, had not gone home to Cooperstown in the spring or summer of 1839, or any other time that year.

The only man to emerge with honor from this cover-up of baseball's true origins was Doubleday himself. After all, he never said he invented baseball.

Peculiar baseball forms persisted well into the 1840s. In one highly popular version the pitcher stood fifteen paces from the batter in an open-ended rectangle. After hitting the ball, the batter ran seven paces to his right, where first base was located. Then he progressed twenty paces down the field to second base. Then he turned and ran fifteen paces to third. Finally, he headed home, which was located thirty paces away. Home was parallel to the batter's base and about five paces behind it. There were no basemen and no outfielders, just roving defensive players called scouts. It was plug baseball at its worst. The great national pastime was waiting not for Albert G. Spalding and his commission to proclaim its origins but for Alexander Joy Cartwright, who truly can be called

the Father of American Baseball, to organize it.

Cartwright did not invent the sport; he simply made it sane and playable. If Spalding had been content to canonize Cartwright and designate him as the man who Americanized an imperfect foreign sport, Spalding might have glorified his country just as well at the cost of far less violence to history. And incidentally, the Baseball Hall of Fame undoubtedly would be located in New York City instead of Cooperstown.

It was Cartwright who concluded that the bases should be set ninety feet apart and that to retire a man the ball should be thrown to a defensive baseman rather than at a base runner. According to many witnesses it happened one Sunday morning in June, 1845. There was a grassy open field between Third Avenue and the railroad cut, about a half mile below the reservoir, at what is now the corner of Lexington Avenue and Thirty-fourth Street. The young men of Manhattan gathered on a weekend to hit a ball until darkness drove them to their carriages. Often they played games of their own invention. Sometimes they worked on Town Ball or Four Old Cat; other times they strictly observed the new rules of English rounders.

They were playing one of the New England games when they saw Cartwright hastily striding down the long dusty road. His enormous stature made him difficult to ignore; he was six feet two inches, very straight in his walk, and wore very handsome chin whiskers. The match in progress halted as he trotted onto the field, waving a set of papers. Cartwright acted, said one observer, as if he had just come into an inheritance. He presented a simple diagram that he and a fellow named Charles M. Wadsworth had worked out.

Not one man in the crowd understood exactly what Cartwright was sputtering over. They all laughed and made snide jokes. However, because they were mostly well-bred enough to listen, however skeptically, they let him draw his diagram in the dirt, and even helped him with it. Then they took the positions he directed them to, though with much hooting. They also complained vigor-

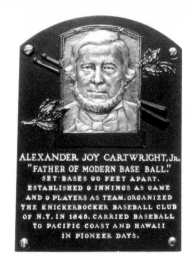

ALEXANDER JOY CARTWRIGHT, Jr.
"FATHER OF MODERN BASE BALL."
SET BASES 90 FEET APART.
ESTABLISHED 9 INNINGS AS GAME
AND 9 PLAYERS AS TEAM. ORGANIZED
THE KNICKERBOCKER BASEBALL CLUB
OF N.Y. IN 1845. CARRIED BASEBALL
TO PACIFIC COAST AND HAWAII
IN PIONEER DAYS.

ously because there were only nine men to a side. After eighteen players were chosen, they protested, the remainder could not play and that was contrary to the practice of the times.

Cartwright decreed that when the ball was struck into the field and knocked down by a defensive man it had to be thrown to first base in order to retire the runner. Scouts would have to stay close to bases and try to retire batters by stepping on the bags. He also limited each side's turn to three outs.

"Damned good game," said Duncan Curry, one of the players. "Where the hell did you come up with it, Alex?"

All week long they struggled with the intricacies of Cartwright's game. They found canvas sacks and drew up a proper infield. The pitcher was placed forty-five feet from home base. (In 1881, the distance was increased to fifty feet. In 1893, it became sixty feet, but a surveyor misreading "60-0" for "60-6," made it sixty feet six inches, the distance it is today.)

The group, which would call itself the Knickerbocker Club, set out the next spring on a trip to New Jersey on what the players called a prospecting tour. As they headed for the Barclay Street ferry dock, they carried their bats and balls stuffed in straw suitcases. The morning was swept clean of clouds and a small wind was drifting down the mighty Hudson. It was a fine day for history making.

The group included Cartwright and Curry, James Lee, William Randolph Wheaton, Edwin Dupignac, Jr., Wilford H. Tucker, Dr. Arthur Randson, Abraham Tucker, James Fisher, and Theodore Vail, who was known to his companions as "Stay-Where-You-Are Vail," suggesting that he had not quite mastered Cartwright's new base-running techniques. The men walked up the dry dirt road through the Jersey countryside, enjoying the fragrance of the blooming flowers. In the tangled hedges and stone fences along the road, orioles were singing. This was a different time and Hoboken was not yet a gritty factory

town but a resort town for tired New Yorkers.

The Knickerbockers stopped next to McCarty's Hotel at a lot called Elysian Fields. There is a plaque there today that commemorates the events of that day and observes, "It is generally considered that until this time the game [baseball] was not seriously regarded." The date was June 19, 1846.

Cartwright pointed out to the young men with him that the nearby inn presented a place to get a warm meal or a cool drink after the game. Perhaps considering this fact himself, the owner of the place had no objection to the Knickerbockers and their opposition, the New York Nine, playing on his meadow. The tourists watched with amusement as the Knickerbocker Club was defeated 23–1 at its own game.

The New York game spread because it was more stylish than the New England game. A team that called itself the Jolly Young Bachelors' Baseball Club became the Brooklyn Excelsiors and challenged the Knicks as well as teams called the Washington Gothams and the Brooklyn Eagles. Eventually, these New York teams were joined by the Atlantic Club of Brooklyn, the New York Empires, the New York Metropolitans, the Putnams, and the Eckford team from the Bronx.

Yet few people paid attention to the New York game in the 1840s. Most athletes thought the Knickerbocker rules to be somewhat soft. Plugging the base runner was still favored by some well into the twentieth century. During one game in 1905, a year in which he won 24 games in the American League, the Philadelphia Athletics' great left-hander, Rube Waddell, tried to hit a runner going to second base. "That's an out where I come from in Pennsylvania," he explained.

A Bostonian in 1850 would have laughed uproariously at what he considered the effeminate sport devised by Alexander J. Cartwright. In New England it was appropriate to have two dozen people play on a side. And though less artistic, perhaps, the New England game did have published rules. "The trouble with the New York

Alexander Joy Cartwright was a quiet, intense man whose mind grasped the fundamental concepts of baseball. More than any other man, he wrote rules that influenced and guided the game toward what it is today. In baseball's Hall of Fame, a bronze plaque honors Cartwright .

game," said Amos Bidwell, a devotee of the New England game, "is that it leaves less room for argument. They have two umpires who are presumed to be infallible. Our choosers can turn to a spectator for advice. Players may depart from the game by simply letting the chooser know that they are going. Our oblong field makes for more scattered play and, hence, more excitement. The fact that our third base is closer to second than it is to fourth base makes a better show of running. The Boston rule for changing the thrower and catcher every three innings makes for less specialization. The New York game will never survive because it lets one man pitch as long as he likes."

Most New Yorkers considered their game strictly for men of the upper classes. Yet the game did not expect or reward gentility. A third baseman who moved in front of a slow-moving shortstop to pick up the ball was being clever, though an Englishman might consider him a poor fellow. This new game was not cricket.

It was, as Albert G. Spalding claimed, a poor man's game and essentially American. The equipment was cheap in those days before gloves. Playing fields could be arranged on vacant lots, of which there were many in mid-nineteenth century America. A group called the Pastime Club from a tavern on Long Island formed a contending team without a drop of blue blood. They were just a bunch of men with gritty necks who gathered on Sundays to pitch horseshoes, swill some ale, and argue about sports. They looked at the Knickerbocker game and found that they did not have the time to play until twenty-one or more runs were scored, the total that gentlemen used to define the end of the game. The lowbrows discovered that playing nine innings suited their time schedule and gave everybody a chance to bat about four times, just enough, they thought.

Other teams of a similar economic level followed. A group of New York policemen formed the New York Manhattans. The New York Phantoms were a team of bartenders. The second team to use the name New York

Metropolitans consisted of schoolteachers and clerks, the Metropolis Club of politicians and journalists, and the New York Pocahontas Club of milkmen and farmers. They did not class themselves with the rich men's teams; they simply liked the sport and played it. Baseball, they found, was a fine sport for gambling. They enjoyed betting small sums of money as much as Cartwright's bunch enjoyed wagering large sums.

The Knickerbockers used gambling terms to describe their game. Time at bat was a hand and a run was an ace. Driving in two runs was a deuce. Because gamblers were fancy men, people who followed sports were called "fans." Every player bet on the outcome of the games in which he played. The umpires (who sat in high chairs on the sidelines, much like tennis officials), bet, too, though occasionally they warned the teams in advance which way they had bet.

In its formative years, baseball had a distinct advantage over other sports in that it was a sport its participants openly enjoyed. Once the rules had been refined to eliminate the rowdyism, it was clean enough to play even before ladies.

In the 1850s, there appeared on the scene one George Wright, the same man who was later to participate in A. G. Spalding's fabrication about Abner Doubleday. He was a sixteen-year-old cricket player with a trim moustache and long blond curls, which men grumbled over and women gushed over. Handsome, dashing, and personable, he also played baseball with a spirit and inventiveness that few people had ever seen. Wright made one-handed catches, and from his position at shortstop often flipped the ball behind his back to his second baseman. He had range and speed. He also understood how to run the bases; he would reach first, take a slight lead, and head for second. Others watched and learned.

The people adored George Wright and they came to watch him and such other heroes of the 1850s as Dickey Pearce and Joe Start.

Some two thousand persons actually paid fifty cents

each to enter Fashion Race Course in 1859 to see the Brooklyn Excelsiors play the Brooklyn Atlantics. It was the first time admission had ever been charged.

The sport was developing fast. As the game became open to the increasing number of Irish immigrants, there was as much a furor over the addition of young Shamus Creighton to the Excelsiors' lineup as there was a century later when Jackie Robinson became the first black to play for a major league team. In some quarters the Irish were considered a bit too rough for what was still supposed to be an elitist's sport. But Creighton could pitch with great speed. America has usually managed to put aside prejudice in the face of proven performance.

George Wright invited his brother, Harry, to join the exclusive Knickerbockers in 1856. When the war was over, the Wright brothers would found a professional baseball team and then a league.

9   America Enters the Ring

Large wisps of cigar smoke hung in the air of the old cotton storage shed as the fighters for the main event were ushered in. They were dressed in tights and they had cloaks thrown around their shoulders. They were both black, as had been every boxer all afternoon. It was almost twilight and the gentlemen in the shed, almost all of them planters, were negotiating big money bets as slaves in expensive livery passed among them offering drinks or fried delicacies from the kitchen. Beyond the crowd, in the doorways, stood other slaves from the plantation, having been rewarded with such a choice location by the favor of either the head overseer or some member of the master's family.

The last fighters of the day were heavyweights who stood five feet nine inches tall and weighed around one hundred ninety pounds. They were not large by today's standards, but both were powerful and sleek. They were fed better than the house servants and far better than

the field hands. The fighters were quartered in cabins with comfortable beds, and some even had other slaves to wait on them. They were valuable housepets.

Some fighters were fighting for their liberty. If they won a specified number of bouts and returned a sufficient amount of money in prizes and wagers to their owner, they were set free. Often the owners regarded the conditions of these agreements highly enough to have them recorded before town clerks. When a slave champion became free, he often received a suit of clothes, a percentage of his winnings, and other benefits from his owner.

It was from this era that Tom Molineaux (sometimes spelled Molyneux) came. He was America's first black athletic hero.

There is as much mystery about Molineaux's origin as that of Justin Morgan's horse Figure. One account contends that Molineaux was born in Georgetown, D. C., and raised to be the personal servant of an urban gentleman who put Molineaux to fighting when he discovered that young Tom was a splendid athlete. Another version holds that Molineaux grew up on a Virginia plantation. Still other sources say that he was the son or the grandson of a freedman, also named Tom Molineaux, who had gained his liberty by being a slave boxer before the Revolution. The controversy over Tom Molineaux's identity reached a point where a writer from *Harper's Weekly* researched the matter in 1858 and found only enough data to suggest that Molineaux was probably a slave on a Virginia plantation who fought his way to freedom.

The name Molineaux or Molyneux appears frequently in the history of American prizefighting. It was customary for black boxers to pretend they were somehow either related or associated with the famed Tom Molineaux, just as Italian, German, and Jewish boxers adopted Irish names in the early 1900s because Irish boxers had been so popular.

Pierce Egan, the first great boxing writer, probably

In one of the first international competitions between the new world and the old, the radically styled yacht *America* sailed to England in 1851 to engage in a series of races that began a world-wide competition. *America* won the race in an astonishing upset, establishing a winning tradition that remains unbroken. The America's Cup, which is bolted to a table in the New York Yacht Club, is a symbol of American dominance in the world of sailing.

persons in Boston and thirty thousand in Jones Woods outside of New York. Thus, he prophesied prizefighting's growing popularity, if not its rise to respectability. In the 1880s, when John L. Sullivan arrived, it became obvious that boxing would perish unless it made its peace with the law. The bare-knuckle era, said one fiery critic, died a much overdue death.

10   Sinking the Queen's Navy

Yachting in America probably began with the Dutch in 1664 with a race around New York Harbor. By 1717 the harbor was filled with sporting boats. So thick were they on a summer's day that it was difficult for merchant ships to find their wharfs. Racing on the water was much in fashion. The gentry had their pleasure barges and the lower classes had their yachts and boats. Even the poor found a skiff or two.

In 1851, a wealthy man created the graceful schooner *America,* which won a singularly ugly cup worth a mere one hundred guineas at the time of the cup's rendering. The cup had a long curlicue handle, a pelican spout, a narrow neck, and a filigreed abdomen. It has been bolted onto a heavy table at the New York Yacht Club's headquarters for nearly one hundred twenty years now. Yachtsmen from countries that used to be part of the British Empire have spent hundreds of millions of dollars trying to pry it loose. It is called the America's Cup and hardly any competitor for it has actually seen it.

The man who helped begin this tradition was, appropriately enough, a fanatic yachtsman, John C. Stevens. His father had been one of the country's first maritime engineers, and the son had been totally captivated by the sea. Stevens, Sr., manufactured steam-driven ships for the open seas. Stevens, Jr., though he went through the ritual of following in his father's business, built experimental sailing ships for racing on Long Island Sound.

It was in the main saloon of Stevens' sporting schooner *Gimcrack* that the New York Yacht Club was formed and the plans for the construction of the *America* revealed. There had been an exchange of international correspondence in the spring of 1850 between Commodore Stevens and Lord Wilton, commander of the Royal Yacht Club. An American boat was invited to come to Britain and participate in a regatta as part of the first World's Fair, to be held in London. Stevens realized that no yacht in the New World could possibly compete against the best of England and Scotland. He commissioned the brilliant designer George Steers to create a vessel capable of defending the nation's honor.

According to *Gleason's Pictorial,* the people who came to witness the laying of the *America's* keel did not leave until after the yacht was launched. Americans of that day desperately wanted to overcome the English on the sea. Britannia might have ruled the waves—her flag was everywhere—but Americana was hot in her wake. John C. Stevens and his seven-man syndicate of New York millionaires were leading the charge.

"She is modeled on the lines of those fast New York packet boats," said *Gleason's* of the *America.* "She is one hundred and one feet, nine inches long and will be rigged rakishly as a schooner. Her mainmast will be eighty-one feet high, her foremast seventy-nine feet, and her bowsprit thirty-two. When completed she will sweep every other craft from the ocean."

Escorted by ferry boats and steamships, *America* slipped past the fuming smokestacks of the William Brown Yard and moved out to sea on June 21, 1851, heading for Le Havre, where she would be refitted for racing. From there she would sail to the Isle of Wight for a showdown with the British in the Queen's Cup. The English, it turned out, had a surprise waiting. Even before the *America* reached port, she would be challenged by a British cutter, the *Laverock.* There had been loose talk in Le Havre that an English ship might meet the American challenger in the channel, simply to test her strength. But the Americans, being somewhat naïve, had dismissed the stories as sheer nonsense. They believed that the British were impeccable sportsmen.

There are numerous accounts of what happened, almost all of them conflicting. Years later Stevens wrote his own to the *New York Times,* and this is probably the most accurate version:

> In coming from Le Havre, we were obliged by the darkness of the night and a thick fog to anchor some five or six miles from Cowes, the royal resort of the Isle of Wight. In the early morning the tide was against us and it was a dead calm. At nine A.M. a gentle breeze sprang up and, with it, gliding along, came the *Laverock,* one of the newest and fastest cutters of her class. The news had spread like lightning that the Yankee Clipper had arrived and the *Laverock* had gone down to show her the way up.
>
> The vessels in the harbor, the wharves and windows of all the houses bordering on them were filled with thousands of spectators, watching with eager eyes the eventful trial they saw we could not escape. The *Laverock* stuck to us, sometimes laying to and sometimes tacking around us, evidently showing she had no intention of quitting us. We were loaded with extra sails, with beef and port and bread enough for an East India voyage and were some four or five inches too deep in the water. We got up our sails with heavy hearts. The wind increased to a five- or six-knot breeze and after waiting until we were ashamed to wait any longer, we let her get about two hundred yards ahead. Then we started in her wake.
>
> During the first five minutes of the test not a sound was heard, save the beating of human hearts or the slight ripple of the water upon her [the *America's*] swordlike stern. The captain was crouched down upon the floor of the cockpit, his seemingly unconscious hand upon the tiller, with his stern, unaltering gaze upon the vessel ahead. The men were motionless as statues, their eyes fixed upon the *Laverock* with an intensity that was nearly unnatural. We worked quickly and surely to windward of her wake. The crisis was past and some dozen deep-drawn breaths proved that the agony was over. Our ship came to anchor perhaps a third of a mile ahead. Our anchor was down roughly twenty minutes before the *Laverock,* and the Earl of Wilton came on board to introduce his family and friends when the other ship was coming to an anchorage.

There were some interesting differences between the *America* and her opponents. British yachts of the era were of heavy displacement, narrow in the beam with extremely deep keels. Their sails were cut from loose-textured, handwoven flax. The *America* was broad with a shallow draft. Her masts were raked sharply, a design that stunned the British. She could set more than five thousand square feet of sail, one-third more than her opponents. Her mainsail and her foresails were laced to her booms and loose fitted. She was a one hundred seventy-ton greyhound. The British had no chance. The age of the Yankee Clipper was beginning. Stevens wrote:

> In our race for the Queen's Cup there were seventeen entries. Our directions from the sailing committee were simple and direct. We were to start from the flagship at Cowes, keep the No Man's Buoy on the starboard hand, and thence make our way around the Isle of Wight and back to the flagship from whence we started.
>
> We got off before the wind and in the midst of a crowd we could not get rid of for the first eight or nine miles. A fresh breeze then sprang up that soon cleared us from our hangers-on and sent us rapidly ahead of every yacht in the royal squadron. At the Needles there was not a yacht that started with us in sight. So that when

somebody asked Her Majesty, the Queen, if she would care to know who was first and she replied that she would, they said that the *America* was. Then she volunteered to know who was second. A high personage told her, "No one." After passing the Needles we were overtaken by the Royal steam yacht *Victoria and Albert*. Her Majesty and family were on board to witness the trial of speed.

After the steamer passed, we had the gratification of tendering our homage to the Queen, after the fashion of her own people, by taking off our hats and dipping our flag. At this time the wind had fallen to a light breeze, and we did not arrive at the flagship until dark. I did not learn until much later when the others arrived, but the cup that we so proudly bear comes by the courtesy of Her Majesty and the Earl of Wilton. It is possible now to toast both the President of the United States and the Queen of England.

In 1857, the Cup was placed in the New York Yacht Club. Twenty-two challenges have been surmounted, and the Cup has never left. The *America* later became a blockade runner and was renamed the *Memphis*. A schooner, supposedly the same boat, was permanently docked at Annapolis in 1929.

The *America* was an American heroine. She was strong, swift, different, and she won with ease, a characteristic her fellow countrymen much admired. Let the British speak extravagantly of sportsmanship. Winning was the American goal.

11 The Gentle Game

Croquet was the first sport to be adopted by American women, creatures who were supposed to suffer silently, listen to their husbands at all times, produce children to populate an under-populated land, and sit quietly in the shadows. Under no circumstances were they to be out on the lawn in the hot sun engaging in physical activities, but that was exactly what many of them were doing. They were engrossed in a sporting craze so fierce that for the next thirty years no home was considered complete or civilized without a croquet lawn.

Criticism was intense and unmerciful. *Harper's Weekly* editorialized, "Ladies have been known to try cricket without much success. Their batting and their running are dreadfully embarrassed by their petticoats, and few of the ladies have the nerve required to stand up to the approach of a swiftly pitched ball. Having been defeated by their gender at men's games they are now turned to something called croquet, which they play endlessly and shamelessly."

The vision of an entire generation of American women debased by sport soon faded. While men were fighting at Gettysburg, croquet, with its slow pace and genteel atmosphere, became the courting game of the North. When the War Between the States ended, croquet was a firmly established institution. Even *Harper's Weekly* relented. No longer seeing it as a threat to society, the magazine praised croquet as "the most delightful opportunity for flirtations and a boon to the health of young ladies who play the sport so well." So popular did croquet become that Captain Mayne Reed, author of the first book on the subject, lamented that the game had lost its aristocratic status.

Croquet was a simple pastime. A player drove the ball from a starting stake through a series of wire wickets and back. Slamming an opponent's ball out of bounds added a slightly savage element that was not at all lost upon the women who played the game with such a passion. They took particular pleasure in driving some man's ball into the distant rough.

Arguments arose over the rules because every manufacturer of croquet equipment included his own list of regulations. So a convention of croquet players, most of them female, was held at Norwich, Connecticut, in

Most nineteenth century sports appealed
only to men, but women had their competitive ventures, too. Women were active in
many areas of athletics, including archery,
tennis, rowing, swimming, and croquet.
Artist Winslow Homer painted several
studies of croquet, including the one at
left in 1866.

1882. The group formed the National Croquet Association. A high tournament game called "roque" was devised and for the first time men and women took part in
a major sporting event. No historical plaque in Norwich
commemorates this unusual event, however.

Hearing that the Americans had taken up their game,
the British were skeptical, if not contemptuous. The
humor magazine *Punch* depicted Yankee croquet players
using Indian war clubs as mallets to stroke ninety-six-
pound cannon balls through triumphal arches.

Later, roque became an extremely competitive masculine game, played on slick bowling greens with short
mallets and hard rubber balls. The wide wickets of croquet were narrowed to make the game more difficult.
Exclusive roque clubs sprang up all over the Eastern
states. Gone was the easy camaraderie and the joyous
spontaneity of croquet. Roque forsook women.

Nevertheless, croquet's greatest significance was that
it liberated females from their athletic closet. Given the
opportunity to compete, they began to search for other
activities that were socially acceptable. It happened
almost a century before Billie Jean King, who would lead
the most successful campaign yet in the fight to liberate
the American female athlete.

12   Bear Market

War! War! War!
The celebrated bull-killing bear,
GENERAL SCOTT,
will fight a bull on Sunday the 15th, at 2 P. M.
at Moquelumne Hill.
The Bear will be chained with a twenty-
foot chain in the middle of the arena.
The bull will be perfectly wild, young,
of the Spanish breed. The bull's horns
will not be sawed off to prevent accidents.
The bull will be quite free in the arena
and not hampered.

The celebrated grizzly General Scott embarked on his bull-baiting career after he
crashed through the upper reaches of the
Sierras, barely at his full growth, with an
arrow half-broken in his left haunch. Some
settler had seen the bear rummaging near his cabin and
shot him with a bow and arrow. General Scott was so
weakened and in such pain that he submitted to anyone
who would relieve him. The bear was fed several bottles
of beer, which made him groggy. The broken arrow was
brusquely removed and whiskey was poured into the
wound. The bear eventually mended.

Notwithstanding the ease with which General Scott fell
into captivity, it usually took great skill to entrap a bear
of his dimensions. The reward was great. An outstanding
specimen was worth between two thousand and two
thousand five hundred dollars on the open market. A man
named Ramon Ortega became famous throughout the
state for his ability as a bearcatcher. He began his career
on a Spanish land grant outside Los Angeles when he
killed a grizzly after it had killed and eaten three of the
four horses Ortega owned. A nephew, Jacinto Damien
Reyes, who spent most of his life as a ranger in the
Cuyama district of the Santa Barbara National Forest,
wrote this about Ortega:

My uncle, Ramon Ortega, went into the canyon
with nothing but a rope and a six-shooter. A few
hours later he came back to the ranch dragging
one of the largest grizzlies ever seen in California. From that time on, Ramon Ortega's favorite
sport was tying up grizzlies and turning them
over for a large fee to the men who promoted
bull-and-bear fights. He was not afraid of any
bear that ever lived. When he found a fresh bear
trail, the critter that used it was as good as finished. My uncle hated bears so much that he
began to raise what he called "The Ortega Fight
Bull," a breed that seemed to deeply enjoy dispatching bears with one flip of their horns.

The first time General Scott faced a bull in the arena the opposition was chained to a stake. The match was over so fast that the crowd in San José hardly remembered what had taken place. The General waddled onto the warm red sand, snorted a few times, stood up to his full eleven-foot height, and broke the bull's neck with one swat of his right paw. Then he rolled over on the ground, looked at the sky, and snorted. Somebody threw him a bottle of beer, which he drained playfully.

Later, he faced unchained bulls, but as the summers went by, he grew fatter and less agile and it was deemed necessary for him to fight a chained bull again. The customers complained loudly. After all, they argued, only once had the bear been badly gored. They insisted that he battle an unchained adversary.

So it would be when General Scott met the beige bull, Conquistador. On the morning of the battle, General Scott had his three or four bottles of beer and was in an especially savage mood. His angry bellowing could be heard by the men who lived in tents two miles away. Surely, Conquistador shivered in his pen.

The arena where the match would take place was a strong wooden structure made of shaggy redwood. The outer enclosure, made of ten-foot-high boards, was one hundred feet in diameter, and the arena proper was forty feet wide, enclosed by a strong, five-barred fence. There were fifty rows of seats to accommodate the large crowd that was expected. As the people entered, about noon, a couple of fiddlers entertained. A reporter said that it reminded him of a theater opening in San Francisco. The audience wore red, white, and blue shirts in honor of what they considered an American production, even though the territory was not then part of the nation. The men, bronzed by the sun and bearded, had pistols and bowie knives in their belts. Some Mexican women, wearing white dresses, puffed "cigaritas in delighted anticipation of the exciting scene that was about to be enacted."

Down the hillside came General Scott, not yet exposed to the public's gaze. His heavy wooden cage was lined with iron and there were bars on the outside. Everyone could hear his roars. There were two pens at the opposite side of the arena. In one of them Conquistador scratched the turf with his front right hoof.

The General was not a big betting favorite. Not only had many of the bulls he killed been tethered, but some that hadn't had had the tips of their horns sawed off. And of course the General was a known lush; he had to have his beer.

"Beer or no beer," said one miner, "there's nary a bull in Calaforny as can whip that there b'ar. He's a mean 'un, drunk or sober. He fights better when he are hung over, make no mistake about that."

A final gong was struck to warn people away from the bear as it was moved forward, deeply depressed at being caged. Some of the bolts connecting the door had slipped out of place. With a howl he flopped out on the sand in a vast ball of fury. As a handler tried to subdue him by pulling on his chain, he slammed large patches of dirt with his hind legs.

By the time the bull was released from his pen, the General had dug himself a pit and was in no mood to leave it. For a moment, Conquistador surveyed the ring, his coat all smooth and glossy. There were several white spots around his head and there were people who protested that this was not the animal they had paid to see. When he saw the bear, he attempted to return to his pen, but there were stakes in his way. He finally decided that he had no choice but to brawl. The General was prepared. The bull charged. The bear grazed him on the groin.

In fury and fear, Conquistador attacked again. This time the General grabbed him by the nose and held on. Acting almost cuddly, the bear rolled over and put his forepaws around Conquistador's neck. Hardly mollified, the bull attacked the bear's private parts. General Scott rolled his challenger over, chewed on him a while, and then let him escape. The bull went off to the far side of the arena, his nose dripping blood. The General went around begging for another beer, thinking the whole miserable business had ended. He was refused. Frustrated, he turned toward the bull, and dragged it around the ring by its right hind leg. The crowd shouted happily at the long-awaited action.

That should have been it, but the General was supposed to be a marathon bull-baiter. So they let another bull into the arena, one fresh and full of murder. The two bulls seemed to understand that the bear was their common enemy. The fresh bull caught the General in the haunch where the arrow had been. Now fully aroused, the bear turned in fury, slaughtering one bull and then the next. Afterward he sat in the middle of the arena, clapping his paws and begging for more beer. A few weeks later a bull killed the General with his first charge.

13   A Tale from the Wild West

The cowboy was a solitary figure and he did not want to spend leisure time outdoors in physical activities. He had enough of that on the job. Instead he headed for the saloon for active card-playing, not a game to be lightly considered in a history of American sport.

The cowboy wanted to be seated in a warm, comfortable saloon with perfumed ladies near him. He longed to forget about cows, horses, sheep, bears, and the other forms of wildlife he contended with in his work. (The Spanish custom, the rodeo, was not yet popular with the Anglo cowboys.) Nevertheless, the cowboy wanted action, and in card playing he found it. Witness this exceptional story taken from *The California Journal,* printed just after the Bear Flag Republic dissolved and California joined the Union in 1850:

> There is such a place as Deadwood, California, and a friend of ours passed through the town just the other day, stopping long enough to witness a trial before the chief officer of the law, vulgarly called the justice of the peace. The case was *Hank versus Breese* and the facts seemed to be that [the two men] had violated the law by playing poker on the Sabbath. The second fact was that Breese had played low down or, in other words, had cheated the plaintiff. The final fact was that the game had broken up in a row, the parties being broken up by the justice, who just happened to be present. It was an important case, both parties being well known and having hosts of friends.

> Twelve of the best in the locality formed the jury. At length an odd-looking genius named Stephen Lick was placed on the stand by the prosecution and the case proceeded.

> "You said you were present during the poker game between the parties, did we understand you correctly, Mr. Lick?" The witness nodded in the affirmative. "Did you observe the progress of the game with any interest?"

> "Reckon I did — liquor was pending upon it," said Lick.

> "What was at stake at the time the row between these two cow fellows took place?"

> "Well, the ante was two bits and Lem Hanks bet a half on his little pair. Then Bill he went in for—"

> "Never mind the details," interrupted the lawyer impatiently, "answer my question."

> "That's what I'm going to do," said the witness, drawing a large black plug of tobacco from his pocket. "You see when Lem dropped his half in the pot, Bill covered it with a big dollar. I could tell this was particular serious business. But from where I stood I could also tell that Bill held just a little pair. Lem, he then took a drink and appeared sort of careless—"

> "Come, come," said the attorney, "just tell us the amount of money at stake when the quarrel commenced."

"Steve," said the judge, familiarly, "you say that when Bill Breese shoved up his dollar, Lem Hanks took a snifter and appeared sort of careless. What did he do then?"

"He saw Bill and lifted him two scads. Bill appeared a little uneasy, but raised Lem a five spot. Lem took another drink and said that the game was getting interesting. At the same time he shook a ten dollar piece into the pot. Bill just said, 'Lem, you kind of suit me and I think I can go twenty dollars better.' Then we took a small drink and Lem spread himself. He thought he'd go thirty better on that twenty dollars. Bill, he then got down to scratch his foot and when he lifted up again he lifted Lem some twenty more. Then Lem begin to look downright distressed and pushed his shirt sleeves up to keep them from getting dirty. Why then Lem lifted him a cool fifty."

"Gentlemen of the jury," said the judge, "that's so. I was there and I seen Lem do it."

"Bill took another look at his hand," said Steve Lick, the witness, "and scratched his foot again. When he came up he asked me for a hundred dollars. I asked him what for and he said he wanted to clean out Lem Hanks. I told him he couldn't do it on his pair of deuces because old Lem had bully sixes. But he said, 'Cover my pile and I'll call him.' Well, I came up with the money and Bill Breese took down Lem's pile. Not too many people know how that could happen. Bill did have deuces first, I'll swear to that."

The lawyers, thinking the witness was about to continue his story to the point of endlessness, requested that he try to be brief. Stephen Lick bit a large piece out of his tobacco plug and continued. "The way of it was this: when I covered the pile, Bill called Lem and said, 'What do you have to say for yourself?' Lem said that he had three of them. 'Three what?' asked Bill. Lem said that he had nice little spots, all in the middle of the card. Bill said that even if he showed them he couldn't win this pot.

"Well, Lem wanted to know how so and he placed his revolver on the table. And Bill said, 'Cause here's four more of the same sort,' putting his revolver out on the table and cocking back the trigger. All that I know is Bill got the pot before he was arrested."

The lawyer for the plaintiff intended to have made a good case in relation to the manner in which defendant's hand became strengthened from a little pair of deuces to four aces, but to do so he would have had to call on somebody to explain where Lem got his three aces.

The judge saw through the case at once. He charged the jury that if they thought there was anything wrong with a man scratching his foot during a game of poker, they could so find. But if they thought such a movement was on the square, they would also be likely to pass over the act of fumbling with his shirt sleeves, as the plaintiff had done. The jury, after being out three minutes, brought in a verdict to the effect that it had been a tie game, and the judge dismissed the case. Thus was the game of Poker saved from calamity in Deadwood, California.

14 A Romantic Hazard

"I think that much the most enjoyable of all races is a steamboat race. . . . Two redhot steamboats raging along, neck and neck, straining every nerve—that is to say, every rivet in every boiler—quaking and shaking and groaning from stem to stern, spouting white steam from the pipes,

The sport of bull-baiting was a favorite of the hardy folk who traveled to California in the mid-nineteenth century to seek their fortunes in the gold fields around Sacramento. The event was a wildly brutal exercise between semiwild beasts that enlarged upon the concept of the cockfight. One has to search all the way back to the Roman circus to find a sport that appeals to the less noble senses of man.

pouring black smoke from the chimneys, raining down sparks, parting the river into long breaks of hissing foam—this is sport that makes a body's very liver curl with enjoyment. A horse race is pretty tame and colorless in comparison."

—Mark Twain, *Life on the Mississippi.*

Magnificent floating palaces coasted along the bayou in the afternoon, the sun illuminating the dazzling gingerbread-like structures. They were finer than any mansion along the shores. Their saloons were heavily carpeted and their steam organs played such tunes as "Long Long Ago," "The Battle of Prague," "Arkansas Traveler," "On a Barren Isle," and "A Life on the Ocean Wave, a Home on the Rolling Deep." The furniture was polished mahogany; the walls were paneled in walnut; there was brass everywhere. They were the architectural visions of their day.

Steamboats were not designed for racing. They were flat-drafted and wide, so they could only lumber along. Their paddle wheels were built for utility, not speed. Yet by the mid-1830s the lower Mississippi had become one of the great race courses of the world.

In order to pursue the sport of steamboat racing, it was necessary to strain boilers right to the brink of their still very limited and unpredictable capacities. Often there were towering explosions that sent great flumes of water skyward. The passengers, more thrilled than the crewmen, sometimes volunteered to throw their trunks in the furnaces just to keep the mighty wheels clanking in the water. In 1835, the *Aurora* sustained a mortal wound from a boiler explosion after the crew had burned most of her structure in a vain attempt to overcome the *Imperial Eagle*. More than forty-nine crewmen were killed or badly scalded, including the bartender, who had not wanted to go along in the first place.

"The object was to prove how fast you could get from here to there," said Twain, who worked as a pilot on the Mississippi. "That's all there was to it, except for the fact that the captain of a fast boat wanted to let people know he was the captain of a fast boat. These steamboats were works of pure American art, high and fine, pleasing and comfortable. Those were old flush times and none of them should have changed."

In 1858, the *Grey Eagle* became famous when it raced the *Itasca* to St. Paul to announce the news that Queen Victoria had sent President James Buchanan a message on the Atlantic cable. It was a grueling race and the *Grey Eagle* barely made it into the wharf ahead of its rival.

The news of such contests spread far beyond the Mississippi Valley and by the 1850s there were steamboats racing on the Great Lakes and on the Sacramento River in California.

The inhabitants along the river banks became downright hostile because it seemed they were forever picking debris and corpses out of the scrubs that lined the river. They would be eating a lunch of corncakes and washing them down with cider, and some damn fool trying to reach Natchez first would slam the sides out of his boilers. It reached the point where the *Daily Alta Californian* thundered about the dangers of this daring racing sport after the *Pearl* and the *Great Enterprise* went on a harrowing trip down the Sacramento delta, throwing sparks that started numerous forest fires.

According to romantic tradition, racing was supposed to be spontaneous—a steamboat captain taking off after the opposition through sheer pride and exuberance. Perhaps the sport began that way but before long the races were planned. Dates and times of upcoming races were published. Crowds always knew when to gather down the river to watch the swiftest and most famous boats. Results were quickly printed in sporting journals. There were even handicappers, who knew that the *Belle of Cincinnati* was quicker than the *Great Star Circle*.

The riverboats were the first product of the Industrial

Revolution significantly to affect sport in America. They were ungainly contraptions, belching fire and hooting horribly. Yet they were seen as floating castles delivering opulence and elegance to their ports of call. "The steamboats brought it all," gushed a Natchez writer. "When a great racehorse was coming to town, he was on board a steamboat. When there was a great cockfight, like as not the cocking main was in the grand saloon of some elegant steamer. When there was nothing else to do there was a card game on board. On slow, warm nights you could hear them racing."

For a country wowed by progress, the romance of the steamboats was hard to resist. Off in the distance one whistle would shriek, and then another, so piercingly that they seemed to tear the leaves off the trees. The sparks crackled upward from the dull black stacks. The wheels, either on the side or at the stern, churned furiously in the dark water. When the steamboats raced past a wharf, urged on by passengers who stayed up all night to feed the fire, everybody in town stayed up, too, with torches in hand to watch the great white palaces charge by, elegant shadows in the night.

15   Ocean-going Opulence

The father of American yachting, George Crowninshield, was a short, pudgy man. In his bright red waistcoats, boots with gold tassels, blue-dyed beaver hats, and hair tied back in a pigtail, he looked a bit bizarre but he seemed to enjoy that.

His family had been in the merchant marine business, outfitting ships for the West Indies trade. After the death of his father, it was left to George to run the business, an older brother, Benjamin, having rushed off to the capital to be Secretary of the Navy. When not attending to business, George would leave Boston Bay on board his favorite ship to look for merchantmen who were floundering in trouble after a storm. Three times he had saved drown-

ing men and once was awarded a gold medal from the Massachusetts Humane Society for his bravery.

Almost all the foreign shipping companies with which Crowninshield dealt had competitive yachts. The American shipping magnate longed to make America a respectable power in ocean racing, then a burgeoning sport in Europe. His first effort was launched on October 21, 1816, from Retire Beckett's shipworks in Salem, Massachusetts. People gathered on the banks around the shipworks to watch the 195-ton brigantine slip into the water. She had cost somewhere between fifty and sixty thousand dollars, a massive fortune at that time, and sported rainbow stripes on one side and a gray herringbone pattern on the other. She was christened Cleopatra's Barge because Crowninshield was especially fond of Shakespeare's play "Antony and Cleopatra," and doted on the passage (Act Two, Scene Two) that began, "The barge she sat in, like a burnished throne, burned on the water. The poop was beaten gold. Purple the sails, and so perfumed that the winds were love-sick with them." The vainglorious Crowninshield sent outfitters into her hold to convert her into a sea-going inn complete with cypress panels and bird's eye maple furnishing. The local citizenry, used to austerity, was utterly amazed at such magnificence. On an unusually warm winter's day, some one thousand nine hundred women and seven hundred men came to visit Cleopatra's Barge. Nothing had been spared. There were elegant settees with velvet cushions, chairs with descriptive plates, mirrors on the walls, and buffets loaded with plates of every kind and the best glass and porcelain.

Investigating this craft, a reporter from the Salem Gazette descended into a magnificent saloon about twenty feet long and twenty feet broad, finished on all sides with a polished wood that was either cypress or mahogany and inlaid with other ornamental woods. The splendid mirrors standing at both ends and a grand chandelier suspended in the center of the saloon "give a richness of effect not easily surpassed," he reported.

The spring of 1817 came to old New England and the

Barge weighed anchor for her maiden voyage. At every port of call Crowninshield held an open house, pouring much wine as he showed off his treasure. There was a wooden Indian just underneath the wheelhouse. The visitors to the *Barge* in foreign lands took it to be some sort of American saint. In the dissolute port of Marseilles one intoxicated Frenchman bowed and kissed the Indian's feet.

By the fall, after sailing against the best of Europe and winning, the ship was once more at the wharf in Salem, with Crowninshield living on board. He was planning another voyage in the spring, this one to the Baltic Sea, where he planned to take on the best yachts from Germany, Denmark, Sweden, Russia, Poland, and Finland. But on November 26, 1817, while dining with a lady friend, Crowninshield was stricken with a heart attack. He called for a glass of gin, but it reached him too late.

The furnishings of the *Barge* were distributed among Crowninshield's relatives and the ship was sold at auction for sixteen thousand dollars, which was extraordinarily cheap. She was purchased by a merchant who immediately pressed her into the Hawaiian sandalwood trade. When she reached the islands she was sold to King Lihoiliho to pay off a ninety thousand dollar debt and was renamed *The Pride of Hawaii*. While the Hawaiian king was in London trying to convince the British that the Hawaiian islands were far too civilized to be incorporated into the British Empire, the ship ground its gorgeous hull into a coral reef off the island of Kauai and settled into ten feet of tropical water. The crew tied ropes around her masts and tried to bring her up on the beach, but they failed. When a savage storm drove part of her hull out of the water, a Yankee skipper, Henry C. Sullivan, inspected her and was amazed at how little deterioration had occurred.

"New England men build their ships soundly," he wrote in a letter to one of Crowninshield's heirs. "If she hadn't been wrecked she would have lasted two hundred years."

16   Run for the Money

For weeks the people of New York City had been stupefied by the offer. A newspaper was actually willing to award one thousand dollars to a man if he could run a ten-mile course in less than an hour. The mania of the age was professional footracing, at least among urbanites.

Indians were renowned as the greatest footracers. Nearly every white man who participated in the sport insisted that he could run with great speed because of some alleged relationship to the Indians. Indeed, in 1835, a man named Louis Bennett, who was half-Scot and half-Seneca, won the first great cash race in Manhattan. Bennett called himself Deerfoot, and to make the act more authentic he ran dressed only in a breechcloth and moccasins and wore a colored feather in his black hair. He could run ten miles so fast that other professional long-distance runners winced in shame.

When the money was put up and the challenge accepted, the populace thronged to watch this race against time. "Without intending it by any means," wrote Philip Howe, who attended the race, "when I rose in the morning I found myself with my son, Robert, in the barouche [carriage], enveloped in clouds of dust . . . on the road to the race course, jostled by every description of vehicle conveying every description of people. The total attendance seemed to be as large as it was when American Eclipse raced against Sir Henry, although I was told that it was really closer to twenty thousand." Deerfoot completed the ten miles in fifty-six minutes, then leaped on a horse and went charging around the track.

In the 1850s, "the Pedestrians" (long-distance runners who took money on top of the table) became the flashing hit of the times. There were dozens of popular champions, most of them running under gaudy pseudonyms— the American Deer, the Welsh Bantam, the Boston Buck, the Bunker Hill Speed Boy, and the Yankee Clipper. Each used his own distinctive colors. A patriot from Boston

Footracing is an ancient sport, but in the 1830s, it became a mania along America's eastern seaboard. One of the greatest of the runners was a half-Scot, half-Seneca who called himself, appropriately, Deerfoot. In an 1835 lithograph, Deerfoot is shown running a professional race through New York City when he was at the height of his popularity.

who called himself the Grand American Union wore a star-spangled shirt, red and white striped shorts, and red, white, and blue shoes.

At these races the crowds were so enormous and their enthusiasm so overwhelming that it was necessary for the contestants to run under heavy police escort. Six mounted officers cleared a path and a dozen on each side kept the crowds back. Indian runners were enormously popular, and when a silver-shirted eccentric from Manhattan called "the Great Gildersleeve" challenged a tribe of Indians to send their six best men against him, the entire population talked of little else during the week of the race.

"The race has monopolized conversation for a week past," reported the *Buffalo Courier*. "The 'redmen,' being from around Buffalo, were the great betting favorites. They were paraded through the streets in carriages, preceded by a band of musicians. As the hour of the race came closer, the two streets, Main and Delaware, were crowded with carriages, horses, and pedestrians wending their way to the course. When we reached it, there was a larger throng than we had seen on any similar occasion."

Despite the madness that surrounded it during the decade of its greatest popularity, long-distance running as a sport all but vanished after the Civil War. In the 1870s, athletic clubs were being built all over the nation, and in the fading footprints of the grand and glorious Peds came a whole new sport, track and field.

17   A Wartime Diversion

"One has to chuckle, just a little, thinking about Doubleday. The generals of that [Union] Army, the good ones and the bad ones alike, were intensely jealous of fame and distinction.

"Here was Doubleday, strictly an average general, never making any great mistakes but never winning any great laurels, either.

When Reynolds was killed at Gettysburg the following year, Meade took good care not to turn his corps over to Doubleday, the ranking division commander. It is fascinating to wonder what the other generals would have said if they could have known that in the end Doubleday was going to be one of the most famous of them all—not for his war record, but for his alleged connection with the origin of the game of baseball, which the soldiers were just then beginning to play in their off hours."

—Bruce Catton, *Mr. Lincoln's Army.*

A thin blue haze rose off what had once been a piece of virgin pasture land. But the grass had long since been trampled into clods of shapeless dirt by the prisoners, who had nothing to do but turn a chunk of North Carolina into fine red dust. Large galvanized pots steamed under pine trees, where men alleged to be cooks were stirring a tasteless gruel and bits of salt pork. There was little meat because the entire Confederate States of America was on short rations. There was some coffee available, barely a half cup per prisoner. With the blockade and the damage to crops, it was difficult for the South to feed her armies in the field, let alone the Union troops she captured.

At first, some of the Union prisoners were put to work in the woods, cutting lumber or working in the nearby fields, but the inhabitants of Salisbury were apprehensive about the possibility of escapees who might steal food. So the prisoners were confined. They were reduced simply to walking back and forth, churning up red dust.

High poles with pointed ends set into the ground formed a stockade wall. To save labor the poles were strung from tree to tree wherever possible. Josephus Clarkson, a Boston ship chandler's apprentice before

In the mid-1800s, the Elysian Fields in Hoboken, New Jersey, were regarded as baseball's finest playing area. This engraving, from *Harper's Weekly,* shows a game in progress from the 1850s, when the nation stood on the brink of the Civil War. Baseball was one of the few customs binding North and South together.

the war, recalled in his diary that one of the Union soldiers wandered over and picked up a pine branch that had dropped on the ground. Another soldier wrapped a stone in a couple of woolen socks and tied the bundle with a bit of string. The soldiers started a baseball game of sorts, although there was much argument over whether to use Town Ball rules or play like New Yorkers.

"To put a man out by Town Ball rules you could plug him as he ran," wrote Clarkson. "Since many of the men were in a weakened condition, it was agreed to play the faster but less harsh New York rules, which intrigued our guards. The game of baseball had been played much in the South, but many of them [the guards] had never seen the sport devised by Mr. Cartwright. Eventually they found proper bats for us to play with and we fashioned a ball that was soft and a great bounder."

While the guns were raging elsewhere, there was a baseball series between the guards at Salisbury, North Carolina, and the Union prisoners. The Southerners, not used to the New York rules, kept forgetting that plugging a runner was not allowed. One player, a pitcher from Texas, was suspended by general agreement because he was "badly laming" too much of the opposition. "He came quite close to knocking the stuffing out of two or three of our fellows," said Clarkson, "and we informed our captors, rather politely, of course, that we would no longer play with a man who could not continue to observe the rules. By and large, baseball was quite a popular pastime of troops on both sides, as a means of relaxing before and after battles."

Even before the War began, social barriers were crumbling quickly and baseball was no longer a pursuit for silk-hatted young urbanites. The Southerners were delighted with the new game. One report insists that during a lull in the fighting numerous members of Stonewall Jackson's second brigade were joined in chasing a hare by some Yankees who waved their hands to show they had no weapons. After the chase ended, the Southerners asked their enemies how to play baseball the New York

way. An innocent game broke out on a sunny hillside.

Baseball was expanding in all directions. Thanks to Alexander Joy Cartwright, it had driven cricket out of Philadelphia and Town Ball out of New England. It had crossed into the Midwest and gone to San Francisco with the wagons. There were twenty-five teams that joined something called the National Association of Baseball Players in 1857. Just as the War was starting, the Brooklyn Excelsiors went on tour through Pennsylvania, New Jersey, Maryland, and Delaware, and when they came back drew a crowd of fifteen thousand people.

In the years following the Civil War, manufacturers constantly searched for new sporting crazes. It became increasingly easy to produce baseball equipment, bicycles, billiard tables, sporting rifles, rods and reels, and gymnastic goods. New markets opened as athletic clubs were completed and college students took to playing something called varsity sports.

There were a number of inventions that stimulated the nation's interest in games. Newspaper publishers purchased new machines that enabled them to print as many as twenty thousand copies an hour. Cables, telegraphs, and telephones permitted sports news to flow in an unending stream to newspapers. The great press lords discovered that America loved the smell of liniment. All sports news was combined in one section. Bat Masterson became sports editor of the *New York Morning Telegraph.* Later there were papers devoted solely to sports, so many, in fact, that it appeared the nation had no other interest.

Before the turn of the century one newspaper observed, "Now men travel to great boxing contests in vestibule limited trains. They sleep at the best hotels. When the time for the contest arrives they find themselves in grand, brilliantly lighted arenas. If they choose to stay home and wait for the next match, they have the news relayed to them instantly by reporters sending their dispatches across great wastelands via cable. Truly this is the age of electronic miracles."

THE PASSIONATE AGE
1866-1919

"The championship stays where it belongs,
in America. And I remain yours truly,
John L. Sullivan, American."

—John L. Sullivan after losing the heavyweight
title to James J. Corbett.

Salutat, by Thomas Eakins, 1898.

1 Playing for Pay

The great amateur baseball teams toured like knights-errant entering the lists. The Washington Olympics, a club made up entirely of men who had been appointed to government jobs so that they might play baseball for this club, went off to challenge the great teams of New York and Brooklyn. They left for the railway station in carriages grander than any in an inaugural parade. All the players wore brand new matching suits. The horses wore plumes of red, white, and blue. Pretty girls, dressed in costumes with patriotic themes, met the players at the railway station to hand them bouquets of roses. A brass band thundered in the background, and a group of Zouaves, special troops dressed like the French Foreign Legion, clicked their heels and saluted as the baseball club marched past.

"When we arrived in different towns," wrote one of the players, "we were greeted always by the mayor and by at least three brass bands. There were welcome signs everywhere. One English journalist covering our tour asked us, 'Why can't you be moderate in anything? Why must you always go mad?' There was no answer. America is mad for baseball."

Whenever there was a match scheduled, people crowded into trains or hired hacks to head for the baseball grounds. There was, said one writer of the period, a flow of bicycles, wagons, and butchers' carts. It seemed sometimes that an entire city was emptying. Pedestrians pushed along, carrying great baskets of food.

At the field, peddlers sold liquor by the drink. There were no fences in those days so the people squatted beyond the outfield boundaries, sitting next to carriages that had been driven through the main gate. Before the game, the competing teams appeared on the veranda of the clubhouse to mingle with the elite, who had been there for hours, partaking of a buffet and sipping mixed drinks. Representatives of the numerous newspapers, sporting journals, and periodicals talked with the players.

It was not easy to keep peace in those days. There were no stands and no fences or other barricades. When the liquor salesmen and bookies had done their jobs, the fans and "the cranks," the lower-bred spectators, often dashed onto the field of honor to protest some offense against their side. It is said that some customers even dashed out to pick up a bat and tried to hit when their favorite team fell behind.

In a game that was billed as the national championship of 1870, a spectator whose love of the Brooklyn Atlantics had become fanatical actually helped decide the game. The Atlantics were playing the nation's first professional club, the Cincinnati Red Stockings, who had been on a triumphant tour of the nation for two summers. (They had beaten one group of alleged athletes 103-8.) In the game with the Brooklyn Atlantics they were leading by two runs with Clarence Smith of Brooklyn on third base and Joe Start, the Atlantics' first baseman and super hero, at bat. After missing a couple of pitches, Start drove a long fly toward Calvin McVey in rightfield. The crowd moved back to give the man room to catch the ball. A man in a carriage even flicked his horses back to allow the outfielder more space. Nevertheless, McVey could not reach the drive.

As McVey leaped to retrieve the ball, a drunken spectator jumped on his back. By the time McVey threw the crank to the turf, scooped up the ball, and returned it to the infield, Smith had scored and Start had gone to third on what was called a triple.

Up stepped Bob Ferguson, later one of the game's great umpires, who batted left-handed to avoid sending the ball toward the great shortstop George Wright. Ferguson struck a hard ground ball (what was then called a "daisy-cutter") between first and second base, scoring the tying run. Then one of the Brooklyn players lined a shot that could have been caught easily had it not been for the jangled nerves of a Cincinnati player. Ferguson scored with the winning run and the president of the Red Stockings wired the following message back home:

"New York, June 14, 1870—Atlantics eight; Cincinnati seven. The finest baseball game ever played. Our boys did nobly, but fortune was against them. Eleven innings played. Though beaten, not disgraced. (signed) Aaron B. Champion, Cincinnati Baseball Club."

Baseball had always been especially big in Cincinnati. The Cincinnati Baseball Club was founded on July 23, 1866, in the law offices of Tilden, Sherman, and Moulton. The occasion was a festive one, culminating in a rollicking round of drinks at a nearby bar. The club was conceived as an amateur organization, but it soon decided that its pursuit of excellence on the field required salaried players.

"It became ascertained that the Cincinnati Baseball Club could not survive if the pretense of amateurism was continued," wrote Champion, a local attorney. "Players would be imported from all sections of the nation and every effort would be made to produce the finest baseball team that America had ever known. It was a drastic step but a necessary one."

Thus the Cincinnati club became the first to openly challenge the amateurism that had existed for years. Before the Civil War, when the great and colorful clubs in New York and Philadelphia started to draw big crowds, athletes were openly recruited. The Eckfords, the Unions, the Excelsiors, the Knickerbockers, the Gothams, the Metropolitans, and the new Athletics of Philadelphia vied with each other to recruit the best players. The new players received prizes from older members. Their expenses were paid by the club and they often were given percentages of the gate receipts. Tickets were as high as fifty cents. Prominent businessmen gave a good amateur player a job as a clerk for forty dollars a week, this in an era when a seasoned clerk could expect to make eleven dollars. These amateurs would make an appearance at their company's office, shake hands with employees, and then take an all-day lunch break.

The Red Stockings changed all that. By 1868 there were four outright professional players playing for Cincinnati. Harry Wright no longer had to be a jeweler because he was getting more money (twelve hundred dollars) as the centerfielder for the Red Stockings. His younger brother George, the shortstop and star of the team, earned fourteen hundred dollars. Dick Hurley, a lad of nineteen with no visible means of support, became baseball's first utility man when he was hired at six hundred dollars per year as a substitute in case any of the nine regular Red Stockings was disabled. Asa Brainard, the pitcher, was expected to work every time the Red Stockings played, though this was less taxing than it seems—underhand pitching was the custom of the day.

Like many challenges to tradition, the Red Stockings' professionalism aroused a furor. "These are nothing but shiftless young men, debasing a fine game with their open greed," said a publication called the *Lakeside Monthly*. "They mock the sacred name of amateurism. They have no shame for what they are doing, neither are they interested in seeking honest labor." However, good money prevailed over bad publicity and the Red Stockings won as many imitators as detractors. A stock brokerage company in Chicago announced that it would sponsor the White Stockings and even pay dividends from the gate receipts.

Harry Wright commissioned Mrs. Zona Bertram of Cincinnati, a seamstress of great renown, to make the Red Stockings' first uniforms. The team decided on knickerbocker pantaloons cut off at the knees with buckles behind. They wore long red stockings. They adopted a jockey-style cap with a wide brim and a more square crown, and they gave up the dickey fronts, much favored in the East, for long-sleeved tunics.

From old photographs the team seems quaint, and its marching song sounds silly today.

"Hurrah! Hurrah! For the Noble game hurrah!
Red Stockings all, we'll toss the ball
And shout our loud hurrah!"

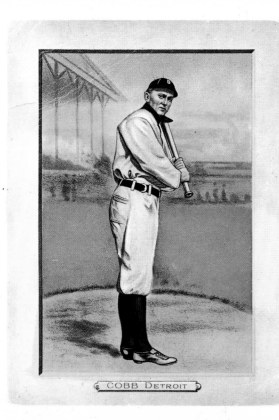

COBB DETROIT

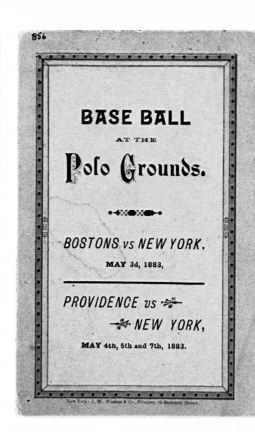

BASE BALL

AT THE

Polo Grounds.

BOSTONS vs NEW YORK,

MAY 3d, 1883,

PROVIDENCE vs NEW YORK,

MAY 4th, 5th and 7th, 1883.

New York: J. W. Weekes & Co., Printers, 75 Beekman Street.

STEAL UP

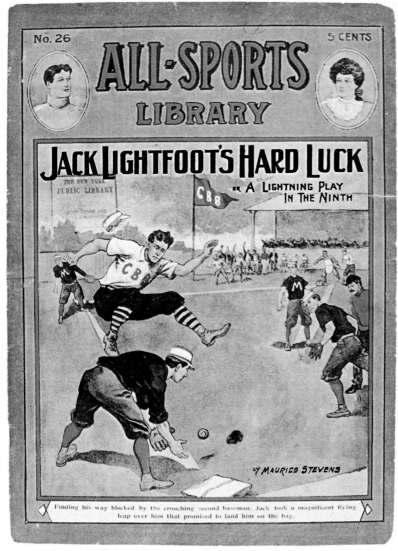

No. 26   5 CENTS

ALL-SPORTS
LIBRARY

JACK LIGHTFOOT'S HARD LUCK

OR A LIGHTNING PLAY
IN THE NINTH

By MAURICE STEVENS

Finding his way blocked by the crouching second baseman, Jack took a magnificent flying
leap over him that promised to land him on the bag.

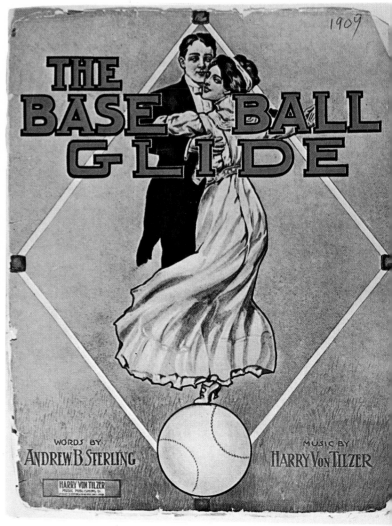

1909

THE BASE BALL GLIDE

WORDS BY
ANDREW B. STERLING

MUSIC BY
HARRY VON TILZER

HARRY VON TILZER
MUSIC PUBLISHING CO.

ADRIAN C. ANSON.
ALLEN & GINTER'S
RICHMOND, Cigarettes, VIRGINIA.

MORIARITY DETROIT AMER.

TY COBB DETROIT AM.

YOUNG, CLEVELAND

CLEVELAND

YOUNG, CLEVELAND

Chance—   Chicago Nat.

Evers—Chicago Nat.

BROWN, Catcher, New York

GEORGE, Pitcher, New York

FOSTER, Centre Field, New York

TIERNEY, Right Field, New York

Often criticized for its conservatism, baseball has only recently experimented with new ways to dress its players. Variety was evident in 1869, however, as this catalog art displays.

It should be remembered that baseball was a violent game of the 1860s and early 1870s, and for many decades thereafter it did not lose its bloodiness. The pretense of a gentleman's game was rapidly disappearing. "Gunpowder for breakfast, lads!" yowled one coach. "That's what the men on this baseball nine eat!"

The Red Stockings were about as gentle as brigands. The players did indeed appear to eat gunpowder for breakfast. When they came down off the train in Philadelphia to play the Athletics, one of the boys at the station shouted, "You bastards gonna git beat." When they rode out to the park on a four-horse, flag-bedecked bus, they were followed by very belligerent young men, some of whom had been drinking. "Go to hell, you little bastards," the Red Stockings shouted. "Just plain go to hell. When we're through with the Athletics, baseball's gonna be dead in this here town." When the Red Stockings rode back from an almost ridiculously easy victory, their bus was stoned. It took several policemen to keep the thugs away from the Red Stockings' horses.

There was nothing to stop the Cincinnati machine during 1869, its first season. It rolled through New York and Massachusetts, outclassing the teams it played. The Red Stockings' first real contest came when they met the Mutuals in New York and won only 4–2. (This was a time when eighty runs in a game was not considered unusual.) When the result was telegraphed to Cincinnati, a crowd of two thousand stood around the Gibson Hotel, shouting, screaming, drinking, lighting red flares, and generally gloating over the defeat of the New Yorkers.

After the victory in New York, the Reds moved through Philadelphia, Washington, Baltimore, Wheeling, and Columbus, finally chugging up the Ohio River on a steamboat to be greeted by a brass band and a banquet so sumptuous that a reporter from the *Cincinnati Enquirer* admitted that he was too embarrassed to reveal all he had eaten as a guest of the club.

The Red Stockings had played sixty-six games from May to November without defeat. They had met hand-picked nines on hostile grounds in Boston, Pittsburgh, Louisville, St. Louis, and San Francisco, though to ensure fairness the Red Stockings had brought along their own umpire.

"Someone asked me today whom I would rather be, President U. S. Grant of the United States or President Champion of the Cincinnati Red Stockings baseball club," said Champion. "I immediately answered him that I would by far rather be the President of the Red Stockings."

It looked as if the Red Stockings would never be beaten. The following season, in 1870, they won twenty-seven more in a row before McVey had that unfortunate experience against the Brooklyn Atlantics.

Rumor had it that one reason the Red Stockings did not do as well in 1870 was because Edward Atwater replaced the redoubtable Dick Hurley as the substitute player. Hurley had been hired away by another team. Other strong professional teams were being organized in 1870, and the players were starting to receive offers Cincinnati could not match. In the winter after the season the Red Stockings were asked to vote, they decided to disband.

As baseball's practitioners were reaching out to further professionalize the sport, the tone of baseball was changing. The rules set down by Alexander Joy Cartwright were constantly being changed, though each new revision caused cries of protest in the clubhouses of the most prominent teams. From the beginnings of the game, baseball devotees were resistant to change, but they were fighting a losing battle.

One debate had arisen over the function of the pitcher. Was he to be a feeder—to use the rounders' term—whose only duty was to put the ball into play, to let the batter hit it? Or was he to be a bona fide member of the defense and help prevent the enemy from getting on base? At first the former view held sway. The first pitch was supposed to be a "square" pitch, a high lob toward the plate. Pitchers were forbidden to "jerk the ball" toward the plate;

that is, they were supposed to throw as stiff-armed as possible. If a man did not deliver the ball directly over the plate, he was chided for using "unfair pitches," called "balls." After a certain number of them, the umpire would signal the runner to first base and credit him with a hit. (In one season it took nine balls to move a man to first base, but this rule was subject to annual change.) If on the other hand a batter dawdled and acted too choosy about the pitches, the umpire would call strikes. Of course, the batter was waiting for the pitch he could hit best, but it was decided he could not take all afternoon. When the rulesmakers cut down the number of pitches a batter could let go, they attempted to compensate the batter. They allowed him to use hand signals to call for the type of pitch he wanted; the pitch had to be down the middle and somewhere between the shoulders and the knees. Unfortunately, few pitchers had good enough control to comply with the batters' requests. Eventually the three-strike, four-ball formula evolved.

The gritty confrontation between pitcher and batter began in earnest when the underhand pitch gave way to the overhand one. The rules stated that the pitcher could not release the ball from beyond a certain point above the waist, but the pitchers forced a change in the rule. They hiked their belts up to their armpits so that no umpire could deny that they were observing the letter of the law when they came in sidearm, with balls thrown at devastating speed. The rulesmakers finally threw up their hands and changed the regulations.

Other changes were taking place increasing the violence of the game. Baserunners were beginning to slide, their spikes up, apparently intending to maim. The purists were outraged but the fans loved it. They screamed with delight as baserunners tore into the bases, defying the men who guarded them. These men who ate gunpowder for breakfast would do anything to win and America urged them on. There were stories of athletes who played the five hours of the first game of a doubleheader in blood-soaked shoes and socks and, after going to the doctor for a few stitches, returned to play the second game.

However, not all the changes in the game made it simply rougher. One season the game added a tenth man, called the "right shortstop," who soon became the "rover," or the "shortfielder." He was supposed to play between first and second base, but the double play was becoming fashionable and the right shortstop interfered with the pivot, so he had no set position. He could stand behind the catcher and retrieve wild pitches and passed balls. A batter might look up and find that he was trying to pull the ball into a forest of outfielders. The right shortstop was phased out after one year.

In 1864, William A. Cummings touched off an enduring argument, namely, does a curveball actually curve? He noted that a ball always appeared to curve in the direction of its spin. After secretly experimenting behind a tavern in Brooklyn, he perfected a pitch with a slow, graceful arc.

Physicists denied the possibility of throwing a curveball. Journalists took sides. Batters, backsore from swinging at the elusive pitch, testified that it damned well did curve. There was a public demonstration in Cincinnati. Poles were set up in a straight line and Tommy Bond was asked to throw a pitch that would bend between them. His first attempt bounced off the lead post. The second pitch did indeed hook and the crowd erupted in exultation.

The introduction of the lively ball touched off another controversy. Some argued that the high scoring the new ball fostered made the game ludicrous. One team could easily make two dozen home runs, and the man who could not score at least one run in an important match usually stood for the drinks. Amazingly, in one game the Chicago White Stockings held an opponent without a run, and for the next twenty years a shutout was known as a Chicago decision. Thereafter the ball was thoroughly deadened, and further dissatisfaction ensued. After one college game went twenty-four innings without a run, the

Copyrighted 1895 by
CALVERT·LITHO·CO.,
DETROIT, MICH.

267.

Bicycle racing was a fad of epidemic proportion in the 1890s. The bizarre print (below) portrays a race in which the competitors seem to bend to a force too strong to resist. At right is an 1898 drawing from the files of the U. S. Patent Office, showing an inventive way to combine cycling with rowing to gain the ultimate means of locomotion.

ball was modified to be neither dead nor hyperactive. The compromise lasted until Babe Ruth emerged as a slugger in the 1920s—when the nation got home run fever again.

Baseball equipment was constantly improving, usually over considerable opposition. In 1875, a catcher for Harvard named Fred Tyng decided to wear a mask to permit him to move closer to the batter and the rest of the players. From his newly advantageous position, he cut down Yale and Princeton runners, whereupon spectators called him a sissy and a cheat. Within two years the equipment was patented, if not universally popular. A short time later catchers were wearing gloves on both hands and playing as close to the batter as possible, especially with men on base.

The first attempt to form a major league of baseball was a wretched failure. Gamblers were involved from the start, some of them heavy investors in the corporations that entered teams. The charter members of the National Association were the New York Mutuals, the Brooklyn Eckfords, the Chicago White Stockings, the Philadelphia Athletics, the Boston Red Stockings, the Troy Haymakers, the Fort Wayne Kekiongas, the Washington Olympic Club, the Forest City Club of Cleveland, and the Forest City Club of Rockford. It was an exercise in anarchy: nobody policed the game. Pool sellers wandered through the crowds and gamblers shouted out the odds to the batters as they stood in the box. Drunkenness among the players was epidemic.

When a game was fixed, everybody was aware of it. On the morning when the news of an "arranged match" got out, there would be a wild dash along the cobbled streets of nearly every league city, as cranks and fans alike searched for their bookies.

Ironically the great crusade for honesty in baseball began with a player raid. Having noted the success of the Boston Red Stockings, William Hulbert plundered their roster for his Chicago team, signing pitcher Albert

Spalding, second baseman Ross Barnes, rightfielder Calvin McVey, and catcher Deacon White. Fresh from that coup, he attempted another. Hulbert sent invitations for representative clubs to meet him on February 2, 1876, at New York's elegant new Grand Central Hotel. The potential franchise holders arrived by carriage.

Hulbert talked privately with each of them and then addressed them as a group, taking the precaution of first locking the door to the meeting room. One of the guests, somewhat astonished at the action, protested loudly. "Gentlemen, you have no occasion for uneasiness or distress," Hulbert reassured them grandiloquently. "I have locked this door simply to prevent any intrusions from without, and incidentally to make it impossible for any of you to go out until I have finished what I have to say to you, which I promise shall not take an hour."

There was a clock on the wall and Hulbert consulted it from time to time as he spoke. In an oration that lasted exactly one hour, he documented everything that was wrong with the game. He proposed that this new league keep careful surveillance of its players. Anyone caught consorting with gamblers would be barred for life. Pool sellers and bookies would have to be kept out of the ball parks, he insisted. No longer would players be permitted to tear up their contracts in midseason and jump to another team.

"The National Association is either unable or unwilling to correct these abuses," he said. "In either event it is unfit to further control the great game of baseball. I have here a new constitution which insures the future of the sport. Gentlemen, with your permission, I give you . . . the National League!"

With that, Hulbert walked to the door, brandished the key, and unlocked the door. There was utter silence in the room for several minutes. Then the gentlemen from Boston, Chicago, Cincinnati, Hartford, Louisville, New York, Philadelphia, and St. Louis stood up and proceeded to a table at the front to sign the constitution. For the first time baseball had a permanent governing force.

Morgan G. Bulkeley was titular president of the National League the first summer, but the power rested with Hulbert. By the second season he succeeded to the title as well. He was strong and energetic. For a start Hulbert banned all alcoholic beverages from the league parks. "I am no temperance leader," he said, "but ladies and children must be allowed to view the competition in a dignified atmosphere. I am adamant about this." Down went the betting booths at the entrances. Private police hired by the league routed gamblers from their seats and threw them into the streets. No longer were the front gates of ballparks adorned with signs that read, "No game played between these two teams is to be trusted."

However, resistance to reform was not long in resurfacing, confronting Hulbert with a crisis that threatened his authority and the integrity of the game.

The best team in the league was the Louisville Grays, led by two acknowledged superstars, centerfielder George Hall and pitcher Jim Devlin. When they left on their final eastern trip of the year, the Grays needed to win only six more games for the championship, having won more than two-thirds of their games already. But they were beaten by the Boston Red Stockings and the Hartford Blues in their first two starts on the road. These were not bad losses but they aroused Hulbert's suspicions. The president dispatched two agents to Hartford for the next match, which Louisville lost by an astounding 7–0 score, only the second time the Grays had been shut out all year.

A couple of days later the two clubs met again and Hulbert was well aware that Hoboken pool sellers had made Hartford the favorite in all three games. The Grays managed a 1–1 tie in a game that ended in the eleventh inning. Back in Boston the following afternoon, they were beaten 3–2, a loss that cut their first place lead to one game. They blundered through two more losses to the Red Stockings, then staggered on to Brooklyn Union Grounds, where third place Hartford won by a 6–3 score. Earlier that day the vice-president of the Louisville club, Charles E. Chase, had received an anonymous telegram warning him that the Blues were a 30–20 favorite in the Hoboken pools and Louisville was being sold out.

Immediately after hearing the score, Chase wired manager Jack Chapman and demanded to know why Al Nichols had been at third base instead of the regular, Bill Hague. The reply came back: "The team captain, George Hall, requested it because Nichols was from Brooklyn and it seemed like a nice thing to let him play before his relatives and neighbors." The owner wondered why the captain would make such a request and why the manager would grant it when the team was in jeopardy of losing a league championship. The next day Chase received another telegram, this one informing him that the last game against Hartford was "crooked and Louisville is to lose." In that game Hall, Nichols, and Devlin seemed to forget how to field ground balls. That evening Chase wired Chapman not to use the three men again. On the way home the Louisville team lost two more, these to the last-place Cincinnati Redlegs, and a couple of exhibitions to minor league professionals in Pittsburgh and Indianapolis.

Hulbert demanded that Chase conduct an investigation as soon as the Grays got off the train. A raging Chase summoned Devlin and Hall, who admitted that the team had played carelessly but attributed it to the long season (fifty games) and the lengthy train trips.

Unconvinced, Chase summoned the entire team to the Grays' clubhouse, where the board of directors was waiting. The players were informed that management wanted to see duplicates of every telegram sent or received by the Louisville players during the 1877 season. Any player who failed to authorize Western Union to provide the duplicates would be immediately suspended from the team and then expelled from the league. The only man to refuse the order was catcher Bill Craver, who was suspended immediately. Everybody else decided to tough it out: they signed.

Within a few days Chase and Hulbert had their evidence. The fixers had gotten to Hall, Devlin, and Nichols.

The players had sold out for five hundred dollars each, and they had made twice as much betting against their teams. No evidence was found to implicate Craver, but for his insubordination he was punished as severely as the bribe takers. All four received the maximum penalty: they were expelled from baseball for life.

2 America on Wheels

The Scottish immigrant Alexander Graham Bell demonstrated his invention, the telephone, in Philadelphia before the visiting Emperor of Brazil, His Majesty, Dom Pedro II, and absolutely astounded the imperial tourist. Dr. Bell spoke a line from Shakespeare into his receiver and a hundred yards away the emperor listened on his receiver and shouted, "I hear, I hear!"

The newspapers reported nothing else for days: science had conquered the problem of long-distance communication in a spectacular way and it was being demonstrated right at the great Centennial Exhibition in Philadelphia, that fantastic display of lights, glitter, and progress. Reporters could not stop writing about the magnificent new gadget at the grand American birthday party. America, they reported, was forging ahead in 1876.

One of the most fascinating machines was an English import, the bicycle. It had been shipped across the Atlantic so that English manufacturers could explore a new market. Unaware that everybody on the western side of the Atlantic was mad for mechanical gimmicks, the English had no idea how the Americans might receive the bicycle. In the 1860s Americans had tried the velocipede, a crude French version of the bicycle, and soon renamed it "the dandy horse," or "the bone-shaker." A jumble of moving parts, many of them useless, it was a hand-driven vehicle operated by a piston rod connected to a crank that was in turn connected to one end of the front wheel axle. Although its inventor, Pierre Lallement, saw the practicality of using some sort of

pedal, he insisted on attaching it to the front wheel.

It must be noted that a man named Brighton Carroll, a New England Yankee, threw in with Lallement. For a while their machine seemed to win some converts. Young men who saw it used in an act by the most skilled acrobats of the day, the Hanlon Brothers, practiced secretly in barns and abandoned lofts. Riding schools and indoor rings were set up. But the bone-shakers produced more wrenched knees and backs than it did gymnasts. The market crumbled when it was learned that these vehicles could not be used in the streets. Lallement went back to France and Carroll disappeared.

The new English machine that appeared on the market was impressive. There was a huge wheel in front and a small one in back. It had real gears. The tires were solid rubber. The bicycle reeked of progress and America was off on its first sporting binge over a mechanical device. Wooden frames gave way to iron ones, which provided more support for the rider's body. India rubber tires were an immense improvement. As riders went stumbling forward from a height of about seven feet, they risked permanent injuries from falls, yet bicycle enthusiasts contended that an afternoon in the sun and wind on board the big wheel of a bicycle would restore one's lost health.

In 1882, six years after the exposition in Philadelphia, there were some twenty thousand cyclists in the United States. By 1890 there were more than one hundred thousand. Clubs were organized in nearly every town in the nation. Once again America had discovered that it could do nothing in moderation. The father of cycling was Charles Pratt, a lawyer who founded the Boston Bicycle Club, and later produced a periodical called *Bicycling World*. In 1880, he commanded the bicyclists of the nation to gather in Newport on May 30, which was then called Decoration Day, to form a national alliance. For days the roads were clogged with daring young men, all heading for Rhode Island's south shore on their two-wheeled machines. The bicyclists jammed the town's

Bicycling was the most popular mass sport in the 1890s, but roller skating was not far behind. Roller rinks were a favorite gathering place for family recreation. For some, waltzing to the music of an organ proved to be too tame. More competitive skaters developed a fairly violent version of roller hockey, as illustrated here in a page from a calendar published in 1878.

hotels; they camped in tents; they found accommodations even in some of the town's finer homes. Before the conclave was over, the League of American Wheelmen was born with some ten thousand members.

There were bicycle parades, competitive drills, hill climbs, and races. On the Fourth of July, 1884, so many people gathered on Boston Common that the planned meeting of the Wheelmen, for which all sorts of competitions had been planned, could not be held. In downtown Manhattan an academy taught businessmen to ride to the accompaniment of a brass marching band. And a man named Thomas Stevens went off on a bicycle trip around the world.

Stevens did much to drive the nation wild over cycling. With only a few days' practice, he set out from his native San Francisco for Boston in April, 1883, arriving there in August. He remained in Massachusetts until he could secure financial backing, then set out to conquer the rest of the world. Great crowds followed him across Europe and the Middle East. He was a guest of the Shah of Persia and continued through India and the Orient, returning to San Francisco in 1887 to a wild municipal celebration.

Despite its popularity, bicycling had yet to achieve its greatest breakthrough. From the start women protested that wheeling was too difficult for them because of the height of the front tire. They were forced to pedal on absurd-looking tricycles if they wished to participate in the national craze. They were ready to abandon the sport until manufacturers offered a light-framed machine with moderate-sized wheels of equal proportions. The frame was indented in the middle to accommodate the fashionable long skirts. This bicycle was simple to operate and it was remarkably safe. "The greatest product of the mechanical age," trumpeted an advertisement. "Wheeling is an abiding national habit, one that will insure the health of everyone who participates." Women were captivated by the new machine, which they immediately called "the safety bicycle."

Bicycling made it permissible for ladies to appear in public in what was called "trouserettes," long pantaloons that gathered at mid-calf. Women also joined such social groups as the Michaux Club of Manhattan, where they performed intricate drills to popular music. Under a mellow October morn, several hundred female cyclists made a road run to Coney Island, riding in single file with male escorts to the port side.

Not only was the safety bike popular with women, but it also turned bicycling into a spectator sport. These machines were manageable enough to race, and racing was the vogue. Velodromes sprung up on the banks of the Connecticut River in West Springfield and East Hartford, and great crowds watched the "scorchers," the racers who would career around the board tracks at full tilt. Once again the nation was confronted with a conflict between amateurism and professionalism. The riders were not competing for prizes, but they were being paid by the manufacturers to convince the public of the virtues of such bikes as the Imperial, the Monarch, and the Columbia. In 1886, after the participants refused to explain their financial arrangements, the American Cyclist Union declared them all professionals.

While the scorchers rode to popularity on the safety bike, a man named Albert Schock insisted on using the high-front-wheel machine and pedaled 1,009.5 miles in seventy-two hours. That style of bike was vanishing, but that kind of bicycling activity, the endurance contest, was just beginning.

The ultimate adventure was the six-day bike race, which flourished in the late nineteenth century and made a stunning comeback during the Depression years. The contestants in these events tried to complete as many laps as possible in the six days. Schock showed up with a safety bike and left all his competitors in the lurch at Madison Square Garden in one such race. The New York State legislature declared the bike races "inhuman" after it learned that each contestant circled the track without relief for one hundred forty-two hours, snatching bits of food from handlers.

While America was going mad over the bicycle, the British decided to capitalize on the American desire for mechanical gadgets by introducing the roller skate, the invention of James L. Plimpton. Even the English nobility had adopted what they called "rinking." When the pastime moved to America, it grew even more popular. Smooth wooden floors were installed in refurbished old warehouses. Women in bustles and flowing dresses accompanied by men in bulky jackets and woolen bell-bottoms skated around and around the floors. By 1885 more than $20 million had been invested in the sport.

Roller rinks became social centers for families. Roller skating was a charming way to pass the time, and promoters kept their facilities so wholesome that churchmen recommended this odd little sport. In Chicago in 1882 it gave birth to a game called "roller polo," hockey played on rollers.

Strangely, the interest in these mechanical sports ended as quickly as it had begun. By 1902, magazines and newspapers were wondering what had happened. Almost every periodical devoted to wheel games had disappeared. John D. Rockefeller invested millions in the American Bicycle Company, only to see the bicycle craze dissipate and his company fail.

In 1905 the *Washington Post* noted that the cycling and roller wheel industry, which had done $30 million in business three years earlier, was almost extinct, grossing less than $6 million for the entire season. The velodromes became boxing arenas when boxing became legal (with the start of gloved fights). The Vanderbilts, J. P. Morgan, Stuyvesant Fish, and others gave away their cycles. They were no longer chic. The cycle brigade of the Manhattan Police Force disbanded. The argument over whether ladies should ride cycles in public was abandoned. Chicago's park commission, no longer threatened by powerful groups such as the League of American Wheelmen, banned Decoration Day races, and no one protested.

Perhaps the bicycle had become too familiar and the country was ready for something new and more sensational. A couple of cycle-shop owners from Dayton, Ohio, brothers named Wilbur and Orville Wright, were experimenting with machines that flew. The automobile was getting better and better. It was inevitable that the airplane and the automobile would become sporting machines.

Left behind from the era of the first mechanical sport was a classic piece of 1890s music, "Daisy Bell." Few people realize it is a sporting song:

> "Daisy, Daisy, give me your answer true,
> I'm half crazy, all for the love of you!
> It won't be a stylish marriage,
> I can't afford a carriage,
> But you'll look sweet upon the seat
> Of a bicycle built for two."

3   A Bit of Doggerel

June 3, 1888, was an idyllic day on San Francisco Bay, with low clouds scudding toward the mountains and ferry boats passing each other on waters as yet undefiled by bridge pilings. The morning was unusually warm, and columnist Ernest Lawrence Thayer was sitting by an open window in the *San Francisco Examiner*'s crowded city room on Third Street, just off Market. Several boys were playing baseball on a nearby vacant lot. It was the first cheerful sight Thayer noticed that morning. The children were playing with great enthusiasm, and as he watched them, the depression that had overcome him of late began to dissipate. Just then an editor came by to remind him that two columns on page four were still distressingly blank. It was up to Thayer to fill them.

Thayer had been with the *Examiner* for about a year now. He had arrived in 1887, when William Randolph Hearst had come home from Harvard to rescue a mundane newspaper that his influential father considered the least important of the vast family holdings. Young

Hearst had brought several of his friends from Harvard with him, including Thayer, who wanted to enjoy the rugged life of a western journalist before going back to New England to run his father's woolen mills. At Harvard he roomed briefly with America's first great press lord. Thayer had edited the *Harvard Lampoon,* which was then, as it is now, a fine college humor magazine. William Randolph Hearst had been its business manager.

Under the slam-bang editorial and promotional techniques of Hearst, the *Examiner* became the nation's most exciting newspaper, but now the fun was ending for Thayer. He felt he had indulged himself shamelessly at the *Examiner,* writing satirical verse and humorous sketches. His New England conscience was bothering him; it was time to consider returning to Worcester and a more serious vocation. So it was that on the morning when Ernest Lawrence Thayer was to produce the most enduring work of his life he was feeling dull and melancholy—anything but inspired.

Mechanically he began his column, scribbling a snide item about the editor of the *Lake County Avalanche,* who had used coarse language to denounce the editor of the *Sonoma Democrat* for using, of all things, coarse language. The story suited Thayer as a lead item, since he doted on comic irony. It was his custom to follow with some bright and senseless doggerel.

Outside, the sounds of those children playing ball with such gusto distracted him from his work. Later he was to admit that his mood changed from melancholy to nostalgia. He began to recall the scenes of his boyhood in Massachusetts. His mind drifted to a dramatic moment of his childhood. There were only two ethnic groups worth mentioning at Worcester Classical High School: the Anglo-Saxon Protestants, the old-line Yankees, of whom Thayer was one of the leaders, and the Irish Catholics, largely newcomers to town, whose undisputed champion was a large, emotional lad named Daniel Casey. Casey was decent, kind, and popular with his peers. He also was an excellent student and, thus, equally

popular with the faculty. However, Casey also had a temper. Thayer was studious and frail. His outlet for anger was satire that tended to debase his victims.

The school was just one year old, so there was no official undergraduate publication. Without authorization, Thayer started a journal, and in the very first issue he ridiculed Daniel Casey, indulging in the then-current Yankee prejudice that all Irishmen were hulking, hot-headed fools. Casey was not amused.

As Thayer sat at his desk now, musing over his column, the picture of the hulking Irishman returned to him. He saw the physically superior Casey standing with clenched fists and grinding teeth, refusing to make the move that would have battered his enemy but also proved his enemy's point. Still smarting over Casey's victory through self-restraint, Thayer tried to slay the dragon all over again. "Casey at the Bat, a Ballad of the Republic, sung in the year 1888," he scratched on paper. He gazed out the window again at the boys at play. Then he wrote:

> *"The outlook wasn't brilliant for the Mudville nine that day.*
> *The score stood four to two with but one inning left to play*
> *And when Cooney died at first and Barrows did the same*
> *A sickly silence fell upon the patrons of the game.*
> *A straggling few got up in deep despair*
> *The rest clung to that hope which springs eternal in the human breast*
> *They thought if only Casey could get a whack at that*
> *We'd put up even money with Casey at the Bat."*

Thayer wrote quickly, anxious to complete the demise of his hero. The dread deed done, Thayer ended the column with an item about a Nebraska editor who had been shot twice with a revolver. He tried to give it a humorous twist but he failed. Then he went back to his room and tried to sleep. A couple of weeks later he boarded a train for New England.

One of the most engaging popular poems in American literature was created by a San Francisco newspaper man, Ernest Lawrence Thayer, in 1888. *Casey at the Bat* has become a sports classic, and in 1946 Walt Disney brought the poem to life in an animated film titled *Make Mine Music.*

The piece reached the East before Thayer did. It was also reprinted all over the West without his knowledge. De Wolf Hopper, the actor, received a copy in the mail a few days before he was to appear at a special performance honoring the 1888 New York Giants' baseball team at Walleck's Theater on Broadway. An hour after receiving the poem, he decided to use it. He memorized the fifty-two lines and gave the first of his more than forty thousand recitations. He went to his grave forever marked as the man who did "Casey at the Bat," having all but abandoned his acting career, though he did play the part of Casey twice in silent movies.

Not until many years later did Thayer admit to being the author, after dozens of fraudulent claims to authorship had been made and a national guessing game had raged over the identity of the model for Casey. Thayer admitted to Hopper when he encountered him at the Worcester Club that the model was Daniel Casey (who, in fact, had never played baseball), but the public refused to credit the truth, having been led to believe that the real Casey could surely be someone of no less stature than the great King Kelly of the Boston Red Stockings. And so Daniel Casey lived out his life a beloved but hardly renowned junior high principal in Worcester.

When Thayer died, an obituary writer for the *Examiner* spoke to the woman whom Thayer had married when he was fifty years old. She declined to comment about "Casey at the Bat" except to deny that Thayer wrote it. To his family Thayer was simply a retired textile merchant when he died. And to judge from the evidence he left, that is how Thayer preferred to be remembered.

4 Football . . . Sort of

Cold winds were sweeping across the field where the two teams came together. Any moment snow would start to fall and cover this patch of New Brunswick, New Jersey. The date was November 6, 1869, and the men from Rutgers wore red turbans to distinguish themselves from the men at Princeton. It was about 3 P.M. and there must have been one hundred spectators.

The players were laying aside their hats, coats, and vests when a grouchy old professor came pedaling past on a bicycle. He paused there for a while and, brandishing his umbrella, rode away shouting, "You men will come to no decent Christian end." The irate old man missed the first intercollegiate football match.

It was part rugby, part soccer, and part American initiative. There were twenty-five men to a side and the winner was the first team to score six goals. Earlier in the day the two captains had met over tea to determine the rules. Both were over six feet tall and weighed around two hundred pounds, big for the men of their era. They were William Gummere of Princeton, later chief justice of the New Jersey Supreme Court, and William Leggett, later a distinguished clergyman for the Dutch Reformed Church. First, they agreed that violence should be kept to a minimum. After some gentlemanly debate, Gummere and Leggett then decided that two men on each side would be designated keepers of the goal. The remainder of each team would be divided into fielders, who would be confined to guarding certain sections of the field, and bulldogs, who would follow the ball up and down the field.

The players from the two schools stood at midfield and tossed a coin. Princeton won. The first kickoff in history was bad; it went dribbling off to one side, totally frustrating Rutgers, the kicking team. But Rutgers soon mastered the problem. John W. Herbert, one of the players, wrote:

> The light and agile Rutgers men pounded down upon it like hounds chasing a rabbit. By driving it with short kicks and dribbles, the other players surrounded the ball and did not permit a Princeton man to get near it. They quickly and craftily forced it down to Old Nassau's goal, where the captains of the enemy's goal were waiting.

The first goal had been scored within five minutes of play. During the intermission, Captain Gummere instructed Jacob Michael, who was later to become dean of faculty at the University of Maryland, to break up Rutgers' massing around the ball. Michael was a young giant of a man, very blond. Sides were changed and Rutgers kicked again. In this period the game was fiercely contested. Time and time again Michael (or Big Mike) charged into Rutgers' primitive mass and scattered the players like a burst bundle of sticks. On one of these plays Princeton obtained the ball and by a kick scored the second goal.

The third goal went to Rutgers and the fourth was kicked by Princeton, Big Mike again bursting through a mass out of which Gummere gained possession of the ball and, with Princeton massed about him, easily dribbled the ball down and through the Rutgers goal posts, making the score once more a tie.

The fifth and sixth goals went to Rutgers, but the feature of this latter period of play is awarded to Big Mike and Large [a future State Senator named George H. Large, who played for Rutgers]. Someone, by a random kick, had driven the ball to one side, where it rolled against the fence, closely followed by Michael.

They reached the fence on which the students were perched and, unable to check their momentum, in a tremendous impact struck the fence, which gave way with a crash and over went its load of yelling students. Every college probably has the humorous tradition of some player who has scored against his own team. The tradition of Rutgers dated from this first game. One of her players, whose identity shall never be revealed, in the sixth period started to kick the ball between his own goal posts. The kick was blocked, but Princeton took advantage of the opportunity and soon made the goal. This turn of the game apparently disorganized Rutgers, because Princeton also scored the next goal after a few minutes of play, thus bringing the total up to four-all.

At this stage Rutgers resorted to the use of craft which has never failed to turn the tide of every close battle. Captain Leggett had noticed that Princeton obtained a great advantage from the taller stature of their men, which enabled them to reach above the others and bat the ball in the air in some advantageous direction. Rutgers was ordered to keep the ball close to the ground. Following this strategem, the Rutgers men determinedly kicked the ninth and tenth goals, thus winning the match six goals to four.

It is still debated today whether the Princeton-Rutgers efforts of that day can be called football. Hands were used, so the game could not have been soccer. But distinctly unlike American football, the players were not permitted to pick up the ball and run with it, so it cannot be said that the game favored by Pop Warner, Knute Rockne, and Bear Bryant, among others, was actually invented that raw, windy afternoon in New Brunswick. Historians are more apt to credit the match between Harvard and McGill universities at Harvard in 1874 as the true start of American football.

Whatever it was that Rutgers and Princeton played, it was an engaging enough pastime to provoke a return engagement the next week. On that occasion Princeton defeated Rutgers, "settling a score of blood," said a Rutgers undergraduate.

5   The Violent Game Degenerates

The yellowing photos show a man with a square, dark, resolute face that stood out from the others in the crowd. From the time he was a freshman answering a call for football players in 1876, the amazing Walter

Yale University's Walter Camp, shown holding the ball in this 1879 team photograph, was responsible for most of football's early rules. His influence over the sport spanned five decades. His selection of the annual All-America team in later years was a popular innovation.

Camp wore a moustache and sideburns. When he played the game he wore a hairband that kept his center-parted black locks in place. His legs were stronger and fuller than his shoulders. As he posed for the photo against the gate where all Yale captains have posed, he looked like an athlete.

Born in New Haven in 1859, the son of well-to-do white Anglo-Saxon Protestant parents, Walter Camp did all the proper things. He studied hard, made good grades, played baseball, swam, ran track, and experimented with the newly imported game of tennis. He was the finest swimmer of his time, winning everything from sprints to five-mile races. He rowed with his class crew. The adventures of Frank Merriwell were allegedly based on the true stories of Walter Camp.

When Eugene Baker, captain of the Yale football squad, tacked up a pen-scrawled plea for football players, it was first answered by Walter Camp, who said that he could be a halfback in this new game. He was close to six feet tall and weighed nearly two hundred pounds. He was exceptionally fast and stronger than he looked. He could punt for distance, drop kick, and kick the ball from placement. It is quite likely that Camp could play the game on its highest levels today.

In his first game for Yale, against Princeton, he returned a punt eighty yards for a touchdown. He took the ball out of a rugby scrum on another play and went fifty yards for another score.

Indomitable as he was as a player, he was even more dynamic in his contribution to the rules of the game. As a junior at Yale he appeared at the game's second rules convention, held at the Massassoit House in Springfield in October, 1878 and helped to push through legislation to keep teams limited to eleven men and to make safeties scoring plays. He pleaded for elimination of the scrum, maintaining that it gave neither side an orderly means of putting the ball into play. In place of everybody locking arms, rugby fashion, and heeling the ball backward, which sometimes took several minutes, he proposed a "scrimmage." The team that had possession of the ball would place it on the ground and one man, called a center, would either snap it back with his hands or kick it back with his heel. "If this rule is adopted," he told the second convention, "it will guarantee possession of the ball and there will be a rapid development of strategic plays designed to advance the ball."

Thus Camp proposed to break down the game into its component plays. But the convention was not convinced that these plays would, simply by being clearly defined, produce the exciting pattern of play Camp promised. The older men wanted to know how a team would be induced to surrender the ball when it could not advance it. Camp had no workable solution, and he was told to go home and find one. He went back to Yale and brooded until the third rules convention, also held at Springfield, on October 12, 1882. This time the convention adopted his proposal, though he had still not come to grips with the problem of extended possession. He insisted that when a team was stalled it would do the honorable, intelligent thing and punt.

Alas, his confidence was misplaced. Instead of promoting a brisk pace, his center snap caused the game to stagnate. "The block game" evolved, whereby a team clung grimly to the ball after it was snapped, refusing to mount an offense. Football reached the depths of dreariness when in the Yale-Princeton game Princeton took the opening kickoff and controlled the ball through the entire first half. Yale men growled and the spectators booed incessantly.

When the rules convention gathered again, such distinguished football men as Edward Peace, John Harlan, and P. T. Bryan asked Camp if he had a solution. "Indeed, I do," the young theoretician replied, "and it's one I think will settle forever such matters as the block game and other problems we have. I hope we can be agreeable."

This time he hit upon the system of yards and downs: "If on three consecutive fair tries or downs a team shall not have advanced the ball five yards, nor lost ten, they must give up the ball to opponents at the spot of the fourth down," he wrote. "When a team advances five yards, it will receive a first down and have as many tries as is required to progress the ball another five yards."

The next debate arose over standardizing a scoring system. In the early 1880s some schools used the old rugby system. Others changed their scoring system from game to game, discussing the matter with each opponent and adopting whatever system was mutually agreeable. Some schools rated field goals and touchdowns equally, either four or five points each. At some schools in the West and Midwest, touchdowns were worth six points. Still other schools, especially in the East, counted one point for every scoring play. It was also the custom to count soccer-style goals. At Yale, Harvard, Princeton, and Columbia, four touchdowns equaled one goal. Even a field goal was superior to a touchdown.

Camp began to rectify this problem by recognizing the essence of this new, American game. "It is my thinking that the future of the game lies in running rather than kicking," Camp said. "If that comes about, then we shall have to award more points for a touchdown and less for field goals. If the running aspect dominates, we will see the day when a touchdown counts twice as much as a field goal."

Camp believed that six points was a fair reward for a touchdown, but he kept the idea to himself, waiting for the proper moment to reveal it. In the meantime, he settled for institutionalizing different values for different scoring plays. After much debate, it was decided to count one point for a safety, two for a touchdown, four for the conversions, and five for field goals.

There were no coaches in the 1880s, at least none recognized as such, but Camp was the uncontested authority on the game, and he continued to be even after Yale began to employ full-time coaches. In time he was to be called "the coach of coaches." As football began to spread to other colleges, Yale men were in great demand because they had studied under the amazing Mr. Camp.

No fewer than eleven Yale men became the first coaches hired by other major universities. Among the Camp protégés was the almost literally immortal Amos Alonzo Stagg, who lived to one hundred and three expounding and expanding on the wisdom of Camp.

Camp sent out all his students with a stalwart ethical credo, one that persists even today, though it provokes more lip service than adherence. It was Walter Camp who first felt that football built character. He wrote:

When it comes to the football field, mind will always win over muscle and brute force. What a gentleman wants is fair play and for the best man to win. If he accepts these principles, he will find his own character greatly enriched. If your opponent takes trifling liberties with you, such as slapping your face, let all such action merely determine you to keep a close watch on the ball.

Don't fail to try to take the ball away from an opponent whenever he is tackled. Make a feature of this and you will succeed oftener than you anticipate. There is no substitute for hard work and effort beyond the call of mere duty. That is what strengthens the soul and ennobles one's character.

It was vainglorious and corny, but the young men of Camp's time devoured such sophistries. It was easy to worship this handsome, haunting man who stood firm against the vices that threatened to destroy both the nation and the game of football.

In 1884, the Princeton team conceived the flying wedge, a murderous formation that placed the ball carrier in the crook of a V-shaped mass. Defenders dropped to the turf before it as if a stampede of buffalo had trampled them. Every team adopted the flying wedge, ignoring a leftover rugby rule that prohibited interference for the ball carrier. Camp denounced the formation as brutal and illegal. In 1885, he tried desperately to curb such a flagrant abuse when he helped pass the first penalty rule—a loss of five

College football was marred by such shocking violence early in the twentieth century that President Theodore Roosevelt threatened to abolish the sport. In this *Harper's Weekly* engraving, an injured player receives attention from a teammate as the riotous scrimmage continues up the field.

yards for crossing the scrimmage line before the ball was snapped. Although everybody agreed that this was a fine idea, no one obeyed it.

"The officials have tacitly decided to ignore this new rule," said Camp. "It could be the ruination of the game. This can only result in football becoming a bully's sport."

Three years later he submitted another rule, this one making it legal for a man to be tackled from the beltline to the top of his knees. Previously, runners could be tackled only from the waist to the neck. This new rule aimed at making contact cleaner and less hazardous, but it had the opposite effect. Lighter and swifter runners were now given the ball, and the wedges grew tighter around them. The style continued unchallenged until the remarkable Pudge Heffelfinger of Yale devised the art of leaping over the apex of the wedge, his sharp cleats flashing in the sunshine.

One man who joined Camp in protesting the needless violence in football was Thomas Woodrow Wilson, a professor at Wesleyan. He later became a football coach at Princeton and a politician of some distinction.

Despite the efforts of Camp and Wilson, football continued to deteriorate into violence and chaos. Some fifty players died of football injuries during a nineteen-year period. The press took the cue and called football "sheer butchery." Because of football's poor image, it was difficult to draw recruits, and so began the practice of paying money to potential players. The tramp athlete came into vogue. These athletes would move from school to school without attending classes or even knowing where the campus was located.

"We have lost," lamented Camp, "the Homeric thrill of human action, the zest of out-of-doors, the contest of speed, of strength, of human intelligence, of courage. Unless steps are taken to reform the sport we shall discover that our precious football is being relegated to the ash heap of history. Brutality has no place in this sport. This is a game that must train its followers, its players and its spectators in the qualities of a successful charac-

ter. They are: knowledge, skill, strength, speed, obedience, initiative, aggressiveness, courage, honor, and morale."

But where Camp saw declining sportsmanship, others found irresistible sport. During the 1890s football became a national sport, despite its brutality or, perhaps, because of it. Teams traveled long distances as more and more schools took up the game. The Michigan team went on a train tour of the East, taking academic tutors along as it played Vermont, Princeton, Dartmouth, Harvard, and Cornell. They attracted crowds of between eight and twelve thousand, considered enormous for the time. After Dartmouth went west to play the Chicago Athletic Club on Thanksgiving Day in 1894, inviting teams from long distances became fashionable. When the Oakland Athletic Club, made up mostly of athletes from the University of California, boarded Pullman cars for the trip east to challenge Michigan, Chicago, and Cornell, the San Francisco Bulletin exulted with regional chauvinism: "Never before has an eleven crossed the Great Divide from the Golden West and it is one from Alta, [Northern] California, that makes the trip. Cover yourselves with glory, lads!" It was the lead story on the front page.

On the day in 1899 when Chicago became the first Western school to defeat an Eastern team, beating Cornell 17–6 on Chicago's Marshall Field, there were approximately five thousand other teams and one hundred twenty thousand players across the country. Newspapers devoted dozens of columns to descriptions of the games and the colorful crowds that attended. The New York Sun proclaimed football a genuine society sport when the Cornelius Vanderbilts and some of the equally important people who were their friends attended a match between Yale and Columbia.

The universities were beginning to see football as a means of making money. Soon after the University of Chicago hired Amos Alonzo Stagg as its full-time coach, Minnesota brought in Henry W. Williams to be its "professor of scientific football." The great autumn hustle

was on. Stagg, a man of impeccable manners and unshakable morals, who abstained from drinking, cursing, smoking, chasing women, and dirty jokes, observed the boom with some taste.

Because of his basic goodness and his deep religious nature Stagg was considered a freak. Coaches at other schools were flagrant in their disrespect for the ideals that Stagg and his teacher, Walter Camp, held to be self-evident. Corruption was everywhere. One young man, whose real name may have been Martin Thayer, played for thirteen years at nine schools under so many pseudonyms that hardly anyone knew who he really was. If he had not applied to one college for the second time, he might never have been caught.

James Hogan, proficient at football at Yale, was expelled after accepting a suite in an exclusive hall, meals at a fashionable eating club, a ten-day trip to Cuba paid by the athletic association, a hundred dollar scholarship, free tuition, a monopoly on the sale of scorecards, and a position as exclusive agent on campus for the American Tobacco Company. He enrolled at the University of Pittsburgh the next year but was apprehended again for similar offenses. Subsequently he played at Allegheny College and Vanderbilt. Sadly, Hogan was not a rare case.

Having deserted the sportsman's ethic and having embraced one of hardly mitigated brutality and opportunism, football began to arouse fervent opposition.

"Football today is a social obsession," wrote Shailer Mathews, dean of the Chicago Divinity School. "Football is a boy-killing, education-prostituting, gladiatorial sport. It teaches virility and courage, but so does war. I do not know what should take its place, but the new game should not require the services of a physician, the maintenance of a hospital, and the celebration of funerals."

The distinguished president of Columbia, Dr. Nicholas Murray Butler, called for all schools to curb their misguided athletic policies. "This is madness and slaughter," he said.

"The game has no social significance, except to give ruffians on our campuses an opportunity to express themselves," said Henry MacCracken, chancellor of New York University. "There seems to be a well nigh universal consent that the present game is intolerable."

There were a dozen deaths in 1902. When a player was killed during an NYU-Union College match in 1905 in front of newsmen from Manhattan, it was impossible to ignore the state into which football had degenerated. A survey of college presidents and medical doctors published by Charles Thwing in the *Journal of the American Medical Association* reported that the majority wanted the game to be abolished.

Dr. Charles Eliot, a sparse and dour man who was president of Harvard and a leader in the crusade against football, liked to tell his audiences that football was to academics what bullfighting was to agriculture.

The issue reached a climax in 1906 when the *Chicago Tribune* printed a series that documented the deaths of eighteen college players, forty-six high school players, and nine semiprofessional players the season before. Without waiting for the figures to be verified (they never were), Columbia announced it was abandoning football in the face of the evidence. Several Southern and Western schools announced they would take steps to reform the rules. Football had become a matter of great national concern. There was even talk that Congress might outlaw it.

6 Teddy Roosevelt to the Rescue

Theodore Roosevelt was a weak and failing child. He suffered from asthma, sinusitis, and heart murmur. His vision was poor and he coughed too much. Relatives thought he would never survive childhood. Yet he defied logic and conquered his infirmities with a remarkable zest that made him a legendary American and, not incidentally, helped him become President.

In 1902, Connie Mack (seated center) organized the Philadelphia Athletics football team, comprised mostly of players from his baseball team. Pitcher Rube Waddell was the football team's star and helped the A's defeat a Pittsburgh team that.had Christy Mathewson at fullback, 12-6, for the professional football championship. The Athletics also engaged in the first night pro football game, at Elmira, New York, in 1902, beating the Kanaweola A.C. 39-0.

Roosevelt rode through the Badlands of the Dakotas, shooting bear and buffalo. He was so fond of boxing that he had a boxing ring installed in the White House basement, where he worked out daily, if not in the ring with a friend or an aide then alone on a punching bag. He was a devoted disciple of Walter Camp's exercise program, the famed "Daily Dozen." In short he was the first President to be fascinated by physical fitness.

In the autumn of 1905, this dedicated Harvard graduate, who wore a crimson tie every Saturday that his old school played football, purchased out of his own pocket eight tickets for the football match between Harvard and "those Yalies." Roosevelt planned to attend the game even though the press and the pulpit in particular considered it beneath the President's station. His assistants presented him with clippings from various newspapers, all of which advised him to stay in Washington and forget football.

The press wanted the President to repudiate football, which had fallen into such discredit that few people thought it would ever regain respectability. Baseball was the national pastime, a relatively graceful and safe sport that ladies and Republicans liked.

Roosevelt was not to be persuaded. His love of football was unquenchable. A year or two earlier he had admonished his Cabinet to "hit the line hard." Those words were inscribed on bronze plaques pinned to gymnasium walls all over the nation. Frequently when he interviewed candidates for government appointments, he asked if they had ever played football. If they had not, he considered their applications a bit longer.

Roosevelt felt so remiss over not having played the game as an undergraduate at Harvard that he often pretended that he had. His legs had been too thin, so he had jumped rope and jogged by the hour, hoping to make himself stronger. But by the time he built himself up, he was ready to graduate. Later, his son played at Harvard and that was some consolation to Teddy.

As President, Roosevelt had already cast himself in the role of football's savior. Having received the Nobel Prize for helping to end the Russo-Japanese War, he considered it well within his prowess to bring peace to the football fields of America. He had summoned Bill Reid of Harvard, James B. Fine of Princeton, and Walter Camp of Yale to what was billed as the White House football conference. There he demanded an end to kicking, punching, biting, and scratching. Football was to be a gentleman's game, he told them. An agreement was drawn up to reform the sport. The season of 1905 commenced and the casualty list across the nation was gratifyingly short. It was at this point that Teddy bought his tickets to the Yale game, feeling fairly confident that football had been rescued.

Yet the momentum of the ban-football forces would prove hard to thwart. On the first day of November, the Harvard coach was notified that the school's Corporation Board had secretly voted to abolish the Yale game. Reid telephoned the school's best known alumnus and ticket holder, who in turn called other alumni with a Presidentially powerful request to help out.

The move caught Dr. Eliot and his allies by surprise. The Corporation Board decided that the Yale-Harvard game could be played and contented itself with cautioning against unnecessary violence on the field.

Unfortunately, the issue was still not resolved. Two days after the Board made its decision, a match between Harvard and Penn ended with Barthol Parker rolling on the ground and moaning after a deliberate kick in the groin from a Penn lineman. Somehow Parker struggled to his feet and with one punch broke both his assailant's jaw and his own hand. The referee did not see the attack on Parker, only his subsequent retaliation. Thus did Parker become the man who almost killed football.

By Sunday morning Reid was on a train heading for the White House. When he arrived he was told that Roosevelt would see him immediately. There was a dinner scheduled with the German ambassador, who wanted to discuss an especially important trade agreement, but the President decided the Ambassador would have to wait.

Then he approached Reid with a visage writhing in consternation. He demanded to know what had happened.

Reid told of the debilitating kick the referee had missed, apparently the only person in the stadium who had. "What would you have done, Mr. President, if you had received such a kick?" Reid asked.

"Well, I believe that in the heat of battle, I would have done exactly what young Mr. Parker did," replied Roosevelt.

Parker got off with an official reprimand from Eliot and a lecture on how Harvard men were supposed to behave. At long last the much-discussed Harvard-Yale game took place, with the President of the United States in the stands, as planned.

The first two periods were uneventful. In the third quarter, Yale was forced to punt. Harvard's Francis Burr signaled for a fair catch, but Yale captain Tom Shevlin chose to ignore the signal. He slammed straight at the ankles of Burr, driving him into Yale fullback Jack Quill, who knocked him over backward. Burr toppled to the turf like a stunned elk. His nose was broken and he was bleeding profusely.

The men of Harvard demanded instant revenge. In the stands fistfights broke out. On the field Harvard and Yale players pushed and shoved each other. Fortunately the band began to play and tempers cooled while Burr was carried off the field on a stretcher. Reid wiped the perspiration from his forehead and slumped forward on the Harvard bench. A runner handed him a message from Major Charles Higginson, a leader of the anti-football faction. "Take the Harvard team off the field and save the honor of our noble institution," it said. Reid declined the request, fully aware that Dr. Eliot was not in the stadium and that the President was. Harvard continued the struggle, but Yale went on to win 6–0. Three days later Dr. Eliot announced that Harvard would not schedule any games for the following season.

The controversy dragged on. Nicholas Murray Butler of Columbia explained that his school abolished the sport "to prevent gentlemen engaged in it from assassinating each other." Others, a majority, defended the game. Reverend Father John Cavanaugh, the brilliant, young new president of Notre Dame, retorted in *Collier's Magazine*, "I would rather see our youth playing football with the danger of an occasional broken collarbone than to see them dedicated to croquet."

When the season ended Roosevelt summoned representatives of Harvard, Yale, and Princeton to the White House and again told them what must be done. He demanded a full code of reform, one that would pacify such academic lions as Eliot and Butler. "Do not report back to me until you have a game that is acceptable to the entire nation," he ordered. "You must act in the public interest. This glorious sport must be freed from brutality and foul play. The future of the republic is dependent upon what you do. The character of future generations is in your hands."

Toward this noble end the representatives of twenty-eight schools gathered at New York University the next spring. They called themselves the Football Conference Committee. The chairman was General Palmer Pierce of the United States Military Academy at West Point. The resident genius at the sessions was Walter Camp of Yale, a distinguished business executive and author, but still the most respected man in football. At last the changes he had been contemplating could be realized.

First of all the college game would be limited to undergraduates. "College football can only be cleansed if eligibility is restricted to sophomores, juniors and seniors, with special instructional teams for entering freshmen," Camp said. "Any man who changes schools must wait one year before becoming eligible for the varsity. The tramp athlete can only be controlled if his path is strewn with obstacles."

Next the rules convention decided to encourage a more wide-open game. A first down would be awarded after an advance of ten yards, within four downs, and the restrictions on the forward pass were liberalized.

Having altered the laws of the game, the rules conference committee considered the matter of enforcement. Camp demanded and received a central board of officials, which assigned impartial officials to each game. These men were empowered to assess penalties under a specified code. If a Yale man kicked a Harvard man in the groin, he would be judged by a referee from Amherst.

The new rules committee did not ban "mass plays" until four years later, when it became illegal for the offense to join hands in its assault on the defense. Two tackles could not form themselves into one human turtle and move forward ahead of the ball carrier. Prodded by Camp, the rules committee also further encouraged the forward pass. It allowed the ball to be passed forward to any point on the field as long as the quarterback was ten yards behind the scrimmage line. Even that restriction vanished in Camp's lifetime.

At first the coaches were slow to change. Teams slogged along on the ground although Camp insisted that the pass would enable light and speedy teams to compete as equals with strong and heavier clubs. Then in 1913 a team from Notre Dame came east to face Army at West Point. The Notre Dame quarterback, Gus Dorais, dazzled the Cadets by flinging passes to an end named Knute Rockne. The Notre Dame attack was so impressive that several members of the Army team, including an injured Dwight Eisenhower, questioned the visitors for hours before they left. "We became convinced that it was a maneuver we had to master," said Eisenhower, who could have won an All-America mention at halfback if he had not been hurt that year. "At the end of the season, we knew it so well that Navy suffered. It was our final game and we came out passing just like Dorais and Rockne."

Through strength of purpose and with a generous assist from a powerful politician, Walter Camp had turned a number of discordant sports into the distinctly American game of football. It was adventurous, fast, and versatile. If it was still at times more bestial than honorable combat, that was a minor problem now that most of the brutality was curbed. Camp was the man who made football work and brought its virtues to the attention of the public. Without him there would have been no Knute Rockne or Frank Leahy, no Bear Bryant or Vince Lombardi.

7   A Vestige of a Dying Era

This was the last great moment of a sport that technology, which had spawned it, destroyed. It was the long, humid summer of 1870, with mosquitoes flitting through the stagnant air on the bayous and inlets of the Mississippi River. The *Natchez*, owned by Captain Thomas P. Leathers, an unreconstructed Confederate, was to race from New Orleans to St. Louis against the *Robert E. Lee*, built and captained by a staunch Unionist, John Cannon. "The war of the rebellion is ending in a sporting event," wrote Edward Horatio Wheeler in *Darcy's Sporting Journal*, leaving no doubt where his allegiance had been. "This is why this is such an important race, one worthy of international coverage."

Sure enough, this, the greatest steamboat race in history, would command attention across the country and beyond. Correspondents would fire off hour by hour reports. Eastern newspapers would flood their readers with front-page news about the race. Great sums of money would be wagered on it as far away as France and England.

More than ten thousand spectators crowded the upper wharf in New Orleans to watch the start. At 5:05 P.M. the *Robert E. Lee* moved out into the current and headed up river, followed in five minutes by the *Natchez*. Cleverly, Cannon had stripped his vessel of extra rigging. He refused to carry freight, and he had cut the passenger list to a hundred. Leathers, on the other hand, had shown little foresight. He carried freight and a load of passengers.

YALE Versus

BRADLEY
1898

Annual Foot Ball Game
NEW HAVEN
NOV. 19, 1898

Official Souvenir Price 50¢

HARVARD

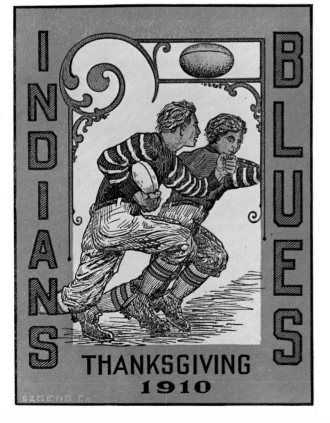

INDIANS

BLUES

THANKSGIVING
1910

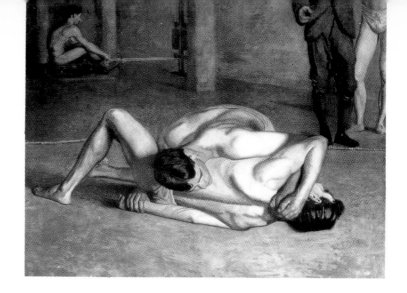

For the first miles the two boats ran close together, but gradually the *Robert E. Lee* pulled away. Off Baton Rouge the *Natchez* was nine miles behind.

Above the bend at Vicksburg, the lead boat got an important assist, causing supporters of the *Natchez* to cry foul. A barge came along side the *Robert E. Lee* to service it. The two boats were lashed together and for several hours, while fuel was transferred from barge to steamboat, the two ships ran as one. The *Natchez* took on fuel in the conventional way, docking at ports along the river, and fell farther behind.

At 11:04 P.M. the *Robert E. Lee* steamed past the wharfs at Memphis while thousands of spectators lined the shores with torches. The *Natchez* followed one hour and three minutes later.

Between Cairo and St. Louis, a distance of twelve hours running time at worst, lay an enormous spread of shoal water. Just above Cairo the captain of the *Robert E. Lee* took on two experienced river pilots who knew the treacherous sandbars well. Slowly and gently the *Robert E. Lee* made her way upstream. When the *Natchez* came close to the shoal waters, she too moved forward under much reduced power. Then a fog settled across the Mississippi and the *Natchez* tied up on a riverbank for more than five hours. The greatest boat race was in effect over.

On the morning of July 4, at 11:33 A.M., the majestic *Robert E. Lee* steamed across the finish line unfettered. She had traveled the distance between New Orleans and St. Louis in three days, eighteen hours, and thirteen minutes, more than five hours better than the previous record. That evening at 6 P.M. the *Natchez* came into port. Her supporters had ready excuses for her defeat, but those served more to save face than to contest the decision. Over forty million dollars in bets was paid off on the winner.

The race was the last glorious gesture of a perishing era. The railroad took over commerce on the river and the steamboats vanished. Left behind was a memorable piece of Americana. Henceforth all great races would be compared to the one between the *Natchez* and the *Robert E. Lee*. It was talked, written, and sung about until almost no one remembered just how lopsided it had all been.

8 Flourishes and Flops

It was a time of trumpets and drums. America sensed that she was an emerging power, and she strutted furiously before the rest of the world. Going over the crest of Niagara Falls in rubber-lined barrels was only the most farfetched of displays in this carnival of American exhibitionism. America was captivated by any sport that might glorify it. When the strongman and wrestler George Hackenschmidt, "the Russian Lion," got off the boat in New York to meet the American champion, Frank Gotch, the populace became fanatical about weight lifting and wrestling.

Hackenschmidt was born in what was then the Russian province of Estonia. His father was the owner of a dye-works. Young George was an apprentice engineer when Dr. Wladislaf von Krajewski, a Polish physician who had ministered to the Czar of Russia, discovered him. A father-son relationship developed, and the two set out to turn weight lifting into a science. By the time Hackenschmidt was twenty-one years old, he was five feet ten inches and two hundred pounds. His chest measured forty-eight inches normally and fifty-one inches expanded. His thighs were twenty-four inches around. When Americans saw him, they would not rest until they could produce such physical specimens themselves.

There followed a surge of strongmen, and a whole generation of Americans lifted weights and ate sunflower seeds to preserve their bodies. Hackenschmidt upheld their faith. He died in 1968 at the age of ninety, and until the moment he took his final breath, his fans claimed he could do everything but stop freight trains with his bare hands and leap tall buildings in a single bound.

Hackenschmidt was admired not only for his enormous strength but for his skill, his command of many holds, and, above all, his intelligence and gentility. Gotch, to his discredit as a sportsman, used every foul tactic against Hackenschmidt. He oiled his body so that his opponent could not catch him. When pinned, Gotch rubbed the oil in the Russian's eyes. He gouged, scratched, and punched. Yet America was not ashamed of Gotch; instead he was thought to be quite clever, except for the fact that he was beaten. Hackenschmidt prevailed, but the cost of victory was high. Before he was through with the series of confrontations against Gotch, he had torn the semilunar cartilage in his right knee and was not the same again. Gotch succeeded him as world champion.

When Gotch retired, his place was taken by Ed (Strangler) Lewis, who paid tribute to Hackenschmidt's pioneer work in the sport. "Until Hackenschmidt toured America there was no interest in wrestling or body building to speak of," said Lewis. "When he went back home with his bad knee, he left behind a whole nation of enthusiastic wrestlers and body builders. By the time World War One broke out, everybody was obsessed with those two sports."

America saw itself as putting on a show for the rest of the globe. And, as often happens to showmen, her search for new material and new wrinkles on the old routines became obsessive. Americans sailed faster, jumped higher, moved quicker, and spent more money than anybody else. Still they were not satisfied.

With a banner flapping over their heads and a Marine Corps band playing martial music in the background, the six contestants in the Great New York to Paris Auto Race, sponsored by the normally sedate *New York Times,* went chugging across the starting line. They were heading west on the first leg of their journey, across the continent to San Francisco, no easy drive in 1906 when paved roads were a rarity. From San Francisco the cars would be shipped to Valdez, Alaska, where the drivers would set out for Nome. They would cross the Bering Strait on ice and proceed to Moscow, Berlin, and Paris —a total of eight thousand miles over badly rutted roads, hardly fit for oxen.

Each car carried a crew of three with heavy clothing for arctic wear and spare parts for the vehicles. The cars rambled through swamplands with no roads, plowing through miles of gumbo mud. They drove even on the tracks of the Trans-Siberian Railroad. Once, the only American car in the race had to back out of a tunnel to avoid a head-on collision with a train.

In addition to the American car, there were three French, one Italian, and one German in the race at the start, but the contest narrowed to two cars, the German and the American. The Americans rolled into Paris four days after the Germans, but because of a thirty-day allowance, they were proclaimed the winners by twenty-six days.

For more than an hour newspapermen stood on the seawall above the Battery in New York waiting for two American fishermen of Norwegian birth, George Harbo and Frank Samuelson, to begin a three thousand mile voyage across the Atlantic. The fishermen had announced to the world that they would row all the way to France in an ordinary eighteen-foot, round-bottomed boat without sails or motor. It was June 6, 1896 and they had spent two years planning for this date. The boat was named *The Fox* after Richard Fox, publisher of the successful *Police Gazette.* It was loaded with five hundred pounds of food, sixty gallons of water, an oil stove, signal flares, five pairs of oars, and a sea anchor. The rowers planned to ride the Gulf Stream all the way to Le Havre.

They moved out smartly and had almost no trouble for weeks. A German passenger ship signaled them, assuming they were shipwrecked, but the Germans were told they weren't wanted.

Several days later a storm broke and the two-man crew

of *The Fox* was forced to stay up for three straight days
bailing out water. On the third day Samuelson looked up
to see a wave the size of a mountain. The boat capsized
but the men were able to stay close to it because each
man wore a life jacket fastened to the boat by a rope.
Just after sundown, they both managed to return to *The
Fox*. They righted the boat and crawled in, their hands
bloodied, their lips blue and puffed. Not a moment too
soon they sighted the Scilly Islands, off the southwest
coast of Britain. They rested there for a day before con-
tinuing to Le Havre. Then they rowed up the Seine to
Paris.

Europe would have acclaimed Harbo and Samuelson
for their sixty-one day voyage if they hadn't called themselves Americans. "We did it for America!" the native
Norwegians cried, and though they were in fact naturalized Americans, the Norwegian press lambasted them.

On a windswept field outside Dayton, Ohio, a crowd
of ten thousand assembled for America's first balloon
race. More than a hundred contestants were gathered
for a massive movement of airships to a destination
outside Chicago. The year was 1876, and though balloons had been used in the recently concluded Civil
War (to observe troop movements), this event was considered the true breakthrough for ballooning. "This is
the greatest race for lighter-than-air," declared Professor
Clampton R. Lowe. "This launches America soundly
into the balloon age."

Roughly three-quarters of the entrants failed to last
through the first mile, impaling themselves on trees and
sinking into nearby fields, to the disgust of Ohio farmers. Several balloons rose majestically, only to float
toward undetermined destinations. Severe crosswinds
took James K. Rothridge toward Toledo, where he spent
two days on the ridge pole of a barn. Another balloon,
sponsored jointly by a Cincinnati newspaper and a
steamship company, came down on a church spire in
Muncie, Indiana. No contestant came close to Chicago.

A reporter who covered the race from start to aborted
finish insisted that despite the mishaps it was an event
to make America proud. After all, hadn't one hundred
airships risen into the air? America exceeded its great
ambitions, only in the ease with which it proclaimed
them fulfilled.

9   The Boston Strong Boy

> *"For a long time I enjoyed the friendship
> of John Lawrence Sullivan. There never
> was a better prize fighter than the Boston
> Strong Boy. When he was in his prime, no
> finer boxer ever stepped into the ring.
> When I went to Africa to hunt wild game,
> Sullivan presented me with a gold mounted
> rabbit's foot. I carried it through my entire
> African trip and there is no question but
> what it brought me plenty of luck. I shall
> carry it to the moment of my death."*
> —Theodore Roosevelt, President and amateur boxer

> *"And John L. Sullivan
>   The Strong Boy of Boston
>   Broke every single rib of Jack Kilrain."*
> —Vachel Lindsay's "John L. Sullivan,
>   The Boston Strong Boy"

As a fighter he was supreme. He could
beat anybody, fighting bare knuckled or
under the new Marquis of Queens-
berry's rules. That much is beyond dispute. John L. Sullivan the boxer left no
room for argument.

It was John L. Sullivan the man who raised the fuss. As
the finest fistfighter in the world, he was America's first
athletic super hero but he also was an arch-villain. Early
in the game he learned that acclaim and notoriety went
hand in hand for a man in his position, and he encour-

aged both. He was, in short, America's first great sports personality.

It is no easy task to isolate the real John L. Sullivan from the many conflicting profiles of him (including his own —he wrote four autobiographies, all slightly different in their estimation of him). He was a reserved, almost shy man who rarely smiled. At five feet ten inches and one hundred eighty pounds, he was stocky, narrow in the shoulders, and given to fat around the waist. His muscles were sleek and flat. He wore his hair closely cropped, contrary to the style of the day. In later years he grew a large black moustache, which complimented an otherwise undistinguished face.

John Lawrence Sullivan was born in Roxbury, Massachusetts, on October 15, 1858. His mother was at least six feet tall and weighed one hundred eighty pounds. People said she was either Italian or Greek, but Sullivan insisted that she was Irish. (She probably was born in Ireland, though not necessarily of Irish parents.) His father, Mike Sullivan, was no bigger than five feet three inches tall but heavily muscled from years of carrying hod, an occupation that his son attempted to follow.

It is doubtful that Sullivan progressed past the fifth grade in school, though after he became the undisputed idol of American youth he liked to present himself as a college graduate. He was about nineteen when he began fistfighting on the stages of Boston theaters and in the tents of suburban towns. "Our family was not well-to-do and it was necessary to pick up what dollars there were in order to eat," he said.

"He was incredibly strong, and when he hit you it was like being run over by a runaway horse," said Mike Donovan, one of the few opponents to last four rounds in a sparring exhibition with Sullivan.

Donovan testified that Sullivan was the greatest natural puncher who ever lived. He was certainly a zestful one. He admitted from time to time that the thing he liked most about boxing was simply the joy of hitting somebody. But when the show was over, young Johnny avoided the saloons and took the money home to his mother in Roxbury.

Then the promoter Billy Madden discovered him and took him on tour. He traveled from Cincinnati to Chicago to Philadelphia to New York, fighting with or without gloves in a series of "pugilistic exhibitions." (Prize fighting as such was illegal in most of the United States.)

It was at this point that tales of his private life began making the rounds, portraying him as the archetypical hard-fighting, hard-drinking, womanizing Irish thug. The image was very successful—worth a lot of money at the gate and sometimes a psychological advantage for him over his opponent—but it was mostly untrue. "Johnny liked his drinks," said Madden in an interview with the *New York World*. "Make no mistake about it. But the stories about his prodigious thirst used to start just before an important bout. It helped convince his opponents that they were about to fight a raving drunk. Sometimes he would come up the aisle weaving and slurring his words. That is not to say he didn't have some bad battles with the bottle after he was through fighting. . . . When he was fighting he kept himself in better shape than that."

Sullivan was only twenty-three when he and Madden wandered into Harry Hill's garden of pleasure in Manhattan. They were watching the pretty girls on the dance floor when Richard Kyle Fox, editor of the *Police Gazette* and the most powerful journalist in American sport, came over to talk. Fox covered three beats in his magazine: sport, theater, and society scandal. Sullivan was already a major figure in sport, and thanks to Fox (with the willing assistance of the fighter himself), would soon become a staple of the scandal mongers.

"Fox was my advisor at the start," wrote Sullivan in one of his autobiographies. "He conceived a plan where he would groom me until I became a person of much national prominence. I had to do what he said, but I trusted him because he was the most intelligent sports promoter of the day. He donated hundreds of prizes to the ring and was the main promoter of Paddy Ryan, then

The lure of the Wild West was a strong one for curious Easterners. Many people traveled West to hunt, and the favorite target was the seemingly abundant American bison. Large and fearsome in appearance, but not particularly bright, the beasts were slaughtered by the thousands in the 1880s. The Indian, as shown in a painting by Charles Russell, had used the buffalo to provide food, shelter, and clothing, but the new adventurers had little reason for their kill except for sport.

the heavyweight champion of the world."

Fox would do anything to build up Sullivan, and in this case the strategy called for tearing him down. According to a legend perpetuated if not first perpetrated by Fox, he despised Sullivan. Supposedly the publisher had or-dered the young fighter to come to his table and bow down, and Sullivan had refused. This was fine melo-drama, precisely what a man of Fox's theatrical bent would conceive as a story to delight Victorian America. But of course it was overblown, if not totally false. "We had some evil words and we had our fallings-out," wrote Sullivan of his relationship with Fox, "but we were never the enemies people thought we were."

From the moment of their meeting, Fox and Sullivan began to build an image of notoriety for the fighter. The Police Gazette ran story after story, some of them amus-ingly bumptious and obviously fictitious, that made John Lawrence Sullivan of Roxbury appear to be the most ter-rifying Irish fistfighter in an era when Irish fistfighters were already shamelessly oversold. According to the Police Gazette, Sullivan was a brawler, a braggart, and the hardest drinker in America. He was so contemptuous of sport and so eager to turn a profit that he would fight in dance halls, theaters, barns, barges, and haylofts. He would punch out lumberjacks, steel-drivers, gandy danc-ers, blacksmiths, town toughs, and gangsters for as little as fifty dollars, taking on all comers and leaving them on their backs. Sometimes he was so drunk he had to be pushed into the ring.

"It is a wonder that he has never killed anyone," said one Police Gazette article. "He hits with such force that quite often his opponent's head hits the deck before his buttocks, there being nothing to cushion the fall."

Richard Kyle Fox gave to John L. Sullivan a sure-fire appeal-through-controversy. He celebrated his fighter with some homeric titles as "the Great John L." and "the Boston Strong Boy." Yet at the same time he continued to denounce him as a cocky brawler and led a crusade to find a man who could beat him.

For his part Sullivan would wear the image of a con-ceited boor wallowing in the decadence of success. On one occasion, in 1883, he showed up at the original Mad-ison Square Garden one-half hour late for the match. He was dressed in evening clothes. While 13,567 people booed loudly, he explained that he felt too ill to fight. He wobbled down the aisle, seemingly drunk. When the customers, who had paid as much as twenty-five dollars a seat, demanded their money back, they were told they had no cause for complaint because "they had seen a great show."

Only in the ring was it possible to find the true Sullivan. The contenders were dragged in one by one and John L. knocked them all flat.

Despite all his bad press, the fans found it impossible to resist this invincible gladiator. When he returned to New York to fight a Fox-picked challenger named Charlie Mitchell, Sullivan was greeted as a hero. Once again the Garden was filled, this time at the astounding top price of fifty dollars. The fans got what they had paid for: the Great John L. dropped Mitchell on his spine. Fox brought in more fodder for his American hero-villain. There was Herbert Slade, a giant Maori native, champion of Aus-tralia and New Zealand. He lasted three rounds. Alf Greenfield, one of the best in England, went two rounds and begged to leave. And so it went.

In 1887, Sullivan toured England, as all outstanding American sportsmen of the nineteenth century did, and talked boxing with the Prince of Wales. The following year, Sullivan fought thirty-nine rounds against Mitchell at Baron Rothschild's estate at Chantilly, France.

After the fight, which was called because of darkness and declared a draw, Sullivan "went on such a bender that he had delirium tremors and was confined to bed for three months," according to the Police Gazette. Actu-ally, Sullivan's vice was overeating, and when he left England he went on a binge that pushed his weight up to two hundred forty pounds. What liquor he consumed was mostly just to wash down the enormous meals.

Thomas Eakins' painting, *Between Rounds,* captures the fascination Americans had for the sport of prizefighting. Boxing clubs were popular and attracted large crowds. While Eakins was bringing sport to the salon with his cool and masterful paintings, young George Bellows was capturing the boisterous mood of the fight crowd in such works as *Stag at Sharkey's,* a lithograph.

Meanwhile, Fox awarded his magazine's diamond belt, symbol of the heavyweight championship of the world, to Jake Kilrain (whose real name was the un-Irishlike John Killion). Only a few months earlier Kilrain had beaten Jem Smith, a co-claimant of the English championship, and the indefatigable Mitchell. A showdown between Kilrain and Sullivan was inevitable. In 1889, Sullivan agreed to the fight, though the *Gazette* insisted he would be too drunk to move.

"As soon as he accepted Kilrain's long standing challenge to fight, London prize rules, at ten thousand dollars a side and the championship, the ring to be pitched somewhere near New Orleans, The Great John L. began to drink heavily again and predict that he would win easily," the *Gazette* said. "With the fight less than two months away, Sullivan is in despicable shape. Some of his backers are prepared to use a gun on him in order to get him into the ring. A tragic state of affairs."

In reality Sullivan had been eating lots of protein, drinking a great deal of water, and preparing diligently for the fight. Duped by the press reports, Kilrain planned to outlast the Boston Strong Boy.

Kilrain would avoid Sullivan's early assaults, assuming that Sullivan's legs, weakened by booze, would collapse in the later rounds.

Sullivan traveled to New Orleans by train from his camp in Belfast, New York, through Cincinnati, and down the Mississippi. When he arrived, the crowd pulled his wagon through the French Quarter to his lodgings at Twenty-Nine North Rampart Street. Kilrain was depressed to find out that Sullivan was sober, working hard, and in excellent shape.

The fight was to be held one hundred four miles north of the city in Mississippi on the thirty-thousand-acre plantation of Colonel Charles W. Rich, who specialized in lumber and cotton. In preparation for the bout, a wooden arena had been built and the promoters had arranged for the police to be elsewhere. At the railroad station, ringside tickets sold for fifteen dollars, entitling the purchaser to round-trip transportation and a camp chair from which to watch the bout. Food and liquor were extra.

On the morning of the fight Sullivan's trainer, William Muldoon, let his fighter loose at the table, as a reward for staying in shape. A writer for the *New York World* was stunned by Sullivan's appetite. The fighter drank no alcohol, but he swilled down three bowls of chicken broth, ate three whole chickens covered with rice and peppers, and two loaves of Louisiana bread. Colonel Rich remarked later that he had never seen a man consume so much food. "He seemed to have less of an interest in spirits than he did in the fried chicken provided," he remarked. "His desire for food is enormous."

Despite the last-minute feast, an extremely fit John L. Sullivan entered the ring wearing his traditional colors of green and white with an American flag twisted into a belt. He wore flesh-colored tights, green knee breeches, and black boots laced high over his ankles. He had a slight bulge on his belly, but he weighed only between one hundred ninety-nine and two hundred four pounds, depending upon which sources are to be believed. Kilrain was described as looking "drawn and worried."

The first six rounds of the fight were uneventful. In the seventh round Kilrain tore Sullivan's ear with a hard left, the first damaging blow of the match. Meanwhile, Sullivan was working on his opponent's rib cage. Every time he swung, the customers gasped. Throughout the fight Sullivan pressed the advantage and Kilrain retreated. The wooden stands shut out the fresh air and the temperature on that humid bayou day reached one hundred four degrees. People collapsed in their seats from the heat and the hearty amount of liquor imbibed.

"Good God," Kilrain asked Sullivan after the twelfth round, "how long can you stay?"

"'Til tomorrow morning, if necessary," said Sullivan. "You'll weaken before I do and—heh, heh—I'll buy you a beer."

Both men turned crimson from the heat, but Kilrain seemed the worse off. He grew darker and darker red as

Sullivan continued to pound his right hand into Kilrain's ribs. The blows could be heard from seventy-five yards away, said one reporter. Apart from the beating to the midsection, Kilrain suffered split lips, a broken nose, and a black right eye. He dripped blood and sweat.

In the forty-fifth round, Sullivan became sick to his stomach. "The booze!" somebody shouted, but it was only a delayed reaction to the enormous pre-fight dinner, and Sullivan managed to keep going.

"Surprised?" asked Sullivan.

"Yes," said Kilrain. "Let's call it a draw."

"No draw," said Sullivan. "You shouldn't have any trouble. You're fighting a drunk, remember?"

By the seventy-sixth round a physician suggested it would be suicide for Kilrain to fight any longer. Jake Kilrain remained in his corner and his manager threw in the sponge. John L. Sullivan was king.

In the same year that Sullivan defeated Kilrain, he granted an interview that revealed much of the man beneath his larger-than-life public image. The interviewer was the *New York World's* Elizabeth Cochrane Seaman, better known under her pen name, Nellie Bly. A veteran reporter who had been around the world to cover wars and marine disasters, she was a celebrity in her own right and certainly the most famous female journalist of her time. She described her meeting with Sullivan this way:

"In his hand he held a light cloth coat. He paused as he entered the room in a half-bashful way and twisted his cap in a very boyish manner. He is said to be a man who roars with great temper, befitting his noted Irish personality. But he seemed perfectly at ease with me. He was far more the gentleman than I expected."

During the interview Sullivan revealed himself as an athlete who was remarkably fussy about his physical well-being. He ate no sweets or potatoes, he said. He had only a small portion of oatmeal in the morning; he consumed warm meat at lunch and cold meat at dinner.

The journalist noted that Sullivan's hands were quite small. She observed that the fingers were straight and shapely and that the closely trimmed nails were pink and oval. She asked to feel his arm: she could not span his bicep with both her hands. Sullivan glowed with adolescent amusement. Then she commented on the smallness of his hands. Sullivan seemed perplexed but not embarrassed. "My friends tell me that my hands are like hams," he said. "I dip them in a mixture of rock salt, white wine, vinegar, and other ingredients to make them tougher."

Clearly, at the time he became champion John L. Sullivan was far from the dissolute brawler the *Police Gazette* had portrayed him to be. But ironically that myth proved to be prophetic. At the height of his success, while he was being handsomely paid by manufacturers to endorse their products (he was the first athlete to do that) and by saloon keepers to visit their establishments, he began to decline. He drank more heavily than before, indulged his tendency to gluttony, and invested unwisely in a succession of saloons. Desperately needing money to clear up some staggering debts, Sullivan agreed to meet James J. Corbett of San Francisco. Corbett was a man of stronger intellect and more disciplined habits. It was 1892, again in New Orleans, and the Great John L., now thirty-three years old, showed up in wretched condition. The fight lasted twenty-one rounds and Corbett won.

When he came staggering to the ropes, overweight and duly punished, Sullivan said, "I fought once too often. But I'm glad that when I had to lose my title, I lost to an American, especially an Irish-American. This man licked me and licked me good. The championship stays where it belongs, in America. And I remain yours truly, John L. Sullivan, American."

The old champion slipped into near obscurity. He ballooned to three hundred thirty-five pounds. He toured on the vaudeville circuit. His drinking got worse. Then one day in 1905 he was reborn. He vowed to stop drinking and became a temperance lecturer.

As a crusader against alcohol, Sullivan at last found a way to redeem his public image. For years he had heard himself denounced. When he lost the championship to Corbett, for example, the *New York Times* ran a front-page editorial applauding his defeat: "Sullivan has been swaggering about as an unconquerable person and the dethronement of a mean and cowardly bully as the idol of the barrooms and stables is a public good that is a fit subject for public congratulations. Corbett is the innovator of a more humane style of fighting, one that may become, in time, legalized."

Suddenly Sullivan was the good guy. "Alcohol is the handwork of the devil and nothing is more foul," he thundered. "It came close to finishing me. I once had more than a million two hundred thousand dollars. Because of booze, I let it slip through my fingers. Don't let it happen to you. My hands are steady and my grip is firm. When I wake in the morning, a whole new wonderful world is waiting for me. I do not need this foul liquid ever again and neither do you. I am yours truly, John L. Sullivan, and in my day I was one of the finest boxers who ever practiced the art."

And so the great John L. lived out his life attaining a measure of the respectability that he had had to abjure as a fighter. His role as temperance leader may have been no closer to the inner man than the role of prizefighter, but at least it was a more serene one. It repaid him with a little of the peace he had lost in becoming the first superstar, the first personality to overwhelm his sport and the public. He was part of the American dream, but his greatest triumph may have been that he wasn't consumed by it.

10 Dr. Naismith's Game

The gymnastics craze of the 1870s had passed, and at the YMCA Training School in Springfield, Massachusetts, there was a general boredom among physical education majors during the long winter months. One of the classes at the institution, later called Springfield College, was especially unruly, much to the concern of Dr. Luther Gulick, the head of the physical training department. After all, in 1891 young people were supposed to act more civilized.

One afternoon Dr. Gulick was chatting with a young instructor, Dr. James Naismith, and the conversation turned to the games Naismith had improvised when he was a child. He told Gulick how he had set strips of old files into a set of hickory flats and thereby fashioned ice skates. "Well," said Dr. Gulick, "unless you have strenuous objections, you're the man to carry out my great project."

"And what is your 'great project?'" asked Naismith, knowing that he was about to be assigned some extra work.

Gulick told him to invent a game that would occupy the unruly group. These students could not be permitted to drift, Naismith was told, because they were studying to be YMCA administrators.

In a book called *Basketball: Its Origins and Development,* Naismith recounted how he first reacted to Gulick's request:

> Knowing the difficulty of the task that was being assigned to me, I immediately began to make excuses to show why I should be left with the classes that I was teaching at the time. I had been instructing in boxing, wrestling, swimming, and canoeing, all sports that I felt proficient in and liked. I tried my best to dissuade Dr. Gulick. It mattered little how much I talked.

There followed a period of experimentation that would have staggered Thomas Alva Edison. Naismith found football unsuitable as an indoor sport because it was not possible to remove the violence from the game. Even soccer proved too rough indoors. The first indoor soccer match at Springfield produced one broken leg and several badly battered thigh muscles. Several windows were also shattered, which did not amuse Dr. Gulick.

N. C. Wyeth was a giant among American illustrators. He created memorable canvases for many of the classic tales in world literature. In 1906, following a commission by General Mills, Wyeth brought his full, romantic storytelling skill to a colorful portrayal of a rodeo bronco buster. In the more sedate East, polo was a popular sport among the wealthy, and sculptor Herbert Haseltine captured its appeal in bronze in a 1909 work.

Next, Dr. Naismith considered the possibility of moving lacrosse indoors. The game would later be played indoors but in nothing so cramped as Naismith's gymnasium. "I had always considered lacrosse the best of all games and still do," said Naismith, a native Canadian and former player for the Montreal Shamrocks. "It just seemed impossible to make an indoor sport of one that required so much space. Besides, the only modification I could think of was to make the 'crosse' itself smaller and more easy to handle in a restricted space. But that would have caused a manufacturing problem that I did not have the means to cope with. So I used the regular two-handed, full-sized 'crosse.'"

The seven Canadians in Naismith's class went at the experimental game as if it were being played on a broad Ontario meadow. Before long the beginners were getting hurt and the experts disgusted. And so, another game was discarded. Two weeks passed and both the students and Dr. Gulick were getting restless.

James Naismith retreated to his office. From below he could hear the sounds of the locker room, where his students were snapping towels at each other and laughing. They seemed happy enough, and Naismith began to understand that this difficult class did not really dislike him. It had just not been stimulated yet. This realization left him less discouraged. He returned to his task with new vigor.

Naismith looked again at American rugby (football), the most popular sport of the day. Its most objectionable feature for his purposes was, he realized, tackling, which produced rather nasty scrapes of the skin when practiced on a gymnasium floor. How to do away with tackling? He decided that his new game would eliminate it by eliminating ball carrying. If a man in possession of the ball could not run with it, he would have to pass. Suddenly, Naismith was elated, confident that he was finally on the right track. Actually, to this point his concerted thinking had produced nothing more than the playground game of "keep-away."

"The next step was to devise some objective for the players," Naismith said. "In all existing games there was some kind of goal and I felt this was essential to sustain interest." From past experience he knew that if he put the goal on the floor, as it was in his indoor soccer and lacrosse games, there would be undue scuffling in front of the goal mouth.

For a while Naismith experimented with a box goal set at a modest height off the floor. With nine men to a side, the defensive team simply fell back, formed a circle around the goal, and would not let the offensive team score. So Naismith decided to elevate the goals above the players' heads. He called the maintenance supervisor, Charles Stebbins, and asked him if he could construct two boxes about eighteen inches square. "Sorry," said Stebbins, "there isn't a spare scrap of lumber anywhere that hasn't been allocated for something. For the game you're talking about, wouldn't peach baskets do? They're larger at the top than they are at the bottom, but they ought to accommodate a soccer ball well enough. I've got a mess of them over in the storage room. I'll have somebody get a couple of them and put them up wherever you want them."

Naismith did not, as legend has it, hang up the peach baskets himself. He let a workman do that. While the workman was tacking them to the lower rail of the balcony, Naismith wrote down the first thirteen rules of the game. He handed them to Elizabeth Lyons, secretary in the athletic department, who typed them neatly. Naismith took the sheet of rules downstairs, tacked it up on the bulletin board, and walked to the gym.

The first reaction to the game of basketball was predictably cynical. Frank Mahan, a member of the football team and a leader of the malcontents in the class, read the paper slowly. Then he snorted derisively. *"Another new game!"* A couple of other men came in, read the rules, looked at the baskets, and signed up without enthusiasm, obviously expecting to be bored again.

There were eighteen men in the class and Naismith

asked two captains to choose up sides. The teams walked onto the floor, not knowing exactly where to stand. Each team was divided into three forwards, three centers, and three guards. Naismith took a center from each side out to midcourt and, as the game's lone official, tossed up the ball in basketball's first tipoff. Immediately everybody began to foul. Since he had not invented the free throw yet, Naismith punished offenders by banishing them to a penalty box until the next basket was made.

Somehow, strategy evolved from the mayhem. The guards tried to pass the ball to the forwards, who took the shots at the basket. The centers stood underneath waiting for rebounds.

The noise from the gymnasium on this cold winter's morning in New England attracted the sport's first spectator. The game had started at 11:30 A.M. and by noon basketball's first fans were watching from the balcony. Some of the spectators had to lift the ball out of the basket after a goal and throw the ball back on the floor. Naismith reminded himself to have the bottoms knocked out of the baskets before the next day's class.

The first slapping, sweaty, aggressive game had captivated the class. The reaction in the locker room afterward was enthusiastic, a ringing affirmation. Naismith was just starting to congratulate himself when he noticed that somebody had ripped the rules off the bulletin board. He brooded for a while, wondering what it meant. Later in the day Mahan peeked into his office, grinning slyly. "You remember those rules that were put on the board, coach? I took them. I knew this game would be a big success and I took them as a souvenir. I went down and paid to have them re-copied. But I'm keeping the original. Is that all right?"

Several years later, when the game was burgeoning, Naismith received a letter from Mahan, by that time a YMCA director. After due consideration, Mahan wrote, he had decided that the celebrated inventor of basketball should have the first set of rules after all. He called upon Naismith to forgive his youthful madness.

An instant hit at Springfield, the infant game made its first tentative forays outside the nest. "At the Christmas vacation [in 1891]," wrote Naismith, "a number of the students went home and some of them started the game at their local YMCAs. There were no printed rules at the time and each student played the game as he remembered it. It was not until January of 1892 that the rules were finally printed in the school paper, *The Triangle*. I remember the headline so well. It said, 'A New Game.' It gave me a great deal of satisfaction to know that I had accomplished what Dr. Gulick asked me to do. I merely hoped at the time that it would persist a few years. I had no idea that it would gain so in popularity."

One day after the students returned from their vacation, Mahan came to Naismith and asked what the sport should be called. At the time the students were calling it "the new game," "Springfield ball," and even "Triangle ball." Mahan insisted that the creator of the game should give it a name. Members of the formerly troublesome class wanted to call it "Naismith ball." Naismith laughingly declined, protesting that his surname on any game would kill it. Then Mahan suggested "basketball." Teacher and student presented the name to the class, and the vote to affirm was unanimous.

Despite the enthusiasm for the sport at Springfield College, basketball spread slowly. Six years later it was still thought of as a YMCA exercise rather than a serious game. The game did not begin to flourish until the children who played it at the YMCAs went on to high school and formed teams. When they reached college, they again took the game with them.

By the mid-1890s, such schools as Geneva, Iowa, Yale, Stanford, Penn, Wesleyan, Trinity, Nebraska, and Kansas had men's varsity teams. And because basketball was a sport in which a woman could perform well and still retain her dignity as a lady, such fine women's institutions as Smith, Vassar, Wellesley, Newcomb, and Bryn Mawr also adopted it.

By 1899 there was an intercollegiate league, and an

Eastern team, Yale, had gone by train to Chicago to meet several Midwestern teams. Still, basketball would remain something of a church-oriented sport until the mid-1900s, when the United States Navy, having limited space for athletic activities on board ship, made it all but mandatory for sailors. Thanks to the navy, basketball became more than just recreation. When early college coaches discovered that the navy had outrecruited them on the high school level, they quite often sat outside naval bases waiting for basketball-playing sailors to receive their discharges.

In 1906 the game got a boost when the wooden baskets were replaced by either metal or rope nets set ten feet off the ground on standards with wooden backboards. But serious problems remained. Spectators were a problem because they were wont to use their hands, their umbrellas, and even baseball bats to interfere with the play. So for years, many games were played inside net cages to prevent the spectators from interfering. After the cages were abandoned, basketball players continued to be called "cagers" and generations of fans never really knew why.

"The many benefits of the game soon became apparent," wrote Naismith. "It demanded and fostered alert minds and supple bodies. Decisions had to be made quickly. Play had to be neat and nimble. It never grew boring as situations changed all the time and players had to perfect tricks of sudden stopping, feint-passing, and side stepping. Furthermore, those anxious to find in sport not only a pastime or a means of character-building, but also health-giving exercise were gratified. The fact that the ball was almost always in the air necessitated frequent stretching and jumping on the part of the players. This was most beneficial for the growing adult."

True, the game was far from well defined yet, but the problems and constant changing of rules never bothered Naismith. He did not pretend that he had given the world a finished sport, only the basis for one.

11 Great Black Hopes

"Wheel about, turn about,
Do just so.
And every time I wheel about,
I jump Jim Crow."

—Thomas D. Rice, the first white performer
to wear blackface makeup in a minstrel
show (circa 1829)

For dreary decades after their legal emancipation from slavery, black athletes plodded along in near-obscurity, mere oddities in white America's sporting life. In football and baseball, the two popular new sports of the post-Civil War era, a few sons of well-to-do black families in the North managed to play for college varsities. But these boys came from a rare and privileged class of blacks. Other black players were reduced to entertaining a white clientele that paid to watch them clown around. Nearly all the best summer resorts had teams of such performers, composed of busboys, gardeners, and waiters from the hotel staff.

"They are comical cusses with a natural sense of mimicry," wrote Rawlin Pierce, a correspondent for *Munsey's Magazine*, after he watched the Cuban Giants of the Argyle Hotel in Babylon, Long Island, perform against another black team in 1882. "They are managed by a darkie, Frank Thompson, and they give a fine performance, worth the price of admission. They do not take the game of baseball as seriously as white folks do, but they are very innovative and they amuse."

The Cuban Giants of the Argyle Hotel rolled their eyeballs, showed their teeth, and strutted shamelessly. Except for the fact that they were earning money to forget their pride and dignity, they were the reincarnation of the plantation slaves who had gathered on front lawns of estates in the antebellum South to entertain the white folks sipping bourbon on the veranda. "We hated some

In the late 1800s, Isaac Murphy, a black who rode to victory in three Kentucky Derbys, was the most famous jockey in the nation. A wealthy man, he is pictured here on a cigarette card popular in that day.

of the shameful things that circumstances forced us to do," wrote George (Chippie) Johnson, first baseman for the Columbia Giants at the turn of the century. "But there was no real choice. To survive, we often gave the white public exactly what they wanted. We also played some damn good baseball."

Only one black athlete of the late nineteenth century was accepted, indeed honored, by white America. He was Isaac Murphy, the greatest jockey of the day, according to no less an authority than Snapper Garrison, a great white jockey, who was also adored. "He's the great one," an uncharacteristically self-effacing Garrison said. "I've got to admit it. Nobody can argue about his ability. He does things I try to copy." The two jockeys competed against each other on June 25, 1890, at Sheepshead Bay, and Murphy, riding a horse named Salvator, beat Garrison, astride Tenny. A champagne company used a color lithograph of the finish in its advertisements and circulated them all over the nation.

Isaac Murphy rode three winners in the Kentucky Derby, a racing event that was rapidly becoming the biggest in America. His record stood for forty years, until 1930, before Earl Sande tied it, and for sixty years before Eddie Arcaro beat it. In 1884, Murphy won on Buchanan, a horse trained by a black, William Bird. Oddly, Murphy had to be coerced to accept the mount. He had ridden Buchanan at Nashville three weeks earlier and the horse had bolted over the rail. On the day of the Derby Murphy refused to get in the saddle. The owners, James Cottrell and Arvin Guest, flattered him, then cajoled him, and finally, threatened to suspend him. Muttering and complaining, Murphy hoisted himself aboard and went on to victory.

Murphy became rich enough to buy horses of his own, many of which he rode himself. He died wealthy and content in the winter of 1896 at his home in Lexington, Kentucky. Later that year another black jockey, William L. Simms, became the first American to win a race in England. He came home a hero. The last black jockey to

win the Kentucky Derby was Jim Winkfield on Alan-a-Dale in 1902.

As quickly as black jockeys rose in fame, they departed. By the 1920s it was rare to see a black face in the jockeys' quarters. "They came and they dominated," said Winkfield in 1923, while still active as a rider. "Then colored kids just stopped thinking about horses. That's all there was to it."

Moses Fleetwood Walker was the first black to play major league baseball. His brother, Welday Wilberforce Walker, was the second. They were both catchers for Toledo when the team was a member of the American Association. When Jackie Robinson's splendid features were cast in bronze and the bust was fastened to the wall at the Baseball Hall of Fame in Cooperstown, New York, it was necessary to note that "Robinson was the first *modern* black to play in the major leagues [emphasis added]." The Walker brothers had preceded him by decades. In 1884, Fleet Walker played forty-two games and batted .263. Welday Walker got into five games as a reserve outfielder (his older brother kept him from catching) and hit .222. There were approximately twenty black men earning a living in professional baseball at the time, the Walkers in the major leagues and the rest in the minors.

After winning thirty-five games for the Newark club, George Stovey, a black pitcher, was purchased by the New York Giants. Then Adrian C. (Cap) Anson of the Chicago National League team reared his unusually prejudiced head. No one has ever explained why Anson disliked blacks so much. He was born in an all-white town in Iowa, but to the knowledge of his closest friends, he had never been injured or offended by a black. Anson's influence on the sport in the 1880s was enormous. When Stovey's contract was purchased, Anson's screaming and shouting could be heard, said one newsman, from Chicago to New York. The league surrendered to his demands and Stovey was barred.

When the Chicago team came to play Toledo, it was

Anson who doomed Fleet Walker and his brother. He refused to take the field until they were banished. The Walker boys did not play that day, and in a week they were gone from baseball entirely.

There was less prejudice against other non-whites in baseball. Indians played frequently, starting with Louis Sockalexis, a Penobscot from Maine. A handsome and dashing player who was highly popular with the fans, Sockalexis was, one legend has it, the reason why the Cleveland team was nicknamed the Indians. He hit .338 in 1897, but he drank a lot and did not last, hitting poorly his second season and drifting out of the game.

Henry Kauhane Oana, allegedly descended from the Polynesian kings of Hawaii, pitched for Detroit a few years before Robinson broke the color barrier for blacks. A couple of Orientals and numerous Cubans with light skin were hired by big league teams. It was not an exclusion of non-whites that baseball clung to so fiercely; it was simply a hatred of blacks.

Banned from the whites' teams, blacks formed their own league. The Cuban Giants became so famous that nearly every black club borrowed their nickname—the Mohawk Giants, the Page Fence Giants, the Baltimore Elite Giants, the Lincoln Giants, the Brooklyn Royal Giants, the Leland Giants, the Original Argyle Cuban Giants, and others. Some of the black ball players were paid well; most were not.

Only a few people, black or white, protested against the segregation of the races in baseball. "The rule that prohibits colored men from competing in so honorable a pastime as baseball is a disgrace to the present age and casts derision on the law of the land which clearly states all men are created equal," wrote Welday Walker in a letter to the governor of Ohio, protesting his ban by the American Association.

Walter Johnson, the gentle, white Idahoan who disproved in advance the theory that nice guys finish last (he won four hundred and sixteen games in the majors), told reporters that he had faced some black pitchers bet-

ter than he, James (Red Ant) Wickware of the Mohawk Giants, for instance. Johnson also ranked himself below Cyclone Joe Williams, a huge right-hander from Texas with a smooth overhand delivery and excellent control.

"If his hair wasn't curly and his skin too bronze," said Walter Johnson, "this fellow Williams would be the very best there is. He was everlastingly breaking off a curve around a batter's knees. He works deliberately and never gets himself excited. It is a shame that these fine fellows and excellent athletes do not get a chance to show their wares in the same competition as the rest of us."

Nobody paid much attention. White writers referred, in print, to the "coon" and "nigger" leagues. Most of the black players accepted their roles as entertainers rather than athletes, and thus several generations of brilliant ball players were lost.

It made no difference to baseball that other sports had not only survived but prospered from some token integration. Fritz Pollard, Inky Williams, Paul Robeson, and Ned Gourdin were allowed to play college football with whites. Harry Wills, Sam Langford, and the incredible Jack Johnson promoted great, albeit largely racist, interest in boxing. But baseball would not relax its unwritten rule against blacks.

At the outbreak of the Civil War, there had been about a quarter of a million free blacks in the South. It is likely that Jack Johnson's father, a janitor and part-time evangelist in Galveston, Texas, was one of them. He was also one of few blacks who could claim pure African ancestry and a clear tracing of his genealogy. His ancestors were Coromantees, from the area of Africa slave traders called the Gold Coast.

Perhaps it was because he knew just who he was and from where his people came that Jack Johnson insisted on his full rights as a human being when most blacks thought it best to be discreetly submissive. His self-assertiveness was even more remarkable for the fact that it became only more flamboyant after he triumphed.

Jack Johnson, who became world heavy-weight champion in 1908, represented a different type of sports figure. A large, virtually unbeatable fighter, he mocked opponents in the ring and outraged the nation out of it. James J. Jeffries, an ex-champion, was called the "Great White Hope" before his unsuccessful attempt to end Johnson's reign in 1910.

He never seemed even tempted to try to moderate it to preserve his success. On the contrary, he was thoroughly audacious, a black man who believed that having reached the top of the world, he could get away with whatever a white man could.

As the first black to hold the heavyweight title, Johnson touched off a shock wave of hysteria that produced the incredible description "the Great White Hope" for any white boxer, no matter how obviously unprepared, who planned to challenge him and, by winning, restore white supremacy to boxing. Johnson was portrayed as a fiend from hell, a dark shadow blotting out American culture, at the very least a dissolute lush. (Billy Sunday proclaimed that liquor had made Johnson's brain "a mud puddle.") From the fervor of the campaign against him it was hard to deny that many people believed it. The hatred would intensify until it destroyed not only the boxer but the man. The only thing it helped create was a legend—of the most famous black of his era.

When Jim Jeffries retired, it was obvious that Johnson was the best heavyweight in the world. A dazzling physical specimen and an extremely powerful boxer who would have been a match for John L. Sullivan in his prime, Johnson was a shining black star on a faded backdrop of second-rate white fighters.

He won the title in 1908 when he went to Sydney, Australia, and defeated a Canadian, Noah Brusso, a champion of sorts who fought under the Irish-sounding name of Tommy Burns.

When the new champion returned home, the crusade of racial hatred against him was already beginning. It gained momentum when Johnson battered two great white heroes. The first was middleweight Stanley Ketchel, whom he faced in 1909. It was a bout between a good big man and a good little man, with the predictable result. After Ketchel landed a right that dropped Johnson to the canvas, the champ arose and hit Ketchel so hard that the challenger's upper teeth went through his lower lip. Ketchel was out for an hour.

Johnson's second highly unpopular conquest was of the amiable, deeply beloved Jeffries, who had been forced out of retirement by public pressure to beat the black man. This fight, one of Tex Rickard's promotions, took place in Reno, Nevada, on July 4, 1910. It was said that Jeffries was sure to win because he had a mission to win, but such fanciful racist propaganda belied the facts. At thirty-five the former champ had been out of boxing for more than six years and he was out of practice. The champion leisurely chopped away at big Jeff and put him away in the fifteenth round.

The search for a Great White Hope was now a national obsession. In 1911, the National Sporting Club advertised "A Great White Hope Tournament, the first of its kind," to be held in New York. "This event will be closely scouted by New York fight managers," the ad promised.

Meanwhile, Johnson flaunted his success, just as if he were a white champion. He opened a saloon in Chicago. He made no secret of his tastes; he liked white women and rather than just sleeping with them, he married them. If he had been covert about the marriages, he might have survived, but Jack Johnson was almost exhibitionistic. He was continually denounced from church pulpits, by black as well as white ministers.

White women proved to be the weapon with which the establishment could destroy him. After his white second wife committed suicide, Johnson was charged with transporting Lucille Cameron, also white, across a state line for immoral purposes. He was arrested, but before the trial, Lucille disqualified herself as a witness by marrying Johnson. So the champion was convicted on lesser charges, to which he pleaded innocent. He jumped bail and managed to elude the authorities, because Rube Foster, the black man who could have been a successful baseball manager but for his race, hid Johnson among Foster's Imperial New York Black Giants. The champion carried the bats and balls to the train station. He would remain an exile until 1920, going to Montreal and then to Europe. In the meantime, he took a fourth white wife.

119

"I didn't court white women because I thought I was too good for the others, like they said. It was just that they always treated me better," he told author John Lardner. "I never had a colored girl that didn't two-time me."

On a blazing afternoon in Havana, Cuba, in 1915, Johnson finally lost his crown, falling before the gargantuan but less than dextrous Jess Willard. The question has always remained: Did Johnson throw the fight? In later years he insisted he had and said so in one of his autobiographies. An emissary from the United States government allegedly visited Johnson in London and told him that his losing the title was part of the government's conditions for dropping charges against him.

"In order to return home and ultimately resume my activities among those who meant most to me, I was willing to make any sacrifice," Johnson wrote. "This desire to wipe out prejudices against me and to still criticism of my conduct included my willingness to permit Willard to acquire the championship and my consent to go to prison for a much reduced term."

As part of the deal Johnson was to receive thirty to thirty-five thousand dollars, to be delivered to his wife at ringside, and also the foreign rights to a film to be made about him.

There were thirty thousand people at Havana's Oriental Race Track on that sweltering day when Johnson climbed into the ring to fight Willard in a bout scheduled for forty-five rounds. No important blows were struck by either man through the first twenty-five rounds. At the start of the twenty-sixth, Johnson had to be called out of his corner by the referee. Willard landed at least three punches and the champion rolled over on his back. A photograph of the event shows Johnson, a dark and sweaty mass, lying down, one knee flexed, his right arm shielding his eyes. Perhaps he was stunned or exhausted. Whatever the case, he sat there an hour while they stacked the money for his payoff.

Johnson left Cuba for England, where he eagerly awaited the call to return home. It never came; neither did the film

rights. He wandered all over Europe, finally going to Spain when World War One broke out. When it was over, he sailed for Mexico. Johnson surrendered to federal authorities in July, 1920, and served a year in prison. He ended his career as an exhibit in Hubert's Celebrated Museum and Flea Circus, amusing the tourists who wandered through New York's Times Square.

12 Spreading the Sports Word

When he arrived in New York City in 1895, fully prepared to do for the morning *New York Journal* what he had done for the *San Francisco Examiner*, William Randolph Hearst was convinced that all sporting material should be gathered into one compact section of a newspaper and not scattered throughout, as was customary. Young Hearst was a confirmed baseball fanatic (one of the lesser known facts about his overpublicized life), and it vexed him to have to turn page after page looking for all the sports results. "It should be that the sports news can be found in one orderly grouping," he wrote in an early memo to *Journal* editors.

He recruited a staff of experts: Charles Dryden for baseball, Ralph Paine for rowing, Paul Armstrong for boxing, and Robert H. Davis, who was the first writer to ghost write for prominent athletes. With typical aggressiveness, Hearst acquired the exclusive rights to the opinions of both contestants in the James J. Corbett-Bob Fitzsimmons heavyweight championship match. With sports coverage, as with so many other items in his newspapers, Hearst was the master packager.

Charles Dana of the *New York Sun* boasted that sports reporting was one of his paper's "strongholds," noting that the *Sun* had once devoted more than an entire page to the opening of a race meeting at Saratoga. Yet neither the *Sun* nor Joseph Pulitzer's *World* thought to put all the sports news together until Hearst's *Journal* led the way.

The first track built especially for car racing was hurried to completion in Indianapolis for a three-day Inaugural Meet on August 19-21, 1909. The *Remy Grand Brassard* was held on the final day. Barney Oldfield, driving his 120-Benz, won the event on a beat-up track that would destroy both cars and men. In Peter Helck's painting, Oldfield is shown defeating Len Zengle's Chadwick and Ralph DePalma's Fiat.

Soon afterward, both the *Sun* and the *World* had sports editors and sports sections. By the late 1890s all the great metropolitan papers had "sporting editors" and trained staffs. They specialized in "sporting extras," which helped to promote boxing and baseball. By 1910, nearly every journal in the nation had a sports section. When the conservative *New York Times* finally accepted the style in 1920, the trend was complete.

The first publisher to recognize the value of sports coverage was Richard Kyle Fox, who had arrived in America from Belfast with five dollars in his pocket in 1875. He earned enough to purchase the *Police Gazette,* subtitled it *The Leading Illustrated Sporting Journal in America,* and increased its circulation to four hundred thousand. True, Fox packed his magazine with "buxom showgirls, scandals, hangings, [and] red-tinted paper" in addition to "a steady stream of sensationalized sporting events." But according to Edward Van Every, "The risqué ladies and scandal were only window dressing. It was as an arbiter of sports news that the *Gazette* came into worldwide prominence. And it was Fox's success that eventually made the heads of even the most conservative of daily papers appreciate the circulation worth . . . in giving increased prominence . . . the world of sports."

As for the scandal and violence in the *Gazette,* some newsstands refused to sell the tabloid, charging that it offended the public morals, but Fox solved his distribution problem by giving bartenders and barbers a special price for selling the *Gazette* at their establishments.

Some newspapers were slow to follow Fox's lead, but after Hearst's innovations, papers began to brag about their coverage of great events. "In all departments of sport, the *World* has taken the lead," said an 1897 promotion ad. "The *World* has continued to be the leading authority on racing, baseball, and boxing, all of which were covered by special and expert correspondents. The great public discussion opened by the *World* as to the propriety of women riding bicycles was one of the features of the summer."

So brilliantly did the daily take over the coverage of sports that the *New York Clipper,* one of the great sporting weeklies of the early years, abandoned the subject entirely, turned to entertainment, and eventually changed its name to *Variety.*

The rise of sporting journalism was directly tied to the development of a national telegraphic network, augmented by the telephone and the wireless. When Sullivan fought Kilrain, in 1889, reporters representing almost all the great journals in the nation showed up in New Orleans for the fight. Some fifty operators stood by to transmit more than a million words of copy on the match. When Sullivan was defeated by Corbett three years later, the number of words trebled. Not only newsrooms but often poolrooms and saloons were equipped with receiving devices. People stood outside such establishments to watch the results being chalked on massive blackboards. In 1922, the World Series was reported on a single circuit that covered twenty-six thousand miles. "Uncle Sam now has an arterial system that is never going to harden," said Thomas Edison.

Thanks to the Atlantic Cable, news could be sent across the ocean to or from England, though hardly in a flash. When the Harvard crew defeated Oxford on the Thames in 1869, the news left London in the late afternoon and arrived in New York at a quarter after one in the morning.

The popularity of sports and the success of sports reporting spilled over into books, plays, songs, and as early as 1894 even movies, all devoted to the nation's great passion. (It was in 1894 that William K. Dickson produced a film entitled "Corbett and Courtney before the Kinetograph.") In the outpouring of sportswriting, a quaint American sporting slang emerged. A baseball, for example, was never called a ball but a "sphere," "pellet," "horsehide," "seed," or "pea." One journal, published in 1901, deplored the fact that baseball writers were mired in what it considered a sea of absurdity and atrocious taste. But at least one foreign observer, an

In the 1880s, two English games were imported to the United States. Tennis and golf were elitist sports as shown in this pen and ink drawing of a rather theatrical Gibson girl and a lithograph showing the first national lawn tennis tournament at New Brighton, Staten Island, September 18, 1880.

FORE!
THE AMERICAN GIRL TO ALL THE WORLD.

Englishman, found it charming. "Never before in the world's history has slang flourished as it has flourished in America," he wrote. "Americans have a natural love of metaphor and imagery. Its pride delights in the mysteries of a technical vocabulary. America has not lost touch with her beginnings. The spirit of adventure is still strong with her. And nowhere is this spirit of adventure stronger than in the sport she indulges herself in. Baseball, poker, and the racecourse, each with its own metaphor, swells the hoard. No baseball player scores a run but what he does not 'dent the platter.' That is typical and so delightful."

Business began to discover the importance of linking itself to sport. The Metropolitan Street Car Company of Atlanta provided a playing ground for members of the Southern League club in 1889. In return, the baseball lads acted as spokesmen for the streetcar line, testifying to its cleanliness, cheapness, and efficiency.

Cigarette and pipe tobacco brands such as Peerless, the Plug Chewing, Croquet, Iroquois, and Our Club Rooms appealed to the sporting trade by picturing boxers, baseball players, and racehorses on cards that were slipped into the tobacco packs. An eager public collected the cards, though before a collector could complete one set another was already on the market.

The Lipton Tea Company ran an endless series of posters entitled "Champion Pugilists of the World." Lipton also solicited the help of John L. Sullivan to promote its product, and the Great John L. obliged. "After a fair test of your product," he said, "both as a muscle and health-building food, I am well convinced it is the best thing of its kind in the market."

Dr. Greene's Nerve Tonic claimed to have cured Harry Brooks, the nation's greatest heel and toe walker, of nervous prostration and exhaustion. Famous hotels and resorts offered purses to the great horseraces. Railroads paid prizefighters, baseball players, cycling stars, and football players to appear in their advertisements. In 1901, the Santa Fe line made a pitch for leisure-class customers by contending that golf was at its best when played "under summer skies in midwinter."

In following years baseball's Ty Cobb endorsed a bewildering number of prep schools. No one ever mentioned that Cobb's higher education lasted only a year.

Among its many contributions to American business, sport can count one of advertising's most enduring slogans. It began when Nabisco's Shredded Wheat advertised itself as "The Breakfast of Champions." The slogan died out, but it was revived by Wheaties and by the turn of the century had become the household phrase it remains today.

13 Something for Everyone

The Scottish game of golf, originated by shepherds, crossed the Atlantic in the early 1880s. It was first demonstrated at the Yonkers-on-Hudson club by John Reid. It seemed a great waste of time to many. "This is a distasteful pastime, strictly for idlers, and no God-fearing citizen will be caught indulging himself in it," said the Rev. R. Lindley McNaughton, rector of St. Swithin's Episcopal Church in Brooklyn.

There were more practical objections too. It took a great deal of expensive property before one could build a golf course, and an extraordinary amount of care to maintain it. Obviously, this was a sport only for the rich, and its exclusivity made it that much more attractive to the few who could afford it. In 1884, the sugar baron Theodore Havemeyer was in the process of capitalizing the Newport Country Club at a staggering cost of one hundred and fifty thousand dollars. His fellow investors included Cornelius C. Vanderbilt, Perry Belmont, and John Jacob Astor. The club's course was completed by 1890, and in 1895 the country's first women's championship was held there. By the turn of the century, membership in the United States Golf Association had soared to 103 clubs.

Harry Vardon of England helped to popularize the

sport in America when he came here for a tour in 1900. Vardon was a popular figure but something less than an egalitarian. "Although none of the American courses could be compared to the classic course of Great Britain, I was not all that disappointed," he said. "The game is in the hand of responsible socialites and they will not let it perish in the New World."

Already golf had become part of the mystique of wealth. Though excluded from the great rolling meadows and the estates of the rich, the public well knew that John D. Rockefeller, Andrew Carnegie, and William Howard Taft played the game with great vigor and enthusiasm. Taft was almost insatiable when it came to golf, far more enthusiastic over it than Dwight D. Eisenhower would ever be.

The first commoner to succeed at the sport was Francis Ouimet, who had dropped out of high school to caddy at the country club across the street from his home in Brookline, Massachusetts. Ouimet defeated Edward (Ted) Ray and Harry Vardon in the U. S. Open in 1913. A heavy mist drifted across Ouimet's home course and later it rained, but eight thousand rubber-coated spectators, an enormous gallery for the day, followed him to victory. In what Harry Cross of the *New York Times* called an "almost mechanical round," he shot a 72, five strokes better than Vardon and six better than Ray.

"The pride in the young American's victory was all the more justified because of the fact that he had won without fluke or flaw in his play," wrote Cross, one of the most literate sportswriters of his day. "Francis Ouimet responded in perfect form to a test of nerve, stamina, and knowledge of golf. All through the crucial journey around the eighteen-hole course, Ouimet never faltered. He appeared absolutely without nerve in playing from tee to fairway, from fairway to green and finishing every hole with a splendid exhibition of putting."

A British critic, Harry Leach, was terribly perturbed by the victory of the commoner. Indeed, he refused to admit it had happened. Leach wrote:

American golfers are telling me that Mr. Francis Ouimet has won the Open golf championship of the United States. This is nonsense. Such a thing was impossible under the circumstances. Consider the facts and you will understand how easy it is to be mistaken about this event. This was the big, wide-open championship of the *second* greatest golfing country on earth. Entered were Harry Vardon—five times open champion of Great Britain and the world, and once American champion, too—and the finest, most splendid player who has ever hit a ball since this marvelous game was mysteriously shaped from chaos. Edward Ray, open champion of Great Britain and of the world last year, who can drive a ball farther than any other man alive, was another of the competitors. How could *your* Francis Ouimet beat these men? It is not that he is an American. Great things in golf have come out of the United States and will come again. But this Ouimet is an amateur and it has become a settled principle at home that no amateur can beat the best of the professionals. Francis Ouimet was only twenty years of age on 8 May last—a youth, a boy. How, then, could Mr. Ouimet win? It is absurd.

Leach's snobbery left American golfers openly antagonistic to their British counterparts, and it was years before the ill feeling subsided. Perhaps America was sensitive to this sort of snub because Americans were themselves just as rigidly expressing their social status through sports. In addition to golf, the rich played at tennis, first introduced on the Staten Island Cricket and Baseball Grounds by Mary Outerbridge, who had picked up a net, racquets, and balls from regimental stores on the island of Bermuda. Not long afterward, Dr. James Dwight and Fred Sears played on a private court they laid out one summer at Nahant, Massachusetts, a resort area near Boston. By 1877, tennis was being played at all the best spas, and it remained the plaything of the very wealthy until the period before World War One.

James Gordon Bennett introduced America to polo. Almost immediately the game fell into the gilded hands of Harry Payne Whitney, who formed teams that won the International Cup three times. Sports reporters rarely covered Cup matches; that was left to society columnists.

America began to dominate yachting mostly because it had so much money to spend on massive ocean racing crafts. J. P. Morgan gave the classic description of the exclusivity of the sport when he pronounced, "If you have to ask how much a yacht costs, you can't afford one." The lower classes had to content themselves with baseball, boxing, and wrestling; the middle class with its love of college football.

While the wealthy frequented such bastions of privilege as the New York Athletic Club for recreation, the YMCA was a catch-all for the less affluent. Public parks began to open (first in Chicago, then in Brooklyn). If you could afford a green's fee, you could even play on a golf course you didn't own—the public links. Not only the rich were taking up sports.

Early in the twentieth century, industry began to promote athletics among its workers as a means of keeping them content. The Wanamaker Department Store in Philadelphia sponsored a track meet for its employees—a meet that eventually became one of the nation's great indoor events, the Millrose Games. The Goodyear Rubber Company of Akron, Ohio, sponsored teams in baseball, football, track, hockey, skating, basketball, volleyball, tennis, and even cricket.

But the ever-increasing popularity of spectator sports among the masses overshadowed all these modest advances in participation sport. In 1903, the future reigning monarch of American spectator sports events, the World Series, was born to instant popularity. The promoters sold 18,801 tickets to the first game, between the Pittsburgh Pirates and Boston Pilgrims in Boston, and thousands more spectators burst onto the playing field.

The Boston police herded back the fans by hosing them with water, but eventually the fringes of the outfield had to be roped off to accommodate the excess crowd. Stadiums that had always seemed adequate were suddenly far too small. When the Series moved to Pittsburgh, the Pirates' Exposition Park, which seated about eighty-five hundred spectators, was mobbed by more than twice that number. Then the Series returned to Boston for the final games, and the customers literally broke down the fences. Others bought their way in and flung ropes over the walls to haul people over at a ticket-scalper's rate of two dollars a head.

The chief producer of this smash hit was a perceptive little man named Barney Dreyfuss, the owner of the National League champion Pirates. In return for an agreement from the American League that it would never place a franchise in Pittsburgh, Dreyfuss offered to match his team against the champs of the rival new league, Henry J. Killilea's Pilgrims. The Pittsburgh players readily agreed to the postseason tournament because Dreyfuss agreed to pay them all the profits. Killilea was less generous to his players, but they agreed to play after he reduced his share of the take from one-half to one-quarter. Boston won the Series, but each Pilgrim received less than his National League counterpart ($1,182.17 to $1,316.25), the first and only time in the World Series that the winning players made less than the losers.

The age of the Great American Spectator had begun. Urbanization had produced a generation of workers seeking release. To accommodate them, construction companies were working overtime expanding old stadiums and building new ones. "America is reaching back for bigness to Greece and Rome," said a magazine writer. "So far we have not surpassed the ancients. But where Athens had one big stadium and Rome several, America is building them by the hundreds. Someday we will be known as the most insane country about sports the world has known. We will not stop until every small town has a stadium seating at least thirty thousand."

America's Jim Thorpe, a Sac and Fox Indian, won both the decathlon and pentathlon in the 1912 Olympics at Stockholm. Recognized by Walter Camp as an All-America football player for the Carlisle Indian School in 1911 and 1912, the powerful Thorpe later starred for the New York Giants' baseball team and became a major figure in the emergence of pro football. In a poll of sportswriters in 1950, Thorpe was overwhelmingly acclaimed the greatest football player of the half century.

Despite the growing commercialization of sports, it was also a time of utter, almost bewildering innocence. In certain quarters, there was much talk of "fair play," in sports. Defeat was said to be preferable to unfair victory. This sporting code was classically expressed by the verse of Grantland Rice:

"For when the One Great Scorer comes
To write against your name
He writes—not that you won or lost—
But how you played the game."

It was a noble sentiment but not a persuasive one. Almost everyone praised it but few honored it. For those who cherished the spiritual value of sport and for those who pretended they did, there was a rude shock in the offing.

14 The "Black Sox" Scandal

"Say it ain't so, Joe!"

—probably an apocryphal line, attributed by Ring Lardner to a Chicago newsboy watching Joe Jackson enter court to testify on his part in the alleged fixing of the 1919 World Series

It was the end of innocence. It was an act so atrocious that no one thought it possible. The war had ended and in the aftermath of the bloodshed America wanted only to be reassured. Instead, she was jolted. Eight of the American League champion Chicago White Sox—Joe Jackson, Buck Weaver, Oscar Felsch, Eddie Cicotte, Claud Williams, Swede Risberg, Fred McMullin, and Chick Gandil—conspired to throw the World Series in return for eighty thousand dollars from gamblers. The ball players never got all their money and they were never convicted of any crime, but their sin was real and in the eyes of the new baseball commissioner, Kenesaw Mountain Landis, unforgivable. He banished the "Black Sox" from baseball for life.

Arnold (Chick) Gandil had winged ears, firm lips, and narrow eyes. He smiled very little. "I have been described as one of the ringleaders of the terrible Black Sox scandal," he said. "There is no question about it, because I was."

He began his baseball career when he was seventeen, running away from his home in Minnesota to join a semi-pro league in Amarillo, Texas. "I was a wild, tough kid," he said. "I did some heavyweight fighting at a hundred fifty dollars a go. I worked in the mines and I was a boiler-maker. I didn't do anything easy. I came up to the Chicago White Sox and they sold me to Washington and Washington sold me to Cleveland and when the White Sox wanted me back, they paid the price."

Like the other players on the White Sox, Gandil despised the owner, Charles Comiskey. The ball players griped most strongly over their salaries, which they considered outrageously low and only one indication of the owner's disdain for them. Risberg said he had heard Comiskey calling the players "shoeshine boys."

"I'd like to blame the whole thing on Comiskey's cheapness, but I can't," Gandil told *Los Angeles Herald–Examiner* columnist Melvin Durslag many years later. "So help me, this man was tight. There were so many times when the best team in baseball played in filthy uniforms because he hated the idea of paying the cleaning bill. On the road we ate like cattle. The salaries were hateful. They made a man feel unwanted.

"I can recall only one real act of generosity on Comiskey's part. He sent around a case of champagne when we won the pennant in 1917. Some of us figured it was something the guys up in the press box couldn't use."

Cicotte won twenty-eight games in 1917, yet in 1919 he was making six thousand dollars, less than half as much as other stars of his caliber. Jackson, one of the finest hitters of the day, made only seven thousand two hundred. According to Gandil, it was all manager Kid Gleason could do to keep the players from revolting against Comiskey during the 1919 season. When the opportunity to rebel came after the regular season, some players seized it. "It was just a matter of trying to pick

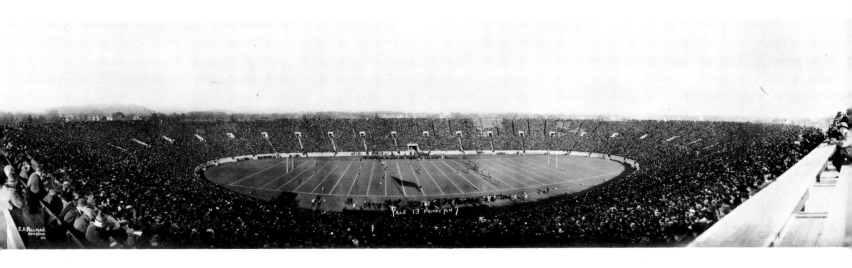

up some easy cash," said Gandil. "Players in my day bet freely. They would sit in lobbies of hotels with gamblers, gabbing away as if nobody would ever stop them. I was, however, surprised when 'Sport' Sullivan [a small-time gambler who represented a big-time gambler, Arnold Rothstein] suggested that we get together a syndicate of seven or eight guys to throw the Series to Cincinnati. I never figured him for a fixer."

Sullivan told Gandil he would give ten thousand dollars to each player Gandil could enlist in the scheme. Gandil knew exactly whom to contact. When he had gathered his conspirators, Gandil told Sullivan they wanted the money in advance. But Arnold Rothstein did not trust his new partners and offered only ten thousand in advance. "I convinced the gang to accept Sullivan and Rothstein's deal," said Gandil.

When Gandil unpacked his bags in Cincinnati before the first game and went out to mingle among the fans, he encountered a clerk who told him that the Series had been dealt away. "The gamblers have gotten to the Chicago players," said the clerk, clearly not knowing whom he was speaking to. Waitresses and bellhops were saying the same thing. So was Kid Gleason, who called his players aside and told them he knew what was going on. Meanwhile, the gamblers were blackmailing the players. "I kept getting all kinds of pressure from Rothstein and Sullivan. They told me that if we didn't go along with the deal . . . they would inform on us," said Gandil. "Oh, how I wanted to go to Kid Gleason and tell him the truth. I wanted to get out of this nightmare. But Sullivan told me it wouldn't be wise to double-cross Rothstein. I called a meeting of the eight players. We weighed the fact that the rumors were going around against the risk of what the gamblers might do."

The eight White Sox decided to take the field and go along with the scheme. Somebody in the stands yelled out, "Hey, Cicotte, there's a guy with a rifle looking for you." That was the highpoint of the conspiracy. By the middle of the Series, the players were quite sure they were not going to get the money they had been promised. The conspirators rebelled against the gamblers and played it straight the rest of the way. Jackson and Weaver batted .375 and .324 respectively, for the Series, and Cicotte won the next to last game, but the Reds took the Series, five games to three.

"I offer no defense for the thing we conspired to do," said Gandil. "It was inexcusable. Even though we decided to forget the gamblers and play the thing on the up and up, we were no different than they were."

For a while nothing extraordinary happened. Gandil left the team to play semipro ball in Bakersfield, California, but only because Comiskey wouldn't grant his request for a two thousand dollar raise. It was not until nearly a year after the Series, in September, that Cicotte confessed what had happened. Apparently, Williams, Jackson, and Felsch also admitted their parts in the plot. A grand jury began hearing the evidence on July 5, 1921, and deliberated fifteen days. It decided not to indict the ball players, who emerged from the court on the shoulders of some of the jurors, to the hearty cheers of the crowd. But the exhilaration was short-lived. Landis, in banning the players, overturned the court's decision.

"Insomuch as we were legally freed, I felt Landis's ruling was unjust," said Gandil. "But I never truthfully resented it because even though the Series wasn't thrown we were guilty of a serious offense.

"Aside from embarrassment and personal qualms, I have never suffered any hardship because of the Chicago Black Sox incident. The doors for jobs outside of baseball have never been closed to me. Our family has lived quietly and we have attended only a few baseball games. . . ."

Gandil outlived all but one of the Black Sox. He spent the last decades of his life working as a plumber in Calistoga, California. Apparently he gained some respectability, for when he died, his family asked that his death notice be omitted from the newspaper, afraid that readers might remember the mistake of his youth and tarnish the dignity of his later years.

THE GOLDEN AGE 1920-1945

"He was unique. There was nobody like him . . . there was never anybody close. He was a god."

—Joe Dugan on Babe Ruth

Red Grange, by Robert Riger, 1962.

Robert Riger

1 A Time for Heroes

It was an era for heroes more than events, and every sport had a Golden Hero; some sports had a dozen. They came forward in an endless procession: Babe Ruth, Bobby Jones, Knute Rockne, Red Grange, Gene Tunney, Johnny Weissmuller, Bill Tilden, Jesse Owens, Lou Gehrig, Bronko Nagurski, and even a horse, Man o' War. The media (it was no longer just the press) made towering giants of flawed human beings and celebrated these innocent deceptions until fact, which should have been easier than ever before to document, became only more artfully and persuasively distorted. In place of a true picture of the athletic giants was a tug of war between scandal and acclaim, the distortions of the former no more than a lightweight counterbalance to those of the latter. Gossips whispered that Babe Ruth was a man of immeasurable lusts, his drinking and womanizing as prodigious as his home runs. Rumors had it that Bill Tilden was a homosexual. There were some people who recalled that Jack Dempsey had been accused of being less than enthusiastic about serving in the armed forces during World War I. But these topics were not considered suitable for the sports page. Stories that revealed shortcomings would have disgusted readers because fans believed in Golden Heroes. The public saw in these athletes exactly what it wanted to see—and no more.

"There is a curious derivation of Gresham's Law that applies to American heroes," wrote Roger Kahn in 1959. "Just as good money drives out bad in economics, so heroic fancy drives out heroic fact and, in the case of heroes, we are often left standing in a forest of chopped-down cherry trees, wondering what our man was actually like. The greater the hero, the more prevalent the fiction. In the end, it seems that all that remains are movie companies, careless writers, and glib story tellers who have busied themselves with obfuscation of fact."

The Golden Age boomed when radio, that unimpeachable on-the-scenes reporter, was enlisted in the obfusca-tion of fact. Suddenly, a fan could be a witness to glory—close enough to the hero to appreciate his majesty but not yet so close as to scrutinize him. The theater of spectator sport, complete with athletic persona, was now playing to a mass audience.

On April 11, 1921, KDKA, the first permanent commercial station in America, aired a description of the Johnny Ray-Johnny Dundee boxing match in Pittsburgh's Motor Square Garden. Also in 1921 Radio Corporation of America, with General David Sarnoff at the controls, brought the Dempsey-Georges Carpentier fight from Jersey City to listeners on a closed circuit that included "halls, theaters, sporting clubs, Elks and Masonic and Knights of Columbus halls." In October, station WJZ in Newark broadcast bulletins of the World Series, Grantland Rice phoning in reports. The Davis Cup was broadcast and so was the University of Chicago-Princeton football game. "People simply have radio fever," wrote Andrew White, editor of *Wireless Age*. "Sport is helping it along."

In six years, major sporting events were broadcast everywhere and everyone was listening. Before the second Jack Dempsey-Gene Tunney fight, in 1927, a New York department store announced that in just two weeks it had sold $90,000 in radio equipment at $22 per unit. At the time $22 was a handsome weekly salary.

The spectating resources of the country were being marshalled in ever-increasing numbers, and the spectators were impressed. For one thing, the bigger the crowd, the larger the prize and the greater the glory to the winner. Purses doubled in the nation's leading horse races in the twenties. When the second Madison Square Garden was constructed, public interest in boxing soared. The celebrated phrase "the Million Dollar Gate" stunned the public only long enough to be replaced by "the Two Million Dollar Gate," which left it breathless. When Tunney and Dempsey first fought, in 1926, Philadelphia merchants and hotel keepers estimated that people attending the match spent over $5,000,000. Motor sports raced

Two important sports stadiums were constructed in 1923, one on each side of the continent. In New York, construction on Yankee Stadium was completed in time for opening day of the baseball season. Appropriately, Babe Ruth hit a home run. In Los Angeles, the 75,000-seat capacity Memorial Coliseum was also completed. In the years to follow, each stadium would host some of America's—and the world's—most important sports events.

forward in 1929 when Ray Keech won the Indianapolis 500 before 160,000 spectators. Gar Wood, another Golden Hero, was getting rich racing his *Miss America* speedboats across the rivers and lakes of the world.

In 1923, the New York American League baseball club opened the most elegant stadium ever built in the United States. The total cost of Yankee Stadium was a staggering $2.5 million. Naturally, Babe Ruth christened the new park with a home run on opening day. He was the king of the Golden Heroes—in the money he made and spent, the feats he accomplished and flubbed, and in the devil-may-care life style he led. Ruth made $1,076,474 from baseball and about a million more from outside sources. One year, though he was making $70,000 and his income taxes were only $1,500, he had to borrow from a couple of teammates who made about $8,000 a year. Money always seemed to float around George Herman Ruth like golden leaves around the boughs of a massive tree in an autumn breeze.

On the day that Jumping Joe Dugan joined the New York Yankees he discovered that his locker was next to Ruth's. (Dugan and Ruth were to be locker-room neighbors for the next seven seasons.) Dugan was one of the finest third basemen in the American League, but to the Babe he was just another friendly member of the grand entourage. Walking into the clubhouse with a stack of mail juggling on both hands, Ruth didn't bother to welcome Dugan to the Yankees. "Here, kid," he said. "Sort through this stuff, will you? Put the letters from broads in one pile and the ones with checks in the other. Throw the other junk away, especially all that sappy stuff from fans."

Dugan handed half the pile to centerfielder Whitey Witt, and the two of them did secretarial work while Ruth, who, as usual was late for practice, dressed quickly. Witt was amazed to see a telegram from producer Flo Ziegfeld, offering Ruth $1,500 a week to be in a show that was to open a month after the baseball season ended.

"Throw it away," said Ruth. "I ain't no actor."

"Are you crazy?" asked Witt, who was making only $3,000 for the entire season. "Make money while you can. For that kind of dough you can learn how to act. That fifteen hundred a week could buy you a whole lot of acting lessons."

"Yeah, yeah, yeah," said Ruth. "And I still wouldn't be no actor. Throw the damn thing away. If I went into show business it would be just another round of booze and broads. I got that now."

Buttoning the top button of his tunic, he hiked off to the playing field to hit home runs, leaving the Great Ziegfeld's telegram crumpled on the locker room floor. During the Golden Age, the playing field was still the greatest stage.

2   The Ruth Is Mighty

"A man may be very imperfect and yet worth a great deal."

—Anthony Trollope

Whatever wrong Babe Ruth did could be excused. Not because he didn't mean it or didn't know better (though often he indeed didn't). Ingenuousness wears thin as an excuse after a while, even for a star ball player. No, there was more to his appeal than the child-hero. It was the man America worshiped—the man whose transgressions could not be segregated from his heroics. Babe Ruth did what he wanted to, and when that proved consistently more delightful than destructive, who could deny him a rampage or two? He was a smashing case for self-indulgence—a natural hero.

True, this most unrestrained of heroes in his youth coped less than happily with the constraints of age. And he died prematurely. The moral could be drawn that his excesses did catch up with him. The hero can be duly deflated, and he has been. Yet his legend persists and,

George Herman Ruth was the finest left-handed pitcher on the Boston Red Sox staff for four seasons but his prowess as a hitter was quickly becoming evident. In 1919 the Red Sox sold Ruth to the New York Yankees, where his skill as a slugger (overleaf) had a profound influence on the game of baseball.

with the recent revival of historical interest in the Babe, it grows. He is not to be dismissed as another dissolute, ill-fated celebrity. He was not only mighty, but courageous, not only ingenuous but good, not only entertaining but inspiring. The Babe deserved to be a hero.

Like all the godlike heroes, a furious gossip raged around him. Seeing his wide flat nose and baleful brows, the public whispered about his origins. Whenever he barnstormed through the South with the Yankees, he was swarmed by black fans who believed the legend that his mother had been black. The newspapers reported that he had been born illegitimately in a room over a saloon in Baltimore that his father owned. According to this version, his mother was either a saloon girl or a prostitute named Ruth whom his father had impregnated and taken pity on, and his father's surname was either Gerhardt or Earhardt.

The real story is that the Babe was the child of Kate Schamberger and George Herman Ruth, Sr., a working class couple who belonged to Baltimore's sizable German-American community. There is some evidence that Ruth's father owned a saloon, though it has been said he worked merely as a bartender. An old photograph shows him standing behind an oak bar in a waiter's uniform, looking exactly like his famous son, displaying the same wide nose and overhanging brow. He appears to have been a man of no greater intellectual calling than his son, and he probably expected no more from the boy than that he turn to an honest trade. The child was not to be cooperative. The younger Ruth was, by his own admission, a bad kid, constantly stealing and fighting. Once, when he had beaten up a newsboy and taken his money, Ruth was turned in by his father. In 1902, in part to keep young George from a worse fate, in part to relieve his rocky marriage of a growing burden, the senior Ruth took the boy to St. Mary's Industrial School, a Catholic-run institution. The Ruths felt no great loss when the doors closed behind their troubled and troublesome eight-year-old.

A biographer who went to look at St. Mary's years after

Ruth's death described it as a pile of bricks as solemn as a prison. Indeed the regimen inside was that of a reform school. Its primary purpose seemed to be simply to discipline the unruly inmates. The school subdued young George enough to teach him to read and write, and he was also schooled in tailoring and shirtmaking, trades that were open to immigrants and their children.

Whatever its accomplishments, the routine was a grim one and left a searing effect on Ruth. He would tell his friends at St. Mary's that his mother would take him home at Christmas. Some Christmases she came and some she did not, but in any case the boy remained at St. Mary's until he was a young man. Some years later, when Ruth was in the major leagues, a teammate, Joe Dugan, heard him whisper between sobs that he must have been an orphan or his parents would never have left him at St. Mary's.

The young Ruth found some succor under the supervision of Brother Matthias, an Irish immigrant who had become an Xaverian brother in America. Brother Matthias had schoolwide responsibility for discipline and physical activity, both areas of interest to Ruth, and he quickly won the boy's respect and affection. "Brother Matt was my father," the Babe told Dugan. "I never had no other."

Brother Matthias was not a baseball genius; you did not have to be a genius to recognize Ruth's talent. Clutching the bat handle down at the knob because that was the way Shoeless Joe Jackson held it, or so somebody told him, he belted the ball with a gusto exceeded only by its consistency. As one of the biggest boys on the team and indisputably the best athlete, he played catcher, despite the fact that he was left-handed and there were no catcher's mitts for lefties. He overcame that obstacle simply by wearing the mitt on his right hand or, sometimes, wearing it on his left and flinging it off when he had to throw to the bases. Before long he took up pitching and shone just as impressively at that position. He was, in short, the consummate baseball natural.

In 1913, Ruth attracted the attention of the Baltimore Orioles, a member of the International League. The next year he signed with the Orioles for $600 a year and a suit of clothes, the first he ever owned. Besides his native talent, Ruth's most fascinating characteristic at this point was his naiveté. Having been cloistered in St. Mary's for most of his life, he had next to no idea of the world outside it. When he made his first road trip with the Orioles, the team bought him his suitcase. He had little to put in it but he carried it proudly. And of course it was his wide-eyed innocence that earned him his famous nickname.

Ruth immediately established himself as a fine young pitcher. Because the Baltimore team had a working agreement with the Cincinnati club of the National League, whereby the Reds had the right to select any man from the Baltimore roster at no cost, it was assumed that Ruth would join the Reds for the end of the 1914 season. However, the Reds chose outfielder George Twombly (whose lifetime average over parts of five seasons would be .211), and Baltimore was able to peddle Ruth to the Boston Red Sox for a handsome profit.

The Red Sox were loaded with pitchers when the Babe arrived, so he did not make the starting rotation immediately. It was not until well into the 1915 season that he became a regular starter, and even after a sensational rookie season (18-8, 2.44 earned run average), he did not pitch in the World Series, in which the Red Sox trounced the Phillies in five games.

The next year he bloomed fully as a pitcher, winning twenty-three, losing only twelve, and leading the league with a 1.75 earned run average. In the Red Sox stretch drive to the pennant that year, Ruth beat the great Walter Johnson five straight times, including a thirteen-inning 1-0 shutout. And in the World Series against Brooklyn, he won the second game 2-1 in fourteen innings.

Even after he became baseball's most famous home run king, Babe Ruth wouldn't lose his prowess as a pitcher. In 1933, when he was nearing the end of his career as a competitive athlete, he would still pitch and win a game

for the New York Yankees. He finished his career as a pitcher with a winning percentage of .671 (94-46), one of the best among the pitchers enshrined in the Baseball Hall of Fame.

"He would have been the greatest left-handed pitcher of the generation," said Ty Cobb, one of the harsher critics of other baseball players, particularly those who competed with him. "I know I always had trouble hitting against him. In fact, he probably gave me more trouble than any other left-handed pitcher of the time."

By 1919, Babe was the finest left-handed pitcher on the Boston Red Sox, and perhaps in the game, yet baseball was beginning to overlook his pitching feats for his prowess at the plate. In 1918, the year he won two games in the World Series and set a record for the most score-less Series innings (twenty-nine), he tied Tilly Walker of Philadelphia for the major league lead in home runs with eleven. That was five short of the American League record, held by Socks Seybold of Philadelphia.

In 1918, Ruth played fifty-nine games in the outfield and thirteen at first base, and started only twenty as a pitcher, half of his total the previous year. In 1919, he started only seventeen games on the mound and played one hundred fifteen in the field. The 60-foot 6-inch corridor from the pitching mound to the plate was tilting toward the latter, about to deliver the force that would topple the strategies of the past like so many duckpins. The Babe came rolling down off the mound to take up the cudgel at the plate and beat the game forward from a grim, tight struggle to an extravaganza of long bashes and high scores.

The assault began in 1919. By Labor Day, the Babe had twenty-three homers, having long since eclipsed Seybold's mark, and was now on the brink of tying Gavvy Cravath's major league home run record of twenty-four, set in 1915. The Red Sox were home for a holiday doubleheader, and Fenway Park was jammed for the occasion with a crowd of celebrants. Vendors sold color portraits of Ruth outside the gate and fans yelled his name before they even reached their seats or the game began. Author Robert Smith, who attended the game with his brother, described the scene:

> Babe pitched and won the first game. During the course of it, while the crowd set up a noise that sounded like the Armistice celebration, he drove a ball into his favorite target, the teeming right-field bleachers, where my brother and I were clutching two bags of peanuts. The ball, before our bulging eyes, struck the seats below us with a whack loud enough, we thought, to carry even above the yells of the fans. The ball bounced high, back over the front wall of the bleachers and into the scrambling crowd on the grass.

An umpire, whose view of the play from first base seemed less than impeccable to Smith, ruled that the ball had not reached the stands but only the overflow of fans who had been clustered in front of them. Thus, Ruth was permitted only a triple, according to the ground rules agreed upon before the game. The customers around the umpire complained bitterly. They signed a petition and gave it to the National Guardsmen, who presented it to the umpire. Foolishly, the beleaguered umpire turned his head toward the bleachers in a hostile gesture. The fans in the bleachers responded by throwing beer bottles, raw fruit, and scraps of paper onto the field. But of course the ruling stood, and Ruth was temporarily thwarted in his home run chase.

In the second game of the Labor Day doubleheader, Ruth moved to leftfield, a perilous position at Fenway Park in those days because of a steep embankment called "Duffy's Cliff" in honor of Duffy Lewis, the player who could negotiate it flawlessly. Still more used to the hill in the infield, Ruth fielded awkwardly on the treacherous terrain, but without incident. In time he would become one of the better outfielders of his day.

At bat the Babe finally produced the record-tying blow, a soaring drive toward the rightfield bleachers. He finished the year with twenty-nine homers, and the baseball world wondered whether the next year he could pass the imposing barrier of thirty. Clearly, there were not yet many who realized just what this young slugger could do.

One who probably did but preferred not to think about it was a theater producer in great need of ready cash—Harry Frazee, who happened to own the Boston Red Sox. He went to Colonel Jake Ruppert, co-owner of the New York Yankees, to ask for a loan of $500,000. "I'm sorry," said Ruppert, realizing only too well that Frazee's interests and investments in the theater were far more dear to him than those in sports. "I can't let you have that kind of money without something in return. Would you be willing to sell me the contract of George Ruth from your Boston baseball team? I'd pay a hundred twenty-five thousand dollars for him and accept a mortgage on the park there for the rest [$375,000]. Done?"

Frazee had already sold a number of his ball players to Ruppert, though none quite of Ruth's caliber. Now he completed "the Rape of the Red Sox," as it came to be called in Boston. And so it was that the dominant city in baseball for the next decades was not Boston but New York, and "the House that Ruth Built," which by all rights should have risen just off Kenmore Square in Boston, became Yankee Stadium in the Bronx.

"If Frazee had had any sense at all, the Red Sox would have won all those pennants," groused Dugan, a fellow exile from Frazee's Boston. "But he was interested only in money. He thought there would be an endless supply of fine players he could peddle. Why, half of those great Yankee clubs were comprised of men he decided to get rid of. The power passed to New York strictly because of a fluke."

In the first step of a meteoric rise that would drive his salary to a peak of $80,000 while the next best paid Yankee was making less than a quarter as much, the Yankees doubled Ruth's salary to $20,000 in 1920. Ruth responded by very nearly doubling his home run production, from twenty-nine to fifty-four. The next best slugger that year (St. Louis's George Sisler) had nineteen.

The nation salivated for news of these Ruthian wonders. The Black Sox scandal festered, but Ruth robbed the headlines with his hitting. Attendance at league matches, which between 1909 and 1918 had not kept pace with the population increase, rose dramatically in the next decade, due in no small part to the Ruthian explosion.

It was not just the style of the game but its personality that changed. Not only had the almighty home run reduced the one-base-at-a-time tactics of bunting, stealing, and short-hitting to near insignificance, but Ruth's happy gusto had overwhelmed the premier player before him, Ty Cobb. Before long baseball was sprouting with happy-go-lucky sluggers like Ruth, dedicated to the long ball even to the point of suffering the heretofore insufferable ignominy of striking out regularly. In another time, when Cobb was the ideal, Hack Wilson, a roly-poly muscle-man, might never have had an opportunity to reach the major leagues. But the Chicago Cubs took a chance on him and he hit fifty-six home runs, the record for the National League.

Baseball officials insisted that their game had not changed but it obviously had, and moreover they seemed to have had a hand in it. Perhaps the cover of the ball was thinner, or a lighter yarn was being used. Maybe the yarn was wound tighter, or the rubber core was enlivened. The difference in the ball was hard to isolate, but it could not be missed. The ball did jump off the bat faster and fly farther. The American League batting average, .248 in 1916, rose to .292 by 1925. Home run production more than tripled in those years, from 142 to 533, and the composite earned run average of pitchers soared from 2.82 to 4.39. Ruth had fomented nothing less than a baseball revolution.

Heywood Broun wrote of the compelling popularity of the new baseball style and its chief exponents:

> The joy of watching Ruth lies in the fact that he
> is so palpably intent upon victory. There is never
> a moment when he is not trying. One feels that

In 1925, two of baseball's most famous players stood together for a portrait. Walter Johnson, the legendary "Big Train" of the Washington Senators, and fiery Ty Cobb of the Detroit Tigers, each approaching middle age, stood confidently and quietly for the photographer, their fires tempered, their fame secure.

no crusader has ever been more firmly convinced of the righteousness of his cause. Babe Ruth has been a considerable factor in breaking down party lines. Even in hostile towns the rooters liked to see Ruth make home runs.

Of course the animal magnetism of the Babe had long since surged beyond the confines of the playing field. Stories proliferated of his prodigious but cheerfully unassuming appetites for food, drink, and women, his generosity, and his amazing stamina. "You've never seen a man eat the way he did," said pitcher and teammate Waite Hoyt. "If you cut that big slob in half most of the concessions at Yankee Stadium would come pouring out. His idea of breakfast was a porterhouse steak, six fried eggs, and fried potatoes washed down by a pot of coffee. Then he'd take a pint of bourbon and mix it with ginger ale and drink it in one gulp. Lou Gehrig's mother used to bring him all kinds of German delicacies. The Babe was nothing but a great big Kraut at heart. His favorite was German pickled eels. He'd eat them with chocolate ice cream between games of a doubleheader. Can you imagine that?"

On one occasion he tottered off the eighteenth green at the Bayside Golf Club in New York, his shirt stuck close to his skin from the humidity. He demanded that the bartender make a "Babe Ruth Special" for him—a Tom Collins made of two-thirds gin, and the rest ice, orange slices, and mixer. Ruth tilted back his head and the drink disappeared, ice and all, in one fantastic slide down his throat. The patrons gasped in amazement. "Make me another," said Ruth.

At one society dinner for charity in Wilmington, Delaware, Ruth was in a refined mood at the start of the evening, but by two in the morning he was drunk and quite smitten by a curly-haired brunette who had been serving him drinks. "I ain't leaving without that broad," he said. The Babe was referred to a Philadelphia boxing promoter, who told him that he knew a place where there were plenty of other ladies. When Ruth was persuaded that

the flesh was better down the road, he permitted himself to be put into a roadster and whisked to Camden, New Jersey.

By nine the next morning the promoter was begging Ruth to leave. The great man was sitting in an easy chair, a girl on each knee, in a room littered with empty champagne bottles. He arrived at Shibe Park in Philadelphia that afternoon without benefit of sleep. One of his teammates suggested that he looked ready for an embalmer. "Don't let my looks fool you, kid," Ruth retorted. "I feel great. Maybe I'll hit one out today."

Sure enough, on his first time at bat he punched an outside pitch into the leftfield stands for a home run. In his next three trips he tripled to deep center, tripled to right, and pulled the ball over the rightfield wall for another home run. Moreover, he made two fine running catches in the outfield. After the game, he washed down six hot dogs with a gallon of beer, stopped for a steak at a nearby restaurant, and headed back to the establishment in Camden, ready for the next night of dissipation. During the entire series in Philadelphia, in which he ruined the Athletics with his bat and glove, he was said to have slept no more than a few hours a night.

To be sure, he could overtax himself. In spring training, 1925, he collapsed from either a stomach ache brought on by overeating or from a more serious social disease. But on the whole he survived his escapades far better than those around him who counseled restraint. His manager on the Yankees, the tiny but crusty Miller Huggins, caused himself at least as much anxiety as he caused the Babe by his valiant but usually futile attempts to discipline him.

Babe's second wife, showgirl Claire Hodgson, had somewhat better luck. With the help of Christy Walsh, a ghostwriter who had done many of the projects Ruth had contracted for, she managed to domesticate her husband, after a fashion. Trust funds were set up by Walsh, and an attorney permitted the Ruths to live in a large apartment on Riverside Drive with a spectacular view of the Hudson

139

River. Every year Claire and Babe threw a big, nostalgic birthday party there.

By this time the Babe was an elder statesman, rapidly becoming an ornament on the Yankees. But surely here was one hero who deserved to rest on his laurels. For eleven of the thirteen years between 1919 and 1931 he led the American League in home runs, for eight in runs, for six in RBIs, and for twelve in slugging percentage. The might of Ruth and his awesome mates on "the Murderers' Row" Yankees as displayed merely in batting practice before the 1927 Series was reliably reported simply to have frightened the National League champion Pittsburgh Pirates into submission. And then there was the legendary incident in the 1932 World Series when the Babe, in response to sizzling abuse from the Chicago Cubs' bench, stepped back from the plate, waved toward the nether regions of Chicago's Wrigley Field, and deposited one of Charlie Root's offerings more or less where he had indicated he would. Some chagrined Cubs' survivors of that rout swear to this day that the flourish of heraldry never happened, but the legend has been verified by more than one neutral observer.

After the 1934 season, with his salary down to $35,000, Ruth marched through the crowds outside Yankee Stadium for the last time. A famous newspaper photo shows him with an anxious expression on his face; he was coming to the end and he knew it. He would be forty before the next season. He had batted .288, the first time he had been under .300 since he collapsed in 1925, and he had hit only twenty-two home runs. He had not dropped that low since he was a pitcher.

Ruth went into the front office to ask Colonel Ruppert about managing the Yankees. The club owner was stunned by the demand. "Root," he said in his stern German accent, "you cannot manage yourself, so vot makes you tink I would let you handle my best players. Go to Newark and manage our farm team dere."

Ruth stomped out of the office. A few weeks later he had his release. Off he went to Boston to be vice-president, assistant manager, and rightfielder for the Braves of the National League. It was mostly a publicity stunt. The team was in trouble and its owner-manager, Judge Emil Fuchs, needed somebody to front for him. The period of exploitation had begun. In mid-June, the Golden Hero of the Golden Age was batting .181 and stumbling pitifully around the outfield. People who had grown up worshiping him bought tickets to boo him. Ruth asked Fuchs's permission to go to a party in New York on the French liner Normandie. Fuchs refused. In the ensuing argument Ruth quit and Fuchs released him.

The last hurrah took place in Pittsburgh on May 25, 1935, two weeks before Ruth was released. The evening before, Ruth had been drinking with a Pittsburgh newsman, stopping at five in the morning. At Forbes Field that afternoon, both men showed up bleary-eyed. The writer told manager Pie Traynor "not to worry about Ruth." Standing nearby was Waite Hoyt, then a relief pitcher with the Pirates. "Don't be too sure about that," he said, remembering the old days in New York with the Yankees. "Even at forty, he's got to be a tough cookie."

In the first inning Ruth hit a home run into the right-field stands off Red Lucas. The next time up he hit one of Guy Bush's sinkerballs onto the roof in right. In the fifth inning he managed a single. In the seventh he hit the first fair ball that ever left Forbes Field on the fly. It was his final home run.

Ruth's name appeared in a major league box score for the last time on May 30, 1935. The Braves were playing the Philadelphia Phillies in a Memorial Day doubleheader. In the opening game, Ruth was the third batter in the lineup. He struck out his first time up, then hurt his leg in the outfield. He did a couple of exercises, then signaled to the bench for a replacement. Out of the dugout raced Hal Lee. Ruth went off the field for the last time. He had wanted to quit as a player after the three-home-run performance in Pittsburgh, but Fuchs would not let him. Numerous Babe Ruth Days were scheduled around the league and he showed up for all of them. He wanted badly to move on to managing or a front-office job, but nobody would give him the opportunity. The other jobs disappeared and he was unemployed for the first time since he left the Industrial Home in Baltimore.

A couple of years later, Ruth was hired by the Brooklyn Dodgers as a first-base coach, but his main job was to take batting practice with the players. He was a sideshow again, attracting a few more customers to Ebbets Field to watch him knock a few over the rightfield wall. When Leo Durocher became the manager, Ruth resigned. The two had been teammates on the Yankees years before and the screechy Durocher irritated the Babe. So Ruth was gone from baseball for good. Thereafter he offered his talents but nobody hired him. The game discarded a man who had revived it and given it a new direction.

Four years after he left baseball, he consented to put on a Yankee uniform again in a charity game. People came out just to see him run around, that wrestler's torso on a dancer's legs. Once he appeared at the old ball park in Hartford. He was in his late forties and the disease that killed him must have been in him already. He took a fee and played first base for a couple of innings, hitting a ball against the wall in his only time at bat. Albert Twombly turned to his seven-year-old son and said, "See that man? Close your eyes and remember how he looked. He was the greatest athlete your country ever knew. Don't forget him."

Cancer of the throat struck Babe Ruth in 1946. "I'm gone," he told Joe Dugan. He died at age fifty-three in 1948.

"He was unique," said Dugan years later. "There was nobody like him. Ty Cobb? Could he pitch? Tris Speaker? The rest? I saw them. I was there. There was never anybody close. He was a god."

They buried Babe Ruth in Mount Pleasant, New York. Joe Dugan was there, carrying the casket, along with Waite Hoyt. "I'd give my right arm for a beer, it's that hot," said Dugan.

"So would the Babe," said Hoyt.

In 1913, two Notre Dame undergraduates, quarterback Gus Dorais and end Knute Rockne, worked toward perfecting the seldom used forward pass. In an important game against Army in New York, the two Notre Dame players put on a passing exhibition that upset the West Point team, impressed the East Coast media, and directly influenced football strategy. Rockne was only warming up for a larger role.

3   Notre Dame Legend

On the Notre Dame calendar of feast days, the holiest date is November 10. It commemorates the day in 1928 when Knute Rockne walked quietly into the locker room at halftime of the game with Army, moved from player to player, offering advice and encouragement, and then gave the most inspiring speech that has ever been derogated by the term "pep talk."

Led by its backfield star, Chris Cable, the brilliant Army team had won all six of its games so far that season. Notre Dame would end the season with four losses, one-third of the losses in Rockne's coaching career. This was the coach's poorest Notre Dame football varsity, and he knew it. On this day the Cadets and Irish were locked in a scoreless tie through the first half. After the grueling first thirty minutes, the Notre Dame players slumped on their benches, in their exhaustion clearly unimpressed by the presence in the locker room of Jimmy Walker, the mayor of New York, and other such notables. Noting the downcast state of his team, Rockne realized he would have to do something drastic if he were to produce a victory for the distinguished subway alumni and the rest of the New York audience that clearly was counting on a Notre Dame victory. It was the time and place for a magnificent performance.

Gently, Rockne began to talk. The famous machine-gun-fire voice was gone, and in its place a strangely tentative cadence. For once the famous locker room orator acted as if he could not easily find the proper words. He glanced hesitantly toward the ceiling while gripping an unlit cigar in his right hand. Then inspiration seemed to strike and he began to glow like a man transfixed by a vision.

"Boys, it will be several years next month since I visited a mighty sick young man in St. Joseph's Hospital," Rockne is supposed to have said. "He was breathing his last few breaths in this world. He was a fine young man, a man who contributed so much to the university they named for Our Lady. There he was on his death bed, and he had just become a Catholic—he wanted so badly to be a complete part of Notre Dame. But boys, he had already brought glory to our school as the greatest back in the nation. His name was George Gipp. Remember that name. Never forget it.

"Years after he died, I met a girl named Irene. She was a town girl and she was the girl that George Gipp would have married. I tried to get her to tell me something about him, something personal that I did not already know. All she would say was, 'George Gipp was a great gentleman.'

"You know, boys, just before he died, George Gipp called me over close to him and in phrases that were barely whispers he said, 'Sometime, Rock, when the team is up against it, when things are wrong and the breaks are beating the boys, tell them to go in there and win one for the Gipper. I don't know where I'll be then, Rock, but I'll know about it and I'll be happy.' Within a few minutes that great Notre Dame gentleman, George Gipp, died."

By this time Rockne's audience was enraptured. It was said even that tears seeped from some of the Irish eyes in that locker room. "Boys," the coach concluded, "I'm firmly convinced that this is the game George Gipp would want us to win for him. Okay, let's go!"

The atmosphere fairly crackled. Football players were converted to holy zealots. They stampeded to the door, and they shocked the Cadets with their fury as the third quarter began. With an offensive line charging forward fanatically, Notre Dame drove relentlessly toward the Army goal, only to be stymied when Fred Collins, who was playing with his left wrist in a cast, fumbled on the two-yard line. The fervor suddenly abated, and by the end of the third period Army led 6-0. Here, Notre Dame's fiery Jack Chevigny commanded the huddle and reminded his teammates that they had a sacred obligation to win this game for George Gipp. "We've got to score," he shouted at them. The tears flowed again, and the crusade swept forward.

Notre Dame mounted a drive that carried fifty-one yards to the Army one-yard line. From there Chevigny ran to glory, clutching the ball, cutting to his left, and plowing straight into an Army tackle whom he carried with him over the goal line. Legend has it that he yelled, "That's one for the Gipper!" as he scored.

The game now was tied, 6-6, ready to be decided by a bit of Rockne inspiration. It came in the person of one Johnny O'Brien, whom Rockne sent into the lineup as the ball rested on the Army thirty-two-yard line. Quarterback Frank Carideo called the play. The tailback took the snap, faked a sweep to the left, and lateraled to another back, Butch Niemiec. He feigned a run, paused, and floated a high, clean spiral beyond the Army secondary to O'Brien. The football bounced crazily off O'Brien's left shoulder pad; he must have moved five yards before he finally brought the ball under control, clutching it to his chest as he rolled across the West Point goal line. In the jubilation that ensued, coach Rockne greeted the new hero at the sidelines with the commendation, "That was one great play, O'Brien," and forever after the inartistic but remarkable receiver was known as "One-Play O'Brien."

It goes without saying that Notre Dame prevailed over Army that day, just as Rockne had over halftime lethargy and other spiritual foes of Notre Dame football. It was left to the nitpicking nonromantics to point out that Rockne had at the very least considerably embellished the final hours of poor George Gipp.

Afraid of the disapproval of his mother, a stern Methodist, Gipp had not in fact converted but only asked a priest to ensure that he was "fixed up" with the Catholic church if he should die. When Gipp lapsed into delirium and the doctor in attendance gave up hope of saving him, the priest gave him both conditional baptism and the last rites. It is likely that Gipp expressed some contentment to Rockne about having resolved doubts he had had about his faith, but there is no indication of any bedside bequests to the Notre Dame football team. In any case, the coach wasn't at his side when Gipp passed away.

Fabricated or otherwise, the Gipp deathbed speech served Rockne well. Some people even insisted that he used the story on at least three different occasions to rouse his teams. Not so, retorted the defenders of the faith.

"I have heard it said that the year after Gipp's death Rockne asked the team to 'win one for the Gipper' in a meeting at a hotel just before a game with Indiana," said Frank Leahy, Rockne's pupil and most illustrious successor. "I have never been able to locate a single person who was either present at that meeting or could recall such a thing being said."

One did not lightly tamper with heroics in the Golden Age.

Knute Rockne was born on March 4, 1888, in Voss, Norway, a village located between Oslo and Bergen. His family name was "Rokne," pronounced "*Rock*-nuh." In 1931, he wrote about a possible kinship to the Irish, but in reality Rockne was about as Irish as a frozen fjord. His father, Lars Rokne, was a carriage maker who came to America to exhibit several of his creations at the Chicago World's Fair. He was so entranced by America that he sent for his wife, two daughters, and five-year-old son, Knute (pronounced "Canute" but Americanized to "Newt"). The younger Rockne attended Northwest Division High School but dropped out in his senior year in order to earn enough money for college. He passed a civil service examination and, by his own account, "became determined to march on the University of Illinois for an education."

Rockne was accepted at Illinois but he decided that it might be better to go to a school where his money would last longer. He chose Notre Dame after a couple of Catholic friends told him that the school appreciated the plight of a poor man, whether he was Protestant or Catholic. He took a high-school equivalency examination, scored 92.5 percent, and maintained a 90.5 percent grade average in the ten subjects he took at Notre Dame.

When he arrived at Notre Dame, a Norwegian Lutheran in an Irish Catholic environment, he was so painfully shy that he hardly talked to anyone except his teachers and roommates. He was no more than five feet eight inches tall, he already had a receding hairline, and he stuttered. He had a sad beagle look to him.

Although he had played football and run track successfully in high school (he was in fact one of the finest trackmen in the school's history), he did not think he was good enough to play college athletics. "Those college players loomed as supermen to me," he said. "They reached heights to which I could not aspire."

His insecurity showed.

"The first time I saw Rockne, he looked like a man far too old for college," said Gus Dorais, who as the quarterback for Notre Dame made a national reputation throwing passes to this prematurely gnarled little end. "He was wearing blue cord pants held up by white leather suspenders. He had on a light blue jersey and a black leather cap. He could have passed for a race track tout. At least that is what I thought he might be."

But of course Rockne proved to be quite a gifted athlete. In the summer of 1913, coach Jesse Harper suggested that Dorais and Rockne practice the forward pass. The two repaired to the hot sands of Cedar Point, on the shores of Lake Erie, where they perfected the maneuver, legal since 1906 but still infrequently and crudely utilized. That fall Dorais and Rockne stunned college football with their proficiency.

Dorais's and Rockne's most famous triumph with the newly potent offensive weapon came against a vaunted Army team, which fell 35-14 before the aerial warfare. Although Notre Dame had already had some fine football teams (and was in fact unbeaten in twenty-seven games between 1910 and 1914), the defeat of Army marked the emergence of the Irish as a fully recognized football power. Rockne was named to the third Walter Camp All-America team that season.

Taken with Notre Dame, Rockne intended to join the faculty upon his graduation. He was a brilliant chemistry

In a drawing for a friend, artist John
Steuart Curry captured the physical struggle
that was football in the first quarter of
the century. At Notre Dame, Knute
Rockne, who became head coach in
1918, was creating a legend (overleaf).
His locker room talks were famous
for their theatrics . . . and for the winning
results they produced.

student, but because he could not stand the smells of the
laboratory, he rejected a post in the chemistry department
and was instead appointed assistant football coach to
Harper. Three seasons later, Rockne was the head man.

At the start Rockne would not acknowledge that he
had a special ability to move people through oratory,
though he had conquered his fear of speaking by his
sophomore year. As late as 1921, when the nation was
beginning to idolize him, he addressed the student body
before a game, and when it shouted emotionally in response to him, he turned to a friend and asked, "Do you
think I reached them?"

Somehow the rumpled, unattractive, unhealthy looking undergraduate had acquired a high style, though he
still looked as unimpressive as ever. Westbrook Pegler
wrote, "He looks like the old punched up preliminary
fighter who becomes a door-tender in a speakeasy and
sits at a shadowy table in the corner near the door at night,
recalling the time he fought Billy Papke in Peoria for fifty
dollars."

Rockne read the description and never talked to Pegler
again, but he did not try to upgrade his appearance until
years later. A friend said Rockne could wear a new hat
and make it look as if it came from a rummage sale.

The fact was that Rockne had acquired a marked self-
confidence. Without it he would have been sleazy; with
it he was rakishly charming. He played at being the common man when in fact he was a brilliant mind and wit. It
couldn't help but shine through.

"I would have hated to have followed him on a speaking program," said humorist Will Rogers. "He was my
dear friend and he told me so many stories that I later
retold and got all kinds of laughs. If there was ever anybody I owed loyalties to it was Rockne. He was the fun-
niest man I ever met."

But Rockne the common man and Rockne the racon-
teur made up only Rockne the entertainer. The real man
lingered beneath these images—a still old-fashioned,
deeply religious, somewhat puritanical soul who de-

"Touchdown"

for Al Alon Chedey
John Steuart Curry Sept. 23d /18.

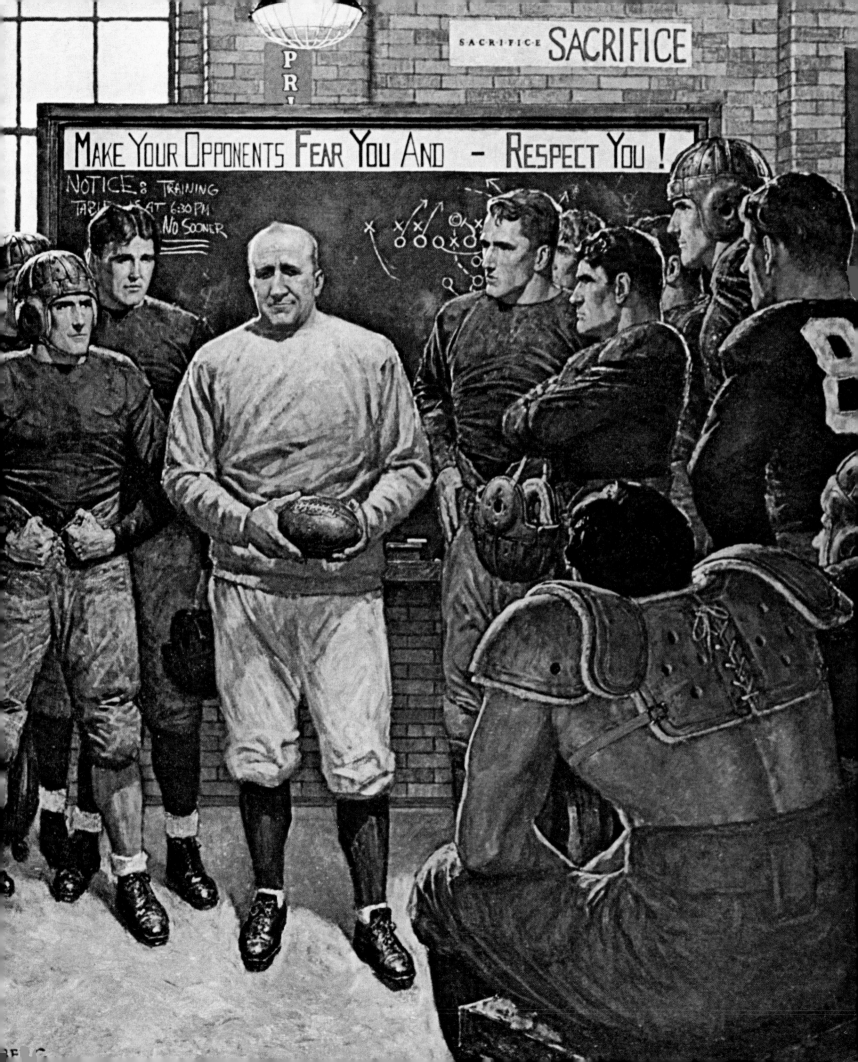

Rockne's death at 43 in a plane crash shocked the nation. The original *Life* magazine saluted Rockne with a 1931 cover.

tested social events (even as he pretended to be a great partygoer) and abhorred drinking, cursing, or carousing. After-hours idlers were contemptuously dubbed "lounge lizards." If he was remarkably tolerant of George Gipp, that noted sinner whose transgressions would have permanently tarnished the Golden Dome had they been publicized, it was also true that Rockne was something of a prude. He liked the fact that there were no women at Notre Dame, believing them to be nothing but a distraction to his athletes. And he insisted that his players wear sweaters and corduroy pants because he thought such clothes had a wholesome appearance.

This was the man who could somehow infuse the power of faith into his players, who could in the words of George Strickler, later the sports editor of the *Chicago Tribune,* "motivate a football team if he did nothing more at halftime than recite the Lord's prayer."

Rockne was the head coach at Notre Dame from 1918 through 1930. He won a hundred and five games, lost twelve, and tied five—a victory percentage of .881. Three of his teams were national champions; five were unbeaten. Then, just when his rule over college football seemed indestructible, he was gone.

On Tuesday, March 31, 1931, Rockne boarded a Fokker tri-motor in Kansas City with five other passengers and two pilots. The plane took off into clear skies and headed west. In a field a few miles southwest of a town called Bazaar, Kansas, a farmer looked up from his work and saw an airplane nose down, spouting a long, ugly trail of black smoke. He heard an explosion and watched the plane come down in sections. There were no survivors.

The nation mourned his death like that of a national leader. President Herbert Hoover telephoned Rockne's widow from the White House and told her, "Every American grieves with you. Coach Rockne so contributed to a cleanness and a high purpose and sportsmanship in athletics that his passing is a national loss." General Douglas MacArthur, the Army chief of staff and a close admirer of Rockne's, called to offer condolences. And the King of Norway announced that the country's best-known American emigrant would be knighted posthumously.

When the casket bearing Rockne's remains was taken off the train in Chicago, more than ten thousand people packed Old Dearborn Street Station and thousands more thronged outside. Every flag in the city was at half mast. Radio stations played funeral music and, intermittently, the Notre Dame victory march around the clock. Pictures of Rockne, swathed in black, were hung in every department store window and every hotel lobby. Some schools closed.

Knute Rockne was buried on the afternoon of April 4, 1931, with six of Rockne's best athletes as pall bearers: Frank Carideo, Marchmont Schwartz, Marty Brill, Moon Mullins, Tom Conley, and Tommy Yarr. Fourteen hundred people tried to enter a Notre Dame church that held six hundred; the overflow listened outside on the lawn. Radio carried the services to all parts of the nation. When the service was over, the bells tolled the Notre Dame victory march in funeral cadence and the coffin was borne to the cemetery next to the campus. The legend of Rockne has yet to be buried.

4   The Manassa Mauler

The moon was riding low in the sky, hiding behind indifferent clouds, when Jack (Doc) Kearns, the most roguish fight manager in history and the manager of the leading heavyweight contender, slipped out the back door of the training headquarters on the shores of Toledo's Maumee Bay. Kearns pushed his way through a litter of bottles, paper plates, and other garbage that had been thrown out the back door. He walked past a couple asleep in a hammock. The training ground building slumped against the wild landscape, seemingly ready to collapse at a slight nudge as Kearns left it. On this sultry July night in 1919, Kearns was the last survivor of a prefight party.

"For the first and only time in my life I had broken up a party, and that was all the more remarkable since I had been the host," he said much later. "It was never like Jack Kearns to stop pouring, for himself or for his guests. But at my plea that I had a championship fight to prepare for, the last of them had finally wandered into the pre-dawn darkness under a full load of whiskey. One broad even leaned on my shoulder and told me she knew Jack Dempsey couldn't lose to Jess Willard. She wasn't telling me anything new. My tiger was as hard as nails and only twenty-four years old. Willard was thirty-seven and fading fast."

Kearns never liked to give a sucker an even break; he intended to win a lot more than just a championship from this match. He had bet $10,000 against 10-1 odds that Dempsey would win the championship in the first round. The $100,000 he stood to win would be considerably more than Willard's guarantee and a fine improvement on Dempsey's own guarantee of $27,500. The hell with being a gallant winner, said Kearns, as he later told his biographer, Oscar Fraley. He intended to be sure his boy won that fight and quickly.

After the last celebrant tottered out the door, Kearns went to a cupboard and took down a can of plaster of Paris he had purchased a few days earlier on a secret trip to Toledo. He poured out the contents of a talcum powder can onto a handkerchief and refilled the can with the plaster of Paris. Kearns marched some fifty yards toward Maumee Bay and dumped the powder and the old plaster of Paris can in the water. The water rippled, bubbled, and swallowed the evidence.

If Kearns is to be believed, he felt no twinges of conscience as he embarked on this, the foulest misdeed of his less than honorable career. "I was a product of my days, when it was every man for himself," he said. "In those times you got away with everything possible. If you turned your head, the other guy had his knuckles wrapped in heavy black bicycle tape or that thick tinfoil they wrapped bulk tea in. It was like hitting a man with a leather-padded mallet. The rules were lax then, officials were not at all fussy, and there were few boxing commissions."

Kearns returned to the headquarters to sleep the sleep of the innocent. A few hours later he tumbled downstairs and discovered that most of the partygoers had returned for more good cheer at breakfast. The couple in the hammock was still there.

As he left for the arena, which had been jerry-built out of Michigan pine to hold 80,000 people, the thermometer read 114 degrees. He made a note to tell Dempsey to conserve his energy. In the dressing room, Dempsey moved like a wild beast, his muscles flexing under his taut skin. He was a dark scowling man, a stereotypical assassin.

Kearns walked into Willard's dressing area to say hello. He noted that Willard's handlers were all inexperienced men; the giant champion did not pay well. Kearns offered them advice on how to wrap Willard's hands. At first Willard was pleased, but then he became suspicious.

"Hey, get away from me, Doc," he grunted.

"Suit yourself," said Kearns. "I was just afraid what these boys might do to you. We want a fair fight, now, don't we?"

Accompanied by Willard's second, Kearns returned to his side of the partition. Kearns ordered his men to pour water on Dempsey's bandages to keep the challenger's hands cool. Kearns told Willard's second that he should have dampened the champion's hands. The second shrugged and said, "Well, you can't tell Jess to do something you know he doesn't want to do." Kearns took a sponge and wet down Dempsey's hands again as he bandaged them. Then he sprinkled the false talcum powder over them. "This is what you should have done for Jess," he said.

"Dempsey was entirely innocent of the whole business," said Kearns. "He never would admit it even after I told about the substitution of the plaster of Paris for the talcum powder. I didn't want him to know. But by the time he entered the ring he must have known that his

149

hands were heavier and harder than they had ever been."

Never in his remaining years did Willard waver in his contention that Dempsey's gloves had been loaded. Anyone who believed otherwise was invited to place his fingers against the dent in Jess's skull from his left cheekbone to the temple. That was what Doc Kearns's cement gloves had done to him, Willard said. He had been dethroned not by a man's fists but by chunks of concrete slammed against his head. "I was robbed by the king of robbers; the greatest one in the history of American sports, the one and only Doc Kearns," he said. "The first time he hit me I knew the gloves were loaded. He knocked me down seven or eight times. Every time he hit me I could feel another bone or two break. As long as I got robbed, I'm glad that I got robbed by the best man in America at stealing. Makes you proud."

The first round ended in what seemed so clearly a knockout that Dempsey left the ring. Willard lay on the canvas. The referee had reached the count of seven. A suspicious person who seemed to be pointing a cylindrical object against the back of the timekeeper ordered him to end the match. Somehow Willard was saved by the bell and revived for the next round. The police were sent to retrieve Dempsey.

"By my watch there were nine seconds left when the first-round bell rang," said Kearns. "Everybody knew that Willard was in no shape to get up in two seconds, three seconds, ten seconds, or even thirty seconds. I could testify until the end of time that the fight did end in the first round and old Jack Kearns was shortchanged a hundred thousand dollars."

If he was, no doubt he deserved it. But perhaps it would have been better if the old con man hadn't been swindled in return. By the end of the third round Willard was a pitiful hulk, his face smeared with blood, which trickled over his huge chest. Dempsey dropped him to the floor and Willard was on all fours, blood dripping from his mouth. When Willard rose, Dempsey pushed the virtually defenseless man into a neutral corner and came frighten-

Jack Dempsey was a raw-boned destroyer, a man who was as hard as the Colorado country from which he had come. On July 4, 1919, he battered 245-pound Jess Willard into submission to win the heavyweight title. Dempsey was described as a savage but after the fight, when someone asked him what his true goal was, he said, "I want to be a gentleman."

ingly close to beating him to death. There was an ugly, hollow sound every time Dempsey hit him. The left side of Willard's face was cut to the bone in thirteen places. He took as ruthless and brutal a beating as any man has ever taken in the ring. His handlers threw the towel in the ring after the third round.

While doctors labored over the fallen champ, whose face had been reduced to a monstrous, bloody smear and whose body was a puzzle of red blotches, Kearns cracked off the bandages from Dempsey's hands. The bandages had hardened so that Dempsey could not unflex his fists, but he seemed not to notice. He was twenty-four years old and champion of the world, and he was a man in a trance. He had no idea what his manager was doing.

Kearns and Dempsey were both products of the old frontier. Kearns had been raised in Seattle and gone off to the Klondike. In the saloons of Nome, Fairbanks, and Anchorage, he met the master swindlers and became a student of the greatest, Willson Mizner. Kearns smuggled Chinese into San Francisco and trafficked in opium. He tried boxing, but until he ran into Dempsey he did not fare well.

William Harrison (Jack) Dempsey was born in a two-room, clapboard cabin outside Manassa, Colorado, on June 24, 1895, the ninth of eleven children. His parents, Cecelia and Hyrum Dempsey, were pioneers, having moved from West Virginia to Colorado on a $300 stake. Cecelia Dempsey was Scottish on her father's side and Cherokee and Jewish on her mother's. Hyrum Dempsey was Kildare Irish. He left the Catholic Church for Mormonism and Mormonism for a homey agnosticism, the philosophy of life he imbued in his children. The Dempsey brood grew up with very little trust in anything save money, and there wasn't much of that.

Hyrum Dempsey more or less failed to support his family as a sharecropper, a hide hunter, a dirt farmer, a gandy dancer, and a small store owner. He housed his family in a series of log shanties with paper windows.

Once a month, while he was out on the Utah plains or the hillsides of Colorado, he and his son, whom he called "Billy" and his wife called "Harry," would drive into town and buy five dollars' worth of staples. They hunted and fished for the rest of their food.

Until he was fifteen young Dempsey never had a piece of candy. His toys were whittled from scrap wood by older brothers. By the time the future heavyweight champion of the world was twelve years old, he had chopped wood, racked balls in a pool hall, worked as a barker in a circus, and had done stoop labor in a beet field. In his spare time he hunted, fished, and trapped. On the whole it was a wretched existence, and like the rest of the Dempsey children, this one would leave home as soon as he was old enough.

Because a famous boxer of the period was named Jack Dempsey, the three Dempsey sons who intended to pursue prizefighting adopted this fighter's first name. First came the oldest, Bernie, who fought many fights throughout the West and taught his younger brothers, Johnny and Billy, how to pound at a canvas bag filled with sawdust. The Dempsey boys used ordinary workmen's gloves stuffed with padding, chewed pine gum constantly to make their jaws strong, and in general went about learning the craft with the determination of men who considered it the only way out of their desperate situation. "One day Bernie dropped a cardboard picture of Jack Johnson out of his cigarette pack," recalled Billy. "Everybody dived for it, but I got it. For years, I carried it with me. I thought Jack Johnson would be the man I'd have to beat for the title. Instead, it was the man who beat Jack Johnson. Strange how things work out."

Billy, the fourth Jack Dempsey, attracted the attention of Kearns by defeating a fine heavyweight, Joe Bond, in Ely, Nevada. Kearns, who had been promoting fights in San Francisco, saw the clipping from the local papers, and to bring Dempsey to the coast, he sent him a railroad ticket and five dollars for meals. Dempsey's train rolled into the Oakland station, and though Kearns was not

In September, 1923, Dempsey fought his greatest fight against a crude but powerful Argentinian, Luis Angel Firpo. In the first round the challenger punched Dempsey through the ropes into the press row. Artist George Bellows, in one of his last—and most famous—paintings, captured the pandemonium of the moment. Dempsey crawled back into the ring and floored the giant Firpo seven times. In the second round, Dempsey put Firpo down two more times before he ended the fight with a short right uppercut.

there to meet it, Dempsey found the ferry slip and paid his way across San Francisco Bay. Kearns's mother took in the road-hardened bum and treated him like a son. Thereupon began a long, amicable relationship between the shrewd manager and malleable fighter, in which they split evenly all Dempsey's earnings. Later the two men would quarrel bitterly, but for now Kearns and Dempsey were good for and to each other.

World War I began just as Dempsey was scratching his way to the top. He got a job in an Oakland shipyard, but because he was too crude to be popular, the government found him a good target for prosecution as a slacker. With the help of an awkwardly presented case against him and a couple of mean lawyers whom Kearns hired, the young fighter won acquittal. But the smear lingered. A newspaper photograph of him wearing shiny leather shoes with his work clothes aroused much comment against him. He was supposed to be slamming rivets into the side of a ship, not lolling about in dressy clothes, said the critics. "I had been at a Liberty Bond rally the night before," he tried to explain, "and somebody from one of the Hearst newspapers wanted to take a picture of me in action at my regular job. It was innocent enough. They took the picture before I had a real chance to change and get into my work clothes. They said I was a slacker. They didn't know that I changed my clothes after that shot, got about four hours sleep, worked a ten-hour day, and fought that night for Liberty Bonds."

The young Dempsey may not have been shirking military service, but he was hardly an attractive figure. He was a seedy, ignorant brawler, disreputable in the ring and outside it. This was the man who battered Jess Willard for the title in 1919. No one should have been shocked that he let himself be used by Kearns as the instrument of one of the most scandalous episodes in the sordid history of the ring. And indeed few people were. Perhaps it was because Willard was more grotesque than awe-inspiring and, considering his shady conquest of Jack Johnson, less than a paradigm of virtue himself.

Georges Carpentier was quite another matter. He was a fine, handsome fighter with a sterling war record. America admired the French for their valiant struggle against the Germans during the war, and Carpentier stood out as a shining example. The slick Tex Rickard matched Carpentier's virtues and Dempsey's depravities and produced the first million-dollar gate in boxing history. The champ met the Frenchman at Boyle's Thirty Acres in New Jersey before some hundred thousand customers, who paid $1,623,380.

As if anybody could forget their contrasting backgrounds, the combatants entered the ring playing their roles to the hilt. Dempsey stalked in with a scowl ferocious enough for a murderer. He had not shaved for several days, and he wore an old pair of trunks and a faded red sleeveless gym shirt that was rank with the sweat of countless workouts. He did not appear to have showered recently. Carpentier, on the other hand, was almost elegant. He was immaculately barbered, and he wore an expensive, expertly tailored silk robe with matching trunks. The crowd was breathless at the sight of such a heroic figure.

Unfortunately, the fight was a mismatch, as most objective observers had predicted. Carpentier was only a light-heavyweight and, though artful, hardly quick enough to escape the meaner and more powerful Dempsey. By the fourth round the champ had him at his mercy. After only thirty-five seconds he felled him with a barrage to the abdomen.

Carpentier was not unconscious but he was in deep distress, curling up on his side while the referee counted to nine. Dempsey hovered in the farthest neutral corner, his face split in a grin that Ray Pearson of the *Chicago Tribune* described as "sardonic." When the Frenchman rose before the count of ten, the champion sprinted out of the corner, slammed a hard left to the belly, and polished off Carpentier with a devastating right to the chin. The challenger fell to the floor with a thud heard fifty rows back. Again Carpentier lay on his side. At the count of eight he made a desperate effort to stand but managed only to raise his body part way from the floor before he plunged forward, rolled over on his back, and took the count.

"C'mon, Doc," said Dempsey to his manager, "let's get out of here. The champagne's cooling off." The victors trotted off to scattered cheers and persistent hisses. In an age of golden, godlike heroes, Jack Dempsey was still an anti-Christ to many.

Finding a worthwhile opponent became something of a problem. When other fighters remembered what he had done to Willard and Carpentier, they thought twice about meeting Dempsey. Oh, there was Sam Langford, nicknamed the "Boston Tar Baby," but the world was not ready for another black champion. Langford was not given a chance. Neither was another black, Harry Wills, who fought Langford fourteen times. "Jack Johnson spoiled it for you people," they told Langford and Wills.

Dempsey toured Europe, discovering he was a bigger hero there than at home. He made the obligatory trip to Hollywood to make two dreadful movies. In both films he was billed as "Daredevil Jack," the movie moguls having deemed his generally accepted nickname, "the Manassa Mauler," too indelicate.

In 1923, Kearns brought off another heist when the citizens of Shelby, Montana, offered a reported $300,000 if Dempsey would defend his championship there against Tommy Gibbons, a weary wanderer. Shelby was a boom town in Montana that liked to think of itself as "the Tulsa of the Northwest" because oil had been discovered there, but boom town or not, it could not afford $300,000 for a fight. Apparently the offer was made less than seriously, but Kearns accepted it and Shelby was stuck.

By the time Kearns was through, he had sacked the town and much of the territory around it. Banks, lending institutions, and businesses failed as they tried desperately to produce the purse. Not surprisingly, the fight did anything but reward their efforts. For fifteen rounds Gibbons actually outboxed a somewhat bored Dempsey, but

156

GENE TUNNEY

the champion fought aggressively when he and Kearns thought it was necessary, and he prevailed on points. Afterward, the champion and his manager, the latter clutching a small black satchel, sprinted to catch a Great Northern Railway train that took them to Great Falls and from there to New York City. They absconded with about $245,000.

Gibbons had said that for a chance at Dempsey he would fight for nothing, and that is exactly what he received. He even had to pay out-of-pocket his own training expenses and his railroad passage back home.

Three months later Dempsey returned to the East, where he finally fought a legitimate challenger in a legitimate promotion and gained the love and respect previously denied him. Luis Angel Firpo, an Argentinian who was called "the Wild Bull of the Pampas," was taller, heavier, and stronger than Dempsey—a perfect foil for the champ, who looked better or at least more heroic against larger men.

The stage was set for perhaps the most furious round in the history of the ring—a three-minute spectacle of sustained violence that sucked the breath out of the Polo Grounds crowd.

Seconds into the fight Firpo decked Dempsey. Shaking his head in disbelief and amazement, the champion climbed back to his feet and clinched with the Argentinian. Then he pushed Firpo away and began to punish him severely with left-right, rapid-fire combinations. The vandalous fury was ablaze in Dempsey now. He dropped Firpo an astonishing seven times, never permitting him to recover from one trip to the mat before dispatching him on another. Miraculously, the challenger rescued himself and, just before the first round ended, laid an overhand right against Dempsey's jaw. As the crowd gasped, the champion tumbled out of the ring, landed on a typewriter in the press section, and rolled into a reporter's lap. The newsmen helped him back into the ring before the referee could count him out.

Less than a minute into the second round the gallant

Firpo was finished, and Dempsey, the shirker of combat until now, had his battle decorations and the adulation they brought.

He chose this time, when he might have solidified his claim to respectability, to rest on his laurels. It was three years before he fought again. When he did he was not only ill-prepared (thirty-one years old and out of shape), but also flirting with dishonor again. True, he was the champ, and as such fervently admired, but a young fellow stood ready to relieve him of both his title and his reputation as a courageous warrior. Dempsey did lose the title, of course, but, to his everlasting credit as a fighter, never his zest for combat.

The man who brought Dempsey's mettle to the fore was the son of a Greenwich Village stevedore—almost as humble origins as Jack's. But by the time he met Dempsey, Gene Tunney was well on his way toward his goal of becoming part of the elite, not only financially but socially. He was educated at parochial schools and attended business college. He was remarkably well read, stern, and rigorously disciplined in his personal life. At eighteen he joined the Marine Corps, having already won a dozen professional fights. He gave a boxing demonstration in front of his officers in France and received permission to take time off from his duties to train for Marine boxing shows. He won the light heavyweight championship of the armed forces in 1919 at Paris. When he returned to America, he met wealthy friends who provided him with country training sites. In the years ahead he would marry Andrew Carnegie's niece; raise four children, one of them a future United States Senator; become a prominent businessman; belong to the best clubs; own a cattle ranch; and earn a million dollars.

As a fighter Tunney was precise. He had the finest, most cutting left jab in the business, and he could deliver a punishing right. He was shrewd and graceful and, perhaps surprisingly for a fighter of his artistry, quite durable. On that September evening in Philadelphia in 1926 when he first met Dempsey, he not only outboxed but outlasted

157

158

America was on a binge in the twenties, unleashing an energy level it had never before experienced. Artist Charles Sheeler captured the essence of this feeling at the quarter century with this stunning painting titled simply, *Pertaining to Yachts and Yachting*.

the floundering champ. Dempsey came out with a rush, intent on destroying his opponent. He succeeded only in attracting the flak of counterpunches; he never could catch the exceptionally clever challenger. At the close of the fight, the 120,000 spectators looked down on Dempsey's teary, purple onion face and watched the crown pass from the mauled Manassa Mauler to a golden boxing hero for the Golden Age.

Woeful though he was in defeat, however, Dempsey still claimed an allegiance from fans not yet ready to embrace the somewhat cool, isolated, even snobbish Tunney.

People came to the dressing room of the loser and mumbled a few fitful words of consolation. They patted his shoulders sympathetically. The former champion slumped forward on a wooden table, his head down, trying to gather his badly scattered thoughts. A blonde woman came up and kissed him on his rudely discolored cheeks. He shook his head. Dempsey's wife called him and asked sympathetically what had happened. He replied with a phrase that would always be a part of the nation's sweaty history. "I forgot to duck," he said.

As Dempsey prepared to leave the stadium, an old man slogged up to him through the rain. He was a tramp whom Dempsey had known years earlier in his hobo days out West. "There shouldn't be no wake," said the tramp, grinning warmly. "What if he is still the champion and what if he ain't? This here's Jack Dempsey, ain't it? Who's better at fighting than he is? He's got dough. He's famous. What's the boxing championship to a man who started the way you did and got all you got? What am I, old pardner? I'm just a tramp, still, but you're Jack Dempsey."

Suddenly Jack Dempsey was adored. In defeat he moved toward a new greatness. He vowed to do what had never been done—to regain the heavyweight title— and he trained for his mission with a dedication few people thought he could muster. No longer was he the arrogant young draft dodger or a villainous assassin but, at thirty-two, a struggling hero. Off he went to prove him-

The Dempsey-Tunney rematch on September 22, 1927, created one of the most widely disputed and controversial moments in American sports. In the famous "long count," Dempsey knocked down Tunney in the seventh round and stood over him in an animal rage. The referee refused to count until Dempsey had retreated to a neutral corner. Obviously hurt, Tunney used the extra moments to regain his senses and resume the fight, which he then went on to win by decision.

self again, and he beat a younger, stronger man, Jack Sharkey. He would never be refined, but he seemed less abrasive now, as both a fighter and a man.

When he moved into the ring against Tunney at Soldier Field in Chicago on September 22, 1927, he was scowling and filled with fury, but he was somehow transformed. Tunney, dancing and jabbing as always, could not touch the primal passions of the fight fans. Dempsey, the inelegant but valiant foot soldier, had the crowd of 100,000 on his side. Dempsey plodded forward, hoping to land a blow that would separate Tunney from his senses. Suddenly, miraculously, he did.

In the seventh round, after sustaining the same sort of punishment he had in the first fight, Dempsey jolted Tunney with a left hook to the head, dropping him to the canvas near the ropes. Tunney sat there in a stupor, gasping for air. Oblivious to the referee, who commanded him to a neutral corner, the challenger stood over the fallen champ, eager for the kill. People at ringside with stopwatches said that Tunney was down for about seventeen seconds. When Dempsey finally realized that he had to retreat, Tunney had enough time to beat the count. He reasserted his mastery over the clumsy challenger and won another decision, in what was forever after known as "the Battle of the Long Count." Later Tunney won a third match with the former champ.

Dempsey wouldn't quit the ring, however. In 1931 he engaged in a series of exhibitions, and the next year, when he was thirty-seven, he fought four rounds against twenty-one-year old Kingfish Levinsky, the noted tie designer. Dempsey took a thorough beating. "I'm through," he said afterward. "I know that. It wasn't the Kingfish that beat me; it was father time." Eventually, he accepted his own verdict. He ended his career with a victory over Bull Curry, a Lebanese-American from Hartford, Connecticut, who took the defeat so hard that he became one of the most financially successful wrestlers of his time.

It took Dempsey some years to find comfort in retirement. His name slowly disappeared from the news-

papers. He owned a restaurant on Times Square. He married again, got divorced again, married for a third time, and had two daughters. When World War II broke out, Jack Dempsey was down front, ready to do what he could to absolve himself of having been in a shipyard during World War I.

The army admired his magnificent physique, but he was forty-six, too old. So he called a senator and got himself a commission in the Coast Guard, where he became a physical fitness director with the rank of commander. A highly fanciful story was told of how he defeated the fleet champion—a bully, of course. Supposedly, Dempsey took a terrible beating in the first round but recovered to knock out his opponent with a perfectly executed right.

Another report claimed that when the Coast Guard swarmed ashore on Okinawa, Dempsey asked to board one of the landing craft for the second wave. Because the authorities were reluctant to risk the life of a famous figure, they denied him permission, but he insisted and they gave in. Then someone recognized him.

"Ain't you Jack Dempsey?" asked one man.

"You're damn right, pardner," he shouted. "They ain't gonna call me no damn draft dodger this time. When this is all over, you're gonna be my guests at my place on Broadway." They waved and he waved back. When the front part of the boat dropped on the sand, Jack Dempsey clutched his rifle and hit the beach. After the men secured the beach and set up headquarters, Jack Dempsey sat there signing autographs. As tarnished as he was, he had the stuff of which golden, godlike heroes were made. Jack Dempsey just took a little longer.

5   King of the Court

Bill Tilden might be the only champion athlete of the past who could succeed in his game today. A comparison of eras in other sports is almost pointless because of fundamental changes in the games themselves. It is fun to speculate but hard to say how Red Grange would sweep the ends against good cornerback-linebacker combinations. Walter Johnson threw a different baseball, mostly against choke-the-bat hitters playing for one or two runs. And basketball has been captured by a race of skilled giants undreamed of in earlier times. Golf, track and field, and swimming have not changed, but the techniques for doing them well have been refined. It is difficult to imagine the Charlie Paddocks and Johnny Weissmullers of the twenties coming within feet, inches, minutes, or seconds of today's phenomenally trained record-breakers; and the less said about those winning U. S. Open scores of 300-plus the better.

No, Bill Tilden may be the only one. You can visualize him stepping onto a contemporary tennis court and, in full command of *his* game, giving almost anyone around today, playing *his* game, a tennis lesson.

It could happen because almost nothing about tennis has changed since Tilden's time. Rules, size of court, height of net, and court surfaces are all the same. The technology of rackets has improved; if he were playing now Tilden would be using a Wilson T-2000; it wouldn't take long for him to make it work his way. The ball is a bit harder; it comes off the racket faster. And from what we can tell of long-ago matches that survive on film, the pace of today's game may be slightly accelerated. There are more top-flight players today than there were in the twenties, and they knock the faster ball around more rapidly. Otherwise, the strokes are Tilden's strokes and the strategy—maneuver the opponent out of position —is one he understood superlatively and delighted in.

All this being so, Tilden could win today because in the years of his greatness he probably played tennis better than any man who ever lived. He is almost invariably at the top of any expert observer's list of the all-time finest players.

Don Budge played on the pro tour with Tilden when Tilden was forty-eight and beat him regularly. But Budge recognized that he was dueling with an incomparable tennis stylist and strategist. Ted Schroeder, U. S. champion and, later, Wimbledon winner and Davis Cupper, played an exhibition against Tilden when Tilden was fifty, in 1943, and Schroeder was soundly whipped, 6-2, 6-2. Almost until he died, just turned sixty, he could rise to an occasion and play a set of beautiful tennis.

The record of active play stretched from 1913, when he won the U. S. mixed doubles title with the redoubtable Mary K. Browne, to 1946, when he helped form the Professional Tennis Players Association.

Within that span he won just about all there was to win, including seven U. S. singles championships, six of them consecutively, three Wimbledons, and seven straight Davis Cups, in the course of which he won thirteen straight singles matches and four of the six doubles he played.

The sublime period was from 1920 through 1926, when the succession of U. S. and Cup victories was fashioned. At the same time, he was winning doubles and mixed doubles, indoor and out, on grass and clay. For this amazing chunk of time he was virtually unbeatable—the more amazing because he got a late start as an athlete and did not win his first major title until he was twenty-seven. At the end of his six-year spurt he was thirty-three.

He won a final Forest Hills at thirty-six, and a last Wimbledon and a last Davis Cup singles at thirty-seven. At thirty-eight he turned pro. Of course, the tour was nothing like it is today, but his name drew 13,600 people to Madison Square Garden to see his debut against Karel Koželuh, the Czech ace. In years to come they would show up to see him thrash Vinnie Richards, and Hans Nüsslein of Germany, and eventually to take his own lickings (at forty) from young Ellsworth Vines. Between 1931 and 1935, aging as he was, he managed to win 340 of 487 pro matches, a .698 percentage.

How did he do it?

First, by perfecting the strokes. He had a tremendous serve, one of the most powerful ever seen. A few fired at

Between 1920 and 1930 Bill Tilden won seven United States and three Wimbledon tennis titles; he was ranked the number one amateur player in the world for six consecutive years. At six feet, two inches and 155 pounds, he was a clever player, a perfectionist who had mastered every stroke. His game was intellectual in concept, but his matches involved the histrionics of a showman. The people loved it. Most experts call him the greatest player of all time.

age forty were clocked at 151 miles per hour. Yet, master of tennis subtleties that he was, he would never have been satisfied with the cannonball as the only shot in his arsenal. He was also proficient with a kick service —what was then called "the American twist"—a high-bouncing topspin serve that broke to the opponent's left, and with the slice, a sidespin serve that took a low bounce while it broke to the opponent's right.

Tilden could be devastating with the big serve, particularly when, with a grand show of impatience, he would take four balls, fire off three aces to win set or match, and negligently throw the unneeded fourth aside as he stalked off the court.

On the other hand, nettled by comments that it was only his serve that enabled him to overpower his long-time rival, "Little Bill" Johnston, he decided to forego the big gun in their quarterfinal match at the U. S. Championships of 1921, and whipped Johnston in an endless exchange of forehand baseline drives.

Like many tennis players, Tilden originally had a problem with his backhand. He could slice it nicely, but not hit with power. His inability to use it aggressively led to his loss in the U. S. finals in 1919, when Johnston exploited the weakness and beat him in straight sets. After that loss, Tilden spent the winter on a friend's indoor court hitting thousands of topspin backhands until he mastered the stroke. By the following summer, 1920, the start of his great streak, his new backhand worked in tandem with his always powerful forehand and, with the big serve gave him his incredible game.

He had finesse as well as power, of course, a full repertory of slices, cuts, and chops; a dropshot that expired obediently close to the net; graceful and accurate lobs. The only shot he never executed superbly was the overhead smash.

Although he had a "big game" and was certainly no stranger to any of the serve-and-volley tactics that have dominated tennis since World War II, Tilden preferred to play in the backcourt rather than rushing the net. He relished the strategic possibilities of tennis, the thrust-and-parry, the maneuvering, the skillful sequence of strokes, which, like moves in chess, eventually set up the foe for the killing shot.

On the court, his footwork was impeccable. He moved easily and perfectly into position for every shot and brought each one off with perfect form. He had a splendid tennis player's build: tall, lean, broad-shouldered, long-legged. And despite an addiction to cigarettes, he had the stamina to play all day. Because he towered over Johnston and such tiny fellows as Cochet, everyone assumed he actually was a big Bill. In fact, he was only a hair over six foot one inch and weighed one hundred fifty-five.

In the long white trousers and white shirts that tennis players wore in those days, he was a lithe and handsome figure, swooping, darting, performing wonderfully or outrageously as the mood struck him, savoring the crowd and stirring it to adoration or goading it to fury as he wished, and often as not psyching his opponent by the audacity of his play.

In the Wimbledon final of 1920 against Australia's Gerald Patterson, the defending champion and the top-ranked player in the world, Tilden lost the first set 6-2. Then he blasted the Aussie in three sets.

At his peak it seemed obvious that some of his five-set matches included a couple of throwaway sets. In his most famous match against Johnston, the finals of the U. S. Championship in 1922, he dropped the first two sets, won one, and then lagged 0-3 in the fourth. Evidently deciding it was time to call a halt to this foolishness, he took the next six games, the fifth set, and the match.

On other occasions he simply indulged himself—to enliven the match, to give the gallery a show, to prolong his own enjoyment of this marvelous game. There was no meanness in it. He always wanted to dominate his opponent but he never wanted to humiliate him. He fancied himself an actor, a playwright, and a novelist (but was embarrassingly inept in his many efforts in these fields), and this sense of himself as performer, dramatist, and cynosure, governed his behavior on court. There was arrogance in it—the disdainful shrug, the sardonic smile on the long, mobile face. But it was innocent, too. For all his posturing, he was a shy and lonely man with few, if any, meaningful relationships in his life. Yet people who knew him also remember generosity and kindness. He was an excellent tennis instructor who gave uncounted hours to developing the skills of promising youngsters. As his homosexuality became more overt and more generally known (as his prowess on the court began to wane), it was customary to sneer that this was the motivation for his interest in young players. But there is no evidence that he ever took advantage of his role as coach.

Still, there were many who found him overbearing, capricious, and outrageous. He was particularly unpopular with the tennis establishment. He would not be dominated by the officialdom of the U. S. Lawn Tennis Association, and he tweaked their noses whenever they tried, most notably in the 1927 Davis Cup match against France. With the singles at 1-1 (Tilden having managed a tough win over Cochet), there was a chance to retain the Cup if Tilden and his friend, Frank T. Hunter, doubles champs of both Wimbledon and Forest Hills that year, could topple Borotra and Brugnon. At this point, with the appalling bad judgment that historically was its hallmark in dealing with Tilden, the USLTA announced that Hunter was being dropped and another player would be matched with Tilden in the doubles. Tilden struck. He sat down to play bridge, his second favorite and second most expert game, and said he would not touch racket to ball until Hunter was restored to doubles duty. Naturally, the officials capitulated, and naturally Tilden and Hunter won. Borotra and Brugnon carried them to five sets, however, and with the nervous energy already expended on the hassle over the pairing, Tilden was not in top form the next day. René Lacoste played the same kind of tenacious tennis now and prevailed in four sets.

Frustrated and dejected by the loss and the impending loss of the Cup—for Johnston could not be expected to defeat Cochet (and didn't)—Tilden nevertheless found himself the crowd's darling. It was his crowd—the Germantown Cricket Club in Philadelphia, where he had started playing—but he had become as inured to applause as to hostility, and he was nonplussed by the warmth of the ovation. Finally, almost in embarrassment, he raised his hands over his head, like a boxer.

It was a moment to remember. For as the years wore on, the magic faded and difficult times began. He endured a hand-to-mouth existence in Hollywood, playing with the stars on sufferance, making hardly enough from pro prizes and lessons to keep going. His homosexuality eventually became humiliatingly public with a trial and conviction for acts with a minor, and after that there was a technical violation of parole.

He never found his way back. Most of the tennis world pretended he did not exist. He was not helped and he was punished beyond his deserts. Yet by the overwhelming force of his example, William Tatem Tilden II changed the game of tennis. He gave it form, style, and—yes—masculine vitality; he was its avatar. If there are no memorials to him anywhere today, he will have to be satisfied with the game itself as his guerdon. More than any other man he made it what it is, and he could still play it brilliantly today.

6 Man o' War

"This is Man o' War! He's the mostest hoss that ever was!"
—Will Harbut, one of history's most famous grooms

Man o' War was the most famous American race horse of all time. Like the two-legged heroes of the time, Man o' War had beauty, charm, uniqueness, and a nickname. He

No horse had ever quite captured the fancy of the American public as did Man o' War, bred by August Belmont I, for whom Belmont Park was named. The storied horse is shown as a two-year-old at Belmont Park in this 1919 painting by F. B. Voss.

was Big Red and he fit with all the other semi-mythological creatures—the Sultan of Swat, the Manassa Mauler, Big Bill, the Galloping Ghost. His ancestry could be traced all the way back to Matchem, the great English stud in whose veins flowed the blood of both the Byerly Turk and the Godolphin Arabian, the founders of the thoroughbred line. He had eye appeal. He was a glistening chestnut red, a thousand pounds of bone and muscle. Man o' War was a picture-book racer. Man o' War was commercial and he was theatrical. He was exactly what racing needed to become a popular sport.

Americans knew racing only as a society sport, obfuscated by technical argot and stigmatized by religious fundamentalists as gambling at its seamiest. In the decades since the large crowds had swarmed to Long Island to watch the fabulous intersectional match races, the sport had drifted into a curious social limbo. But Man o' War, the first American thoroughbred to be compared with the English champions, was to set eight records and stir the public as no horse ever had.

Man o' War was foaled at the Sanford Stakes in Kentucky and sold to Samuel D. Riddle, who went to upstate New York to attend a race meeting at Saratoga and came away with a genuine immortal.

Man o' War won twenty of twenty-one races, campaigning only in 1919 and 1920 as a two- and three-year-old colt. He broke with a perceptible leap and simply drew away until the opposition wallowed in the thin curtain of his dust. The only jockey who ever beat him knew the fear of being in front of him. "I heard something right behind me and I knew it was Big Red coming at me," said Willie Knapp, who rode a horse called—of all incredible things—Upset to victory over Man o' War on August 13, 1919. The wonder horse of the generation was beaten because an inexperienced starter named C. H. Pettingill was at the tape and Man o' War was left at the post. It was the seventh race of Man o' War's career and he would not lose again.

"We'd passed the quarter pole and were going to the eighth pole, I guess it was," said Knapp. "I looked back and there was Loftus riding like a crazy man and yelling, 'Move out, Willie! I'm coming through!' So I yelled back at him, 'Take off! Take off me, you bum, or I'll put you through the rail.' Then I set down to riding and we beat him."

Several years later, Knapp was sharing a few drinks with a young reporter and made what he considered to be an obvious joke—that if he had known what a significant horse Man o' War was going to be, he would have pulled up and let him through. The story made the pages of the New York Sun and the jockey spent the rest of his racing career trying to refute it.

Despite the one defeat, Man o' War's record was impressive. He started eleven races as a three-year-old and won them all, setting American records in two of them. In three races he carried more than 130 pounds. When his burden reached 138 pounds, Riddle retired him. Man o' War was still only three years old. Because of his retirement no one ever would know for sure if he was the greatest of all American race horses.

He beat only one older horse, Sir Barton, in the last race of his career, the Kenilworth Gold Cup in Canada. But he easily outdistanced some of the best horses in his age group, whipping Hoodwink by one-hundred lengths, Donnaconna by twenty, and Damask by fifteen. In the Dwyer Stakes at New York's Aqueduct Raceway, he ran the juices right out of a chestnut colt named John P. Grier, who would have been the champion in any other year. John P. Grier was leading by a head at the three-sixteenth pole, but at the end of the race Man o' War put on an extra burst of speed and his opponent simply flattened out, acknowledging, as horses often do, that he had been beaten.

His owner retired him to Faraway Farms in Lexington, Kentucky, where he became not only one of the greatest sires in the history of the sport, but a notable tourist attraction. His birthday party was usually attended by the governor.

As time went on, Man o' War's groom, the gentle and eloquent Will Harbut, became almost as big a celebrity as his equine friend. More than one million people listened as the old groom introduced Man o' War with a colorful, carefully constructed narrative, which expanded with the years.

On one afternoon, Joe Palmer, the racing columnist for the *New York Tribune,* was escorting Britain's Lord Halifax through the Bluegrass Country. The tour ended at Man o' War's stall. Will Harbut had no idea who the visiting Englishman was, nor would he have been particularly impressed if he had. He had once shut the gates on the wife of a United States cabinet officer because it was Man o' War's feeding time. But since Halifax obviously loved horses, the old groom gave him the full treatment. The ambassador from London was mesmerized. The talk lasted nearly half an hour and Lord Halifax, according to Palmer, never took his eyes off the groom, who was extolling the glories of Man o' War and of his sons and daughters. Palmer compared the oration to Tennyson's comments on the passing of King Arthur.

Harbut soared to that poetic tag line that made him famous: "He broke all the records and he broke down all the other horses, so there wasn't nothing for him to do but retire. He's got everything a horse ought to have and he's got it in Kentucky where a horse ought to have it. He's just the *mostest* horse there ever was! Stand still, Red, let the man take a look at you."

There had been some apprehension that Harbut's studied dialect might not be understood. At the conclusion, Lord Halifax said, "Mister Harbut, that was most remarkable. It was truly worth coming halfway around the world to hear. My deepest thanks."

People said that Man o' War and Will Harbut could not live without each other, and they were right. The same year that Big Red died, at the age of thirty, his dearest friend and constant companion had a stroke. Presumably, said Palmer, they ascended into heaven together, old Will leading Big Red by the halter.

7   Tarzan in the Water

The name evokes the image not of a powerful swimmer churning through the water like a human torpedo but of a half-naked man swinging through a jungle, yodeling in a fashion designed to break up a lawn party. Yet in the gilded years of sporting heroes Johnny Weissmuller was not a monosyllabic actor with a chimpanzee for a co-worker but the most powerful and versatile swimmer the country had ever produced. He won five gold medals in two successive Olympic festivals, three in 1924 and two in 1928. He won sixty-seven world championships and fifty-two national titles. He overwhelmed the sport. Only then did he trade his swim trunks for a loincloth, and the rigors of competitive swimming for the luxury of Hollywood stardom.

Weissmuller was the son of a saloon owner on Chicago's South Side who had a tendency to drink up his profits and indulge his friends in free booze. He would stagger home in the middle of the night, scream at his wife, and beat his two sons. The legend is that Johnny Weissmuller learned to swim when he was eight years old after his father flew into a drunken rage and threw him out of the house. It was an exceptionally warm night and the child wandered to Fullerton Beach on the shores of Lake Michigan. He was playing on some rocks when he slipped into deep water. His head disappeared for more than a minute; when it reappeared, he was swimming with a natural crawl stroke.

The elder Weissmuller died when Johnny started high school. In order to help his mother and brother, the boy dropped out of school and got a job as an elevator operator and bellhop at the Chicago Plaza Hotel. With little hope of bettering himself, he was scared and depressed. Then he met an old grammar school friend who was swimming for the Illinois Athletic Club under Bill Bachrach. The friend introduced Weissmuller to Bachrach, who added Weissmuller to his training program.

The first air race was held in Rheims, France, in 1909 and was won by American air pioneer Glenn Curtis. The sport reached its zenith in the thirties in the Cleveland National Air Races. A frequent winner was the dashing Roscoe Turner, shown here receiving the Charles E. Thompson trophy after winning the race in 1939 at a speed of 282.516 miles per hour over the 300-mile course. Turner won the race three times, in 1934, 1938, and 1939.

Bachrach was an obese man, at 350 pounds certainly more an imposing than an inspiring physical presence. Like most successful coaches, he was a tyrant. "You need to go on a real training program," he told Weissmuller with no trace of self-consciousness. "You change your stroke and do everything I tell you, to the letter. You will not question me and you will not give me any excuses. Everything you think you know about swimming is wrong. . . ."

The hours of training dragged without mercy. On numerous occasions Weissmuller told his coach he was quitting but Bachrach ignored him. Dutifully, Weissmuller showed up every day and learned to stifle his complaints as he learned to swim. Finally, one evening when the swimmer poked his head out of the water he saw his coach grinning faintly.

"You are going to be a world champion," Bachrach told him.

"How soon?" Weissmuller asked.

"When I tell you," Bachrach said, the grin disappearing.

After Weissmuller won the 100-yard freestyle title in the 1921 Central States AAU championships, defeating Abe Seigel, the defending champion, Bachrach pulled his disciple out of competition. He had bet a wealthy swimming fanatic from Des Moines, Iowa, that an unknown kid from Chicago could break any record from fifty yards to a half mile. "Pick your distance, bring your own stopwatch, and I'll provide the listed records, which you can verify by calling the sports department of the *Chicago Tribune,*" said Bachrach. The wagerers picked the 50-yard race and Weissmuller swam the distance in 23 seconds, a fifth of a second less than the existing record. Soon afterward, at the AAU nationals, Weissmuller swam the same distance in 23.2. He could have gone faster, he said, had his hair not gotten in his eyes. Before the year ended, he had broken the record for the 150-yard freestyle with a 1:27.4 clocking at Brighton Beach in New York.

It was then that Bachrach discovered Weissmuller's main distraction, girls. The new champion fell in love with a beach bunny named Lorelei Murphy. "I'm trying to make you famous and all you want to do is chase girls," complained the coach. "You're coming with me to Honolulu and you're going to swim your fanny off against Duke Kahanamoku. . . . You know who the Duke is, don't you?" And so Lorelei Murphy was left on the beach as Weissmuller went off to confront the premier swimmer of the day.

In Honolulu there were plenty of enticing females, but Bachrach kept his man swimming. One morning Kahanamoku wandered over to the edge of the pool as Johnny splashed flawlessly through a 100-yard workout. Kahanamoku looked at his watch and shook his head in disbelief. He slammed his watch against his palm and shook his head again. "Damn thing must be broken," said the Duke. "It stopped at fifty-two and two-fifth seconds." Bachrach offered his timepiece, which showed the same result. Shortly thereafter, Kahanamoku left Hawaii without swimming against Weissmuller, and he did not return until the young dynamo had gone. Despite a series of romantic adventures and lesser competition than Kahanamoku would have provided, Weissmuller set thirteen world records in five days. His reputation both as a swimmer and a lover would provoke Westbrook Pegler to write, "The man proves conclusively that it is possible to be a great champion in two sports."

Weissmuller was twenty when he jumped into the water for the finals of the 100-meter freestyle race at the 1924 Olympics in Paris. He faced Borg of Sweden, Katsuo of Japan, and the two Hawaiian brothers, Duke and Sam Kahanamoku, the stiffest competition of his career.

At the gun they went off like five torpedoes. Weissmuller surged ahead of the Kahanamoku brothers and left the others struggling behind. Weissmuller was home in fifty-nine seconds flat, a world record. Duke was second, Sam third. The three top finishers threw their arms around one another in a memorable pose. Then Weissmuller set world records in the 400-meter freestyle and in the 800-meter relay. Four years later in Amsterdam, he gave a repeat performance. From his first Olympic event through the following decade he never lost a race.

On one of a number of tours he took after the 1928 games, Weissmuller found himself in Los Angeles at a cocktail party hosted by Douglas Fairbanks, Sr. The actor enjoyed boasting that all the best athletes were his close friends and Weissmuller enjoyed the attention. The next day the impressionable young swimmer was Fairbanks's guest on the sound stage at the filming of "The Black Prince." At lunchtime he and Fairbanks sat with producer Sol Lesser.

"How would you like to be the first talking Tarzan?" Lesser asked Fairbanks. "It's going to be a smash hit for somebody."

"What about this man right here?" Fairbanks suggested. "I'm just not the Tarzan type. This lad has a great name as a swimmer and he looks like Tarzan should."

"Naw," said Lesser. "He's a fine-looking kid, but not what you'd be in the part."

A couple years later, Weissmuller married a dancer, Bobbi Ernst, and, his competitive career at a close, started to think of ways he could keep swimming and still earn a living. Only a day later Bachrach turned up the answer. He handed Weissmuller a contract and ordered him to sign it. Having learned by now to trust his coach's orders, Weissmuller did as he was told and asked questions afterward.

"What did I sign?" he wanted to know.

"You are a professional swimmer now," Bachrach said. "The makers of BVD swimsuits will pay you five hundred dollars a week to promote their products. You're married and you need some income. Now that you're a pro, I can't handle you anymore. You've done everything an amateur can do anyway. Trust me again, okay?"

As a "goodwill ambassador" for BVD Weissmuller returned to Hollywood, where the company set up a shop on Sunset Boulevard at the Athletic Club. Cyril Hume, a prominent screen writer who had been assigned to do the first script for Edgar Rice Burroughs's *Tarzan of the Apes* watched Johnny and Bobbi playfully racing in the pool one day and asked Weissmuller to test for the lead in the film. He won the job over more than one hundred applicants and signed for a guarantee of no less than $500 a week for seven years.

Success was a mixed blessing. He lived the lavish, turbulent life of a movie star, and some four marriages and nineteen Tarzan movies after his arrival in Hollywood, it was difficult to remember the athlete who gave rise to the movie idol. The tinsel of Hollywood immortalized his name, but it diluted the memory of the marvelous swimmer. Here was a hero for whom the glitter obscured the gold.

8 Merriwell in Knickers

Before Bobby Jones, the amateur golfer in America was considered an affluent fop who could not sign his full legal name without two hyphens and an apostrophe. He was the sort of fellow who if dissatisfied with his play would sooner buy the course and redesign it than overhaul his game. Jones was different. He was undeniably a Georgia gentleman, but there was a winning gallantry about him. This Frank Merriwell on a meadow adhered scrupulously to the rules and he won. He was young, forthright, remarkably good looking, and personally charming. As he became the nation's finest golfer, he shined as its foremost sportsman.

Once, paired with an aging Harry Vardon in the Open, Jones skulled a chip shot across the green into a bunker. "Did you ever see a worse shot than that, Mr. Vardon?" he asked. "Good god, no!" Vardon shot back. Jones liked that story.

During the first round of the 1925 Open, he called a penalty stroke on himself for accidentally advancing his ball a quarter of an inch. No one was looking, and it

would have been easy to ignore it. But he did not, and his integrity cost him. He finished in a tie with Willie MacFarlane and lost the playoff.

Yet such honesty could never be confused with innocence. This Golden Boy was never the patsy. In one tournament final he was talking to his nearest competitor just before the order came to tee up. They chatted amiably. Then the other man employed an insipid piece of gamesmanship. "Hey, Bobby," he said. "Let's just have a nice friendly game of golf. I really don't care who wins this thing. Let's just enjoy ourselves."

Jones bridled at such hypocrisy. He knew his opponent to be as intent on winning as any contender should be. To pretend otherwise, to misjudge Bobby Jones's manners for ingenuousness, was an insult. Jones drilled the fellow off the course in the final round.

As a golfer, Jones was fluid, graceful, and consistent. As a sportsman he was confident and decent. It made for an irresistible combination. Paul Gallico wrote of him, "I have found only one sports figure who could stand up in every way as a gentleman as well as a celebrity, a fine, decent human being as well as a newsprint personage, and one who never once since I have known him has let me down in my estimate of him."

To those who remembered him as a child, it seemed something of a miracle that this man could have become the paragon of an athlete. He was a stunted youngster, with a head too large for his frail body. He had a digestive ailment that doctors believed would kill him before he reached maturity. Yet this sickly child grew up to win thirteen national championships—five United States Amateur titles, four United States Open titles, three British Open titles, and one British Amateur title. In the last nine years of his career he competed in twelve open tournaments and finished first or second in eleven of them. The *pièce de resistance,* of course, was his Grand Slam in 1930, a sports masterpiece that even an America plunging into financial ruin could not help but celebrate. In retirement he helped to transform a botanical garden in

Augusta, Georgia, into the most celebrated golf course in the nation, and he founded a tournament with only one name that would do it justice—the Masters. In short, he gave golf a stature in the country that it had never had before; he made it a major sport.

And yet, he never played the game for money. "I once asked him why he didn't turn professional," said Walter Hagen, the biggest name in the field before Jones. "He asked why I *had.* I couldn't give him a real answer. The truth is that none of us could make much money until he started winning tournaments. A first-place finish used to be worth a thousand dollars until he came along. He never won a cent in prize money, but when he left, prizes were up around five thousand dollars. That's the effect Bobby Jones had on golf.

"Now, I had no financial problems because I made thirty thousand dollars a year—big, big money then —representing a country club in Florida. "What Bobby did was bring huge galleries out to watch tournaments. He created the golf craze in America. He had everything that made people happy. His swing was graceful. He was phenomenally accurate with his putter. They admired him as much for his modesty as they ever would admire me for my brashness. Bobby brought those galleries onto the courses and they never left. They called him the Emperor Jones. Now, I'm not a modest man, but what he did was to give thousands of professionals who followed me a chance to do their stuff in front of an audience."

Like many a sports hero, he was the son of a frustrated athlete. His father was good enough when he graduated from the University of Georgia to sign a contract with the Brooklyn baseball club, but on his way to training camp, *his* father, Bobby's grandfather, stopped him at the station and informed him that his career would be law. Sport was pure nonsense, the would-be ball player was told, not a fit occupation for Georgia's upper middle class white citizens. It was to compensate for the loss of his athletic career that Bobby's father turned to golf.

In the summer of 1908, when Bobby was almost six

and just strong enough to lead doctors to believe he might survive, his parents rented quarters next to the East Lake golf course near Atlanta. Bobby could look out his window and see men and women whacking balls across the bright green fairway.

According to Grantland Rice, the gospel writer of the Golden Era, it was on a humid morning in July, 1909, when Stewart Maiden noticed Bobby Jones for the first time. The Scot was giving lessons to a group of women when he noticed the youth with the large head and thin body punching away with a badly nicked old cleek. Rice insisted that the conversation went like this:

"Who are ye, wee one?"

"I'm Bobby Jones, son of Colonel Bobby Jones who comes out here every summer. You know that the Colonel is quite good."

Soon after he met Maiden, Jones won a six-hole tournament for boys under ten at East Lake. He was presented with a three-inch-high cup, which he would later display in his library right in the middle of his expensive international trophies.

He won a junior tournament in Atlanta at the age of nine and, competing against adults just three years later, ran off three Georgia club championships in a row. The next season he produced three more victories and went on to the Georgia state championship.

Although Bobby Jones was barely a high school kid, the newspapers treated him like a national figure. In the summer of 1916 the fourteen-year-old boy golfer who stood just five feet four inches attracted more attention than the invasion of Belgium. At the Merion Cricket Club in Philadelphia, Bobby led the first qualifying round of the National Amateur with a score of 74, which was considered brilliant in an age when golfers used hickory-shafted clubs. Unfortunately, like many prodigies, Jones had a more quickly maturing game than personality. After winning a first-round match from Eben Byers, a former champion, and his next contest from Frank Dyer, one of the favorites in the field, Jones met frustration he couldn't cope with in his match against Bob Gardner, a former Yale pole vaulter who was the defending American champion. The two contestants presented a striking contrast—Gardner tall, handsome and gracious, Jones a small, unpolished schoolboy. Gardner treated Jones like a mature athlete, but the boy was not as good to himself. In his autobiography, *Golf Is My Game,* Jones wrote later:

I was one down as we stood on the sixth tee [in the afternoon round]. On the next three holes, he destroyed me with a series of the most amazing recovery shots my still young eyes had ever seen. I reverted to immaturity. I felt that I had been badly treated by luck. I had been denied something that was rightly mine. I didn't half try to hit the next tee shot, and I didn't half try on any shot thereafter. In short, I quit.

He did not outgrow adolescence quickly or easily.

On a summer afternoon in 1923, a deeply depressed Robert Tyre Jones slumped in a creaking wicker chair in the clubhouse at Inwood Country Club on Long Island, absolutely convinced that he would never win a major title and that it might not be a bad idea to go home to Georgia and forget about golf. He had completed his final round in the United States Open with a bogey, bogey, double bogey, squandering a three-stroke lead and leaving him in a tie with Bobby Cruickshank. His head hung low and he clenched and unclenched his fists, attempting without success to keep his temper. "I'm no champion," he told Oscar Bane Keeler, the *Atlanta Constitution* editor. "Anybody who finished like I did can't hope to be a champion. I'm a dirty yellow dog. That's what I am. What's more I'm a gutless failure and I always will be."

"Robert!" said Keeler, who normally used the diminutive to address his young friend. "You are a dirty yellow dog only if you think you are." Perhaps that was a turning point. Within twenty-four hours Jones had recovered from his sloppy finish in the final round and beaten Cruickshank by two strokes in an eighteen-hole playoff.

It was the first of his fourteen major championships.

In the spring of 1930, he told friends that he was playing golf as well as it could be played. It was not a boast, simply an honest assessment. Who knew better than the nation's leading expert on golf? "I was brimming with confidence," he wrote. "I had turned twenty-eight that spring and considered myself at my physical prime. I do not say that I expected a Grand Slam, but I knew if it would ever happen to me this was the year I would do it."

Jones gained all the confidence he needed when he survived some difficult opponents in the early rounds and then defeated Roger Wethered, 7 and 6, in the final round of the British Amateur at St. Andrews, the Scottish golf course. It may have been the most important tournament of his life. In all he played seven matches, some of which he came perilously close to losing. Two nights before the end of the tournament he was so nervous that he had a couple of glasses of sherry to calm himself. He was a bit tipsy as he walked to the first hole for his semifinal match.

"My eyes were the slightest bit out of focus," he said. "I really began to get panicky. . . . I could not get that sherry out of my eyes until more than half the round had been played. . . . I kept missing putts all over the place and finally even fluffed a short pitch at the thirteenth hole. . . . I found myself two down with five to play."

Somehow, Jones won that semifinal match in eighteen holes, and in thirty holes took the championship the next day.

After the tournament, Bob and Mary Jones flew off to Paris for a week of rest before he assaulted the British Open. "I'm looking forward to the Open," said Jones, "but conquering St. Andrews was the biggest thrill of my life."

When he returned to England, he discovered that he had become a national hero. Crowds trailed after him on the fairways and clustered around him in the tees and greens. Business people kept knocking, ever so pleasantly on his hotel door, begging him to say that everybody he knew in America loved a particular kind of chocolate bar or could not wait for Repeal in order to consume a certain gin. Jones insisted that having just begun to practice law, he meant to make it his life's work and had no intention of making money from his golfing exploits.

At Hoylake, in the British Open, Jones started brilliantly with rounds of 70 and 72 and then wandered off, shooting 74 and 75, a total of 291. He was sitting very still in the clubhouse at sunset as Leo Diegel and MacDonald Smith made runs at him and failed. As he left the clubhouse, more than twenty-five thousand Englishmen stood outside and applauded. He sailed home and discovered that America was equally enthusiastic over him, even while the stock market had crashed and unemployment had leaped to thirty per cent. Half way to the Grand Slam, he commanded the attention of the sports world.

The afternoon was exceedingly hot when Jones stepped out of the clubhouse at the Interlaken Country Club in Minneapolis to begin his pursuit of the United States Open title. The temperature was 103 degrees and rising. Several players would be overcome by the heat, including Cyril Tolley, one of Jones's closest British friends and a man who had faced him with great valor in the British Amateur.

Jones began the round wearing light gray plus fours, a shirt with a collar, and a red foulard four-in-hand tie. A dozen red-dyed tees were in one pocket of his trousers. When he finished the round, his plus fours were black with perspiration and red-streaked down one side. Fortunately, Keeler was present to cut away the expensive tie with a pocket knife.

In the second round, Jones made one of the game's most storied shots. He topped a fairway wood and the ball moved toward a rather impressive water hazard. Spectators insisted that the ball escaped it by bouncing off a lily pad, and it hopped up just short of the green. Jones shot a 73 on the second round, remaining in contention, two shots behind Horton Smith.

In the third round the heat diminished and Jones shot a

Robert Tyre Jones, Jr., was the world's greatest golfer in the Golden Age. From 1923 to 1930 he won five United States Amateur titles, four U.S. Opens, three British Opens, and one British Amateur. In 1930 he achieved the only grand slam in golf history by winning the four major championships. Two months later, at age twenty-eight, he retired from competitive golf. Below, he is shown winning the 1927 British Open Golf Championship.

173

68, moving five strokes in front of the field. On the last day, he dropped a 42-foot putt on the seventy-second hole for a 75 and a two-stroke victory at 285.

The final conquest in Jones's Grand Slam was in the United States Amateur at Merion, a course he had clearly mastered. Jones was at the top of his form now, and nobody could approach him. He defeated Ross Somerville and Fred Hoblitzel by five and four margins the first day. Next he posted a six and five decision over Fay Coleman and a ten and nine over Jess Sweetser.

There were at least thirty thousand people on the course, the largest gallery in American golfing history for the clinching round. Jones disposed of Gene Homans, eight and seven, and the fans swarmed in worship around their hero.

"I felt the wonderful feeling of release from tension and relaxation that I had wanted so badly for so long a time," Jones wrote. "I wasn't quite certain what had happened or what I had done. I only knew that I had completed a period of most strenuous effort and that at this point, nothing more remained to be done, and that on this particular project, at least, there could never at any time in the future be anything else to do."

Two months after the Grand Slam, Bobby Jones retired, having no more worlds to conquer. The world's four great tournaments would change with the times. Jones himself would give birth to one of the new prestige events. It was originally called the Augusta National Invitational Tournament. Later, his friends, Grantland Rice, O. B. Keeler, and Clifford Roberts called it the Masters. It was Bobby Jones's epitaph.

9   Fixture at First

Watching Lou Gehrig it was easy to believe he was the only first baseman the Yankees would ever need. Year in, year out, anytime the Yanks were scheduled, he played. Every game, almost every inning. Eventually he achieved a total of 2,130 consecutive games —thirteen entire seasons, plus pieces of 1925 and 1939, and, for good measure, thirty-four World Series games and an indeterminate number of exhibitions. The sporting press unimaginatively but unarguably labeled him the Iron Man or the Iron Horse, and, indeed, he seemed permanent, indestructible.

Actually, many players have had longer careers and played in hundreds more games than the Iron Horse, but all of them, even the most Spartan, sat down occasionally. They were hobbled by injuries, immobilized by ills, aches, or pains. Or they fell into slumps, were replaced by a sub, or skipped the second game of a doubleheader in August. Gehrig played on.

His consecutive-game streak was impressive as an athletic performance, but more than that it bespoke character. Only a dedicated man could have established such an unreachable, unbreakable record—only a consistent man, a faithful man. This is not sentimentality. You could talk that way about Gehrig. For the fans who rooted him on, his record was a shared experience. Lou was the guy who showed up for work every day, pulled his weight, took his lumps, never complained, and somehow managed to perform at the top of his bent. He was the plugger glorified. Everyone understood what such effort cost, and in the Depression days that were most of Gehrig's career, everyone respected it.

He was built for the task. In an era of somewhat smaller athletes, Gehrig's six-foot, 200-pound frame loomed large. He had big shoulders, a broad back, and powerful thighs. The Yankee pin stripes curved and bent around the bulk of him like contour lines on a map. And when all this power was concentrated on the swinging of a bat, the bludgeoned ball flew on a line to the far reaches of the Stadium, screaming with pain.

Gehrig and Ruth were an interesting pair to watch. The Babe batted third, behind Earle Combs and Mark Koenig in the old days. He was a strong man, but built like a top.

In the spring of 1923, a Yankees' scout watched a baseball game between Columbia University and Rutgers. Columbia's first baseman, a powerful young man named Lou Gehrig, hit three towering home runs. In June, Gehrig was wearing Yankees' pinstripes and playing alongside his idol, Babe Ruth. In his first full season Gehrig hit .295. In the next twelve years he would never hit below .300. His most lasting claim to fame—playing in 2,130 consecutive games—earned him the nickname of the "Iron Horse."

All his weight was in the barrel chest and robust belly. Below the waist he tapered sharply. He stood at the plate with feet and ankles touching, the torso bent slightly forward, the head cocked as though looking around a corner to see what the pitcher was up to. When he swung and missed it was almost as entertaining in its explosive futility as when he connected. The great bat flailed, the body twisted, the legs corkscrewed. He would end up so skewed around that he almost faced the catcher.

Gehrig followed. He planted himself solidly on those oaken legs, his stance open, his bat held high and motionless. He too could topple himself with a mighty miss, but generally he was well balanced, not easily fooled by a pitch, and not often struck out. Some pitchers are said to have argued that it was the better part of wisdom to walk Ruth and take your chances with Gehrig. This would appear to be the hopeless answer to an agonizing choice. However much of a terror the Babe may have been, Lou was one of the great power hitters of all time. He is among the top five for lifetime extra-base hits (1,190), runs batted in (1,990), and slugging percentage (.632), and among the top ten for total bases (5,059). He averaged a remarkable .92 runs batted in per game, a figure equaled (by Hank Greenberg and a turn-of-the-century player, Sam Thompson), but never exceeded.

None of it came easy. Lou worked hard all his life, first to escape the poverty of his youth, then to mature his skills as a ball player, and finally to overcome the fears and uncertainties that plagued him.

He was the only surviving child of German-immigrant parents who settled in New York City and made a meager living from a succession of menial jobs. Much was made of the boy, and much expected of him. He grew up big and strong, awkward, left-handed, and painfully unsure of himself socially.

He enrolled at Columbia University, principally because his parents were janitors there, but did not graduate. As he later said, in one of his few attempts at a joke, he got his only BA playing for the Yankees. He was a foot-

ball tackle and running back, a baseball pitcher and first baseman. And a long-ball hitter. Andy Coakley, the Columbia coach, who won twenty games for Connie Mack's 1905 Athletics, told Paul Kirchell, the discerning Yankees' scout, that his clumsy *bube* was a potential big leaguer. Krichell saw Lou pound a ball halfway across the campus and signed him for the Yankees with a $1,500 bonus.

"Columbia Lou," they called him, not because he reminded anyone of a sophisticated collegian but because almost any academic affiliation was noteworthy among the still largely unschooled professional ball players of 1923. Moe Berg, the erudite, nonhitting catcher from Princeton, ebullient Frankie Frisch, the Fordham Flash, and Theodore Amar Lyons, the superb right-hander who leaped directly from the Baylor campus into twenty-one years of servitude with the White Sox, were among the few college-educated big leaguers around. Most ball players and, indeed, most Americans went to work early (their college, they said, was Hard Knocks), or attended obscure academic groves such as Casey Stengel's Kankakee dental school.

Lou spent most of his first two years in Hartford, learning to handle the glove, to survive batting slumps, and to overcome the fits of loneliness, homesickness, and despair that assailed him. In 1925, however, Miller Huggins, the wizened little manager, decided he was seasoned enough to play in New York.

This was not a distinguished year for the Yankees. After three straight Series against their New York rivals, John McGraw's Giants, they had lost the 1924 pennant to Washington, the first ever for the fabulous, but now declining, Walter Johnson. The spring of 1925 was disrupted by Babe Ruth's monumental bellyache and then by his childish rebellions against Huggins's authority. Finally arriving late one day for a game, he was suspended by the Little Miller and fined a spectacular $5,000.

Ruth eventually repented and reformed, but by then it was clear that the real trouble lay elsewhere. The team simply was wearing out. Outfielder Whitey Witt, shortstop Everett Scott, catcher Wally Schang, pitcher Joe Bush were at the end of the line. Disintegrating over the course of the season, the club finished a poor seventh, 28½ games out.

One change in the lineup—almost unnoticed at the time—was made on June 2. Wally Pipp, a smooth fielder and a respectable .281 hitter who had been playing first base for the Yanks since 1915, was seized by the most famous headache in baseball history. He was told to pop some aspirin and take the day off. "Columbia Lou" could play first. (Actually, this was the second game of his streak. He had pinch-hit for shortstop Peewee Wanninger the day before.)

Pipp, of course, never got his job back. He was banished to Cincinnati the following year, while Gehrig became a Yankee fixture.

In 1927, Ruth and Gehrig were the mightiest one-two punch baseball had ever seen. The Babe blasted his incredible sixty home runs in 154 games, and Lou plodded along behind with forty-seven. He also hit .373 and led the league with 175 runs batted in, an extraordinary performance considering how many times Ruth must have cleared the bases ahead of him.

This was very much the pattern. Lou was fated always to be in the Babe's shadow. Not that his achievements were inconsiderable—only that the Babe was Ruthian in all his dimensions. In the early days, Ruth and Gehrig occasionally barnstormed through the sun belt, playing postseason exhibitions with the Bustin' Babes and Larrupin' Lous. Ruth loved the hoopla: crowds, adulation, kids, clowning, cowboy hats, big cars. It was all part of his gargantuan life style. And Lou? Well, Lou hung back, hit his homers, and grinned his pleasant dimpled grin.

Eventually there was coolness between them. Babe couldn't help being Babe, but his spontaneity, his expansiveness, his magnetism, his big appetites—all the easy, natural things about him—were a trial to Lou. Gehrig worried. Through all the years of his greatness he was never free of the fear that, one day, overnight, his baseball skills might vanish. He didn't want to be like Babe, and he couldn't have been if he'd tried, but he must have wished—jealously—for enough of the Babe's insouciance to exorcise his demon.

Lou's career, like that of all ball players, is encoded in numbers. In 1928, a .374 batting average; in 1931, 46 homers, tying Ruth for the league lead; in 1932, four homers in one game and an unheard-of fifth lost through a circus catch by Al Simmons; in 1934, league batting and home-run leader. He was the league leader four times in runs and RBI, had a record 23 homers with the bases loaded, and was the American League's most valuable player four times.

And inexorably, year by year, the consecutive games piled up. Actually, it was not until he was halfway along, seven seasons or so, that anyone realized what was happening. After that everyone began to count. The record was 1,307, set by Deacon Scott, the willowy shortstop whose best years were with the Red Sox and whose final ones were with the Yankees.

Gehrig passed Scott in 1933. Thereafter, the record would be whatever his dedication could make it. He was not immune to illness or injury. Along the way he had his share of colds and sore muscles, but he shook them off, and he never suffered anything severe enough to disable him—at least nothing he talked bout. Later, in the course of X-rays to diagnose the illness that killed him, a number of old finger fractures were discovered. He had played through them, without a murmur, letting them heal "on the job."

Only once did he accept help to keep the streak alive. This was in July, 1934, the day—as the record book shows—he played shortstop. The Yanks were in Detroit, and the day before, while running the bases against the Tigers, Lou had been suddenly seized with a back pain that doubled him over. Unable even to straighten up, he left the field and spent a miserable night trying to get himself in shape.

In the clubhouse next day he was still in agony. Clearly he couldn't play. Then someone had the bright notion of changing the lineup card to let Lou lead off in Frank Crosetti's spot as shortstop. One time at bat would preserve the streak and give him another day to nurse the back.

Shortstop Gehrig singled, struggled to first, and withdrew. The back got better. He was well enough to play the next day, and the next, and a thousand game days after that. As for the strange seizure, well, perhaps that had been lumbago.

Or perhaps not. Possibly it had been the first warning of amyotrophic lateral sclerosis, a progressive, degenerative disease of the nerve cells of the spinal cord. The cells thicken, the muscles begin to atrophy. Once it hits, there is no way to stop it.

The earliest symptom is loss of coordination. Lou first began to falter in 1938. The great skills did, at last, begin to desert him. He finished the season with an uncharacteristically low .295 batting average. By 1939, the trouble had him cruelly in its grip, and eight games into the season, in Detroit, he told Joe McCarthy to take him out. This time no ruse would keep him going. There would be no ninth game, no two thousand one hundred thirty-first. A man named Babe Dahlgren played first base that day.

It is not often that a tragedy ends so publicly, or that there is time to perform the rites of passage. The memorable ceremony at Yankee Stadium in July, after the club came home from its road trip, was a true catharsis. Lou saw himself in perspective and considered himself blessed. There was the hug of reconciliation from the Babe. And there was an outpouring of affection and regard from 62,000 fans, surrogates for millions more who had watched the Iron Man through the years and wished him well.

As long as he could, he worked with the New York City Parole Commission, and he died in 1941, just short of his thirty-eighth birthday.

177

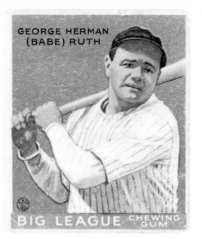
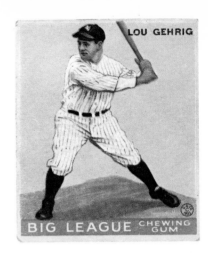

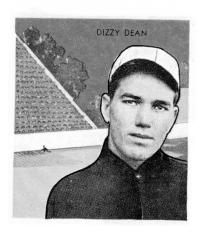

DIZZY DEAN

As escapist entertainment, only the motion picture exceeded baseball in the Great Depression. The game showcased tremendous talent, such as Babe Ruth, Lou Gehrig, and Dizzy Dean. In New York, people stood in line for hours to watch this scene at Yankee Stadium—two men on base, Gehrig at bat, and George Selkirk on deck.

On May 2, 1939, in Detroit, one of baseball's greatest individual records came to an end. After playing in 2,130 consecutive games, Lou Gehrig took himself out of the Yankees' lineup. Later that year, in special ceremonies at Yankee Stadium, 61,808 fans gathered to honor the man who was dying of a rare disease. They chanted, "We love you, Lou." Hesitatingly, Gehrig spoke, "I may have been given a bad break, but I have an awful lot to live for. Today I consider myself the luckiest man on the face of the earth."

10   The Los Angeles Games

Cinema capital of the world, yes, but Los Angeles in the twenties and early thirties was hardly of significance on the American sports scene. It had the Rose Bowl in neighboring Pasadena, true. But the jet age was not yet at hand: flights from one coast to another took twelve to sixteen hours, and those major professional leagues then in existence, in baseball, football, and hockey, gave no thought to establishing franchises on the West Coast. The nearest race track to Los Angeles of any consequence was Agua Caliente, across the border in Mexico; Santa Anita and Hollywood Park had not yet opened. There had been several heavyweight championship prizefights in Los Angeles in 1906 and 1907, but none since.

Thus it is not hard to understand that there existed an enthusiasm, perhaps even a lust, in Los Angeles to host the Olympic Games, a spectacle of international consequence and impact, one befitting a metropolis that boasted, justifiably, of its position as the center of the imaginative, creative world of movie making.

Los Angeles representatives wanted the Olympic Games of 1924, and a delegation journeyed to Antwerp for the Games of 1920 to present their bid to the International Olympic Committee.

That august body did not exactly jump with joy. Since the principal Olympic participants, other than the United States, were European countries, the distance to travel and the enormous expense in getting teams to California militated against the Los Angeles effort. The Olympics had been in the U. S. once before, at St. Louis in 1904, and that had been a sorry experience. Only nine nations made the trip. Britain sent one athlete, France none, Germany seven. There were Americans galore. One historian called the track and field competition a dual meet between the New York A. C. and the Chicago A. A. (The U. S. won twenty-three of the twenty-five track and field events, finishing one-two-three in eighteen. Americans won every medal—gold, silver, and bronze—in wrestling, boxing, archery, cycling, and gymnastics. They lost only one medal, a bronze, in rowing.

It was not surprising, then, that the IOC, in 1921, turned down the Los Angeles invitation and voted to award the 1924 Games to Paris. At that same session, the IOC also decided on the site of the 1928 Olympics: Amsterdam.

Disappointed but not defeated, the California Olympiad Association tried again, and in 1923 the IOC gave the 1932 games to Los Angeles. Almost immediately elaborate preparations began for the staging of what William May Garland, the leader of the California organizers, predicted would be "an achievement of world magnitude and excellence, against which to measure the future in Olympic enterprise." This was no idle Hollywood boast. At election time in November of 1928, Californians voted favorably on an Olympic Bond Act that provided one million dollars in state aid for the Games. The Los Angeles Coliseum, which had opened in 1923, was enlarged to 105,000 seats.

For the first time since the modern Olympic Games began in 1896 there was to be an Olympic Village. When completed, the village consisted of 550 cottages built on 250 acres in a beautiful, hilly area some ten minutes from the stadium, with separate dining facilities and headquarters for each participating nation. F. A. M. Webster, the distinguished British athletics historian, wrote that the Olympic Village "proved to the world that Olympism is an instrument for physical and cultural advancement which is something stronger than the prosaic prejudices of race, creed or colour."

A swimming stadium was constructed to seat 12,000. The rowing course had seats for 17,000. The Olympic Auditorium held 10,000 for boxing and wrestling.

Two other innovations marked the Los Angeles Games. A modern communications system was created to provide results and other pertinent information to the news media. And for the first time in Olympic history, the entire proceedings would be recorded for posterity by camera.

This was a great Hollywood extravaganza. It was planned well, certainly better than any of its predecessors and it served as a model for later Games. Los Angeles was big league then, as now.

Not even the economic depression, which had staggered the world in 1929, stopped the Los Angeles organizers. Quickly they advised the national committees of the various countries that facilities at Olympic Village would cost but two dollars per day per athlete. Reduced transportation rates were arranged, making the trip from Europe possible for $500.

And so they came to California, some fourteen hundred athletes from thirty-nine nations to compete in fourteen major branches of sport.

When the competition began the show quickly belonged to an eighteen-year-old girl described by Paul Gallico as "a hard-bitten, hawk-nosed, thin-mouthed little hoyden from Texas." She was Mildred Ella Didrikson, nicknamed Babe because she could hit a baseball a mile. Babe had already demonstrated to the sports world that she could do most things better than any other woman—better than many men, for that matter. As the years wore on, she earned recognition as the greatest woman athlete of our time.

A year before the Olympics, at the age of seventeen, Babe had led a Texas basketball team to the National AAU championship. That year, too, she was the national champion in the hurdles and the long jump.

Two weeks before the Olympic Games, at the 1932 National AAU women's track and field championships, where the American team would be chosen for Los Angeles, Babe Didrikson won four events—the hurdles, shot put, javelin throw, and baseball throw. She tied for first in a fifth, the high jump, and placed fourth in the discus throw. She scored twenty-five points for the Employers Casualty A.A. of Dallas. The defending champion, the Illinois Women's A.C., with twenty-two athletes, mus-

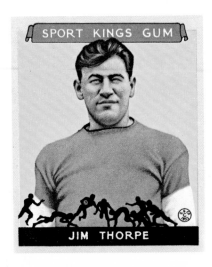

JIM THORPE

WILLIAM T. TILDEN

RED GRANGE

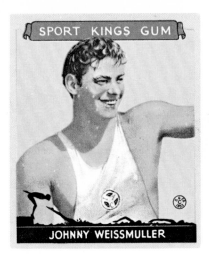

JOHNNY WEISSMULLER

"BABE" DIDRICKSON

CLIFF BATTLES

Promotional art has long made an attractive alliance with sport. Shown here is the official poster for the 1932 Olympics, which were staged in Los Angeles. Tobacco and chewing gum trading cards continued to flourish, proclaiming venerable sports professionals as well as young amateurs. Orange crate labels were an art form in their own right and many featured the glory of athletics and competition as symbols.

The star of the tenth Olympiad, staged at
Memorial Coliseum in Los Angeles,
was a young woman named Babe
Didrikson. A slim, muscular, long-legged
Texan, Didrikson took three medals,
winning the javelin throw with a world
record effort, the eighty-meter hurdles
in an Olympic record, and finishing
second in the high jump. Later she would
make her most significant impact in
the game of golf.

tered twenty-four points, and so this one-woman team
from Texas captured the U. S. championship on her own.

There were five individual events for women on the
1932 Olympic track and field program and Babe Didrikson wanted to compete in all. The U. S. Olympic authorities said no, three only, and that decision represented
her first source of discontent at Los Angeles.

The second irritant came in the opening ceremony. The
official uniform for American women in the parade of
athletes included white stockings. Babe had never worn
stockings of any hue, and she didn't like them. She shed
them after the parade and got down to the business at
hand. Her three events were the hurdles, the javelin, and
the high jump.

When records are broken in short distance races such
as the sprints or hurdles, usually they are lowered by a
tenth of a second, on rare occasions by a fifth. Miss Didrikson won the hurdles in time that was a half-second better
than the world record. She brought the mark down from
12.2 seconds to 11.7.

The listed world record for the javelin was 132 feet
⅞ inches, although Germany's Ellen Braunmiller, the
favorite to triumph in Los Angeles, had a pending mark
of 146-5. The young lady from Port Arthur, Texas, out-
threw the German girl by seven inches, with a toss of
143-4, 11 feet better than the listed mark. Babe claimed
she had never thrown the javelin until the U. S. championships weeks earlier.

Finally, there was the high jump, and this brought frustration to the Babe. Six contenders remained in the competition, three of them Americans, when the bar was
raised to 5 feet 3 inches (the world record was 5-3⅛).
Three were successful, Jean Shiley, who had tied for the
U. S. title with Miss Didrikson weeks earlier; Eva Dawes,
a Canadian; and Babe. Now, they were at a record height
of 5-5. Miss Shiley cleared. Miss Didrikson cleared. The
Canadian girl failed. Next, 5-5¼. Miss Shiley cleared.
Miss Didrikson cleared.

Then, in a never-to-be-explained decision, the judges

decided Babe had dived over the bar, head first, a procedure outside the rules at that time but now legitimate. They disallowed Babe's 5-5¼, declared Miss Shiley the champion, and put Miss Didrikson second at 5-5. Never clarified was why all Babe's earlier jumps—all "dives" —were tolerated. It was eleven years before the women's world record was raised to as high as 5-7¼. Some onlookers in Los Angeles believe Babe would have attained that height that day had she been permitted to continue.

Babe became the darling of the press, including the giants of the trade at that time—Gallico, Grantland Rice, Westbrook Pegler, and others. She had never played golf but Rice was convinced she could murder the ball. They lured her to a course one morning while the Olympics were still in progress and Rice was a prophet with honor: she murdered the ball. How good she was is now an American legend. Suffice to say that in the annual Associated Press poll for woman athlete of the year, Babe Didrikson was chosen for track and field in 1932 and for golf in 1945, 1946, 1947, 1950, and 1954. And in another AP poll in the early fifties, she was the choice of the nation's experts as woman athlete of the first half of the twentieth century.

But these games were too big an event for any one athlete to dominate, not even as heroic a figure as Babe. Like any Games, these had political incidents, rhubarbs over questionable gamesmanship, controversies of all kinds. The legendary Paavo Nurmi of Finland, the winner of nine gold medals (to this day more than any other individual has won) in the Games of 1920, 1924, and 1928, hoped to cap his career by annexing the marathon championship at Los Angeles. On arrival in Los Angeles, however, the chairman of the Finnish Athletic Union was informed that because of certain irregularities regarding expenses in Europe, the famed distance runner had been declared ineligible. The fans—attendance for the track program averaged sixty thousand per day—had looked forward to seeing Nurmi run. They were not happy about his suspension.

Most memorable of the events on the men's track program was the 5,000-meter run. No American ever had won the Olympic 5,000 but Ralph Hill, an Oregonian, was considered to have a chance against two outstanding Finns, Lauri Lehtinen, the world record holder, and Lauri Virtanen. These three paced the field until, with little more than a lap to go, Virtanen began to fade. Hill dogged Lehtinen's tracks until the home stretch. Then, as they raced down the final straightaway, Hill attempted to pass Lehtinen on the outside. The Finn veered out, preventing his foe from going by, whereupon Hill tried to get past on the inside. But Lehtinen now veered in, and again the American's course was blocked. They went across the finish line almost as one. They were given the same time, but photos confirmed that Lehtinen was slightly ahead, and the Finn was announced as the winner.

The pro-American crowd booed heartlessly, whereupon Bill Henry, the public address announcer, said, "Remember, please, these people are our guests." The boos ceased, giving way to spirited applause. Lehtinen disclaimed any willful intent to impede Hill's progress, apologized, and later sought to pull Hill up to the victor's stand with him when medals were awarded.

In swimming the United States was jolted by the emergence of Japan as the new world power in the sport. Only Buster Crabbe, later of movie fame, prevented a Japanese sweep of the men's events. He won the 400-meter freestyle. American women swimmers were dominant, however, with Helene Madison acquiring three gold medals and Eleanor Holm another.

Throughout the program, records in measured sports fell in profusion and the caliber of the competition in others was superb, to a degree never before experienced in the Olympic Games. Olympic veterans were quick to credit the fine California weather, the excellent training and living arrangements for the athletes, and the splendid facilities.

At the closing ceremonies, the one-thousand-voice

choir sang "Aloha," and the sound of "Taps" from a single bugler ended the most successful and finest Olympic Games yet held, another American triumph.

11   It Began with Papa Bear

George Halas was professional football's first absolute monarch. From the moment he appeared on center stage, he was an autocrat and a perfectionist. He was not a golden hero but he collected golden heroes, and when he was not quite seventy, he would discover that his game was the golden game of a new age.

Not that professional football was George Halas's idea. Years before him Connie Mack had fielded a football team called the Philadelphia Athletics at the end of the baseball season. His star pitcher, Rube Waddell, was one of the players. Christy Mathewson, who played football at Bucknell before becoming a great pitcher for the New York Giants, also played with a couple of pro football teams. Professional squads played throughout the East and Midwest. However, the games were haphazardly scheduled and the players were mostly tramp athletes. Playing football was a low profession at the time, just one jump above hustling pool. It was Halas who had the inspiration to reform this disreputable and disorderly arrangement into a respectable national league. He was the first to understand that professional football could be more than a raunchy roadshow.

The father of modern pro football, "the Papa Bear," as he was to be known, grew up in Chicago's rugged Bohemian neighborhood on 18th Street and Ashland Avenue. His parents were Slavic immigrants from Pilsen, part of what would eventually be Czechoslovakia. His father was a prosperous tailor in downtown Chicago who when he died left his family nicely off because it owned one of the town's first apartment buildings (which had all of thirty tenants). Young George went off to play three sports at the University of Illinois and finally signed a con-

tract with the New York Yankees. He was the starting rightfielder during the opening two weeks of the 1919 season and managed two loud fouls off Walter Johnson in the opener before finally popping up. That was apparently the high point of his major league career. After twelve games he was hitting .091 and fighting a leg injury he had sustained in spring practice. The Yankees shipped him down to the minors but did not, as legend has it, replace him with Babe Ruth. (The Babe was still with the Boston Red Sox that year.) In the minor leagues Halas decided he could do better at football, so he joined the Staley Starchmakers of Decatur, Illinois, for the enticing sum of fifty dollars a game plus five dollars a day in meal money on the road. Halas had been a halfback and an end at Illinois and at Great Lakes Naval Training Station.

Although it was still a period of noble amateurism in football, and the Staley Starchmakers were not oversubscribed, Halas plunged into promoting the club. In the spring before the 1920 season, he toured college campuses, promising college men who would join him on the Starchmakers a year-round job at the Staley Starch Works plus a share of the receipts from the team's games. Remarkably, he found people who were willing to join him. Then he approached the owners and operators of other factory teams. While in Canton, Ohio, he met Ralph Hays, who owned a Hupmobile agency. Hays had been sponsoring a town team called the Canton Bulldogs, an outfit that counted among its employees the brilliant Indian athlete from Carlisle College, Jim Thorpe. "I told Ralph we ought to get some people together and form a league," Halas said. "That would make scheduling all that more easy. He said that he would write letters to other teams and see what could be done."

On September 17, 1920, the representatives of eleven teams gathered at Hays's agency and brought Halas's vision to life. Since only two folding chairs were available the founding fathers of pro football sat on the running boards, fenders, and hoods of two sedans as well. In less than a day the American Professional Football

George Halas, who played football for
Bob Zuppke at the University of Illinois,
was moved by a quote from the famed
coach that lamented the fact that
most college players graduated just as
they were learning the game. Halas,
and a few other pioneers, met in Canton,
Ohio, in 1920 to lay the foundation for
a professional league. Halas's franchise
became the Chicago Bears.

Association was organized with Jim Thorpe as its first
president. (The league's name was changed to the National
Football League the next year.)

Thorpe seemed a sensible choice. He was not only
the nation's best football player, but its most famous athlete, having won all sorts of medals as a trackman at the
1912 Olympics in Stockholm. King Gustav V of Sweden
had told him, "You, sir, are the greatest athlete in the
world." The glory faded rather quickly after his medals
were taken away because he once had been paid to play
semipro baseball. Nevertheless, as the most illustrious
player in the league, he made a suitable figurehead, if not
a very effective commissioner. He understood his role
and, for the price of no more than four hundred and fifty
dollars a year, accepted it.

The original franchises cost one hundred dollars each.
Two of the first thirteen exist today, the St. Louis Cardinals
and Halas's Chicago Bears. The Cardinals started out in
Racine, the Bears in Decatur. The other teams were the
Canton Bulldogs, Rochester Jeffersons, Dayton Triangles,
Akron Steels, Hammond Pros, Cleveland Panthers, Rock
Island Independents, Buffalo All Americans, Chicago
Tigers, Columbus Panhandles, and Detroit Heralds. Pro
football had a perilous beginning. A team would show
up for a game only to learn that its scheduled opponent
had made a prior agreement to be playing elsewhere.

The *Akron Beacon* recounted the league's early difficulties: "The less hardy were discouraged and the survivors concluded that there must be administration, as
well as artistic talent, to create healthy growth. In April
of the next year, the league reorganized and elected Joe
Carr, an experienced sports promoter, as its new president. It was the smartest move major league football had
made to date. Carr guided the league with remarkable
foresight until his death in 1939. He was professional
football's balance wheel through the stormy years of its
first two decades, a fair and impartial ruler." The second
year, the Chicago Tigers, and Hammond dropped out.
and Green Bay, and Cincinnati joined.

On January 1, 1929, a player ran sixty-three yards the wrong way with a fumbled ball in the Rose Bowl game to set up a score that resulted in his team's loss. In a moment of excited confusion, Roy Riegels, captain-elect and center for the University of California, committed one of sport's classic goofs. Georgia Tech won the game 8-7 and in the years to follow, nothing would be remembered of the contest except Riegels's infamous run.

The owner of the Staley Starch Works gave the franchise to Halas to be rid of the drain the football team had placed on the company payroll. Halas immediately took the team to Chicago, where there were at least more potential customers than in Decatur. The city fathers of Chicago did not welcome Halas home.

In addition to playing end for his team, Halas served as its coach, owner, team captain, press agent, ticket seller, trainer, groundskeeper, and traveling secretary. Halas and his partner, a halfback named Dutch Sternaman, paid the players in cash every Thursday morning. The partners had an agreement: neither would receive any money if there was not enough from the gate to meet the payroll. Often Halas and Sternaman went without funds in order to keep the team alive.

In 1930, after partners seriously disagreed over Halas's coaching technique, a neutral force, Ralph Jones of Lake Forest, was brought in. Jones won the league championship in 1932 but resigned because he lacked confidence in the future of professional football. Jones had a right to be alarmed. The Bears lost $18,000 that season and Lake Forest was willing to take him back as coach at $3,500 a year, a fair salary in the middle of the Depression.

A few weeks later Halas learned that Sternaman could be bought out for $38,000. The young entrepreneur borrowed from his mother, the mother of George Trafton (the original center for the Bears), an old school friend, and one of his players (whose father happened to be a millionaire). Still he was short. In desperation he turned to Charles Bidwill, who at the time was attempting to purchase the Chicago Cardinals. Bidwill provided not only the rest of the money for Halas to buy the team but a loan for operating expenses.

As he was juggling the team's finances, Halas was trying manfully to stir up some interest in the new pro game. On Sunday nights after a game, he would sit down at a typewriter and do game stories himself, a different one for each of the eight papers, none of which covered his games. Then he would trot from newspaper office to newspaper office, only to see his copy crumpled and thrown into wastebaskets. Finally he found a backer. Don Maxwell, sports editor of the *Tribune*, was fascinated by Halas. The two men would go out drinking two or three nights a week. One Monday morning in 1925, Halas awoke to discover that the Chicago Bears were the featured story in the *Tribune* sports section.

"Max," said Halas, "I can't thank you enough for that eight-column headline. It was absolutely wonderful."

"Don't thank me at all," said Maxwell. "I did it for the newspaper. It was a dull damn news day, as most Mondays are this time of year, and the Bears gave us a good change of pace. That's all."

A love affair developed between the Chicago Bears and the *Chicago Tribune* that lasted over the decades.

The most important early breakthrough came in 1925, when Halas signed Red Grange, the greatest college player of the period, and an instant shot of class for the fledgling pro league. Grange came to the Bears via his agent, the wily, colorful C. C. (Cash and Carry) Pyle. It was Pyle who arranged a two-month barnstorming tour for Grange and the Bears, part of which called for seventeen games in twenty days. The crowds totaled more than three hundred sixty thousand, and the profit was close to one hundred thousand dollars for Grange, one hundred thousand dollars for the Bears, and fifty thousand dollars for Pyle. It was the first time that Halas had shown a real profit.

This fantasy tour opened in Florida in the midst of a great land boom there. When the Bears reached Miami, they discovered that a battalion of carpenters had built an instant 30,000-seat stadium. Once the Chicago team had performed, the same workmen ripped up the structure. Grange and his teammates brought down the house.

The legend of Harold (Red) Grange, "the Galloping Ghost," fit perfectly into the Golden Age. Beset by personal problems and his family's financial difficulties in his childhood, he overcame these and assorted other obstacles to rise to the top. His mother, always in fragile health, died at home when Grange was a youth, and he discovered the body. The family had little money and Grange decided that staying home, in the small town of Wheaton, Illinois, would not improve his position. He quit school and left home, but his father picked him up hitchhiking along the highway, slapped him once, lectured him for hours, and brought him home. The frustrated youth entered Wheaton High School, where he found some outlet for his energies in averaging five touchdowns a game.

Grange was overwhelmed with offers from colleges, but he wanted to play only for Bob Zuppke at Illinois. The first day of practice he saw one hundred fifty candidates for the freshmen team on the field and returned to his fraternity house convinced he was not good enough. Zuppke came for him. "Don't worry," said the coach. "I'm assigning you to the seventh team. That's no pressure on you there. Just come on out and practice and maybe someday you'll get into a game for a minute or two. Now just relax. You're safe and well. What more do you want?"

The next year he catapulted from the seventh team to the first, as Zuppke had planned he would. He flitted about a football field with an uncanny knack for eluding tacklers. "He's out there somewhere and when you go to grab him he's gone like a ghost," wrote Grantland Rice.

On a brutally hot day in October, 1924, he carved a name for himself when he returned the opening kickoff against Michigan 95 yards for a touchdown, then scored four more touchdowns on runs from scrimmage of 67, 56, 45, and 15 yards. In all, he rushed for 3,637 yards in his college career and into the gilded heavens of sports heroes with Babe Ruth, Knute Rockne, Jack Dempsey, Bobby Jones, and Bill Tilden.

"All he can do is run," said Fielding Yost of Michigan.

"All Galli-Curci can do is sing," retorted Zuppke.

His $100,000-a-year guarantee to play for the Bears would not be approached in earning power by a first-year player until Joe Namath signed with the New York Jets for $440,000 forty years later. (Grange's deal was probably more lucrative, considering the sharply increased taxes and the sharply decreased value of the dollar in Namath's day.) Grange moved immediately into the Bears' backfield when his eligibility at Illinois ended. He played against the Cardinals on Thanksgiving Day and brought 36,000 fans to Wrigley Field. Suddenly, the National Football League had status. A couple of weeks later in New York the Bears drew 65,000 cash customers, who watched them beat the Giants in the snow.

Grange was so extraordinarily popular that the next year Pyle decided to form an entire league around him. It was called the American Football League, the first of three ill-starred organizations of that name that challenged the NFL before a fourth won recognition in 1966. Grange played for the New York Yankees and made a handsome profit, though the team failed dismally. When Grange's personal-service contract with Pyle expired, he rejoined the Bears and played six seasons. In that muscle-bending period of one-platoon football, he developed into an even better defensive back than an offensive one.

When Grange retired in 1935, professional football was about to become a different game. The great gods of the game had been the running backs—Grange, Clark Hinkle, Ernie Nevers, Bronko Nagurski, and Beattie Feathers. But the ball had been slimmed down and the rulesmakers had decreed that a pass could be released from any point behind the line of scrimmage instead of five yards back. Thus the seeds were planted that would transform the game into the wildly popular spectacle of the fifties and sixties. Fittingly, Halas spearheaded the new movement. "The changes are good for the game," he said. "The colleges get all the attention, so we have to do something."

In 1939, in becoming the first man to trade players for a first-round draft pick, he brought to the Bears one of the finest of the early passers, Columbia's Sid Luckman. As field marshal of the Bears' revolutionary T-formation the

BRONKO NAGURSKI *the* Living Legend

A new era in professional football was signaled when Red Grange turned professional in 1925. College players from around the nation signed with the pros, joining a league that had twenty-six teams from coast to coast in 1926. Two of the greatest players of the era were Bronko Nagurski, the two-time All-America from Minnesota who played with the Chicago Bears, and Dutch Clark, a remarkable runner from Colorado State who almost single-handedly sustained the Detroit Lions in the thirties.

next year, Luckman guided Chicago to its incredible 73–0 victory over Washington in the championship game, by far the most lopsided championship contest in the history of the NFL.

It would be more than another thirty years after this, probably his greatest triumph, that Halas would relinquish his one-man rule of the Bears. By then pro football's rush to pass had left Halas somewhat behind the times, or at least the style. Nor did the autocratic Papa Bear fare particularly well with the more assertive players and coaches of football's big money days. Yet even then there was no denying the man's contributions. More than any one man, he saw pro football through the Golden Age to a golden age of its own.

12   All That's Golden Doesn't Glitter

The cruelty of economic catastrophe had come crashing down on the nation. The newspapers were filled with stories of suicides, of hoboes living in jungles along railroad tracks, of lower class farmers and miners suffering from malnutrition. The golden era of prosperity had vanished. More than sixty per cent of the people made less than the $2,000 annual salary that an average family needed to purchase the barest necessities.

The stock market, eaten by credit in the form of brokers' loans, disintegrated when millions of small deals were called in. The economy had been unbalanced for a long time, but nobody knew it. Too few people had too much and too many had too little. America was in the astounding position of being torn apart by overproduction and underconsumption. The same prices were maintained even in the wake of receding sales. In order to cut costs, factories laid men off, thereby reducing the nation's buying power. The man who introduced a low-priced car named after Knute Rockne lost $22 million and put a pistol to his temple.

In three years, after the great crash of 1929, stocks on

Red Grange never quite fulfilled the promise of his college derring-do as a professional. Injured early in his career with the Chicago Bears, he spent another year vainly attempting to sustain a rival league to the NFL. He ended his career after the 1934 season, knowing his influence had helped establish pro football as a serious business. About the same time, young Walt Disney was busily developing a character who would become a giant in American mythology. Mickey Mouse, as this 1936 movie poster shows, could do it all, no matter what the obstacles.

the big board were worth eleven per cent of their previous value. More than three hundred thousand people were evicted from their homes and farms. Investors lost more than one hundred billion dollars. People with some small cash reserves actually bought jobs from those a little less fortunate. One source estimated that 34 million men, women, and children in urban areas were without any income at all. On the farm it cost more money to ship an animal to market than a farmer received in payment. Since bullets were expensive, sheep ranchers killed their sheep by slitting their throats in the fields.

With a massive supply of labor, wages were cut to the point at which a dollar a day was considered a healthy salary. Factory girls worked for as little as twenty cents a day. Welfare lists stretched on and on but the Hoover Administration continued to oppose welfare aid through four cruel Depression winters. Doctors refused to treat the sick unless they could guarantee payment in advance.

In the midst of this economic chaos, bowling leagues flourished, movie attendance increased, and miniature golf courses sprouted everywhere. The Boston and Maine Railroad organized the first ski trains, and they were jammed.

A number of the lower minor leagues were forced to suspend operations, but the big leagues survived well enough, though salaries and costs were trimmed. Commissioner K. M. Landis took a voluntary pay cut from $65,000 to $45,000. The man who won the American League batting championship in 1933, Jimmy Foxx, was asked to take a pay cut because the Philadelphia Athletics were trying to stay afloat. Admission prices dropped and the people came to the ball park to forget their problems with a few hours of heroic illusion. "Major league baseball has done as much as any one thing in this country to keep up the spirit of the people," said the newly elected president, Franklin Roosevelt.

It was a desperate time that spawned sadistic entertainment forms: marathon dances, six-day bike races, and battles royal. The last involved a dozen blindfolded

© Walt Disney Productions

boxers who were herded into the ring and permitted to slug one another senseless. In fact, thousands of half-starved young men tried to make money as prizefighters. They poured into the big cities on buses and trains, eager to fight in order to live. As boxing became one of the favorite amusements in the Depression, small clubs sprang up in every dark, gritty neighborhood. Admission was a quarter and most of the fights were winner-take-all. The loser walked away bloodied and hungry.

With Franklin Roosevelt came a bewildering assortment of alphabet agencies such as the WPA (the Works Progress Administration) that brought truckloads of formerly unemployed workers to build federal parks, swimming pools, gymnasiums, football stadiums, playgrounds, fishing wharves and other recreation areas. The workers cleaned the lakes, turned impassable forests into sunny glades, and laid down basketball courts for city kids. Although some of them leaned on their shovels, as the hoary joke went, they created facilities where nothing had been before.

Out of the dust and hunger of a national disgrace came other mass movements. The Young Men's Christian Association and the Young Men's Hebrew Association flourished, followed by the Catholic Youth Organization. All had basketball teams playing in church halls.

As a means of combating juvenile crime, which was epidemic as fewer children found a decent meal on their tables, Bishop Bernard Sheil founded the Golden Gloves program. Contestants were fed and given boxing instruction. At first Sheil could not convince his immediate superior, George Cardinal Mundelein, that this sort of activity was altogether healthy. Sheil was also fretful that the Cardinal might not see it as a proper activity for the Roman Catholic Church to sponsor.

"Your Eminence," said Bishop Sheil, "I want to run the biggest boxing tournament our city has ever seen."

"Well," said Cardinal Mundelein, suppressing the urge to laugh, "this is the first time I ever knew a soul could be saved by a punch in the nose. But you have permission to do whatever you think will best serve the youth of Chicago. . . ."

In the realm of professional sport, technology continued its struggle against tradition, boosted rather than inhibited by the Depression.

Larry MacPhail, the general manager of the Cincinnati Reds and a soldier of fortune who once engaged in a freelance plot to capture the Kaiser, was anxious to recapture some of the business he had lost during the Depression. On May 24, 1935, President Roosevelt pushed a button that ignited 632 lamps illuminating Crosley Field in Cincinnati and the Reds ran onto the field to defeat the Philadelphia Phillies 4-1. A crowd of 20,422, roughly ten times that of an ordinary afternoon game with Philadelphia, was present. Most baseball people were not impressed, however.

"There is no chance whatsoever of night baseball ever becoming popular in the bigger cities," said Clark Griffith, owner of the Washington Senators. "People there who are educated to see the best there is will stand for only the best. High class baseball cannot be played at night under artificial light. Furthermore, the benefits derived from attending the game are due largely to fresh air and sunshine. Night air and electric lights are a poor substitute and they will never be accepted by a discerning public."

The working man, who couldn't get to the ball park during the day, didn't quite see it that way, of course, and night baseball caught on. As escapist as it was during the Depression, spectator sport was slowly taking note of the real world.

13   Hero at Munich

There was no question that the 1936 Games were to symbolize the cultural advantages of the New Order in Germany. The five Olympic rings were surmounted by the highly stylized German eagle, which had become more angular and unfriendly in its renderings by Hitler's artists. The dual symbol was everywhere in Berlin, pasted on every sign post on the Olympic grounds, nailed to every street lamp, fastened to the Brandenburg Gate. Rumors and press reports abounded of book burnings, concentration camp openings, and the persecution of Jewish citizens of Germany.

If Jews, Gypsies, and Slavs were hated by the masterminds of the Third Reich, blacks were utterly beneath comment. Dr. Julius Streicher, one of the Third Reich's leading anti-Semites, told a guest at an embassy party in Berlin, "They are little more than trained baboons." He ridiculed the blacks on the American team as "America's black auxiliary."

Into this milieu of racism moved James Cleveland Owens, a dignified, intelligent product of the black ghetto of Cleveland. He was born in Danville, Alabama, in 1913. His parents called him "J. C." and his friends converted the initials to "Jesse." As a child of seven he picked cotton just before the family moved to Ohio.

In 1933, at East Technical High School in Cleveland, he ran the 100-meter dash in 10.3 seconds and the 100-yard sprint in 9.4. The first timing was unofficial; the second stood as a national high school record for thirty-four years.

Owens was twenty-one years old when he entered Ohio State, in a class with a hundred other freshmen. He had been recruited by Larry Snyder, the track coach at OSU, though Snyder knew that Owens had had little formal coaching in track. Still, in May, 1935, Owens competed in a track meet in which he not only tied the world record for the 100-yard dash but set world records in the broad jump, 220-yard hurdles, and 220-yard dash. It remains one of the most astonishing one-day individual performances in the history of track and field.

Snyder discovered an emotional side to Jesse Owens. To other whites he was so self-effacing that he earned the most gratuitous of compliments, but Snyder found a passionate pride in his runner. The two engaged in violently

inspirational premeet talks that often reduced both to tears. Snyder persuaded Owens that he could be a leader of his race, not merely a token credit to it.

In the Olympic tryouts early in July, 1936, Jesse Owens qualified in all four events he entered. Fortunately, Snyder was able to go with Owens to Berlin. They crossed the Atlantic on the S. S. Manhattan. It was a folksy voyage. All the Olympians spent a great deal of time together on the trip, and the members of the team voted miler Glenn Cunningham the most popular athlete. Second was Jesse Owens, who gloried in the honor.

"It was much different in those days," he said. "To simply be noticed was a big thing for a black. People on the ship knew who I was. They were constantly after me. They even took two pairs of my track shoes as souvenirs. I had a keen appreciation of what it meant to be black. Never forget that. German magazines had been doing stories on me. People on the ship followed me constantly. For a college man I was old. As a human I was young. All I could think of was the fact that I was black and other people seemed to love me. I knew I wanted that for me and for my people. It was a different world then."

The public attention made Jesse Owens newly aware of his own importance. Even the Nazis were using his image on posters to advertise the Olympic Games. Despite the rampant racism in Germany, Owens was favored by the German people. When the American showed up for practice sessions at the stadium, the crowd chanted, "Yes-sa . . . Yes-sa—Ovenns!" Autograph hounds would not let him rest.

"I became determined to do what was expected of me," he said. "The training conditions in Berlin were far from ideal, but American blacks were greatly loved by the German people. The first day that I arrived at the stadium, the Chancellor arose when I passed. I nodded my head, as I would to any head of state hosting the Games, and he waved his hand at me. I waved back."

It is even true, if impartial observers can be believed, that Hitler did not pointedly snub the black American

athletes, as legend has it. On the first day of competition, the Chancellor was seated in his loge when Hans Wollke broke the shotput record and became the first German to win a gold medal. He and the bronze medal winner, another German, Gerhard Stock, were led to Hitler's box for personal congratulations. Later Hitler greeted Tilly Fleischer and Luise Kreuger, first- and second-place winners in the women's javelin throw.

Only one event was left, the high jump. When the only Germans entered were quickly eliminated, Hitler left. Three Americans were vying for first place—two blacks, Cornelius Johnson and David Albritton, and one white, Delos Thurber.

That evening the president of the International Olympic Committee, Count Baillet-Latour, sent word to Hitler that as simply a guest of honor at the Games and not a critic of them, he had no business publicly honoring any of the winners, German or foreigners. Meekly, Hitler noted that henceforth he would congratulate German winners in private, noting that he had overstepped the boundaries of international relations. The next day, Jesse Owens won the 100-meter sprint, the first of his four gold medals. At no time did Hitler refuse to shake his hand. Hitler had, as instructed, consigned himself to the role of spectator and congratulated no one throughout the remainder of the Olympics. Snubbed or not, Jesse Owens streaked off to victories in the 100 meters, in the 200 meters, in the broad jump, and as part of the 400-meter relay team.

All that remained for Owens to win was wealth. There were stories in America that he would return to instant riches. Why, Eddie Cantor was going to pay him $40,000 for ten weeks! So Snyder and Owens boarded the *Queen Mary* and sailed off to a ticker-tape welcome in Manhattan. The famous tap dancer Bill (Bojangles) Robinson told Owens to sit tight and wait. Owens waited; nothing happened. He ran against a racehorse in Havana, Cuba. He led a dance band. He ran against white baseball players whom he gave a head start. He raced dogs, cars, and antelopes. And so he gained a reputation for being an opportunist. He lost $25,000 on an all-black baseball team in 1940, at the same time that young Bill Veeck was trying, and failing, to purchase the Philadelphia Phillies and stock them with Buck Leonard, Monte Irvin, Jackie Robinson, Roy Campanella, James (Cool Papa) Bell, Judy Johnson, Josh Gibson, and other stars of the old Negro National League. Veeck was denied permission to invest in a team because blacks were not acceptable. And neither was Jesse Owens, who ended up taking a series of public relations jobs in his quest for stature and respectability.

When the civil rights movement reached its zenith, it was fashionable, if not obligatory, to deride him as an "Uncle Tom." Owens countered with the classic defense that such slogans and values of the sixties were less than just when applied to less enlightened times. "All I did was buckle down and prove to myself that I had the ability to think as well as run," he said. "I know that I have succeeded. I'm not mad at anyone. In my time, few blacks considered that I had done anything wrong.

"A man must have dignity off the athletic field," he conceded. "But that has nothing to do with color. All men who star in athletics have to walk ten feet tall when they aren't competing. Thousands of kids will emulate a sports star, if he's white or black or red or yellow or what have you. I found that out a generation after I stopped running and hundreds—no, thousands—of white kids told me what black kids had been telling me: that they respected me and wanted to be like Jesse Owens. That is a responsibility that cannot be denied."

14　The Brown Bomber

When Joe Louis came along in 1934 there were few black athletes in organized American sports. Baseball was totally white. Pro football, just begin-

In May, 1925, Nelson B. Sherrill of the University of Pennsylvania vaulted over a bar thirteen feet in height, a world indoor record. Using Sherrill as his model, sculptor R. Tait McKenzie had created this small, bronze masterpiece two years earlier.

ning to stabilize and make a dollar, was white because most of the schools that produced the players were white. The same was true of basketball—as limited as its exposure was. Golf and tennis—those were rich men's sports, so how could a colored boy play them? Might as well expect to see him on a horse, playing polo.

There were a few black track stars. Eddie Tolan of Michigan and Ralph Metcalfe of Marquette did beautifully in the 1932 Olympics at Los Angeles, winning gold and silver medals for the U.S.A. in the sprints. Metcalfe also won medals in the 100 meters and 400-meter relay in 1936.

An underworld of black baseball existed: Fly-by-night Negro leagues, sometimes playing on skin diamonds in third-rate parks, sometimes luxuriating in a major-league stadium on an off date, and a gaggle of gypsy barnstormers, twelve- or fourteen-man squads jammed into a few limping autos or a decrepit bus and covering a couple of hundred miles to play two or even three games in a single day. Miraculously, famous names emerged: the Kansas City Monarchs, the Homestead Grays, the Pittsburgh Elite Giants, the New York Black Yankees. Major league all-stars occasionally encountered them on the exhibition circuit and acknowledged that a Satchel Paige or a Josh Gibson could hold their own with anyone.

Why couldn't they, then? Why didn't they get the chance? Well, that was the way things were. When you came right down to it, the whole country accepted the Southern view of black folks. Oh, they might not be so paranoid here or there. But essentially segregation and inequality of opportunity were built into America's way of life, and there was no real push for change anywhere, not from whites, not from blacks.

Boxing was different. This was dirty, crooked, cruel business. If a couple of colored boys wanted to knock each other's head off for a few fast rounds, why not? (Of course, everyone knew their heads were hard as ivory. The way to beat a colored was body punches; they couldn't take it "downstairs.")

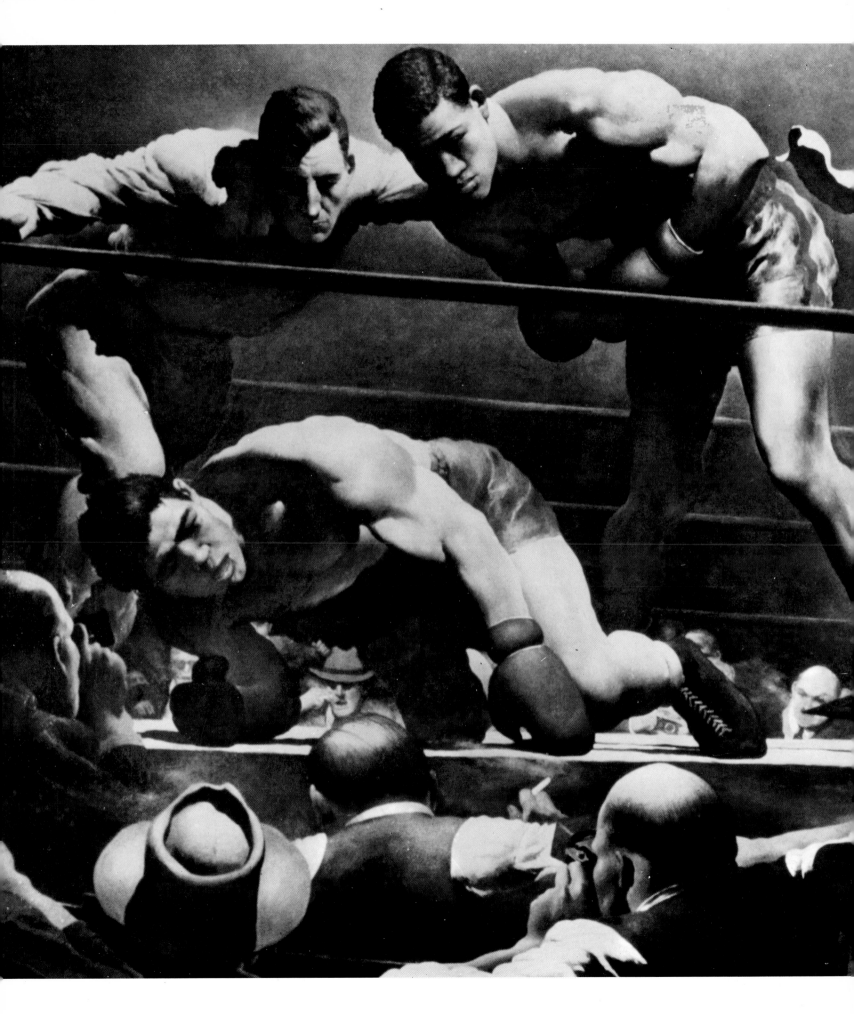

Max Schmeling, a former world heavyweight champion, first met Joe Louis in 1936 and knocked out the supposedly invincible young fighter in twelve rounds. When they were rematched in 1938, Louis was the heavyweight champion. In one of boxing's most dramatic fights, Louis literally demolished the German in less than one round. Writer Bob Considine described Schmeling as "a man caught and mangled in the whirring claws of a mad and feverish machine." Artist Robert Riggs captured Louis's triumphant moment.

Many white fighters wouldn't fight blacks. John L. Sullivan considered it a point of honor not to. "Drawing the color line" was the phrase. Jack Dempsey drew the color line against Harry Wills, one of the few heavies around who could have given him a real scrap. Sam Langford, by all accounts an extraordinary fighter, languished in poverty, unable to get shots at titles he rated.

There were a few black champions in the twenties, exceptions. Tiger Flowers, the middleweight, was indeed a Negro, but Kid Chocolate, the featherweight, and Battling Siki, the light-heavy, were exotics. The Kid was a Cuban, Siki an African, "the Fighting Senegalese." He wore his crown six months. He won it from Georges Carpentier, nicely recovered from his blasting by Dempsey, then was persuaded to risk it against Mike McTigue in Dublin on St. Patrick's Day. He did not win.

Joe Louis had a lot to atone for when he first showed up with his devastating talent for knocking out whites and blacks alike. The press, hugging itself for its fair-mindedness, lectured this sober, unlettered youth over and over again on his responsibilities to colored people everywhere, promising that by sobriety and good conduct he could remove the stain of Johnson's transgressions and become "a credit to his race." It was an insufferably sanctimonious performance, the more so because it was accepted everywhere as appropriate comment and because, under the ministrations of whites, boxing was floundering through perhaps the most unsavory period of its corrupt and rapacious existence.

The retirement of Gene Tunney as undefeated champion, and the death of flamboyant Tex Rickard, holder of the New York boxing monopoly, had left the game in disarray. Prohibition-era gangsters muscled in on fighters, managers, and promoters, and rumors of dives and betting coups were rampant. State boxing commissions, run for the most part by pompous or amiable hacks, seemed powerless to control the chaos.

Most outrageous was the sordid and cynical manipulation of Primo Carnera into the heavyweight championship in 1933. "Da Preem" was a circus strong man from Italy who stood six foot five and three-quarter inches (the mob surrounded him with short guys and said he was six feet eight and a quarter) and weighed 265 or so. Sadly, his size was the only impressive thing about him. A fighter he was not. He was a gentle, trusting soul who could not box and could not punch, but who, in his innocence, believed that the swan-diving palookas fattening his spurious record were being clubbed into submission by the fury of his attack.

The jewel in this crown of deceit was his phantom knockout of Jack Sharkey, a journeyman heavyweight who had succeeded to the title but who was openly suspected of surrendering to Carnera for a payoff larger than he could have accrued in the career remaining to him as a thirty-year-old champ.

Carnera was butchered a year later by Max Baer— twelve bloody knockdowns in eleven rounds. And a year after that James J. Braddock, a fading, nonworking pug making his living with a longshoreman's hook on the Jersey piers, was pronounced a fit contender for the title, and promptly relieved Baer of it, on points, in fifteen rounds. What do you call someone like that? "The Cinderella Man."

Joseph Louis Barrow, an Alabama-born migrant to the slums and factories of Detroit, decided he wanted to be a fighter about the time Carnera's invisible uppercut was felling Sharkey. He knocked out Jack Kracken in one round, his first professional win, about the time Baer was ruining Carnera. And the year Braddock was crowned, he was making steady progress through the ranks and edging into contention as a challenger. Already he was known as "the Brown Bomber."

Curiously, for all the self-righteous preaching of the press, Joe Louis was one of the few people in boxing who was on the level. By great good fortune, he had acquired as managers John Roxborough and Julian Black. This interesting pair were entrepreneurs who had made big money and useful connections through bailbonding, numbers, gambling, speakeasies, politics, and the rackets—the kind of free private enterprise open to aspiring blacks. They had standing in the black communities of Detroit and Chicago, and enough leverage with other shadowy powers to keep the mob from messing with their fighter.

Louis was also fortunate to have Mike Jacobs as his promotional mentor. Uncle Mike, a ticket broker and proprietor of the 20th Century Sporting Club, was maneuvering to wrest control of New York boxing from Madison Square Garden, which, with Rickard gone, was losing its edge. Jacobs, who had been associated with Tex in some of the master's capers in bygone days, needed no lessons in cunning. He stayed clear of the mob and he signed Louis before either of them knew for sure what the other could do for him.

As a result of this shrewd management, Joe's record was impeccable. It included the usual stiffs—you couldn't bring a boy like Louis along too fast—but there was never any doubt that when one of his punches landed, eyes glazed and knees buckled.

For the refinement of his talent, Louis had the redoubtable Jack Blackburn to thank. A tough, dangerous, alcoholic man, Blackburn was nonetheless a hell of a trainer. An old lightweight himself, he knew the art of boxing and how to impart it to his impassive, twenty-year-old charge.

They hit it off well. Blackburn was strict and Joe needed the comfort of disciplined instruction. They called each other "Chappie." Blackburn taught Louis balance, first of all. Louis was always solidly planted to throw or take a punch. Then his left jab was sharpened. This was no tentative, pawing, pushing left hand; it had real snap. Fending off the jab created openings for Louis's power, his jolting right and his devastating left hook.

Louis was not a dancer. He had a shuffling gait. He stalked his opponent implacably, his face expressionless behind the bulge of his gloves. He held his hands high, and for all the slow shuffle-shuffle of his feet, his hands struck fast. His punches never traveled far; no looping

Primo Carnera, an Italian giant, was one of the poorest of heavyweight champions. He was a crude fighter, with little skill, building his reputation on questionable fights. Budd Schulberg would write a best-selling novel, *The Harder They Fall,* based on the sordid story of the exploited Italian. Below, a bronze by Mahonri M. Young, titled *Groggy*.

rights, no fancy, Sugar Ray-style combinations. Mostly he was a counterpuncher. He waited for the lead, for the fatal opening, than bang! The most comfortable thing in the world was to watch him, knowing you wouldn't have to take those numbing, punishing, short jolts to head and body.

By the middle of 1935 Louis was fighting reputable opponents. In June, in Uncle Mike's first big outdoor promotion, he sped the decline of Carnera with a relentless attack on that great, ill-defended body, and when the giant wilted he flattened him with destructive blows to the head that pulped the flesh and sent the mouthpiece flying.

This qualified him for bigger names. He polished off the pathetic King (or Kingfish; it didn't matter) Levinsky in one, knocked out a terrified Max Baer in four, and felled the old Basque woodchopper, Paulino Uzcudun, also in four.

Early in 1936 he was matched with Max Schmeling. It was skillful promotion. Schmeling was a ringwise veteran of 31, never too impressive, but an ex-champ nonetheless. He did not figure to be too tough to handle, and yet a win for Joe would be respectable. More than that, international pride and prejudice were involved. Schmeling was inevitably a symbol of Aryan supremacy, a member of the Nazi master race already beginning to persecute Jews and contemptuous of Negroes.

Schmeling really wasn't much of a Nazi. He'd been coming to the States since the late twenties and this looked like one more good payday. That's all. As for Louis, he had a double burden. Before the verdict was even in on whether he was a credit to his race, he was expected to uphold the honor of the whole U.S.A., white as well as black, against the Hun. In the simplistic world of the sports pages this match between good and evil produced a number of columns, though not on the basis of anything Joe said. Perhaps because he was always sparing with words, he never let anyone put them in his mouth, never let anyone fast-talk him into an attitude or a position. He was not a brilliant man, but he had a sure sense of himself and he never betrayed it. He never lent his innate dignity to a cheap or easy quote.

Well, whatever their ideologies, Schmeling knocked Louis out in twelve. The old campaigner had watched the Paulino match and said he had seen something. He had, indeed. Louis was a mite careless about carrying his left lower than he should. So every time the left sagged, the Black Uhlan came in with a right cross to the chops. Chappie was working the corner, but young Joe couldn't shift gears that fast. He sustained his first professional shellacking.

Louis then stopped flabby Jack Sharkey in three and went through a blur of lesser lights. Despite the Schmeling setback, he was obviously the best young heavy around. He was due for a shot at the title, and after some contractual chess, whose significance time has dimmed, he and Braddock were brought together at Comiskey Park in Chicago in June, 1937.

It went eight. Louis was twenty-three, 197¼ pounds, at the peak of his form. Braddock was 197 and old. There was no television, of course, but movies showed it all. Louis used his left to knock Braddock's left lead out of the way. Braddock's arm swung back dreamily under the force of the blow, exposing the left side of his face and chest. Louis's right moved in a short, straight line, hitting the Cinderella Man a crushing blast on the jaw and dropping him. The black man was champion.

The first of his twenty-five title defenses was against Tommy Farr, a hard rock who could not win but would not go down. Joe won the decision in fifteen.

The chief unfinished business—Schmeling—was dispatched in 1938. There was even more talk about Nazis and race, but Louis wasn't interested. He was going to win this one for Louis. From the opening bell, he was on the attack, smashing through Schmeling's defenses with heavy blows. The round never ended. He dropped the German four times, and before he could do more damage a white towel of surrender flew from Schmeling's corner.

As every champion has found, there just aren't enough

quality heavyweights around to keep a man busy. Louis took on anyone, including a number who didn't belong in the same ring with him. Some thought "Two-Ton" Tony Galento might ruffle him with his butting, heeling, brawling style. But Tony's mediocrity as a boxer made him a standing target for Louis's relentlessly accurate fists, and he was cut to ribbons in four.

In December, 1940, the Bum-of-the-Month campaign began: Al McCoy, Red Burman, Gus Dorazio, Abe Simon, Tony Musto, Buddy Baer—names notable almost entirely for their association with Joe Louis. It was ludicrous, but no one minded. This was the only way you could see the champ in action.

Billy Conn gave him a scare late in the year, but pressed his luck and was bombed out in the thirteenth. Three fights later, Joe was in the army for the duration.

He was thirty-two when he whipped Billy again in 1946 and beginning to drift into those difficult, desultory final years that plague aging kings. For all the money he had earned, there was little to show and he was in trouble with the Internal Revenue Service for back taxes. His marriage had disintegrated and so had his investments.

He whipped Jersey Joe Walcott twice, and retired. Then, because there was money out there and he needed it, he unretired. Ezzard Charles decisioned him, he had some paydays with nobodies, and finally, in 1951, when he was thirty-seven years old, the young tiger, Rocky Marciano, took him apart. By then there were black athletes performing as professionals throughout America. Joe Louis didn't bring it about, but he sure helped by his example.

15   Joe and Ted

In an athlete, "class" is a blend of superlative talent and an admirable personality. The talent must extend the length of a career. Consistency at a high level of performance is part of its attraction, and so is style — grace, bearing, economy of motion,

202

Joe DiMaggio was perhaps the finest baseball player of his day. He could do it all—hit for power and average, throw, field, and run. Jimmy Cannon wrote, "He is a ball player without flaw, a ball player of exceptional purity." In 1,736 games he batted .325 and hit 361 home runs. In his thirteen seasons the Yankees won ten pennants and nine World Series. He was elected to baseball's Hall of Fame in 1955.

execution with a touch of elegance. Withal, the talent must be applied competitively, as nexus of the team spirit and spearhead of its effort.

The personality will be admirable if it includes in its mix verve, pride without arrogance, a jot of self-deprecating humor, a regard for truth, and a professional demeanor, win or lose. Too much? A paragon? Not at all. Though never commonplace, examples are not far to seek: In baseball, Pie Traynor, Charlie Gehringer, Pee Wee Reese, Stan Musial, Hank Aaron, Brooks Robinson.

"Class" has always existed, but it has been of interest—an accolade worth conferring—in the last thirty or forty years because of the changing status of the professional athlete, because of his gradual elevation to something like social distinction.

Few old-time ball players had class. Most of them were hicks, tobacco-chewers, and roughnecks, too vulgar for the beau geste or the beau monde. This is not to put them down but to say that, whatever their talents, the America of their time paid them poorly, shunted them to second-rate hotels and workingmen's bars, and scorned their bucolic manners, smelly cigars, and nickel tips.

Class may be innate, but its beauty is that it can be acquired.

This leads to the parallel careers of Joe DiMaggio and Ted Williams. Both were Californians. Everyone thinks of DiMaggio as a Fisherman's Wharf San Franciscan, but actually he was born in the industrial city of Martinez, across the Bay. Williams was from San Diego. Both played in the Pacific Coast League when it was one of the ornaments of organized baseball. Together with the International League in the East and the American Association in the Midwest, it formed the top tier of the extensive minor-league structure—triple A.

The Pacific Coast sent many fine players to the majors, and because the weather was benign from Seattle to San Diego it was hospitable to veterans, warming the bones sufficiently to lengthen waning careers by two or three seasons. About the time DiMaggio and Williams were coming up, you could see Pepper Martin, Tony Lazzeri, Bill Cissell, and guys like that playing out the string.

DiMaggio and Williams never faced each other on the West Coast. DiMaggio was four years older and in 1936, when he was in his rookie season with the Yanks, the gangling young Williams, six-three and 148 pounds, was signing with the Padres. Williams moved up to the Red Sox in 1939, taking over rightfield from Ben Chapman. Doc Cramer and Joe Vosmik, two of the many established but aging players acquired in Tom Yawkey's early efforts to buy a pennant winner, were in center and left.

Thereafter, DiMaggio and Williams met head to head for ten seasons (both missing three years during World War II). DiMaggio bowed out after the 1951 season. Williams kept going through 1960, missing almost all of 1952 and 1953 while serving a second hitch with the military in Korea.

They were, of course, entirely different men, but as contemporaries, as the two greatest outfielders of all time, their performances and personalities were endlessly compared.

At the outset there were superficial similarities between them. Both were gifted athletes with a quirky outlook on life. DiMaggio was a morose youth of twenty-two when he came up—silent, withdrawn, suspicious of big-city ways, tight with a dollar (although he was one ball player among many in that regard), and with a glittering eye for opportunities to make a dollar more. Williams was twenty-one, full of juvenile insecurities that expressed themselves in brashness and pop-off comments, which promptly earned him the magisterial disapproval of Boston's rather exacting sporting press. Mostly, of course, it was the gaucheness of immaturity, the rookiness of rookies. As players they were something else again.

DiMaggio joined the Yankees with his superb talents already developed to an extraordinary degree. He really was breathtaking; he did so much so well. He was tall and rangy, and covered the vast acreage of centerfield with aplomb, running gracefully, seemingly without

In 1937, Wilbur Shaw captured his first Indianapolis 500 in a car he built himself, powered by the Offenhauser engine that dominated the race for thirty years. His time was four hours and twenty-four minutes, at an average speed of 113.58 miles per hour. Shaw also won the 1939 and 1940 races, driving a Maserati. War rumors filled the air, but America's peace-time Navy was often more interested in fighting of another kind, as portrayed in Fletcher Martin's 1938 painting, *A Lad from the Fleet*.

effort. His judgment of fly balls was superb. He fielded ground balls with precision—the rolling or one-bounce singles, the tricky doubles, the triples headed for the far reaches of left or right center—and until his shoulder was injured he could throw with the best of them, long and low and to the right base.

At the plate he stood with bat held high and motionless, and feet wide apart. He was a wrist hitter, swinging swiftly and smoothly at the last moment, with the ball almost, as they say, in the catcher's mitt. He turned into the ball, snapped his wrists on impact, and, classic right-handed pull hitter that he was, completed his swing with a wide arc of follow-through. Oddly, it was all done without passion. Neither his face nor his demeanor betrayed any surge of excitement, no matter what the situation. He ran the bases efficiently, and if, as happened several hundred times, he was running four of them, he made his lap at a steady pace, elbows pumping, his head cocked to one side. Crossing the plate and heading for the bench with those same long strides, he acknowledged applause with a tug at the bill of his cap and ducked down the dugout stairs. A tip of the hat: It was one of the major differences between them.

Williams wanted to be the greatest hitter who ever lived, and he almost made it. Certainly no one other than Cobb and Hornsby studied the technique of hitting so intensively, so single-mindedly. No one worked harder to perfect his swing. No one knew more accurately the boundaries of that air space called the strike zone.

He has the numbers to prove it: six times American League batting champion; a phenomenal .406 batting average in 1941, the last time .400 was reached in either major league; a lifetime average of .344 (Tris Speaker's level); and a lifetime .634 slugging average (total bases divided by number of times at bat) second only to Babe Ruth's. He lost a sixth batting championship to George Kell on the last day of the 1949 season, .3429 to .34275, and a seventh to Bobby Avila in 1954 because he was fourteen at-bats shy of the required 400.

There seems no doubt that had he played during the nearly five seasons lost to military service—three when he was twenty-five to twenty-seven years old and two when he was thirty-four and thirty-five—his record would be even more remarkable. As a hitter who averaged 30 homers a season for seventeen years, it does not seem unreasonable to say that he would have at least another 150 to add to his already considerable total of 521.

Speculation changes not a single figure in the tabulations on Williams, but it is interesting to note to what peaks he aspired and tantalizing to see how close he came. As Williams himself has pointed out, the .388 of 1957 *might* have been a second .400 season if the thirty-nine-year-old slugger had been able to beat out even six "leg hits" in the course of his 132 games.

Whatever his totals, he was beautiful to watch at the plate. He was in constant motion, stepping into the box, digging his left foot into the dirt to get anchored, wriggling his hips, stepping out of the box, tapping his spikes, dusting his hands; in again, resettling himself, the bat waving in half swings and nervous circles, his hands clasping and unclasping, as though he were trying to squeeze juice out of the wood.

When he connected, that marvelous swing brought the fat part of the bat onto the ball—no superfluous motion here—and the right hand pulled the bat around his body in a full-circle follow-through. Home runs usually went deep into the rightfield stands, doubles on a line between right- and centerfielders. That's where his power was. The Boudreau Shift (all four infielders on the right side of the diamond) *did* make sense, because Ted really couldn't hit effectively to left—on the few occasions he was disposed to try.

As for the rest, there's no getting away from it: He was an indifferent outfielder. Flies he should have caught eluded him. He misplayed balls. He didn't back up the infield. It wasn't that he was inept, like such good-hit-no-field performers as Babe Herman and Smead Jolley. He could catch a ball and he had a strong and accurate arm.

205

In 1939, war seemed inevitable in Europe. But in the United States—and especially in Boston—all attention was focused on a young rookie from San Diego, California. Ted Williams would become a fixture on the Red Sox for nineteen seasons, and lay claim to being the greatest hitter who ever lived. In 2,292 games his lifetime batting average was .344. He was the last batter to hit over .400, averaging .406 in 1941. Williams was one of the most controversial and complex players in the game. When he retired in 1960 at age forty-two, he had not compromised his attitudes.

But he was negligent. Fielding just didn't impress him as a very important part of the game and he gave it none of the intensity he brought to hitting.

Furthermore, he had a temper and his tantrums were not pretty to watch. There was nothing imaginative about them. It was the usual juvenile ball player nonsense of throwing bats, kicking dirt, storming around the dugout, and slouching and sulking in the field. The acerbic Boston press got on him early and never let up, and Williams never forgave them. Boston fans wanted to like him.

Whatever opportunities there were for truce or reconciliation passed. And Williams's reaction to the constant criticism and booing and abuse was to become balkier and more intransigent and more remote. He stubbornly refused to respond to cheers with a tip of the cap, even before the home folks, even on the occasion of the incredible home run in his last time at bat, his farewell to baseball after nineteen years. Throughout those years he was hooted and booed, partly as punishment for his past insolence to fandom, partly to see if he could be goaded into new outrages. Unfortunately, sometimes he could.

Thus, there was more psychic pain in his career than in DiMaggio's. Joe probably could have retreated into his shell, a brooding, frozen-faced fellow, if he had encountered hostility in New York. But Joe was in the Yankee tradition—earnest, striving, and proficient, like Lou Gehrig. He never compiled the record Williams did, but he was the more complete ball player, and many insist he was the better. He led the league a couple of times in hitting, in RBIs, in homers. The year Ted hit .406, Joe had his own remarkable performance, a hitting streak of fifty-six consecutive games. In the course of it he batted .408, and the day after it was broken he started again, on a string of sixteen.

More than this, he led the Yankees. He took over from Gehrig and eventually passed on the baton to Mickey Mantle. It was a position of pride and he bore it responsibly. He did not do it all himself, but he was a more than incidental contributor to the ten pennants and nine world's championships the Yankees enjoyed in his thirteen years with them.

Under the warm sun of New York's approval, first of his talents and then of his leadership, he relaxed, mellowed, expanded, cracked a smile, learned to chat easily with the writers, and was never at a loss for the sportsmanlike quip. Read the columns of the time. They all said it: He had class.

DiMaggio retired after the 1951 season, a champion. The 1946 pennant would be the only one in Williams's long career. In 1960, his last year, the Sox languished in seventh, the beginning of another spell of misery. About the only point of interest was his departure—the awkward, not-entirely-successful effort to let bygones be bygones. That final game had the perfect home-run ending, the ovation as he was sent to leftfield and then recalled—a last look at the Splendid Splinter and a last wringing of how many thousand hearts as he still could not find it in himself to tip his cap.

And yet, it may not have mattered after all, this sticking point. For there was a reprise. Thickened in body, even bulging here and there, he came back from a nonbaseball retirement at fifty-one to manage the Washington Senators, a dismal team in a town that for sixty-eight years had rarely had anything else.

Curiously—it seemed curious, but maybe it wasn't—he was a fine manager. With his humpty-dumpty players, who decamped in 1972 to become the Texas Rangers, he was patient, helpful, and a steadying influence, a calm and dedicated leader. While DiMaggio was making it big in television commercials—gray-haired, assured, a figure to inspire confidence—his old foe was buried in the lower regions of the American League. Under the unremitting sun of east Texas, he worked with his young players. He showed them how, and he never alibied or ran them down.

Make no mistake, he was still Ted Williams and some of the prickles were there. But now, you would have to say, he had class.

THE
ELECTRONIC
AGE
1946-1976

"There was no way our league
should have survived. It was saved
by the television network's
fascination with pro football."

—Joe Foss, first commissioner of the
American Football League

Computerizd Football Player. Color
transparency fed into an electronic scanner.

1 TV and Sports: Love at First Sight

At 2:30 P.M. on May 17, 1939, an anonymous engineer threw switches on a board located in the RCA building in Manhattan. Some eight miles away a large panel truck equipped with odd-looking cameras was parked beneath the stands at Columbia University's Baker Field, where Columbia was playing Princeton in an Ivy League baseball game. It took a great deal of electricity to activate the Iconoscope television camera that was perched above the third-base side of the diamond. The light waves to be transmitted flowed from a nearby flagpole across the island of Manhattan to the eighty-eighth floor of the Empire State Building. Suddenly, station W2XBS was on the air with the first live telecast of a sporting event.

"Good afternoon, ladies and gentlemen," said Bill Stern, one of the reigning radio announcers of the time. "Welcome to the first telecast of a sporting event. I'm not sure what it is we're doing here, but I certainly hope it turns out well for you people who are watching." He took a deep breath and continued. Sitting at a table on top of the grandstand, Stern had no idea what the camera was doing.

"There was no such thing as a monitor in those days," he recalled later. "I had no idea where the damned camera was going. I didn't even know if it could keep up with the play. I just did a radio broadcast and hoped the television experimentalists could cope with that. They didn't. Radio had been around too long and its practitioners had grown too wise. Television was a youthful, bumbling media. The camera, it turned out, couldn't follow the play."

The Iconoscope was the most sophisticated television camera of the day, but it was almost worthless for this assignment because its scope was so narrow that it could not focus on the pitcher and the batter at the same time. The camera was moving back and forth, dizzily trying to follow the ball as it zoomed to and from the plate. When a player hit the ball, the camera searched for it in bewilderment bordering on panic.

Only the most select audience attended this event. The viewers were a cluster of anxious executives in a Manhattan studio, several thousand visitors to the World's Fair in Flushing, Queens, and an undetermined number of the metropolitan area's few thousand television subscribers, each of whom had paid six hundred dollars and more for a set whose circular screen was ten inches in diameter. At the World's Fair, the audience gazing at the mystifying flecks on the screen had been assured that this was the ultimate in modern living, so everyone pretended to be thoroughly entertained. The people applauded when Ken Pill hit a home run in the tenth inning for Princeton, breaking up a 1-1 tie.

An anonymous critic for the *New York Times* was less impressed by the show. "The players were running around like white flies on the screen," he wrote. "When the ball flashed across the grass it appeared comet-like, a white pinpoint on a dim screen. The commentator, Bill Stern, saved the day, otherwise there would have been no way to follow the play or to tell where the ball went. It was not a success. It is difficult to see how this sort of thing can catch the public fancy."

Clearly, the *Times* underestimated this medium. As soon as the war was over, television sets could be constructed from materials that had previously been limited. Within a year after the Japanese delegation signed the documents on the bridge of the battleship *Missouri,* people were huddled in darkened living rooms—no lights, please—to watch boxing matches telecast from the St. Nicholas Arena. Within a decade, the tube was a staple in most middle-class homes, as Americans en masse indulged that delicious fantasy of in effect sneaking into the ball park without paying.

It was a fantastically profitable adventure. Advertisers, who reached a truly mass audience through a riveting medium, hungered for air time to sell their wares. Net-

Post-war America was ripe for the excitement of major league sport. In one of his many memorable paintings, Norman Rockwell caught the raw naiveté of a baseball rookie reporting on his first day of spring training. In another view of baseball, modern American primitive painter Ralph Fasanella summoned all the color and atmosphere of New York's Polo Grounds on a summer's day in 1947 (overleaf).

works snapped up broadcast rights for the most arcane spectacles. Big league teams and leagues sprouted across the country. And the athletes, whose services prompted this extravaganza, reaped the profit, too, basking in the security of lucrative multi-year contracts and television endorsements. Television meant more money for everyone. By the time of the Bicentennial televised sports were a $200 million business.

It was overwhelming. Television not only transmitted sports events but determined them, from time outs to franchise shifts. In 1964, when the Columbia Broadcasting System bought a controlling share of the New York Yankees, then still a successful team, hardly anyone protested that the interests of the network made it an unsuitable owner for a professional sports franchise. Television and pro sports had lived together for years, so who could object if they wanted to get married?

True, it hadn't always been an honorable relationship. Television lusted after sport, and some felt sport surrendered her honor too easily. There was that sordid business of television-studio boxing, for example, when television raped the fight game with its insatiable demand for fighters to fill its every-day-of-the-week broadcasts. Television turned championship golf from match play to medal play and dumped blue dye in the water hazards. Television prompted the baseball Braves to move from Boston to Milwaukee and then to Atlanta, to the dismay of the fans in the deserted cities. And it was television that put baseball's World Series into prime time, which in the middle of October is not always prime baseball weather.

These were not isolated abuses, yet like some unliberated wife clinging to her chauvinist husband, sport nagged a little but never thought of walking out. How could she? Why should she? It was a luxurious, even glamorous dependence. And television was less tyrannical than it could have been.

"When you consider that few franchises in baseball could exist without television revenue and when you

stop to think how dependent we are upon them," said Walter O'Malley, chairman of the board and president of the Los Angeles Dodgers, "you have to give the television people your admiration for their remarkable restraint. They could demand a whole lot more . . . and get it . . . but they don't."

"If you look at the record you'll see that television meddles far less today than it did in its formative years," concurred Roone Arledge, the American Broadcasting Company's grand vizier of sport. "The newspapers and magazines make a big deal out of things that happened twenty years ago."

The issue had been settled soon after Bill Stern appended his narration to the hazy video transmission of that Columbia-Princeton game: Television provided spectator sports with spectators in amounts to dwarf any previous draws. Television, for better or worse, was irresistible.

2 The Black Pioneer

They stood face to face — the odd couple who altered the character of American sport. One was a jowly white fundamentalist with long, bushy eyebrows that dominated an otherwise indomitable face; the other was a remarkably handsome, young black man whose lips poised halfway between a smile and a grimace, as if he wanted to convey both pleasure and pain on this auspicious occasion. Columnist Red Smith insisted that here in the paneled office of the president of the Brooklyn Dodgers baseball team a portrait of a gaunt and tired Abraham Lincoln observed this pivotal moment in American sports from the wall next to Branch Rickey's desk.

The black man was Jack Roosevelt Robinson, whom black entertainer Bill (Bojangles) Robinson called "Ty Cobb in Technicolor." The white man was Branch Rickey, one of those rare individuals who can cultivate money and morality (principal and principle, if you will) without conflict. As he climbed to fame and fortune as a baseball executive Rickey never abandoned certain moral precepts, among them that major league baseball should be integrated. Happily, it would prove to be quite a pragmatic (read "profitable") venture. This was the beginning.

Rickey was supposed to be founding an all-black corporation called the United States League, in cooperation with some black promoters of the old Negro National League. By this proposed scheme, Rickey would own the Brooklyn Brown Dodgers, who would play at home when the white club was on the road. Robinson was amazed to learn that the plan was a sham. Rickey wanted him to play for the regular Brooklyn Dodgers in the National League, but first he wanted to know if Robinson was the right man for the job.

He reminded the young black that only a few years earlier Henry Benjamin (Hank) Greenberg, the first Jewish superstar in baseball, had been vilified because he had refused to play on the Jewish Day of Atonement, Yom Kippur. Rickey warned that as a black man, Robinson could expect far worse treatment.

The Brooklyn owner gave flawless impersonations of the white waiters, room clerks, railroad conductors, and opposing ball players who would abuse Robinson.

"Suppose they throw at your head?" said Rickey.

"Mister Rickey," said Robinson, "they've been throwing at my head for a long time."

"Suppose I'm an opposing player in the heat of an important ball game. Suppose I jump and yell, 'You dirty nigger bastard.' What do you do then? How does that affect you? How do you respond? Doesn't that burn your guts out? Doesn't that make you want to kill him?"

Robinson's lips drew into a tight line. "Do you want a man who is afraid to fight back?" Robinson shouted, his high-pitched voice soaring an octave. "Is that what you want? If it is, you have the wrong nigger, Mister Rickey. That's not Jackie Robinson. My mother taught me to be something bigger than that. I'd love to play major league baseball, but not on those grounds. I'd rather shine shoes

The black athlete had an enormous impact on post-war sports in America. At UCLA, two gifted men, Jackie Robinson and Kenny Washington, starred in football, baseball, and track. Washington (13) and UCLA football teammate Woody Strode were signed to professional contracts by the Los Angeles Rams in 1946. They were the first black men to play in the modern National Football League.

or keep doing what I'm doing now. Please excuse me."

Savagely, Rickey turned the corner of his desk, took off his jacket, and threw it across the room. "No," he roared, "I want somebody with guts enough to fight back. I want the strongest black man of the decade. I want a man who knows his destiny. I want a man who fights back with base hits and stolen bases and fielding plays that amaze everybody. I want nothing else, at least not at first. After the black man becomes accepted and idolized in the major leagues, what you do is your own business. Do you understand what it will take at first? You'll have to swallow your own ego and act humble when that may not be your style. Other black people are going to have to be asked to ease up and not make a big thing out of you. This is going to take a whole lot of finesse, but when it ends, you'll see what's been done and you'll be proud you had guts enough to make the sacrifice.

"Now, I'm playing against you in the World Series. I'm a hot-headed, red-necked player. I want to win that game, so I go into you spikes first. But you don't give an inch of ground. Remember, you're Jackie Robinson and you don't give an inch to anyone. You jab the ball right into my ribs and the umpire yells, 'Out.' I flare up. I stand there. All I see is your black face. So I stand and, in my desire to win, I punch you right in your damned black cheek and call you 'nigger.' What do you do?"

For a second Robinson shook his head back and forth in consternation. He looked up. Arthur Mann, a former newspaperman turned publicity director, was in the room taking notes. He remembers that Robinson could not speak. Instead tears trickled down his cheeks.

"What do you do?" screamed Rickey.

"I guess I turn the other cheek, don't I, Mister Rickey?" he shouted. "I guess that's all there is for a black boy to do. Well, I tell you this: I'll be a black boy turning the other cheek so long as it is necessary. When it isn't necessary anymore, you can be damned sure this is one black boy who will never turn the other cheek. I'll do what you say because I know you are right. I'll do everything I have

to do. But I won't do it one second longer than it's needed. Is that what you want to hear?"

"Indeed it is," said Rickey, smiling and weeping at the same time. "You're the man. You're the man I thought you were. God bless you and keep you, young man. You're hired."

Robinson shook Rickey's hand and got up to leave. Within an hour Jackie Robinson signed a contract with the Dodgers' Montreal farm team. He received a $3,500 bonus for signing. His salary with the Montreal Royals of the International League would be $600 a month.

There were twenty-five reporters present at the press conference. Robinson answered questions with an easy confidence. It was true, he said, that he grew up on Pasadena's Pepper Street with other blacks, a few Mexicans, and some tough Japanese. His record with the local authorities was on file. He'd gone through Muir High School and Pasadena City College with fair marks. It was also true that at UCLA he was a far better football player than student; his intelligence quotient was higher than his marks. When his football eligibility was done, he left. His mother wanted him to be a lawyer. He had wanted to be a physical-education director. Now he was going to be the first modern major league baseball player of his race. One writer said the mood of the press at the gathering was not hostile; it was mostly indifferent. The real hostility came later.

On October 24, 1945, the commissioner of the minor leagues, William Bramham, was distressingly nasty. "Father Divine will have to look to his laurels," Bramham said. "Rickey is strictly a carpetbagger. We can all expect Rickey Temple to be constructed in Harlem soon. There being no written rule to the contrary that I know of, Robinson's contract with the Montreal club will be promulgated just as any other." Later Bramham admitted that he had anticipated this day but had hoped it would never come. He was convinced that blacks were faster than whites and thus would soon rule baseball. Bramham foresaw the destruction of the game.

215

In 1946, Paul Brown was efficiently
organizing the Cleveland entry in the
new All-America Football Conference.
Two of his most important players were
fullback Marion Motley, below, and
guard Bill Willis, two blacks who would
become standouts in pro football.
A year later, a Brooklyn Dodgers' shirt,
depicted opposite by Donald Moss, would
be worn by a black man for the first time.

Other baseball officials were equally distressed. "You will never see Negroes in our league as long as our good old Jim Crow laws are in service," said Alvin Gardner, president of the Texas league.

"Robinson will not make the grade in the major leagues. He is a thousand-to-one shot at best. The Negro players simply don't have the brains or the skills," said Jimmy Powers, sports editor of the *New York Daily News*. The commissioner of baseball, the former governor and senator from Kentucky, the honorable Happy Chandler, withheld comment.

"It has become apparent that not everyone who prattles of tolerance and racial equality has precisely the same understanding of the terms," observed Red Smith.

The next spring marked the beginning of Jack Roosevelt Robinson's ordeal. When he went to train with the Montreal club at Sanford, Florida, some twenty miles north of Daytona Beach, Robinson was not welcome in town.

"We don't want no Nigras mixin' with no white folks in Sanford," said the sheriff. "Robinson, boy, you gotta be outta here as soon as you through practicin'."

In Deland, Florida, for an exhibition match with the Indianapolis Indians of the American Association, Robinson slid across the plate in the first inning of the game and a policeman jumped on the field and arrested him.

"You gotta get out of here or I am putting you in jail," the law officer shouted. When Robinson started to laugh, the lawman dragged him toward the Montreal bench.

"We ain't having Nigras mix with white boys in this town," the policeman told Clay Hopper, the Royals' manager. "Nobody named Branch Rickey is gonna change our way of livin'. Nigras and whites can't sit together. They can't play games together or they gonna start wantin' to sleep together. You knows what that means. Now tell that Nigra to git." Jackie Robinson got up and left.

In one exhibition game in Birmingham, Alabama, a Syracuse player held up a black cat and shouted, "Hey,

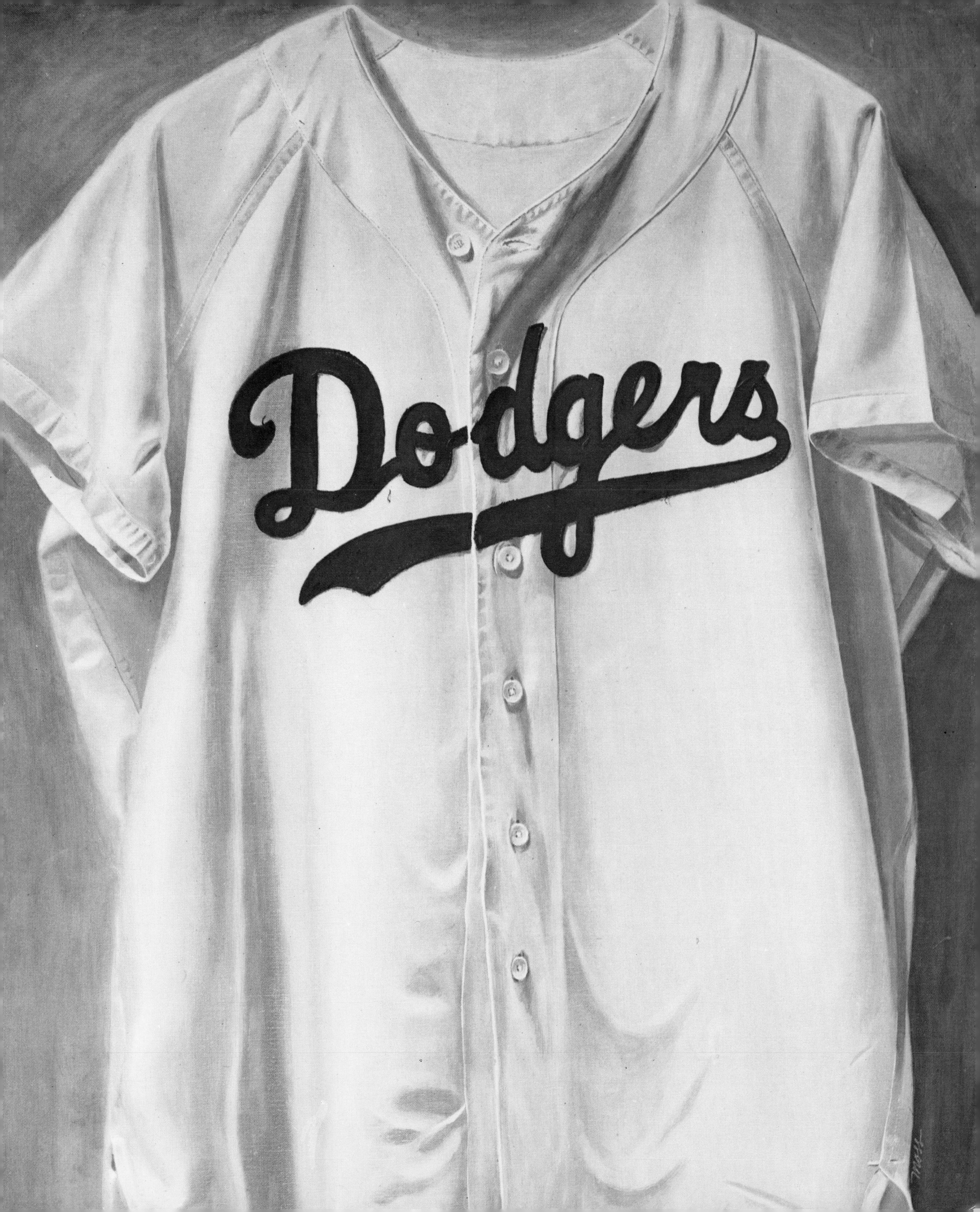
Dodgers

Robinson, here's your brother!" Robinson shrugged.

Spring training ended and the tension eased slightly. In the opening game of the regular season, Robinson started off shakily. He made an error in the field and grounded out his first time up on a pitch he knew he should have hit for at least a single. The deprecative on-lookers in the stands were agreeing that those "nigger boys" really could not play the game seriously when Robinson settled down. He hit a home run with two men on base, singled three times, stole two bases, scored four runs, and twice rattled Jersey City pitchers into balks. Montreal won 14-1.

"Don't worry about this man," said Hopper on the telephone to Rickey after the game that night. "He's a great athlete, a great competitor, and a fine human being. I mean that as sincerely as I can say it. He's all right. I'm proud to be his manager."

The major league color line was broken the next spring, in 1947, when Jackie Robinson joined the Brooklyn Dodgers. Jackie was asked to play first base, since the Dodgers already had the redoubtable Eddie Stanky at second. Stanky was a feisty, no-holds-barred competitor from Mobile, Alabama. The shortstop was Harold (Pee Wee) Reese, from Louisville, Kentucky. When Ben Chapman, the manager of the Philadelphia Phillies, abused Robinson, it was Stanky who ran over to the Phillies' dugout and shouted, "Chapman, you gutless bastard, you know he's under orders not to yell back at you. Why don't you pick on somebody who can fight back? I've got no respect for you at all." On the field, Reese draped his arm around Robinson's shoulder and said, "He's a damned Dodger—just like me."

Not all the Dodgers greeted their new teammate as lovingly. When Robinson reported to the Dodgers that spring, a petition was circulated asking Rickey to reconsider his decision to integrate. Dixie Walker, a native of Alabama, led the protest but it was stifled when the petition reached pitcher Kirby Higbe, a hard-swinging Southerner who later became an evangelist. "Ol' Hig ain't gonna sign nothin' that keeps a qualified man from making a decent livin'," he said at a clubhouse meeting. "The old man [Rickey] has been good to me. If he thinks this Robinson fella can play baseball with us and help us and if he thinks it will be good for baseball, well, I'm not signin' that petition. That's all there is to it."

Later, Walker asked to be traded. His brother, Harry, was alleged to be the ringleader of an abortive strike by the St. Louis Cardinals. Some of the Cardinals reportedly had threatened to walk off the field if forced to play against Robinson. "I had some problems the first year," Robinson readily conceded. "Enos Slaughter from North Carolina spiked me at first base. But he'd spiked a lot of tough new players. . . . Don't forget I had never played first base before. My foot was over the bag and he came down on it. I never thought there was anything racial about that."

Slaughter said as much years later. "He could have been my own brother and if he had put his heel out in my path, he would have run the risk of getting hurt, too," said Slaughter.

"There was opposition from some Southern whites," Robinson said. "I expected that. But other Southern whites went out of their way to befriend me and make me feel I belonged. Many of the Northern whites seemed aloof and disinterested. One of them told me that they were afraid that within ten years blacks would dominate baseball because we all seemed to run so much faster than whites. I told him that was an unfounded fear."

The baseball quota system saw to that. Within two years Robinson was joined by other blacks, yet one manager predicted that no more than four blacks would ever appear in a major league lineup at one time. He was proved wrong, but it was a long time before blacks were judged strictly on merit.

Robinson was still very much the exception. He had good speed, but his greatest asset was quickness and his knack for flustering pitchers with his constant fidgeting when he reached base. He led the National League with

In 1947, Jackie Robinson became major league baseball's first black player when Branch Rickey brought him up from Montreal. The historic event put Robinson on the cover of *Life* magazine and his addition to the Dodgers' roster brought them immediate success at the box office and in the National League standings.

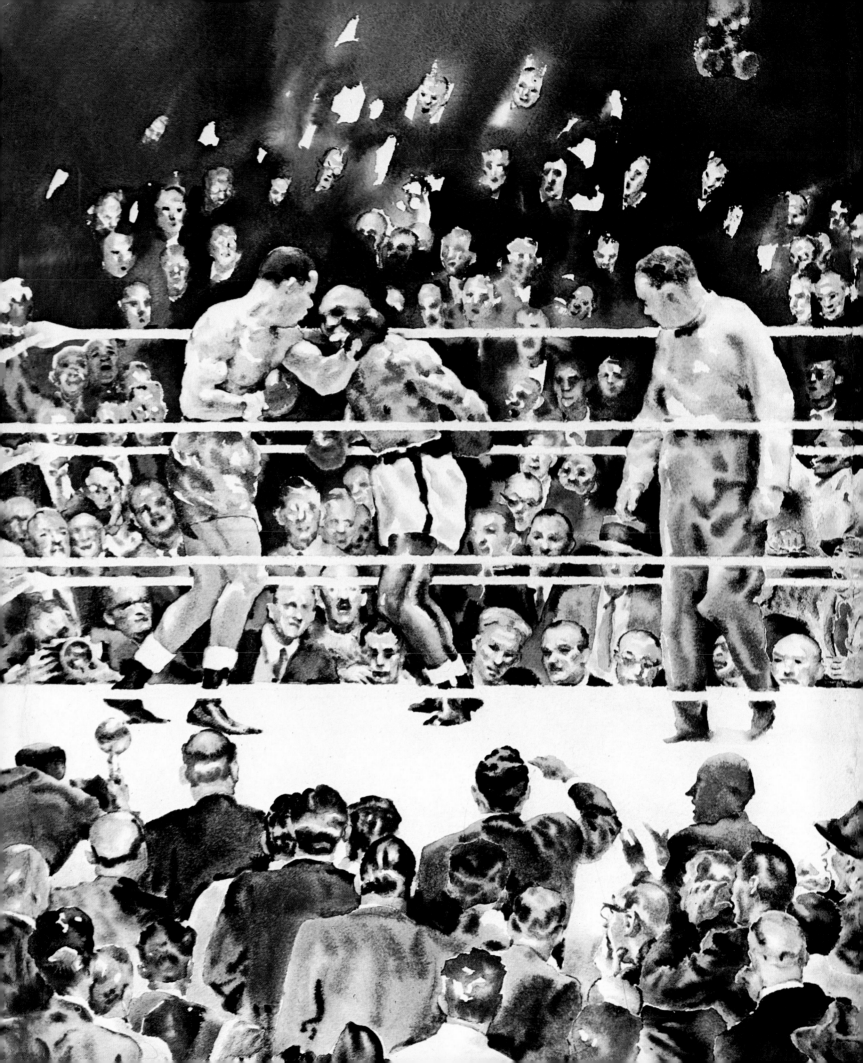

The nation was settling back to normal as the memory of World War II receded. In places like Campo, California, sandlot baseball games were a favorite way to spend an afternoon. But big time sports were of great interest, and in June, 1948, the rematch of Joe Louis and Jersey Joe Walcott captivated the country. Louis had won a close decision over Walcott six months earlier. This time, with the nation's full attention, he knocked out Walcott in eleven rounds to retain his title and continue his long reign as as heavyweight champion.

twenty-nine stolen bases in 1947 and with thirty-seven in 1949, the year he also led the league in batting with a .342 average and was voted its most valuable player.

By this time he was shedding the restraints that Rickey had imposed on him. He was even thrown out of a game, for suggesting to the plate umpire that he had choked on a call. The real Robinson was beginning to show, and not everybody liked this abrasive revolutionary. "He was a hotheaded popoff, a poor loser, and an acid-tongued agitator, that quick-tempered, blazing-eyed man with the big number forty-two on his back," wrote the *New York Daily News's* Dick Young.

In a way, this was progress—being disliked for his personality rather than his skin color. "Maybe I wasn't the ideal man for the job that Mr. Rickey thought I was," recalled Robinson when his career had ended. "But all that garbage I stored my first couple of years just had to break through. Enough garbage was enough. I had to be able to bitch when I thought I had a bitch coming. I found I played better when I let off steam."

Over a ten-season career Jack Roosevelt Robinson batted .311, played five positions, and qualified for the Hall of Fame. Supposedly, he was selected on his contributions as a ball player, not as a pioneer.

Anyone who ever saw him spear ground balls, or knock out his base hits, or, best of all, steal home with that seemingly mad, impetuous scamper, can understand such reasoning. But anyone who weighs the significance to baseball and to sport of the movement he led cannot but conclude that Jackie Robinson's place in the history of sport is as a black man first and an athlete second.

3 Miracle at Coogan's Bluff

You know the story. The New York Giants, given up for dead in August, went storming through the final months of the 1951 baseball season and made up a thirteen and a half game deficit on the league-

leading Brooklyn Dodgers. The Giants seemed to have won the pennant with a victory at Boston on the final day but meanwhile the faltering, floundering, yes—say it—choking Brooklyn Dodgers were swallowing manfully and in fourteen nervous innings beating the Phillies in the cold, swirling mist at Shibe Park in Philadelphia. The regular season was finished with the Giants and Dodgers tied for the pennant, so the two teams engaged in a best-of-three playoff. The teams divided the first two games and stood tied 1-1 in the top of the eighth of the finale in the Polo Grounds.

Red Smith re-created the play-by-play: "Here's Pee Wee Reese hitting safely in the eighth. Here's Duke Snider singling Reese to third. Here's Sal Maglie wild-pitching a run home. Here's Andy Pafko slashing a hit through Thomson for another score. Here's Billy Cox batting still another run home. Where does the hit go? Where else? Through Thomson at third."

That's not Hank Thompson, who also played some third base for the Giants that year, but Robert Brown Thomson, the first game's hero (two-run, game-winning homer), the second game's goat (two errors in the field and some bloopers on the basepaths), and the third game's . . . well, let's not get ahead of the story.

So the Dodgers lead handily, 4-1. The Giants are down without a murmur in the eighth, and—no need to prolong things—the Dodgers follow suit in the top of the ninth.

And so dawned the most famous bottom of the ninth in the history of baseball. This half-inning would move Red Smith to stammer, "Now it is done. Now the story ends. And there is no way to tell it. The art of fiction is dead. Reality has strangled invention. Only the utterly impossible, the inexpressibly fantastic can ever be plausible again. Yet, the story remains to be told, the story of how the Giants won the 1951 pennant in the National League. Maybe this is the way to tell it: Bobby Thomson, a young Scot from Staten Island, delivered a timely hit in the ninth inning of an enjoyable game of baseball before 34,320 witnesses in the Polo Grounds."

The unfortunate sportswriter, unhinged by this manic-depressive event and season, gyrated wildly between overstatement and understatement. The rest of us, not blessed with a muse as enervating as the event itself, have recourse only to the facts.

Alvin Dark led off with a single through the right side of the infield—"a seeing-eye" base hit, to be scrupulously accurate about it. Oddly, Brooklyn first baseman Gil Hodges held the bag against Dark, though with the Giants three runs down the baserunner obviously would not be running until the ball was hit. Sure enough, the next man up, Don Mueller, slashed one to the right of Hodges—some say he could have had it had he been playing off the bag—and the Giants had men on first and second. Monte Irvin was next; overswinging, he popped up. But Whitey Lockman revived the rally with a slicing double to left, scoring Dark and sending Mueller sliding into third.

Time out. Mueller, who broke his ankle, is relieved by a pinch runner. Brooklyn pitcher Don Newcombe, who lost his fastball, gives way to Ralph Branca. While the ace reliever is trudging in from the bullpen in deep left-field, while he's firing in his warmups to Rube Walker, while the crowd senses one of those precipices of decision, and while the nation edges closer to its black-and-white Motorolas, this traditional narrative pauses for a little traditional second-guessing.

Brooklyn manager Charlie Dressen didn't have to bring in Branca. He had Clem Labine (winning pitcher the day before) and the formidable Preacher Roe (22-3 that year with a 3.04 ERA, best on the staff) both warming up in the bullpen. He chose Branca because he wanted a right-hander for the right-handed-hitting Thomson, because Branca was his best man in relief, and because pitching coach Clyde Sukeforth recommended him. Then Dressen instructed Branca to pitch to Thomson, though there was one out and a walk would have filled the bases to make possible a game-ending double play. Dressen followed the conventional strategy of trying to keep the winning run off base. No one really knows whether the manager was influenced one way or the other by the fact that a rookie named Willie Mays was on deck.

O.K. The other strategies having been considered, and for better or worse rejected, the play may now proceed. Thomson steps in, a tall but not lanky fellow with a nondescript stance—neither open nor closed, not much crouch, no bat waggling or other such distractions. Branca leans forward for the sign, unbends to begin the windup, and flings a high hard one over the plate at the letters. Thomson watches it for a strike. And again: the same pitch.

But this time Thomson whips the bat around and connects. It's a curling drive to left—not bombastically but sharply hit. And in an instant it's gone, lodged in the lower leftfield stands of the Polo Grounds, less than 350 feet from home plate. It is not a grand blast, but a modest shot; not an explosion, only a pop. Yet the circumstances are such that nothing more is needed to start the landslide.

Thomson whoops around the bases, while in the third base coach's box manager Leo Durocher jumps in glee and bratty second baseman Eddie Stanky, who has rushed all the way from the Giants' dugout, attacks him. The crowd has invaded the field, mindlessly dancing to release its pent-up tension. In the press box, Giants' broadcaster Russ Hodges surrenders the microphone in exhaustion to a colleague after screaming insanely, "The Giants win the pennant!!" over and over again. Only the devastated Dodgers are transfixed. They melt toward the clubhouse in centerfield. Ralph Branca can be seen on the clubhouse steps, slumped against the wall, crying.

4 Track and Field and Possible Dreams

On May 6, 1954, the following announcement was made at a dual track and field meet between the British Amateur Athletic Association and Oxford University at Oxford, England:

"The result of event number nine: R. G. Bannister, AAA and formerly of Exeter and Merton Colleges, with a time which is a new meeting and track record, and which, subject to ratification, will be a new English native, British national, British all-comers, European, British Empire, and world record. The time was three minutes fifty-nine point four seconds."

Some fifty words or so, and never once did the announcer say that one of the most improbable dreams in all sport had just come true. Man had run the mile in less than four minutes.

Perhaps the public address man kept his cool, but everywhere else people bubbled over. Evening newspapers heralded the feat of Roger Gilbert Bannister with page one banner headlines. Wall Street brokers read the startling news on their ticker tapes. Arthur Daley, sports columnist of the New York Times, likened Bannister's accomplishment to Sir Edmund Hillary's ascent of Mount Everest. "Two of mankind's supposedly unscalable peaks were surmounted at almost the same time," he wrote later. Life magazine led its next issue with Bannister, subordinating the story of the fall of Dienbienphu to Indochina rebels.

For generations many respected and qualified observers had thought the sub-four-minute mile beyond the reach of man. Among them were coaches and former athletes, physiologists intrigued with the study of man's ability to punish his body, mathematicians and other scientists who calculated the limits of the possible with graphs and charts.

But there were optimists, too. Three of them were Wes Santee, a student at the University of Kansas; John Landy, an Australian whose hobby was collecting butterflies; and Bannister, who was completing his work toward a medical degree.

Santee and Landy ranked with Bannister—really, ahead of him—as the world's best milers. All had at one time or another flirted with the seemingly impenetrable world record of 4:01.4, which had been established nine

On May 6, 1954, a 25-year-old English medical student broke track's magic barrier. Roger Bannister became the first man to run a mile in under four minutes when he won a race at Oxford, England, in three minutes, 59.4 seconds.

years earlier in 1945 by Gunder Hagg of Sweden.

Each of these three, continents apart, believed he could run the sub-four-minute mile. Undeniably, they were in a race to be first. Santee was poised for a major race in Dayton, Ohio, one June day in 1953. For fear the American might succeed, Bannister ran in a hastily arranged, almost secret special mile that morning at a schoolboy meet in Surrey. Both attempts failed. In the Australian summer months, between late November, 1953, and early March, 1954, Landy ran no less than twelve-mile races. He got as close as 4:02.0.

Bannister's mile at Oxford was his first of the season. He had trained steadily, whenever he could get away from his duties at St. Mary's Hospital in London. Cross winds, with gusts up to twenty-five miles per hour, threatened the record bid but when the weather cleared somewhat, shortly before race time, the Briton decided to go ahead. Chris Brasher and Chris Chataway, British AAA teammates and runners of international stature, were in the race with pre-planned roles. Brasher took the lead at the outset and held it for 880 yards; Bannister, running in his wake, was clocked in 57.5 seconds for the first 440 yards and 1:58.2 at the half-mile. Here, Chataway eased into the lead, with Bannister tightly behind him. At three-quarters, the time was 3:00.5. A final quarter in 59.4 would do it.

With 300 yards to go, Bannister forged ahead of Chataway. He ran with every ounce of reserve strength he could summon. He was straining, his head wobbling a bit, as he sped through the tape and dropped exhausted into the arms of two officials. He had negotiated the final lap in 58.9, and there it was, a mile in 3:59.4.

It was a superhuman effort. Or was it? Forty-six days later, in Turku, Finland, a smiling and serene Landy snapped the tape at the end of a mile in 3:58.0, almost a second and a half faster than Bannister's time at Oxford. Track fans laughingly suggested that at that rate 3:50 would soon fall. Well, in 1975 it did. John Walker of New Zealand achieved 3:49.4 at Goteborg, Sweden.

What happened in the years between Bannister and Walker? Across the board, in all track and field events, there have been improvements in the preparation of the athlete. Diet is better. The use of weights in training to strengthen the body has been widely adopted. Coaching techniques are more sophisticated. Athletes work out for up to two and a half hours a day; "we trained a half hour a day," says Bannister.

Pole vaulting has enjoyed a bull market mostly because of improved equipment. The introduction of the fiber glass pole, which virtually catapults the vaulter, made a shambles of the record book. The world mark stood around 16 feet for more than twenty years until John Uelses, forsaking the aluminum pole then in vogue, rode a fiber glass to a height of 16 feet ¼ inch in 1962. Don Bragg, the dethroned champion, screamed in protest to no avail; the international fathers who govern the sport approved the new equipment and soon vaulters were reaching for the moon. In a year and a half, the record was up to 17 feet and by 1970 it was 18.

Vaulting demonstrates that improved equipment advances performance; shot putting illustrates the benefits of new techniques. For generations it was conventional for the shot putter to launch his effort from a position at right angles to the direction in which he would throw. Parry O'Brien became the first 60-footer because he introduced the practice of beginning with his back to the toeboard, from which the competitor propels the shot. Thus he was putting the force of his weight, strength, and agility into a 180-degree turn rather than one of a mere 90 degrees. The O'Brien technique was universally adopted and led to greater and greater performances. In the mid-seventies, Brian Oldfield, a professional, pioneered still another procedure. He whirled within the narrow circle, as though he were a discus thrower, and then let go. He attained a distance of 75 feet, almost three feet farther than man had propelled the 16-pound shot before.

The most fascinating factor in the postwar spree of

Many runners followed Roger Bannister across the four-minute threshold, including the first American, Don Bowden, who ran the mile in 3:58.7 in 1957. In a sudden rush of achievement, other long-challenged marks fell to Americans in the fifties, including the sixty-foot shot put, the seven-foot high jump, and the sixteen-foot pole vault. In *The Milers,* Jim Jonson dramatized track's best-known event.

record setting in track and field has been the athletes' growing confidence that no record is unbreakable. The challenge of record-breaking has been shown to be far more psychological than physical. Bannister and his rivals proved that. Bannister broke the four-minute barrier, and there was a flood of sub-four-minute miles thereafter. At the same time several shotputters were striving for the first 60-footer, while wondering whether it could ever be achieved. O'Brien held the world record of 59 feet 2¼ inches. On April 24, less than two weeks before Bannister's mile, he did 59 feet 9¼ inches. It was an exhibition, however, so the mark was not considered a record. On May 1, Stan Lampert reached 59 feet 5⅞ inches. Suddenly, O'Brien had all the incentive he needed. Not only had his record been broken but he realized that 60 feet was well within his range (and Lampert's). Competing in Los Angeles on May 8, two days after the Bannister mile, O'Brien staked a board in the earth just short of the 60-foot mark. On the marker he had written, "Lampert 59-5⅞." With that self-goading reminder, he unleashed a toss of 60 feet 5¼ inches.

In the high jump, one of the more intriguing and suspenseful events to the spectator, the world record stood at 6 feet 11 inches for more than a decade. When it finally was surpassed, it was by only a half-inch, to 6 feet 11½ inches. Immediately after the record jump, the man who did it, 1952 Olympic champion Walt Davis, asked to have the crossbar raised to 7 feet. But he failed three times at that seemingly stratospheric height.

Three years later a nineteen-year-old junior college freshman from Los Angeles, Charles Dumas, won an Olympic trial meet in the high jump with a leap of 6 feet 10½ inches. Like Davis, he then requested the privilege of trying to do what man had never done before. Dumas tried once, failed, tried a second time, and made it. Suddenly, high jumpers seemed skybound. Twenty years later high school boys were jumping 7 feet. By then one needed to do 7 feet 1 inch just to qualify for the Olympics. In 1973, Dwight Stones, another Californian, lifted the world record to 7 feet 6½ inches, and talked of 7 feet 8 inches.

A special niche in the assault on the limits of the possible belongs to a man from Long Island who attended the University of Kansas, a discus thrower named Al Oerter. He was responsible not only for another psychological breakthrough but also for an unparalleled Olympic accomplishment: he captured the gold medal in his event at four consecutive Games. He made the team in 1956 at age twenty and triumphed with a record Olympic toss of 184 feet 10½ inches. Nobody had yet reached the magical peak of 200 feet. In the 1960 Olympics, Oerter was up to 194 feet 2 inches in defeating two former world record holders. In 1962, Oerter became the first man to throw the discus over 200 feet; he surpassed the figure by five inches. Instead of retiring at that lofty plateau he won his third Olympic crown in 1964, and then, at age thirty-two, made it an incredible four in a row with the best toss of his career, 212 feet 6½ inches. By 1975, America's John Powell had the world mark up to 226 feet 8 inches.

The limits to our conception of the possible have proven to be as great as the limits of possibility itself. The American athletic woods are filled with saplings soon to grow great. One day they'll put the shot 80 feet and pole vault 20 feet. They'll run the mile in 3:30. Science will not determine what an athlete can and cannot do until it determines the limits of what he thinks he can do.

5   To the Red Line and Beyond

It is not an overstatement to say that professional ice hockey in the seventies is a game made possible by the institution of the center-ice red line in 1943-44. There is more to it than that, of course, but it seems certain that the headlong, bang-it-into-the-corner-and-chase-it attack of today would not be so popular if players could not pass half the length of the rink.

Players of the pre-red line era would high-stick you for saying it, but their game was somewhat statelier than that played today. And more artful. The puck-carrying team could not pass forward over its blue line, so someone, usually the center, had to stickhandle the puck out of the defensive zone and into center ice. Waiting for the puck carrier just over the line was a poke-checking enemy center. A clever one, such as Frank Boucher of the New York Rangers, or Pit Lepine of the Montreal Canadiens, or Johnny Gottselig of the Chicago Black Hawks, could dominate the center zone, breaking up attacks before they got organized. Once the red line was established, a pass to mid-rink, a stride or two beyond, and a head-man pass over the foe's blue line—well, the puck would be shot on goal before the old poke-checking center knew where it was.

Since anyone could bang the puck half the length of the ice legally, it was almost impossible to pin a team in its own zone anymore. Forecheckers did not dare venture too deeply down ice to hawk the puck; a quick pass could snap it to a winger hanging out by the boards, just inside the red line, and a sprint, or a pass, or a long drive into a corner could have the enemy swarming around the net before the checkers could get back to help their defensemen. So the last men out of the opponent's defensive zone as the action shifted to the other end of the rink were less likely to backcheck energetically than to start hanging around *their* side of the red line, hoping for a pass-out and another lightning change of direction in the flow of the game.

All this meant an entirely new job description for defensemen. They became the real two-way players of hockey: aggressive, physical, taking part in the action in all areas of the ice. On defense they had to be quicker, more alert, more responsive to rapid shifts of play. Because the red line was now the first barrier an opponent could not overstep without incurring an offside, defensemen began to meet the play in center zone, rather than behind their own blue line. Thus, they had to be able to skate backward fast enough in their half of the rink to

In the northeastern United States, cold weather directly influences sport. Ice hockey and skiing are traditional favorites, but one of the most popular sports is ice boating. As shown in this painting by New Jersey artist Stanley Meltzoff, a hard freeze on the Navesink River near Red Bank has brought out several classes of ice boats, including a nineteenth century Class A boat.

keep between a racing wing and the goal. They had to be able, at rink's end, to turn swiftly right or left, close with their man, pin him or take the puck, and accelerate or pass out of danger. On offense they had to be able to stickhandle well enough to fend off harassing checkers, pass well enough to lead a flying winger, and shoot with speed and accuracy on power plays within the opponent's blue line. And when the attack went awry, they immediately had to become defensemen again, re-establishing position in front of their goal before the enemy swooped down, shooting.

As this wide-open, end-to-end hockey required defensemen to play more and more like forwards, it was natural that an integrated five-man attack would evolve, but instead the first decade or so of postwar play saw the arrival of the game's true superstars and the formation of several of the superb forward lines of all time. Hockey had not yet understood the profundity of its red-line innovation. It had upset the balance of the game without fully altering the concept of how the game should be played.

With all deference to the great players of the prewar era, there just never had been anyone quite like the three number 9's: Maurice (the Rocket) Richard of the Canadiens, Gordie Howe of the Red Wings, and Bobby Hull of the Hawks. Or, for that matter, like Montreal's Jean Beliveau and Doug Harvey, Detroit's Red Kelly and Marcel Pronovost, or Toronto's Tim Horton. Or combinations like Detroit's Production Line, Sid Abel, Ted Lindsay, and Howe; Montreal's Elmer Lach, Toe Blake, and Richard; or even Chicago's Bentley brothers, Max and Doug, and Wee Willie Mosienko.

They played the old-style game better than ever. They were extraordinarily expert and brilliantly deceptive in their playmaking, passing, and shooting, and they could roll over or evade anything in their way. The image of Richard bulling his way down the right-wing alley was always fearsome. Over the blue line he stormed, taking a flip from Lach or Blake, leaning goalward, legs wide

to counter the hampering, encircling weight of the defenseman, raven hair neatly parted and seldom ruffled, and dark eyes blazing. And finally the deadly left-handed shot.

The five-man attack operated perhaps first and certainly most formally with the power play. The man advantage gained through a penalty gave the wide-open offense almost total control of the ice. The four-man box defense might prevail with luck and some inspired play, but the time-killing center-ice keepaway stickhandling—"ragging the puck"—just wasn't a defensive option anymore. From mid-ice the puck flew into a corner, the wings went after it, the center trailed, looking for position in front of the net, and the defensemen took the points, inside the blue line on opposite sides of the rink.

The Canadiens' power play, quarterbacked by Doug Harvey on one point, Boom-Boom Geoffrion at the other, and Richard, Dickie Moore, and Beliveau (or Bert Olmstead) weaving patterns inside, was so efficient it could score two or three goals in the course of one penalty. It broke so many games apart that the league finally, in 1956-57, instituted a rule permitting the penalized player to return to the game as soon as a goal was scored against his team.

The power-play pattern was utilized generally in offensive play. Defensemen could not play point quite so audaciously in the regular back-and-forth of a game, but they often carried the puck out of their own end, rushed it beyond the red line, and passed off, or shot a head-man pass over the blue line to a streaking wing, or slammed it into a corner. Because the game was so open, defensemen often did better to stay with their forwards up ice, keeping passes short and accurate, rather than hanging back cautiously in the defense zone and risking interception of a long sliding pass.

The game went on in this manner for some twenty postwar years. It was a game totally dominated by Montreal and Detroit. In the twenty-seven years between 1943 and 1969 these two teams led the league twenty-

Bernie Parent takes off the mask at 12:15
today in the Grand Court when he
accepts the 1975 John Wanamaker Athletic Award
on behalf of himself and the Philadelphia Flyers.
The Stanley Cup stays in Philadelphia
for another year and the victory is even sweeter
the second time around. Join
John Wanamaker in a rousing cheer
for the man behind the mask and the team
behind the man who did it.

John Wanamaker

four times. Because of the manipulations that make lesser teams eligible for Stanley Cup competition, Toronto became a winner four times in the sixties, and Chicago and Boston won once in a while as well. But the Canadiens have been first in the league twelve times, first in their division eight times, and Stanley Cup champions eighteen times. Now that the NHL has expanded to sixteen teams in four divisions, it is unlikely that any dynasty will arise to threaten the Canadiens' record or longevity.

What has emerged in the seventies, however, is a style of play initiated by the Philadelphia Flyers and so far executed successfully only by them. This is chase-the-puck-with-a-vengeance, and it challenges even the smooth-skating expertise of the Canadiens. The expansion of the league has inevitably resulted not so much in a deterioration as in a coarsening of play. The fast-paced, see-saw action, the minute-and-a half turns on the ice, the hasty change of lines on the fly have all added a measure of hysteria to the game, but no poise.

Philadelphia's contribution has been to add rigor and resolution to the haphazardness of corner play. Digging for the puck in these "pits"—like the hand-to-hand combat between National Football League linemen—is punishing business, and whatever theory may say about the way it should be undertaken, there are more than a few forwards and defensemen around the league who have no stomach for it. Philadelphia's extremely physical team has determined to put its hand in the fire. The pain attendant on extracting the puck from a melee is to be borne by all forwards as payment for the opportunity to win control and to pass the puck out to the teammate with the quick stick in the goal mouth. No one is exempt, or wishes to be. Every Flyer does his job. And to the extent that he does it willingly and eagerly, he intimidates less resolute opponents more surely than the blatant brawling and fouling that preoccupy most analysts of the Philadelphia mystique. It is not subtle hockey. Its lessons are plain for all to see. The story of the National Hockey League in the late seventies and beyond will be the re-

sponse, the countervailing force, it offers the Philadelphia Flyers.

6 From Casey to the Amazing Mets

Beyond the rococo arches of the moldering ball park the gray sky held a yellowish-brown sun. It was an eerie day, the last day—or what seemed like the last day—of National League baseball in New York. The fans were in an ornery mood. They had been led to believe that two of baseball's great imperishables were the Brooklyn Dodgers and the New York Giants. But within a few hours both would be moving to the West Coast.

In recent years, two big league franchises had moved: the Boston Braves to Milwaukee and the Philadelphia Athletics to Kansas City. But the Dodgers and Giants were supposed to be different. The Dodgers were making money and the Giants were not in distress. Their moving was not a matter of survival, critics charged, but of greed.

Walter O'Malley, owner of the Dodgers, had a debt-free baseball team with real estate holdings worth some five million dollars. His team was drawing well, and it had a radio-television contract for $580,000 in Brooklyn —one of the best in baseball. In Los Angeles the figure would be $1 million to start. The normally staid and proper game of baseball was chasing the almighty dollar across the country, or so it seemed, and there were those who found it a grubby and disgusting spectacle. Somehow a ball team seemed to owe more to its loyal fans.

One protester walked through the aisles at the Polo Grounds, carrying a banner that read, "Stay, team, stay! Go, Horace, go!" The slogan referred to the owner of the Giants, the shy, pink-complexioned Horace Stoneham, who was cast as O'Malley's henchman in this perfidious move West, and who now, too scared or depressed to mingle with the twelve thousand spectators of the Giants' last game, observed the proceedings from a dressing room in distant centerfield.

When the final out was made and the New York Giants ceased to be, a kid jumped out of the stands and literally stole second base, escaping with it across the outfield. Two rivals moved in on him and he lateraled to a friend. Meanwhile in the infield, fans clawed with fingernails and pen knives and dug up home plate and the pitcher's rubber. They tore away the green canvas screen behind home plate and made off with the padding on the dugout benches. They dismantled the little awning over the right-field bullpen. They ripped down signs and smashed up seats. Somebody even started a fire from broken kindling. Then the crowd sang "Auld Lang Syne" on the dressing room step and yelled for Stoneham's scalp, cursing the owner roundly. In the general bereavement at the passing of the New York National League teams, the mourners were as angry as they were grief-stricken. And they had no trouble finding scapegoats for the tragedy, even though, as usual there was enough blame for all to share.

It was true that O'Malley and his Dodgers were doing just fine in Brooklyn, but their continued success was less than assured. At a time when the great American stadium-and-arena building boom was beginning, the Dodgers' Ebbets Field stood as a 32,000-seat hovel in a rapidly deteriorating neighborhood.

"My first feeling was that the park could either be drastically improved or replaced on the same site," O'Malley said. "I inquired about the possibility of having the Dodgers play their home games at Yankee Stadium while this was being done. However, studies informed me that Brooklyn would soon be an unsuitable place for night games. In other words, the Dodgers could look forward to a steady decline in attendance unless something was done. I went to Norman Bel Geddes, the architect, and he told me that such a new stadium would be a financial impossibility."

Instead, Bel Geddes suggested a domed stadium. The idea appealed to O'Malley but not to the New York State and City governments, which procrastinated over various sites O'Malley suggested and failed to authorize the assis-

The Brooklyn Dodgers and New York Giants abandoned the East Coast in favor of the West Coast in 1958. The idea of leaving New York City disfranchised of a National League team distressed many Americans and created a vitriolic eastern press. The agony was completed when historic Ebbetts Field was razed to make way for an apartment complex. In the months to follow, the Polo Grounds also suffered the same fate.

tance he needed to build the new ball park. O'Malley did not wait for the words to be spelled out on his office wall; he leased Roosevelt Stadium in Jersey City for three years with the intention of having the Dodgers play seven games a year there. He sold Ebbets Field for three million dollars and leased it back for five years. "At that point," O'Malley admitted, "I had no intention of staying in Brooklyn."

In the winter of 1957 he visited Los Angeles and talked to Mayor Norris Paulson and Los Angeles County Supervisor Kenneth Hahn. Soon after O'Malley announced that the Dodgers had purchased both the Los Angeles Angels of the Pacific Coast League and their home stadium, Wrigley Field, from the Chicago Cubs. Then O'Malley turned toward Stoneham. "I explained to Horace that if we took our rivalry to California it would flourish as it never had before," said O'Malley. "I believe I explained this possibility to Mayor Paulson, who in turn may have called George Christopher, his opposite number in San Francisco. I do know that Christopher flew all the way across the country just to talk to Stoneham. After all, his [Stoneham's] attendance had dropped from one million one hundred fifty-five thousand to less than half that in just three years. He had trouble and there were four million people living in the nine counties around San Francisco Bay. It was something to look at."

Robert Moses, park commissioner of New York, offered O'Malley some park department land in Flushing Meadow. It was a fine offer, but Los Angeles had promised to deed over Chavez Ravine, a three hundred-acre tract of ancient houses and tangled weeds on a hillside only two miles from Los Angeles City Hall.

New Yorkers, who like other provincials are never as angry as when their naiveté is exposed, found it hard to accept that there was no higher law to keep the Dodgers and Giants in New York, to make hard-hearted, tight-fisted Walter O'Malley into Santa Claus. Those most jaundiced of baseball fans, the New York sportswriters, escorted the teams to both California ports, as if there were hope for a last-minute reprieve, only to find that baseball was in fact the business that most grown-ups had cynically declared but never quite believed it to be.

And so as baseball broke away from its traditional battlegrounds, the upper Eastern quadrant of the United States, it again betrayed that wholesome but essentially false and therefore unhealthy image it had in the minds of many—as nothing more than the national pastime. Walter O'Malley wasn't the villain; he was merely the messenger who brought the bad news.

To an outsider the cries of woe from New Yorkers who had lost the Dodgers and Giants may have seemed as unconvincing as those desperate pleas for money the city was already beginning to make. New York already had all the money and baseball it needed, or acted as if it did. Any town that spent money the way New York did didn't deserve more; and any town that disdained the Yankees, as New York seemed to, surely had more than its share of baseball wealth. Say what you like about the gray efficiency of the Yankees, the fact remained that they were pinstripe sophisticates in a city that proclaimed itself almost uniquely capable of appreciating such class. Any knowledgeable observer of New York might justly have suspected that had it been the Yankees who decided to relocate three thousand miles away, the protest might have been more genteel but the shock no less profound. Quite simply, New York believed it deserved a perennial world champion, just as it deserved marvelous Willie Mays, his Giants, and the class of the National League, the Dodgers. Just as it deserved to spend money it didn't have.

In this citadel of arrogance there flourished a sportsman who, though the top man in his field, remained as unassuming as the comic strip character he seemed cut out to be. Charles Dillon Stengel was not only a humanizing influence on the stony image of the New York Yankees but the kind of homey figure baseball needed as it competed against newer, slicker competitors.

Major league baseball became a truly national sport with the move to California. Baseball had a lot of big names in the fifties and sixties, but none exceeded the Giants' Willie Mays. New York City may have lost the Giants and Dodgers but they still had the American League colossus of the New York Yankees and their irascible manager, Casey Stengel. After winning nine World Series championships in twelve years, Stengel was asked to resign in 1960 at age seventy. In 1962, Stengel became the first manager of the New York Mets' National League expansion franchise.

On casual inspection, the old man looked like a gargoyle carved by an inexperienced artist. The face was crude and drooping, even when it was new; the old photographs of him in a series of major league uniforms indicated that clearly. His eyes were watery and mournful; his ears were large and foolish, giving him the look of a basset hound. His hands were hopelessly gnarled and his legs looked like two Christmas stockings stuffed with oranges.

He satisfied the public's image of a baseball team's manager. He was witty, often unfathomable, occasionally cruel, always entertaining. But Casey Stengel (his nickname came from his home town Kansas City or "K.C.," not from his mother's Irish ancestors) knew the game he was playing. He knew that his media personality was not really himself, and the high-powered communications media accepted this and respected him for it. For Stengel understood the entertainment value of sport as well as any man they covered.

Early one morning—it could have been 2 A.M.—when Stengel was between jobs in the early 1960s, he sat in the tower at Wrigley Field in Los Angeles. The more he drank the more lucid he became. A young baseball writer was utterly amazed to discover that the old man could be coherent. "That jargon of yours is just a joke, isn't it?" he asked.

"Son," said Stengel in a gravelly voice, "that is going to be our little secret, isn't it? They wouldn't pay any attention to me if they knew."

Ironically, Stengel was devilishly difficult to capture in print or even on film. The best journalists tried to translate or transcribe him, but the shattered syntax and fumbling verbosity that was Stengelese never reproduced quite right. Red Smith got it down as well as any:

"After bein' a manager that had had major league clubs in the National League and in the American League and in minor leagues I would have to say to come back and run the Yankees I was, uh, very thrilled with some of the men that

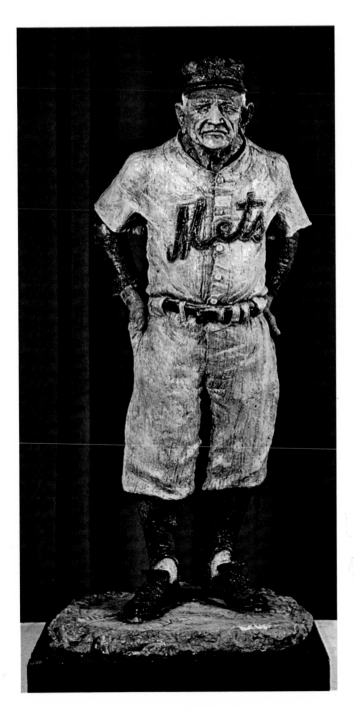

235

I saw today. I don't wanta go back into the years at the present time, but I'll start in the last three years since I bin manager. We had Mister DiMaggio that walked out there today and when I tell you that DiMaggio with the cheers he received every one of them shoulda bin given by myself and I shoulda yelled all winter during my off-season because of the success that the club had with him at bat and the wonderful ketches that he made in the outfield.

"I also had Tommy Handricks [Henrich] who was one of the greatest hitters that I ever saw in my life to walk up to the plate and get the ball that he wanted in a pinch and I also had Mister Keller [Charlie] who was one of the greatest outfielders I ever saw in my life as far as puttin' effort inta his work—strong, just wouldn't give in and he always believed and all three of those men, that a manager run a ball club which is an amazing thing."

In his inimitably roundabout style this clever comic was making the somewhat drab point (loosely translated) that he was the most successful manager of his time because he had the best team. From 1949 through 1960, Stengel's tenure as Yankees' manager, the team won ten American League pennants and seven World Series, including five straight. After Stengel was eased out in 1960, there was enough residue of talent left for Stengel's successors, Ralph Houk and Yogi Berra, to win four more pennants and two world championships in a row before the dynasty toppled.

At the root of the empire was the willingness of co-owners Dan Topping and Del Webb to give general manager George Weiss the authority (and, more important, the money) to find and develop talent. Many New York superstars were uncovered by the Yankees' superscouts—Paul Krichell, Joe Devine, and Bill Essick—and expertly developed by New York's farm teams. But despite permission to do so from his bosses, Weiss didn't really buy championship teams. Rather he patched them together. When the talent-laden Yankees needed just a bit more help, Weiss always seemed to be there with a John Mize, Johnny Hopp, Enos Slaughter, Johnny Sain, Jim Konstanty, Eddie Robinson, Suitcase Simpson, Bobby Shantz, or Luis Arroyo—all good men but something less than Hall of Fame candidates, at least not from their tenure with the Yanks.

Clearly, there was more to those infuriatingly successful Yankees of the fifties than Mantle, Berra, and Ford. And there was more to managing them, despite Stengel's assertion to the contrary, than watching the stars perform. With his rich mixture of ingredients Stengel concocted winning lineups like a baseball Merlin. In 1949, when the Yankees suffered seventy-three incapacitating injuries, including the bone spur ailment that kept DiMaggio out for the season's first sixty-five games, Stengel used seven different first basemen. And somehow the Yankees kept winning. Trainer Gus Mauch later marveled, "It was hard to believe but Casey would take a guy out of the original lineup and the substitute would do better than the original. He moved players around, he switched positions, he did everything, and everything seemed to work."

Don Larsen's perfect game, Mickey Mantle's prodigious blasts, Roger Maris's sixty-one homers, Whitey Ford's record skein of scoreless World Series innings—all great moments befitting a great team. But it takes more to build a dynasty, and if that extra ingredient was not Stengel's masterful manipulations, well, there were those who swore that the man didn't just look a wizard.

At seventy he was deemed too old or infirm to continue and was asked to retire. Reporters wanted to know if he had been fired. "Wait a minute fellas, for crissakes, I'll tell ya," Stengel said, stepping forward with his face all scrunched up and his hands thrust deep into his pockets. He never looked quite so young or defiant. "Mister Webb and Mister Topping have started a program for the Yankees. They need a solution as to when to discharge a man on account of age. Me? Well, my services are no

When Charles Dillon Stengel died in 1975 at the age of 85, the sports world mourned the passing of one of its most unique characters. Paul Conrad, editorial cartoonist for the *Los Angeles Times*, drew this eloquent tribute.

longer required by this club and I told them that if that was their idea, not to worry about me. Quit, fired, discharged, use whatever you damn please. You don't see my crying about it, do you? If I had been wronged, I'd be the first man to say it."

"What will you do now, Casey?" asked a writer.

"Have another drink!" he shouted. "All my writers into the bar and I'll have a bourbon and soda. Keep them coming at five-minute intervals, will ya?"

The truth was that the Yankees were closer to senility than the old man. By 1965, the team was plummeting to the second division, from which depths it would take a good decade to emerge, while Stengel was polishing off his acting career with his zaniest role yet, as maestro of the masterfully inept New York Mets. After a decade of showing the Yankees how to win, Casey Stengel moved crosstown and showed them how to lose.

Robert Lipsyte, the former *New York Times* columnist, contrasted the fans of the two teams. Yankees' fans, he said, were mostly businessmen in gray flannel suits who frequented Sardi's and the Stock Exchange. Mets' fans were laborers with families, small apartments, and one good suit, which they never wore to the Polo Grounds, the Mets' first home, because there might be pigeon droppings on the seats.

In 1962, their first season, the Mets looked a lot like Yankees' rejects. They had not only the old Yankees' manager but the general manager, George Weiss; the trainer, Gus Mauch; numerous other former Yankees' employees; and one of the Bronx Bombers' first basemen, Marv Throneberry, the crown prince of klutz. They did not have Mickey Mantle, Roger Maris, or Whitey Ford.

After they won their first exhibition game, Stengel started his postgame speech to reporters with the comment, "They're amazin'!" And so they were, during that first season, losing a record 120 games.

They were so desperately incompetent that they couldn't even clown proficiently, which was just as

well, or they would have been less entertaining. Broadcaster Ralph Kiner had Clarence (Choo Choo) Coleman on the radio one day after he'd had a big game—three singles. Kiner wisely spent most of the interview talking about Choo Choo rather than entrusting that task to the none-too-articulate Coleman himself. Finally, he asked the catcher what he thought was a safe question—how he got his nickname. Choo Choo was quiet for a minute, then admitted, "I don't know." The Mets were easily stumped.

Then there was the erratic shortstop, Elio Chacon. He's the guy who'd had a new sports car for all of a week when somebody spotted it outside the Polo Grounds, both headlights and tail lights smashed, two fenders twisted, one door handle gone, and a crack in the windshield. "How did that happen?" a writer asked. "Parking," replied Chacon.

The charm of ineptness tends to grow with one's remoteness from it, and old Mets' fans have been known to sentimentalize the pathos that they found nothing more nor less than pathetic at the time. But there was no doubt that New York fell in love with its Mets, whether because of their bumbling or in spite of it.

One day, between games of a doubleheader, the Mets' management opened the centerfield gates and some four hundred signmakers marched onto the field, carrying banners proclaiming such sentiments as "Hit One Into the Darkness, Harkness," and "Know Why the Mets Are Such Good Losers?—Practice Makes Perfect." And their magic wasn't confined just to New York. In his book *The Amazing Mets*, Jerry Mitchell wrote, "The Mets found fans everywhere they went. They became sentimental favorites all over baseball, people rooting for their home team first and the Mets second." Roger Angell wrote, "This was a new recognition that perfection is admirable but a trifle inhuman, that a stumbling kind of sentimentality can be so much more warming. Most of all, perhaps, those exultant yells for the Mets also were yells for ourselves . . . there is more Met than Yankee in us."

In 1969, the Amazing Mets became truly amazing, winning the National League championship. *Jock* magazine, a New York City sports publication, used a cover on its inaugural issue that was meant as parody but turned out to be fact. In the subsequent World Series with Baltimore, luck played a major role as the Mets upset the Orioles. Artist Seymour Leichman, in a lithograph titled *Fate Takes a Hand*, offers his version of a critical play.

Maybe so, but the charm is being an underdog, not a loser. When the underdog turns winner—world champ, moreover—then it is proclaimed Destiny's Darling, and everyone else's as well. It happened to the Mets a short eight years after their laughable first season.

Suddenly, they had a marvelous young pitching staff, timely hitting, inspired fielding, and, most captivating of all, that winning magic that transforms dinky ground balls into base hits, Punch-and-Judy hitters into key men in the clutch, a ninth-place also-ran of 1968 into the Amazing Mets of 1969.

Those who lived through that heady experience often point to one play that symbolized it—a bit of inspired madness that may have been the turning point of the World Series. It came in the fourth game, when the favored Baltimore Orioles, trailing 2-1 in games, appeared on the verge of regaining the control they had unaccountably lost after their win in game one of the Series. The Mets led 1-0 in the top of the eighth inning, and the Orioles had runners on first and third against Mets' ace Tom Seaver with one out. The batter was Brooks Robinson, as steady and reliable a batter as one could want at a moment like this.

Robinson plastered one of Seaver's offerings on a vicious line drive to right-centerfield—a solid base hit, it seemed, but no more so if fielded properly. Disdaining such cut-your-losses prudence, Ron Swoboda, the Mets' musclebound rightfielder, noted for bizarre but usually not fortuitous fielding adventures, rushed in and flung himself headfirst at the ball, his left arm wrenching across his head in a crude attempt at a backhand stab. He made it! Sprawled full-length on the grass, he clutched the ball in the web of his glove—an impossible, foolish play transformed into genius. Had he missed, as he should have, more than one run would have scored and the Mets would have gone to the bottom of the ninth behind. Even though he made it, the runner from third scored. So the strategic gain from the catch hardly justified the gamble. But spirit sometimes compensates for foolishness, and

October 1969   60 Cents

Jock

New York

NEW YORK METS
1969
CHAMPIONS

Ben Hogan's determination and unemotionalism did not warm the affection of galleryites. But his determination led him to his greatest victories. He won four U.S. Opens, two PGAs, two Masters, and one British Open, and many of his achievements came after a 1949 automobile accident that almost killed him. At right is the fifteenth hole at Cypress Point, Pebble Beach, California, considered one of golf's most beautiful—and intimidating—golf holes.

Swoboda's spirit rekindled the Mets. They put down the Orioles with no further scoring, recovered to win in ten, and took the Series the next day.

When it was all over, and the Mets' fans wrecked Shea Stadium in vengeful exhilaration, the Mets' leftfielder, Cleon Jones, observed, "Some people might not believe in us. But then some people still believe the world is flat." One would have had to have been almost that obstinate not to yield to the mystique of the Mets.

7   Arnie's Army and Other Success Stories

On the morning of February 2, 1949, Ben Hogan, thirty-six, and his wife, Valerie, were on their way home to Fort Worth, Texas, from Phoenix, Arizona, and the pressures of the tournament-a-week winter golf tour. Suddenly, out of the ground haze in the low, rolling hill and sagebrush country near Van Horn, Texas, a Greyhound bus loomed. It was traveling in the opposite direction but it was in the Hogans' lane. The vehicles hit head on. Trying to protect his wife, Hogan threw himself across the seat in front of her. He suffered a double fracture of the pelvis, a fractured collarbone, a broken ankle bone, and a broken rib. If he hadn't reacted to protect his wife, he probably would have been killed. The crash drove the steering wheel through the driver's seat.

Ben Hogan recovered from an accident few men would have survived. A month after the crash, blood clots formed and doctors performed two-hour abdominal surgery, tying off the major veins in Hogan's legs. They doubted he would walk normally again, let alone play tournament golf. But golf was his passion. Seventeen months after the accident, Bantam Ben Hogan won his second U.S. Open, at Merion. The next year, 1951, he took both the Open and the Masters. From 1948 through 1954, Hogan never failed to win at least one of golf's four major tournaments each year—the Masters, the Professional Golfers' Association championship, the U.S.

Open, the British Open. And so the Electronic Age of golf, which began in the tragic crippling of the game's finest player, produced one of the most inspiring success stories in the Electronic Age of sport.

Hogan didn't play golf; he attacked it. Even in practice he drove himself as if he were competing in a sudden-death playoff, whacking shot after shot carefully, methodically, with controlled fury. He smoked cigarettes almost constantly when he wasn't shooting. He seldom spoke, and when he did it was only to his caddy or his playing partner. Small talk didn't suit this man. The Scots nicknamed him "the Wee Ice Mon" after he won the British Open. "His expression never changed," Herbert Warren Wind wrote in *The Story of American Golf*. "His walk never changed. His silence never changed."

Wind wrote:

> "[He was] not only the outstanding golfer but the outstanding athlete of the postwar decade. He was perhaps the best golfer pound-for-pound who ever lived. He was a thrilling golfer. He expected perfection from himself and was always thinking in terms of the flawless shot, not the good shot. The green was not his target on his approaches, nor the quarter of the green around the pin. The flag was his target, and he drilled for it. He fully intended to be inside the other man, on every shot."

As he neared sixty his nerves, tested so hard over so many years, began to unravel. His hands shook over putts, he fought himself, and he lost. In 1971, at fifty-eight, he played the last tournament of his career, the Houston Champions International. He liked the course and had shot sixty-seven and sixty-five in practice rounds. But when he began the tournament play, the touch was gone. On the fourth hole he strained his bad knee. By the twelfth hole he was eleven over par, and he asked for a cart to drive him back to the clubhouse. As he left, he said to a friend, "Don't ever get old."

Hogan's major contemporary, "Slammin'" Sammy

Snead, took Ben's advice. He was still playing well in the 1970s, when he was in his sixties. Perhaps his secret was his approach to the sport, as casual as Hogan's was intense. He didn't burn himself up. Bob Green, longtime golf writer of the *Associated Press*, said of Snead, "The colorful, sweet-swinging Virginia hillbilly was a man everyone loved. He had a captivating backwoods personality, a picture swing, and was immune to polish." And pressure, it seemed. Toddling around the course in one of his brightly banded straw hats, he seemed as carefree as any vacationer out for a leisurely round. He ambled his way to three Masters, three PGAs, and one British Open. But perhaps it was in the major disappointment of his career—his failure to win the U.S. Open, though he came close four or five times—that he best expressed his sanguine philosophy. "It gives you the eeriest feeling sometimes," he drawled, "like you don't have anything to do with the way a tournament comes out. I've won many a tournament I had no business winning. Everything just went right. On the other hand I've had tournaments [like the Opens] snatched right out of my hands when by all rights they should have been mine. It's destiny."

In the years before the glare of television cameras glamorized them and golf became a living-room sport, professional golfers were itinerants whose wanderings were recorded by a couple dozen journalists and followed by a few thousand fans. A golfer who won some six thousand dollars over the twenty-five scheduled tournaments would be the fifth biggest moneymaker on the tour.

The Electronic Age changed golf perhaps more than any other sport, and as golf became a television show, Arnold Palmer became the star. A tousle-haired Pennsylvanian, who wore a quizzical, almost hurt expression when he sprinted between shots, Palmer was handsome and charismatic. People followed him in flocks. Arnie's Army, they were called, and they tromped after him

fanatically. No golfer before or since has had such a gallery.

When he hit into the woods and silently cursed his shot, he looked like every golfer. But only momentarily. For Palmer was a natural athlete—a solid 185 pounds with large, strong hands and arms. His first major victory was the 1954 National Amateur, and he attained national prominence when he won the 1958 Masters, the first of four triumphs he was to score at Augusta. His second big win, in 1960, was especially dramatic. Palmer needed a birdie on either the seventeenth or eighteenth hole at Cherry Hills in Denver to tie Ken Venturi, who had finished with a 283, for the lead. Palmer got his birdie on seventeen, dropping in a twenty-seven-foot putt. On the par-four eighteenth, Palmer put his second shot two feet to the right of the pin. It spun around and came to rest five feet from the hole and a little below it. Palmer dropped in the putt. For a moment he didn't realize what he'd done: birdie, birdie: victory. He snatched the ball from the cup, took a normal step, then began jumping and whooping as wildly as his Army around him.

Palmer was the first man to win one million dollars on the tour, and he handled it as brilliantly as he played. He leased his own plane, set up his own company, invested well, and hired a staff of five to help run things. His wife, Winnie, personable and bright, was a notable asset, too.

Strangely, like Hogan, Palmer might have wanted to win too much. He slumped in 1963 and again in 1965. He probably was fighting himself and his nerves more than he was distracted by new business deals, which the press immediately suggested was the cause of his slump. In 1969, after not having won that year on the tour and shooting an 82 in the first round of the PGA, he withdrew, announcing that he wouldn't play again until the bursitis in his hip was gone. He returned and won the first two events on the fall tour, whereupon the *Associated Press* named him athlete of the decade. But the Palmer glory days were mostly over by then. Other top golfers came

Arnold Palmer joined the pro golf tour in the late fifties, and his personal magnetism and style helped turn it into a rich extravaganza. No performer ever captivated his audience as did the ebullient Palmer, a bold and daring player who virtually assaulted golf courses. His fans were legion and Arnie's Army was a familiar sight at the big tournaments. Palmer became golf's first tournament millionaire.

along—Billy Casper, Gary Player, Lee Trevino, the venerable Julius Boros, and such toothpaste-smile kids as Johnny Miller and Ben Crenshaw.

But after the Palmer magic of the early sixties, there was really just one name in golf: Jack Nicklaus. It used to be Fat Jack Nicklaus, and he was the lurking presence who always seemed to be spoiling things for the svelte and popular Palmer. Jack didn't have an army of his own. He didn't have the looks and he didn't have the flow. But even the oldtimers conceded he drove the ball higher, straighter, and farther than any man who ever lived.

Nicklaus came to full bloom in the 1965 Masters, shooting a record 271 for seventy-two holes, three strokes better than Hogan's old mark. In the four rounds, he needed a fairway wood just once; incredibly, he never used a club longer than a five-iron for his approaches on the par-four holes. Bobby Jones put it quite succinctly. "Palmer and Player," Jones said, "played superbly [in the 1965 Masters]. But Nicklaus played a game with which I'm not familiar."

Nicklaus had been stunning people for years. As an amateur in 1960, he shot a 269 at Merion, eighteen strokes better than Hogan had shot in winning the National Open ten years earlier. In 1962, in Nicklaus's first try as a professional, he beat Palmer in an eighteen-hole playoff at Oakmont, Pennsylvania, for the U.S. Open title, and a few months later he stopped Palmer again in the World Series of Golf. By the end of 1975, he had won five Masters, four PGAs, three U.S. Opens, and two British Opens.

At first Nicklaus was so businesslike he often looked grim. He seldom smiled. But as people got to know him, they liked him. Behind the chilly facade was a friendly, pleasant man who was gracious in defeat as well as victory. He found a new haberdasher eventually, lost weight, and let his hair grow modishly long. And he finally won the galleries.

Between tournaments, Nicklaus spent considerable time working on the construction of golf courses, for

Public acceptance came slowly to Jack Nicklaus, but not success. Nicklaus was a marvel of golf precision from the time he joined the pro tour in the early sixties, a portly young man with a crew cut and little color. Nicklaus changed his image later and became one of the pro tour's most popular players—in addition to its richest. The fifteenth hole at Oakmont Country Club near Pittsburgh (below) as interpreted in the style of René Magritte by artist Donald Moss, has been called one of the eighteen best golf holes in America.

which he had an unusually strong aptitude. He also built a new home for his wife, Barbara, and their five children, complete with a swimming pool, athletic field, and a grass tennis court. Two miles away were the offices of Golden Bear, Inc. Unlike Hogan and Palmer, and despite the distractions, he seemed in no danger of losing his competitive edge. Herbert Warren Wind wrote:

> There were flaws and inconsistencies in Nicklaus's game, but when he was in full flight it is really to be wondered if anyone in the history of golf has ever been capable of such sustained passages of outrageous brilliance.

Probably not. And Jack Nicklaus, the most enduring golfer of the booming Electronic Age of golf, continued to reap the full benefits of his brilliance.

Gone were the romantic wanderers of the 1930s. Television and golfer-businessmen such as Palmer and Nicklaus had changed it all.

8 Pro Football: The National Mania

The winter sun had long disappeared and the two best professional football teams had not yet finished their engagement. The Baltimore Colts and New York Giants had produced sixty minutes of nearly perfect football, but they had not yet produced a decision. The score was tied 17-17; now there would be a sudden-death overtime to resolve the issue.

The 64,185 people seated in Arctic-like cold at Yankee Stadium were not so much witnesses to the spectacle as participants in it. The true audience was the fifty million television viewers across the nation who saw the spectacle of pro football at its most compelling—an icy drama [what Hamilton (Tex) Maule of *Sports Illustrated* called "the best football game ever played"] enacted before a riveted audience.

This event more than any other helped transform pro football from a minority sect to a state religion. Within

Professional football grew steadily in popularity during the 1950s. The twelve-team league cultivated exciting rivalries, but, more important, the game adapted perfectly to television. In December, 1958, the Baltimore Colts played the New York Giants for the NFL championship. The game, won by the Colts in a dramatic sudden-death overtime period, was televised nationally. Pro football's fire was lit.

twenty years more Americans would be watching pro football's championship game, the Super Bowl, than baseball's hallowed World Series. And pro football would contend that it was the national sport.

Why this boom? That Colts-Giants game, which began it, provides some answers.

Start with a star—Johnny Unitas, a humble-looking hero who wore inelegant high-top shoes and carried a football with all the grace of a blue-collar worker toting his lunch pail. True, he could throw the ball as well as the best passers, but even that facility was only part of his appeal. Here was an athlete who was captivating because he was in charge—the quintessential quarterback. He called the plays, and—miraculously, if you stopped to think about it—his ten teammates did what he told them and his eleven opponents did as he expected them to. Though perhaps the least athletic athlete on the field, Unitas could and eventually did control the game.

"To control," "to quarterback"—the verbs have become synonymous. Baseball's catchers, basketball's playmakers, industry's executives, the President try to control, to quarterback their teams. The quarterback has power. On this day in 1958, Unitas gave football's first mass audience a thrilling lesson in quarterback control.

His control was hotly contested. In 1958, many experts considered the New York Giants the best team in professional football—certainly the best defensive team. The Giants had twice stifled the frighteningly efficient, if vulnerably predictable, offense of the Cleveland Browns, including the magnificent running back, Jim Brown. Fifteen years later, when a middle linebacker could be as publicized as the flashiest running back, the Miami Dolphins would celebrate a "No-Name Defense." But in 1958, defense still took a small "d." Anonymity signified insignificance, so it was a breakthrough when the Giants' defensive line emerged as a famous "front four": Jim Katcavage, Rosey Grier, Dick Modzelewski, and Andy Robustelli. And everyone knew that middle linebacker Sam Huff quarterbacked the defense.

The best quarterback against the best defense: like sudden-death overtime itself, a useful oversimplification of a complex contest. The finish, in detail:

The Giants won the toss to start the overtime and elected to receive. Frank Gifford ran on first down and gained four yards. Quarterback Charlie Conerly threw toward end Bob Schnelker and missed. Third down—the crucible in pro football, as the nation was beginning to understand. Finding his receivers covered, Conerly tucked the ball against his chest and tried to run the six yards for the first down. Linebacker Bill Pellington spun him sideways and middle guard Don Shinnick knocked him down. The quarterback bounced along the icy turf, his thirty-four-year-old body feeling every bruise, and came to rest a foot short. The Giants were forced to kick.

Enter John Unitas, and the beginning of what Maule dubbed "the Thirteen Steps to Glory." The sequence began after Carl Taseff returned Don Chandler's punt to the Baltimore 20-yard line.

(1) Unitas sends L. G. Dupre to the right on a sweep for a first down at the 30-yard line. (2) He throws deep to Lennie Moore—incomplete. (3) Back to Dupre for three yards on a draw. (4) Third-and-seven, big play. Unitas saw linebacker Harland Svare neglecting the flat to stay with end Raymond Berry, John's favorite target, so the Colts' quarterback hits fullback Alan Ameche on a swing pass. First down on the Colts' 40. (5) Dupre on a sweep to the right turns inside for a four-yard gain. (6) Crunch. Modzelewski thunders into the backfield and drops Unitas for an eight-yard loss. (7) The key play. On third-and-long Unitas hits Berry on a hook pattern for a first down on the New York 43-yard line. The drive is resuscitated; the Giants are shrinking toward their goal line. The director and star of this eerie passion play, under lemon lights on a darkening plain, is back in control. (8) He hands the ball to Ameche on a trap play, and the fullback scoots twenty yards to the New York 20. "We'd run this once or twice in the game," said Unitas later. "It wasn't considered a long gainer. Usually we figured it for about five yards at

best. The way Modzelewski had been crashing into our backfield, I figured it was time for a trap. I hit it right."

(9) A pause. Dupre off tackle for no gain. (10) It's beginning to snow on the Giants. Raymond Berry clutches a slant pass on the New York 8-yard line. (11) Ameche nudges it off right tackle to the 7.

No need for the star now. The master upstager, the bane of drama in pro football until the rulesmakers moved the goal posts back to the end line of the end zone, the field goal kicker is primed on the sideline. Without Steve Myhra, the Colts would already have lost; his field goal with seven seconds left in regulation time tied the score. But with him they seem destined to win unheroically. This game is one mechanized snap, spot, and kick from being over.

Not so fast. This is third down, not fourth, and Unitas won't relinquish the spotlight. (12) In a daring, wholly unnecessary, but wonderfully successful gamble, he throws for the first down to tight end Jim Mutscheller on the 1-yard line.

(13) Stringing out the inevitable? No such charge can be sustained against the master impresario. Ameche bores through a gaping hole, and the drama is done, completed with a just and decisive ending.

There was nothing for fifty million viewers to do but watch the closing credits and marvel at the production. As Johnny Unitas romped off stage that evening, the theater of pro football opened for a long run.

One summer day in 1959, the sunshine reflected in great pools on the patio of the Sheraton West Hotel in Los Angeles. Ladies in puffy chiffon dresses moved through the crowd, passing out press releases that explained the start of a great adventure. Everywhere on the patio very rich men laughed contentedly, as one does after making an especially satisfying investment. These were no longer just rich men; they were owners of pro football franchises.

A public relations man for the new American Football League pointed at a draped easel and announced to the press, "Gentlemen, I give you the Los Angeles Chargers." A cloth fell away, revealing a promotion poster with the team's name emblazoned on it. "Why that nickname?" the press inquired. "We're the Chargers," explained one press agent, "because when everybody yells "Charge!" they'll be talking about our football team."

"Actually," interjected another press agent, "a charger is a large and powerful war horse. That's the kind of animal the ancient knights used to ride into battle."

A third explanation was offered. "Mr. [Barron] Hilton [owner of the team] also is president of a new charge card firm called Carte Blanche," said yet another press agent. "So we felt 'Charger' was appropriate." Besides, someone pointed out, if the Buffalo team could be known as the Bills, the Los Angeles club could call itself the Chargers.

Of such gentle humor and confusion was the American Football League born. Before a football could be thrown, the humor deteriorated further and the confusion deepened. Within a few days, the new franchise in Minneapolis-St. Paul dropped out to join the National Football League, and the NFL placed a team in Dallas to compete against the AFL entry there. The war was on. Before it was over and the hatchet was buried in a grand merger celebrated by the first Super Bowl, the two leagues and their television-network sponsors would begin to redefine the financial parameters not only of football but of all televised sports.

In 1959, each NFL team was making two hundred thousand dollars on the television rights to its games. Two years later, NFL commissioner Pete Rozelle, the sports guru of the Electronic Age, announced that the NFL had signed a two-year contract with the Columbia Broadcasting System for $9.3 million.

In the beginning, the American Football League got just the scraps from the table, but that was the difference between starvation and survival. "There was no way our league should have survived," said Joe Foss, the first

In 1959, a group of determined men gathered to create a second professional football league. The American Football League began play in 1960 with eight teams. Lamar Hunt, the original planner, would see his dream become a reality. In 1972, Hunt became the first member of the AFL to be inducted into the Pro Football Hall of Fame (award presenter William H. Sullivan, Jr. is at left).

commissioner. "It was saved by the television network's fascination with professional football. The American Broadcasting Company gave us $1,785,000 for the first year. Now that doesn't sound like a lot of money in view of what happened afterward, but it was quite a piece of change for a new league just getting started."

In its fervent quest to put pro football on television, ABC chose not to be deterred by the rather serious problems of the fledgling league. Harry Wismer, owner of the New York Titans, was so drastically under-capitalized that he ran the club from his Manhattan apartment. The Boston Patriots conducted their first draft with a football magazine as their only source of information. The Oakland Raiders and the Houston Oilers had to play in high school stadiums, the Patriots in Braves Field, a deserted major league baseball park with no parking facilities.

For a time the new league barely survived, losing most of its draft choices to the established league. But the new league persevered and prevailed. When it won a $36 million multiyear contract with the National Broadcasting Company in 1964, its survival was assured. Now began the second phase of the Great Alphabet War, NFL-CBS versus AFL-NBC.

AFL games were scheduled so they could be seen in many cities after the NFL home games went off the air. In an attempt to deprive the new league of its television underpinnings, CBS began to schedule doubleheaders, following up a home game with a nationally significant match.

The AFL fought back. In New York Sonny Werblin succeeded Wismer as head of the failing Titans. Werblin admitted he knew nothing about football as it was played on the field. But he presumed to understand show business, and football as a product to be sold was show business, he contended. Werblin did for his new team what a producer might for a flagging out of town show before its opening in New York. He changed the name from the discredited "Titans" to the presumably more vibrant "Jets." He booked them into the new Shea

Stadium (appropriately, right underneath the airport glide path). Most of all, he gave the cast a face lift, importing big names (and not-so-big names) at stars' salaries. Werblin believed people were impressed by large sums of money.

He gave $50,000 to Cosmo Iacavazzi, a tailback from Princeton; $150,000 to quarterback Bill Schweikert of Virginia Military Institute; and $200,000 for Heisman trophy winner John Huarte of Notre Dame. In a moment of inspired madness, Werblin lavished $427,000 in money and worldly goods on Joe Namath, a sleepy-eyed, brassy country boy from Beaver Falls, Pennsylvania, by way of Bear Bryant's football finishing school at the University of Alabama. "Glamour begins in the backfield," Werblin informed the press. "That's where the money has to be spent if the American Football League is going to make good."

Buttressed by NBC money, the AFL outbid the NFL for other top college stars as well. Some six years after the AFL was founded, the NFL was, if not exactly suing for peace, at least willing to consider accommodation. Both leagues and both networks were weary of the war that had sent costs skyrocketing. They had spent as much as they cared to.

On the rainy spring morning of April 6, 1966, in Dallas, Lamar Hunt and Tex Schramm held a secret meeting in a United Air Lines lounge at Love Field. Hunt was owner of the Kansas City Chiefs (formerly the Dallas Texans) of the AFL. Schramm was president of the NFL's Dallas Cowboys. "We sat there for a while and had coffee and doughnuts like two people who were getting ready to fly off to Honolulu," said Hunt. "Then we got up separately and walked to Schramm's car. We did it as inconspicuously as possible for fear that some newsman might see us and know what we were up to. We sat and talked for an hour and a half. Both of us knew what the other wanted. The fight between the two leagues had been a stalemate and everyone knew it. There was no reason to hold off a merger any longer."

On the last day in May Hunt presented a twenty-six-point proposal for a merger to the NFL. On June 8, 1966, negotiations were satisfactorily concluded, and at 6:15 P.M. at the Warwick Hotel in New York, it was announced that the AFL would be integrated into the NFL as a separate conference.

To the fans the item of greatest interest in the merger was the establishment of a playoff game between the champions of the two leagues. Hunt agreed to the title NFL-AFL World Championship Game, but it bothered him. How could you fit all those words into a headline? Baseball had the World Series; College football had the Rose Bowl. These were titles you could deal with, he mused.

"My little daughter plays with this crazy toy that bounces here and there," said Hunt. "She calls it a 'Super Ball'. That thought keeps running through my mind. I keep thinking of that ball. The same phrase keeps coming to mind—Super Ball, Super Bowl. That is what we ought to call this game—the Super Bowl."

Other classic sports events had taken years to develop, but this was the Electronic Age, the age of instant classics. Television started the countdown to what is called "Super Sunday," and a nation mad for pro football awaited the fateful day as if the first "Super Bowl" held almost cosmic significance.

Instead, it merely proved what almost everyone had taken for granted—that the NFL was decidedly the better league, for the time being at least. The Green Bay Packers, upholders of NFL supremacy, punished the Kansas City Chiefs, the AFL challengers, 35-10. The nation would have to wait another two years before the Super Bowl lived up to its billing.

In the meantime, all hailed the merger and, as far as the game on the field was concerned, a brilliant dictator who treated football like a holy war and who, though far from saintly, was well on his way to sainthood.

Vince Lombardi grinned at the world through a fortress of teeth. He was warmth and meanness incongruously combined. His subordinates suffered under the lash and came away marveling at the love they found in Lombardi-ism. This coldly passionate man produced the finest football teams of the time. When pro football established the Super Bowl to deify the champions of the sport, it seemed to turn instinctively to Lombardi.

"I guess I'm a typical product of Vince Lombardi," testified guard Jerry Kramer. "I don't ever want to finish second in anything I do. What I learned from Lombardi I'll be using the rest of my life."

"I was thirty-six years old when I went to Green Bay," recalled Emlen Tunnell. "I thought I had acquired a little sophistication. But those pep talks of his—God! When I heard those pep talks, I'd cry and go out and try to kill people. Nobody else has ever been able to do that to me."

"Lombardi treats us all the same," said defensive tackle Henry Jordan, "—like dogs."

The tyrannical coach transformed Paul Hornung from a poorly trained quarterback into a running back who set a record for points scored the year after Lombardi took charge. He made an ordinary fullback, Ray Nitschke, into the finest middle linebacker in the game. And in a seventeenth-round draft choice from a school (Alabama) that won only one game, he developed a brilliant quarterback, Bart Starr.

Lombardi came to the Packers in 1959, when he was forty-five years old. He found a team that had won only one game the season before, and a franchise on the verge of collapse.

"He yelled so long and loud during the first week of summer camp," said receiver Max McGee, "that he lost his voice. He made injured players run in practice. No one could interfere and he took suggestions from no one. He was determined to sink or swim on his own. He told everybody that they could cross him once and maybe they'd get by. To cross him twice was to write your name on the waiver list."

The Packers leaped to 7-5 respectability in Lombardi's

first year, but the coach was dissatisfied. On the Monday
after the season ended, Lombardi showed up at the club
office with game films and bulging ledgers, ready to go
to work on the next season. "The Packers," he said,
"should have won more games. They failed because they
were unaccustomed to winning."

In 1960, Lombardi accustomed the Packers to winning.
Green Bay improved to 8-4, won its conference title, and
came within four points of the Philadelphia Eagles for
the National Football League championship. The Lombardi dynasty was about to take root.

In 1961, the Packers romped to the Western Conference title and ravaged the New York Giants 37-0 for
the championship. At halftime, with the score 24-0,
Giants' coach Allie Sherman didn't even bother to give
a chalk talk. "What can you say?" he asked helplessly.
Starr threw three touchdown passes. Hornung scored
nineteen points and ran for eighty-nine yards. Nitschke
led the defense that intercepted six passes from New York
quarterback Y. A. Tittle.

The next year, in frigid, blustery Yankee Stadium (such
conditions would soon be called "Packer weather"),
Green Bay beat New York again for the championship,
16-7. The Giants' offense, which had been shut out in
1961, still couldn't score (New York's only score came on
a blocked punt). Green Bay fullback Jim Taylor, who cut
his tongue when hit by linebacker Sam Huff early in the
game and swallowed blood the rest of the way, gained
eighty-five yards in thirty-one carries, and scored Green
Bay's only touchdown. The winning points came from
guard Jerry Kramer, who had become the kicking spe-
cialist when Hornung was injured earlier in the season.
Kramer made field goals of 26, 9, and 36 yards. The
Giants had no replies.

There followed a two-year hiatus, when Green Bay,
though a winner, deferred to the Chicago Bears and the
Baltimore Colts in the Western Conference race. In 1965,
"the Pack was back," as its highly enthusiastic followers
in Green Bay liked to say. In the championship game that

While the Packers became the dominant team in pro football, Jim Brown of the Cleveland Browns was proving himself as the dominant individual. At six feet two inches and 228 pounds, Brown was a superior runner, a man with speed and power who was seldom injured. In nine seasons he led the NFL in rushing eight times. When he retired in 1965 to pursue a Hollywood acting career, he held numerous records, including the most yards gained by rushing in a game, season, and career.

season, the Packers checked Cleveland 23-12, frustrating Jimmy Brown, the greatest fullback of all time, in his final game.

The next year it wasn't as easy. Against the Dallas Cowboys in Dallas in its fifth NFL title game, Green Bay seemed comfortably ahead, 34-20, with just ten minutes left. But Don Meredith passed sixty-eight yards to Frank Clarke for a touchdown. Then the Cowboys regained the ball and drove toward a score that would have tied the game. They reached the Green Bay 2-yard line with just thirty seconds left. Meredith rolled right to throw, but linebacker Dave Robinson rushed him, and the pass went wild. Green Bay safety Tom Brown intercepted, and the Packers were champs again.

Oh, yes, the Super Bowl. It was hard to make the Packers' 35–10 thrashing of the Chiefs sound like the real championship game. Less than a master diplomat, Lombardi failed to. As he stood in the locker room lovingly patting the game ball, which his team had presented to him, he told the press, "The Chiefs are a good team but they don't compare with the top teams in the NFL. Dallas is a better team. That's what you wanted me to say, isn't it? Now I've said it."

The next year the most rabid AFL partisan would have found it difficult to dispute Lombardi's assessment. The Packers and Cowboys engaged in one of the most heroic struggles for the NFL championship, and the Super Bowl proved a marked anticlimax again.

It was sixteen degrees below zero at 8 A.M. in Green Bay on December 31, 1967, the date of the NFL championship rematch between the Packers and Cowboys. By game time it had warmed up to minus thirteen. It was not Cowboy weather. But then it seemed even a little excessive for Packer weather. Henry Jordan quipped, "Lombardi got down on his hands and knees and prayed for cold and he stayed down too long."

Television, which had all but perfected its coverage of football, what with split screens, isolated cameras, and the omnipresent instant replay, could not adequately report the cold. It discerned the white, billowy breaths of the players and fans, the quarterbacks and receivers tucking their hands into their jerseys, the players fumbling the ball as they slid about on the frozen field. But it did not show chill, or numbness, or pain. As the twilight deepened and the cold intensified, the cameras seemed to transform the players into unfeeling hulks who lumbered around the field. It was difficult to tell that these were men playing football. Yet even without a faithful rendering of the searing cold, the spectacle as transmitted by television was compelling. The nation watched in fascination as the two best football teams performed this bizarre rite of manhood.

After the first quarter or so, when the Packers struck for two touchdowns, the Cowboys had the better of it. At halftime the Green Bay lead had shrunk to 14–10. On the first play of the fourth quarter, Dallas produced the go-ahead touchdown, and the Cowboys' defense, which had stifled Starr and company for nearly half the game now, seemed capable of protecting the lead. For some ten minutes, the Dallas defense continued its domination. Then, with four minutes fifty seconds to play, Green Bay gained the ball on its 32-yard line.

As if spurred by the realization that this would be their last possession, the Packers began to move. In three plays they were at the Dallas 42, and the fans, huddled in silence since the early scores, began to revive. A halfback option play lost nine yards, but the imperturbable Starr got his first down with two modest passes to halfback Donny Anderson. From the Dallas 30, journeyman Chuck Mercein (Yale, New York Giants, Westchester Bulldogs), trundled past a linebacker who had slipped on the frozen turf and reached the 11 with 1:11 to play. A trap play with Mercein carrying made eight when the ice felled Cowboys' defensive end George Andrie. Donny Anderson moved the ball to the 1 for a first down, but now the treacherous footing victimized the Packers and two thrusts made no more than a foot.

The Packers took their last time out. There were sixteen

seconds to go. Green Bay had two downs but time for only one play.

Later, nobody dared suggest that Lombardi should have ordered a field goal. One didn't question this man. It was not just that he succeeded but that he made success seem inevitable. Before that fateful final play, one might have believed that Dallas would hold one last time. But afterward—after the chink in the line had been exposed and exploited—it all seemed predetermined.

It seemed that Jethro Pugh, a mammoth defense tackle who would narrowly avoid losing some fingers from the frostbite he was incurring this day, was a bit too high in his stance. Guard Jerry Kramer submarined him, and quarterback Starr plunged across the goal line with the winning score.

Another Super Bowl, another romp, and the warrior Lombardi retired in triumph, winner of ninety-nine games, six conference titles, and five championships in nine years at Green Bay. A few years later he was dead from cancer, and amidst the many honors bestowed on him in memoriam, the National Football League named its ultimate prize, the Super Bowl trophy after him. It was a fitting tribute.

After the first Super Bowl, Packers' coach Vince Lombardi had all but stated that the American Football League was inferior to the National Football League. After the second Super Bowl—a 33–14 Green Bay rout of Oakland—it became an article of faith. Then Joe Willie Namath, who was never known for bowing to the conventional wisdom, predicted that the AFL (i.e. his New York Jets) would win Super Bowl III.

It was probably true that the Chiefs and Raiders also had defiantly predicted victory. But this was more than another rash prediction from another brash underdog. Namath was a swinger at a time when the Lombardi ethic of team, religion, and family was the prescribed morality for football players. True, some didn't subscribe to it, but they were the losers. Namath had the effrontery to live a life of lavish self-indulgence and win. He had a white llama rug in his penthouse apartment and he hosted get-togethers and parties. "A get-together," he explained, "is when the guys come over to eat steaks and play cards; a party is when there are girls." There were many girls—all young and beautiful—who came to Namath's parties. Broadway Joe even went so far as to suggest that his sexual adventures helped his play. Few football coaches concurred in that opinion, or dared to say so if they did, but there were at least two notable ones who endorsed Namath without qualification. "The greatest athlete I ever coached," testified his college coach, Bear Bryant. "He's a winner," agreed Weeb Ewbank, his coach on the Jets. "He doesn't know how to lose."

It was all too much for many NFL traditionalists to bear. Yes, he was talented, they conceded, but he threw too many interceptions. He lacked discipline, they insisted. Only an emotionally unstable post-adolescent would feel the need to grow a Fu Manchu moustache, and only a shameless huckster would shave it off on television for thousands of dollars. Joe Namath was an insult to the American success story, and the NFL champion Baltimore Colts would teach him a lesson. And few observers doubted that wouldn't happen.

Even if one didn't subscribe to this Puritanical condemnation of a fellow who was less than the iconoclast he was said to be, it was hard to credit Namath's predictions of victory. The Colts, who had lost only one game, were the class of the NFL. They had destroyed the Cleveland Browns in the championship game 34-0. Their zone pass defense had stymied more potent passing attacks than the Jets'. And their defensive line had proved all but impenetrable. Pro football technicians as well as moralists expected Namath to be humbled in Super Bowl III.

And then came one of pro football's greatest upsets—surely its most glorified. Perhaps Bob Oates of the *Los Angeles Times* best captured the shock of the morning after when he wrote, "Think of the biggest surprise you've ever had. Then forget it. Joe Namath beat the National

256

Football League here [in Miami] Sunday.''

Suddenly, the Namath style was no longer cocky self-indulgence but brilliant innovation. ''He is a new kind of passer,'' wrote Oates, ''the most natural passer you have ever seen. Unlike such classic stylists as Unitas and Norm Van Brocklin, who came to prominence by setting up, stepping forward, and throwing over the top, Namath throws without planting his feet. He retreats into the pocket with his left side turned downfield. Then he wheels, pivoting on either foot, and throws with his body—with his hips and shoulders as well as his arm. Namath looks like a quarterback who can last forever. . . .''

Namath didn't decimate the Colts; he just beat them with a workmanlike precision that gave the lie to those who had contended he was too flighty to succeed against a top-notch NFL defense. He led his team on one eighty-yard touchdown march, and drove it into position for three field goals. He completed seventeen of twenty-eight passes, and he was not intercepted. Meanwhile, the Jets picked off three passes from Baltimore quarterback Earl Morrall, whom Namath had had the audacity to rate as inferior to many AFL passers. By the fourth quarter it was 16–0 Jets, and across the country the self-appointed guardians of goodness, decency, and NFL supremacy were squirming in agony.

Under John Unitas in the last quarter, the Colts managed to score, making the final score a less-lopsided 16–7. But the verdict was indisputable. ''Congratulations to the American Football League,'' said a gallant Joe Namath. And, allowing himself a jab at the writers who had belittled him, he crowed, ''I hope they all eat their pencils and pads.''

A year later the fuss over NFL-AFL parity had subsided and the two leagues officially merged into the American and National Conferences with three old NFL teams—Baltimore, Cleveland, and Pittsburgh—joining the AFC. Pro football settled down for the seventies with six divisions and an elaborate playoff system, all of which quickly made the old AFL-NFL rivalry obsolete. NBC and CBS retained equal shares of the spoils, and ABC, shut out of pro football since the early sixties, made a big splash with Monday night football. There would still be squabbles over home game blackouts and player reserve-clause restrictions, but on the whole pro football, reared by its guardian angel, television, was a quite prosperous, solid citizen in American sports now. The tenth anniversary of the Super Bowl provided the most entertaining show yet. The Steelers and Cowboys exhibited a thrilling display of not only all the fundamentals, expertly executed, but a zesty array of blocked punts, tipped passes, and the other fascinating vagaries of the game. ''Don't ever tell me again that the Super Bowl is dull,'' shouted one defiant fan as the excitement reached a climax. And the television ratings were higher than ever, the highest in the history of the medium, in fact.

9   The Ultimate Big Man

> ''I have never seen
> an eagle with a beard
> but if there is
> in some strange
> corner of the world
> and the Hindu
> belief is true,
> you will return
> and beat your wings
> violently
> over my grave.''
> —To Bill Russell *by Tom Meschery, poet and basketball player*

Not long ago, when they had just escaped the greasy food and the long bus rides of the old Negro Leagues, black men in the major leagues were happy simply to fly first class and get a chance. No more all-

In professional basketball, size is relative. Seven-foot giants are common while six-foot men are regarded as pygmies. In the sixties, two of the best of the giants were Bill Russell of the Boston Celtics, number six, and Wilt Chamberlain of the Los Angeles Lakers, number thirteen. Below, Elaine de Kooning's abstract-impressionist canvas captures the high speed action of the game.

night rides, small crowds, low pay, and fourth-rate hotels. They were content to suffer lesser indignities so as, in the words of Branch Rickey, "not to ruin the chances of others." But as their numbers grew and their accomplishments increased in magnitude, the first faint whispers of dissent were heard.

Blacks began to notice with some resentment that a white athlete could earn fifty thousand dollars in endorsements after a good year, while blacks, at best limited to commercials aimed solely at the black market, made almost nothing. Unsympathetic white Madison Avenue contended that white people had most of the money and would certainly not buy products endorsed by blacks. It was not an altogether convincing explanation.

One winter day the entertainment chairman for a Boston social club called the office of the Boston Celtics, champions of the National Basketball Association. He offered to pay Bob Cousy fifteen hundred dollars to be the guest speaker at his group's annual sports night.

Cousy was unavailable, so the Celtics offered to substitute Bill Russell. After all, Russell had been the league's most valuable player. The entertainment chairman called Russell and offered him five hundred dollars.

"He was messing with the wrong black man," said Russell. "I loved and respected Bob Cousy. In fact, I loved and respected Bob Cousy so much that I would not work for one penny less than he would work for. Cousy saw my logic, but the man from that social club didn't."

It may not be that the revolt of the black athlete began with Bill Russell, but he certainly gave it impetus. It disturbed white America when Jackie Robinson turned out to be a man of temper and independence, not at all the imperturbable character that Branch Rickey had created. Bill Russell, a 6-foot 10-inch seemingly affable giant, with an overpowering smile and a marvelous cackling, crowing laugh, proved almost as disconcerting.

First he denigrated the great American jock dream. He told people that playing basketball was simply a means to an end for him and essentially meaningless in the sweep of history. That was a bit far from the gratitude white America had in mind for a black man who was finally getting his piece of the spoils of big-time sports. The suggestion that the major leagues were of something less than cosmic importance was considered gratuitous when it came from a white athlete. From a black it was nasty impertinence—biting the feeding hand, as it were. America did not like to be reminded that it still expected its athletes, its blacks, and especially its black athletes to nuzzle the palm of its affluence.

Not only did Russell refuse, but he followed up with an active and conspicuous interest in the touchiest racial-political matters. "The basic problem in black America is the destruction of racial pride," he said. "One could say that we've been victims of psychological warfare in the sense that this is a white country and all the emphasis is on being white—whiter than white.

"There was a sense of self-degradation. We believed what the white man told us, that we were inferior. When I look at the struggle of the American black, I can't help but be very proud. With what we've been given to work with—and we've been given damn little—we've done a magnificent job of surviving. We still have a long way to go and we have to believe we can do it. Egotism is important. When somebody asks me if I think I'm a real good basketball player, I tell him, 'Hell, no, I'm a great basketball player.' The black man has to beat his chest as hard as he can beat it."

Somebody once asked Russell to name his all-time NBA team. He ticked off Oscar Robertson, Jerry West, Elgin Baylor, and Bob Pettit, and then, when he paused, his questioner asked, "O.K., who's the center?" Russell stroked his goatee, squealed his laugh, and with no further hesitation answered simply, "Me."

He appreciated himself and his heritage, and he made no bones about it. He grew the goatee at a time when such facial adornment was a bona fide act of militant assertiveness. He considered it merely stylish. He ran on about Africa and the high civilization of his ancestors

before they were sold into slavery. He invested his play-off money in a Liberian rubber plant. And he aimed some of his most pointed activism at his profession. He drew a fine for exposing the fact that the NBA had a gentlemen's agreement to limit the numbers of blacks on a team—a quota system, pure and simple. Once when Russell and several black colleagues were refused service in a coffee shop on Lexington Avenue in New York, he decided that he would not play that evening in the scheduled exhibition. If a man wasn't good enough to be served a soggy egg salad on rye, he reasoned, then he certainly wasn't good enough to play. So Russell didn't.

As the black movement worked a bloodless revolution in the land within a single generation—no more keenly felt than in major league sports—Russell was one of the leaders. To attain that stature it was necessary for him to be almost as good on the basketball court as Jackie Robinson had been on the baseball diamond. But the fact was that Russell was better; he dominated and changed his sport, whereas Robinson merely excelled at his.

Ironically, this remarkable activist, whose mission in life seemed to extend far beyond reordering the exertions of ten men on a hardwood floor, affected the game of basketball more than the institution of basketball or of sports in general. He was one among many of a new breed of black athletes, albeit one of the first and most distinguished. But as a basketball player he was unique.

Well before Russell, the game was dominated by a big man. The first was a 6-foot 10-inch Croatian-Lithuanian center with thick glasses and crude moves (by today's standards), George Mikan. He revived a sport that was struggling to survive. He began the process of reshaping it from a game of workmanlike earnestness to a captivating spectacle of leaping, soaring giants.

"Tireless and amazingly agile for his size," Time magazine reported in 1949, "Mikan kept wearing down fresh men sent in to guard him. He gobbled up rebounds from both backboards, made blind passes on the fast break, fed the ball to his teammates from his pivot slot. Because of such players as George Mikan, pro basketball is gradually taking on a big-league glow."

Into the mid-1950s the sport belonged to Mikan and his Minneapolis Lakers. After the 1953-54 season, in which they won a third straight title, Mikan retired, only to play again in 1955-56, a shadow of his former self. Into this void moved Dolph Schayes and the Syracuse Nationals, then Paul Arizin and the Philadelphia Warriors, and, finally and most definitively, Bill Russell and the Boston Celtics, one of sport's most amazing dynasties.

The seeds were planted in 1950, six years before Russell's arrival, when owner Walter Brown hired Arnold (Red) Auerbach to coach the Celtics. Immediately, the new coach felt pressured by the Boston fans to draft Bob Cousy, a consensus All-America at Holy Cross of Worcester, Massachusetts, and as such a hero in Boston. Auerbach snarled at Brown, "Am I supposed to win or am I supposed to draft local yokels?"

Brown agreed with his coach. The flashy Cousy, who passed behind his back while on the run, dribbled between his legs, and left fans (and sometimes teammates) gaping almost stupidly at his ball handling, seemed more like a stuntman than a solid pro prospect. Only through the vagaries of the draft did the Celtics end up with the hometown hotshot, and they weren't happy about it. Brown turned a Celtic green. "I thought I'd got stung," he said. "I'd had a bellyful of hometown heroes."

Of course, the Cooz, as Boston fans called him, proved to be as disciplined as he was innovative, and he quickly became the court general of the Celtics. Cousy directed a crew of Bill Sharman, the quintessential shooter, his partner at guard; Easy Ed Macauley at center; musclemen forwards Jim Loscutoff and Bob Brannum, and Frank Ramsey, the first of the NBA's great "sixth men," those supersubs whose warmups consisted of sitting on the bench. This team was mightily entertaining, pouring in points consistently enough to win six consecutive NBA scoring titles. But Boston always finished second or third in the Eastern Division and couldn't survive the playoffs.

What the Celts had in offense they lacked in defense and on the backboards. Until Bill Russell.

A late bloomer, Russell had failed to make his high school team as a sophomore. As a senior he never scored more than fourteen points in a game (he wouldn't score much in college or the pros either), but an assistant coach at the University of San Francisco who spotted him liked his aggressiveness and the school offered him a scholarship. In Russell's own estimation he was far too scared and immature to make good, but he progressed astonishingly in his freshman year. When he moved to the varsity he taught himself how to play defense and became the leader of a team that won an unprecedented fifty-five straight games and two national championships. After playing on the United States Olympic team in 1956, Russell was drafted by the St. Louis Hawks, who traded him to Boston for Ed Macauley and Cliff Hagen.

In Boston the skinny center joined Loscutoff, Sharman, Cousy, and another rookie, Tom (Ack-Ack) Heinsohn, on the starting five, and the Celtics immediately won the championship.

Boston briefly lost its touch in the 1957-58 playoffs, losing to Bob Pettit and the St. Louis Hawks after Russell hurt his ankle in the third game of the final round. But the Celtics then reeled off an incredible eight straight NBA championships, and ten of eleven, the last two with Russell as coach and Auerbach as general manager.

These were the Celtics who would sweep down the court in an irresistible green wave, not so much led as unleashed by the spindly giant. He would soar for a rebound, turn in the air, and flick the outlet pass to Cousy or Sam Jones. Then, while the big man loped down court (only once in awhile would he bring the ball down himself, in a high, wild, almost uncontrolled dribble), the attention would shift to droopy-eyed "Sad Sam" Jones, stopping in full flight to toss in a soft bank shot. Or to John Havlicek, splashing to the bucket on a drive. Or to Heinsohn, whipping in his outrageous hook from the corner. Or to Don Nelson, pounding the offensive boards in the

Attendance at horse tracks around the nation swelled in the fifties, sixties, and seventies. Beautiful surroundings, improved racing conditions, and innovations such as the exactas attracted the people. So did the horses, and millions cheered and millions were bet as great thoroughbreds such as Swaps, Nashua, Bold Ruler, Kelso, and Secretariat sustained the racing traditions of the nation.

unlikely event that his teammates missed the mark. They didn't display Russell then. Oh, occasionally he'd hit that awkward, tentative, definitively lefthanded jumper or hook. But for the most part he stood in the low post, setting picks for the Celts who were whizzing about him, passing off when the ball came his way. He was the seemingly motionless hub of a spinning wheel.

It was on defense that the hub began to sparkle. Then the Celtics seemed to radiate from him like so many spokes, four more to add to the two that were his arms. Those spidery limbs seemed to reach to the foul line from his command post under the basket. And when a driver steered injudiciously into the key, there they were, warding him off. Or better yet the eagle casually kept to his perch, seemingly uninterested in the prey around him, then swooped in for the kill on a vulnerable shot.

Russell enjoyed his greatest successes against the other great big man of the day, of all-time, Wilt Chamberlain. Eventually, in their later years as players and in retirement, the differences in their style seemed to blur and the adversaries began to be regarded as they always should have been—simply the two greatest big men in the history of the game. But when they competed against one another, their every difference was scrutinized for its place in the great Chamberlain versus Russell debate. Who was better, basketball fans asked endlessly, the man who once scored 100 points in a game but who played on only two championship teams (and those when he concentrated more on defense and rebounding), or the man who averaged in the teens but was a perennial winner? The answer seems obvious enough now, when fans recognize that the essence of this high-scoring game is, paradoxically enough, defense every bit as much as it is pouring the ball through the hoop. But in the high-flying years of the sixties, when the craze for bigger men and more points was just peaking, Chamberlain had his adherents. They failed to realize that when the two giants did battle one had enlisted an army of support troops whereas the other towered vulnerably alone.

And so game after game, season after season, the Celtics mastered pro ball. The portly Auerbach would savor, not to say gloat over, his victory cigar, and the giant black man would hunch beside him on the bench, observing the slack finish of yet another Boston romp. Not that the go-go Celtics ran away with all their titles. But the sheer profusion of them made each new triumph seem inevitable.

The 1961-62 season was typical. The playoff finals between the Celtics and Lakers went as far as it could— to the seventh game. The seventh game went as far as *it* could—to the last seconds with the score tied 100–100. The Lakers had the ball. But the Celtics held, and won in overtime, after Lakers' guard Frank Selvy's jump shot in the final seconds of regulation time hit the rim, tantalizingly, and fell away. No doubt the eagle was glaring at it.

10   No Longer Separate, Almost Equal

The role of women in sports has reflected the status of women in society. Even in the 1970s, with vast and accelerated improvements underway, professional women athletes are still traveling second class—compared to men—in terms of money, press coverage, fan interest, sponsorship, working conditions, and the attention and concern of the owners and underwriters of commercial sport.

Professional tennis and golf are the only games at which women can earn a living wage, and the best most of them can do is about one quarter the income of the best males. Women skiers can convert Olympic triumphs into endorsement money, and figure skaters usually can do well as ice-show entertainers. There are one or two fairly successful female jockeys, some professional women bowlers, and perhaps there may one day be major league women baseball players, if any of the young girls now playing Little League can average .300 and hit

the curve. Otherwise, in the sports open to women, there is no job market for track and field athletes, speed skaters, gymnasts, fencers, canoeists, swimmers and divers, and equestriennes, although, in truth, there is virtually nothing here for men, either.

No one argues that women should or can play pro football or hockey. But there would seem to be no reason why noncontact sports now exclusively male preserves could not be played by women if they were introduced to them, like boys, at an early age and were as patiently coached.

The Russians are making this point across the board, as Americans captivated by the lissome gymnastics of Olga Korbut—if not the shot-putting of Tamara Press— can see. American, Australian, and Japanese swimming coaches know that phenomenal performances can be elicited from teen-age girl water sprites. And skiing is an almost completely unisex sport. A Jean-Claude Killy can make more money than a Rosie Mittermaier, but essentially skiing is without social or athletic distinctions. Its comparatively recent development (since the mid-thirties) has meant that there was no tradition of male dominance. Women have had parity from the beginning, and as a result skiing has become, even more than golf and tennis, the sport that men and women can enjoy as equals. Helmeted, goggled, and otherwise accoutered in standard gear, women are indistinguishable from men on the slopes.

Figure skating, on the other hand, although a rigorous athletic skill, perpetuates and accentuates sexual differences. A certain amount of the acclaim for Sonja Henie, Barbara Ann Scott, Peggy Fleming, and Dorothy Hamill has been rooted in their feminine grace and charm.

It was an exaggerated notion of femininity, of course, that relegated women to a fatuous role athletically throughout the later Victorian era, when organized sports got their first big push, and even quite far into the twentieth century. (It was not until the Amsterdam Olympics of 1928 that women were permitted to compete in track

Since the twenties, when Helen Wills became the champion of women's tennis, America has seen a succession of talented women athletes. But it was not until the seventies, when women's liberation opened new vistas for the female athlete, that women began to dramatically assert themselves. Their leader was tennis champion Billie Jean King, who assaulted the barriers of sports' masculine domination with skill, talent, and personality.

and field events.) It was considered immodest and inappropriate for refined, well-bred women to indulge in violent exercise, to grunt and strain and sweat and extend themselves, as any healthful exercise requires—and certainly not in competition. These strictures did not apply to the lower orders of society, but then it was not expected that such women would have time to spare from a life of toil to engage in athletics.

For confirmation all one has to do is look at period photographs or art: genre scenes of ladies in ankle-length skirts and big hats playing pat-ball tennis, or trying to swat a golf ball while encased in corsets and stays.

Perhaps the first significant dent in this suffocating athletic confinement was made by Eleanora Sears, a wealthy, well-born, ebullient young Bostonian who liked sports and didn't give a hoot for anyone's opinion of her enthusiasms. She was born in the 1880s, a time when archery, croquet, lawn tennis, and, for the womenfolk of country squires, the hunt were about the only sports available to women. She nonetheless saw no reason not to play any game she wished, or to play it less than well. She promptly began to burn up the tennis courts of Boston. Her ground strokes had power, she moved with zip, and she covered the whole court scrambling for retrieves. She appalled everyone.

Nonsense, she said, and plunged into swimming, sailing, and canoeing. She was a fine shot with a rifle and a superb, hell-for-leather horsewoman. As fast automobiles and motorboats became the rage, she drove them. And she mastered golf, although she never competed for a title. In her forties she took up long-distance walking. In her fifties she won a singles championship at squash. By her splendid example she helped establish the image of the active sportswoman as a wholesome and respectable one.

But still a genteel one. Except for Suzanne Lenglen's brief tour as a tennis pro in the twenties, women's sports were almost exclusively for well-to-do amateurs until after World War II. On high school and collegiate levels

across the United States, athletic programs for women were boringly unimaginative and severely limited. There was some tennis (where there were courts), some swimming and diving (where there were pools), some perverted and abysmally inactive basketball, a touch of volleyball, a good deal of calisthenics, and a certain amount of field hockey performed in bloomers and middie blouses. It's a wonder American women grew up with any muscle tone at all.

Tennis was the first sport at which women excelled, and while its enthusiasts did not—and still do not—consider them important, they were competing in singles, doubles, and mixed doubles at most big tournaments well before World War I. There was, fortunately, a nucleus of strong players to give the game panache: May Sutton Bundy; Hazel Hotchkiss, who, as Mrs. George Wightman, donated the cup for international women's play; Mary K. Browne, beneficent doubles partner of the youthful Tilden; Elizabeth Ryan, a doubles winner at Wimbledon a record twelve times, and Molla Bjurstedt Mallory, eight times U.S. singles champion and the best American woman player before Helen Wills. In their pleated skirts, white stockings, and long sleeves, they played a steady baseline game and prepared the way for Wills and Lenglen.

Tennis was already embroiled in the pernicious business of paying its amateurs under the table. By hypocritically ignoring its own ethical standards while rewarding its better players handsomely, tennis managed to delay for many years discussion and establishment of an appropriate and equitable pay scale for men as well as women.

Meanwhile, however, there was no lack of first-rate American women players: Helen Hull Jacobs, who succeeded Helen Wills Moody Roark, Alice Marble, Pauline Betz, Margaret Osborne du Pont, Althea Gibson, in the late fifties the first black woman to win U.S. and Wimbledon singles championships; Darlene Hard, and, most significantly, Billie Jean Moffitt King.

Ms. King has been significant because she was willing,

In the second half of the twentieth century, American sport came full circle. Spectator games continued to attract wide audiences, but even larger numbers of people sought the joy of individual sport. Camping, sailing, hang gliding, cycling, skiing, jogging—all enjoyed tremendous popularity as people found new ways to fill their leisure hours.
Sport had gone back to the basics. There still was sport for the spectator, but now there also was sport for the participant.

in the years of her supremacy, to stick her neck out and exert leadership in an unpopular fight for better wages, hours, and working conditions for women players. She did not do it all herself, but as the champ she used her own considerable clout to get larger purses, a better-organized tour, better press coverage, and, incidentally, to beat the pants off the old male chauvinist, hustling Bobby Riggs. All women's tennis, professional and amateur, has gained thereby.

Women's pro golf has also made good progress, although it took many more years to get where it is, with a circuit of thirty-four tournaments and prizes totaling $2.5 million, aside from television specials and other extras.

There were women professionals but no interest in the professional game until the extraordinary Mildred Didrikson Zaharias took over in 1947 and made it her own—exciting, fun, and completely big league.

Babe Didrikson, in her short, brilliant, and often unhappy life, made all the points there are to be made about women and sports. She burst on the scene in the Depression days of 1932, coming out of nowhere—Port Arthur, Texas—to win five events at the National AAU championships, tie for first in a sixth, and finish fourth in a seventh. She was a lanky, long-muscled youngster of nineteen with a lantern jaw, a twangy voice, and a natural aptitude for the labors of track and field. She was a sprinter over several distances, two kinds of hurdler, a high jumper, and a javelin thrower who launched her missile like an arrow, seldom more than ten feet off the ground but for prodigious distances.

She was enjoyed for her talents, her good humor, and back-country candor, but also derogated as the typically androgynous female track star. This is the ugliest of the stereotypes with which women athletes have had to contend. It is a vestige of the etiquette that required women to be ladies first and athletes incidentally, and an active, full-flowering snobbism that finds running, jumping women vulgar, declassé, and—snickering—not quite *women*.

Interestingly, of course, it often has been the strong, middle- or lower-class girls, often the children of immigrants, who find track and field one of the few outlets available for their physical vitality. And since they have brought no particular social graces to their specialties, they have been easy victims of the condescensions of their social betters.

Most of America came to acquire an affectionate regard for Babe as a woman, as well as for the transcendent athlete she was, and by the time of her death from cancer at forty-three, the talk had dwindled to a mutter and the stereotype had disappeared as much as such things ever do.

Babe went from the AAU meet to the Los Angeles Olympics, amazed everyone there, later unofficially broke every track and field record for women in the book, and then decided to see what else she could do. Her legend grew phenomenally, yet it seems certain that she could swim, dive, ride a horse, shoot a gun, heave a baseball, and pop the five-ball in a side pocket with skill and accuracy, if not with style.

In 1934 she took up golf, won everything in sight as an amateur (it was at this time that her most bitter encounters with country-club discrimination and hostility occurred), and in 1947 turned pro. The circuit was pretty primitive in those days, but the Babe was a joy to watch and they came to see her. She won thirty-three tournaments, including three U.S. Opens, made a pile of money, and to her own intense pleasure learned to use a bit of makeup on her lean and lively face and to wear a stylish dress. The women pros of the seventies have won greater recognition and undoubtedly are better golfers, but they have much to thank Babe for.

The woman athlete is no longer unusual, no longer a freak, and she plays her games with greater knowledge, grace, and skill than perhaps any of her predecessors. If she has yet a distance to go in gaining public acceptance and a commensurate reward, the way is at least and at last open to her.

John Wooden is honored in the basketball Hall of Fame as both player and coach, the only individual so distinguished. As a guard at Purdue, he was an All America three times. As the coach at UCLA, his teams won seven consecutive NCAA titles and ten in twelve years. Family, religion, self discipline, and team purpose over individual gain were the tenets of his coaching philosophy. In basketball's volatile arena, Wooden reigned in unwavering style.

11 The College Game

By almost anyone's measure, it was the most amazing streak in sports history, greater even than those of the New York Yankees and the Boston Celtics. Not only did John Wooden's UCLA Bruins win ten national collegiate basketball championships, seven of them in a row, they did it without losing a game in tournament play. The Yankees and the Celtics could be champions of the world by winning four of seven games. One loss in NCAA basketball tourney play and you were on your way home from Provo, Utah, or Albuquerque, New Mexico, or College Park, Maryland, to wait for next year.

Great players came and went at UCLA: the intimidating centers—Lew Alcindor (now Kareem Abdul-Jabbar) and Bill Walton; the slick and powerful forwards—Sidney Wicks, Curtis Rowe, Keith Wilkes, and Dave Meyers; the quick and crafty guards—Walt Hazzard (now Mahdi Abdul-Rahman), Gail Goodrich, Mike Warren, Lucius Allen, and Henry Bibby. But one constant remained: John Robert Wooden, who taught like a professor and coached like a dictator.

Despite a blandly diplomatic public image, Wooden was a fiery man. His enormous self-pride, much like Vince Lombardi's, drove him to greatness. "There's no way you can have consistent success without players," he said. "No one can win without material. But not everyone can win with material. For the most part, we've done what we were supposed to do." It was a clinical but deadly accurate description of a perfectionist's passion—to make the probable all but unavoidable.

The huge success was a long time coming. Wooden, an All-America guard at Purdue in the 1930s, came to UCLA from Indiana State in 1948. Most of his teams were good ones; none was great, until 1964. That was "the Year of the Gnats."

Wooden's shrimpy, crew cut kids—Hazzard, Goodrich, Jack Hirsch, Fred Slaughter, Keith Erickson, Kenny Washington, Doug McIntosh—ran, pressed, and harassed their way to the Bruins' first national championship. Thereafter, Wooden won with little teams, with intermediate teams, with gigantic teams. He won with overwhelming players and average players.

He won through a decade of campus protest and social change that many coaches couldn't even survive. A few players quit his team, challenging his methods on and off the court. Wooden bent a little but no more. And on the court the Bruins embraced his system; they were his apostles of order and cohesiveness.

"My teams have to play *my* way," he said. "They can't be individuals. Eventually, they learn when they can shoot, when they can dribble, and when they can't. I'm not blowing my own horn when I say this, but I think my teams, for the most part, play closer to their level of potential than most teams. I don't generally want teams of heights and depths. I want consistency."

In a free-flowing game, which forever tempts a player and a team to abandon the straight and narrow, Wooden's players and teams were examples of discipline and order. They controlled a game so completely that they seemed to make the clock tick. On offense no wild fast breaks, those perilous flings that produce turnovers as often as crip lay-ups. On defense no audacious steals, but no free shots either. Precise, organized, poised. As the man said, consistent. Most championship teams glitter; Wooden's glowed.

Wooden's greatest competitor and rival was Kentucky's "Baron of the Bluegrass," Adolph Rupp, who coached such players as Ralph Beard, Alex Groza, Bill Spivey, Cliff Hagen, Lou Tsioropoulos, Frank Ramsey, Johnny Cox, Cotton Nash, Louie Dampier, and Dan Issel. Rupp's teams won four national championships and just missed a fifth. Like Wooden, Rupp was a dictator, but he flaunted it. He ordered strict silence on the practice court. "Why should boys constantly chatter in a class in basketball," he asked, "any more than they do in a class in English? Why should they whistle and sing? If you let 'em talk and

The colorful spectacle of college football grips the nation each autumn and is culminated on January 1 when the important bowl games are played. The college mystique includes pep rallies, card stunts, marching bands, All-America teams, Heisman trophy candidates, and arguments about who's number one. Once in an infrequent while a truly spectacular collegian captures the attention of sports fans. O. J. Simpson of USC (and later the Buffalo Bills) was one of those men.

wisecrack around, they don't concentrate. I tell the boys if they want to talk we've got a student union for visiting purposes. And if they want to whistle, there's a music academy."

Nobody had the stranglehold on college football in the Electronic Age that Wooden and Rupp had on college basketball. Rather, football on America's campuses was a mélange of coaches and formations—Wilkinson, Bryant, Parseghian, McKay, Hayes, Royal, the single wing, the straight T, the wing T, the split T, the wishbone T, the veer T, the I, the pro set, the full house.

Bud Wilkinson's Oklahoma teams dominated the 1950s. From 1953 to 1957, they won forty-seven straight games, a record. And from 1948 through 1957, they lost only seven games, perhaps an equally impressive achievement.

Soft-spoken and personable, Wilkinson enjoyed the game as he mastered it, and his players enjoyed him. "I always wanted to win," he said, "but I wanted to have fun, too. Once my players saw that winning was the most fun of all, they worked hard at it. I didn't drive them; I didn't have to. You can motivate players better with kind words than you can with a whip."

Wilkinson's teams overwhelmed an opponent with speed and quickness rather than brute force, employing a split-T formation that Wilkinson had learned from Missouri coach Don Faurot. Wilkinson had fresh personnel in the game at all times, so the hit-and-run Sooners were a tireless, perpetual motion machine.

After Notre Dame beat Oklahoma 7-0, the Sooners' first loss in 48 games (and first shutout in 123), Wilkinson explained, "Well, we couldn't have gone on winning forever." The rest of college football had been starting to wonder.

The 1960s and the first half of the 1970s belonged mostly to six coaches—Paul (Bear) Bryant of Alabama, John McKay of USC, Ara Parseghian of Notre Dame, Darrell Royal of Texas, Woody Hayes of Ohio State, and Bob Devaney of Nebraska. The Notre Dame-USC series

grew to be the most interesting in the sport, the Hayes-McKay battles in the Rose Bowl a close second. But the most exciting game—both for its perfection and its imperfection—may have been the final game of 1973, Notre Dame and Parseghian versus Alabama and Bryant, in the Sugar Bowl. A national championship was at stake; both teams were unbeaten and untied. There were eighty-five thousand people in the stands and an estimated forty-five million watching on home television.

The lead changed hands seven times. Notre Dame went ahead 24-23 on Bob Thomas's fourth-quarter field goal. But Alabama still had time for one last miracle. It failed to move, but a sixty-nine yard Crimson Tide punt pinned Notre Dame near its own goal line. Suddenly, it was third down and eight yards to go for the Irish from their 2-yard line.

Everybody assumed that Parseghian would order his team to stay on the ground for one more play, then punt. This was the coach who in 1966 had passed up a chance to beat Michigan State, opting for a thoroughly anticlimactic 10-10 tie because it preserved Notre Dame's number-one ranking. But this time Parseghian lived dangerously. Notre Dame quarterback Tom Clements faded back into the end zone to pass and found Robin Weber on a thirty-five yard pass, clinching the win. Somebody in the stand unfurled a banner that read, "God Made Notre Dame No. 1."

Being number one, something of an obsession in all sports throughout the Electronic Age, applied both to college football's teams and its players. The footballers had to rely on the concurrence of wire service polls for determining the top team in the nation. But the choice of the most valuable player was entrusted quite definitely, if arbitrarily, to the New York Athletic Club in New York, which awarded its Heisman trophy to the player it considered the game's top star of the year. Unlike college basketball, which chose its top team with an end-of-season playoff, football seemed to favor the Oscar award approach.

Ohio State's Archie Griffin, a modest little man with amazing strength, won two Heisman trophies. No one else did that. But probably the most memorable number one of the generation was O. J. Simpson, the Trojan horse of USC. Operating at tailback in John McKay's I formation in 1967 and 1968, he carried the ball thirty or forty times a game. "Why not?" McKay would ask jauntily. "He doesn't belong to a union. And the ball isn't very heavy, anyway."

Nothing seemed to weigh down Simpson. In mud he was almost as spritely as on solid ground. Perhaps his secret was his running instinct, that indefinable sense that seemed to spirit him away from danger before he really understood it was there. He was supernaturally fast.

Simpson ran USC to a national championship in 1967 and into two Rose Bowls. Against UCLA and its Heisman trophy winning quarterback, Gary Beban, in 1967, he made two remarkable touchdown runs, one of which, a sixty-four yard effort, moved a writer to say, "The thrill of it will live to the last day of the last man alive who saw it."

The face of college football began to change in the mid-1970s. Devaney and Parseghian retired; McKay jumped to a fat pro contract; Royal was finding it harder to beat the world at Texas. Among the titans, only Bryant and Hayes were flourishing, Bryant in that muted, mumbling way of his, Hayes in his full flower of bombast. Hayes's critics called for his retirement. Bryant was in no such danger. His rumpled face and pork-pie hat had almost become Alabama's state symbols. Asked whether he might follow Parseghian into retirement, Bryant seemed to isolate the allure not only of coaching college sports but of college sports themselves when he said, "No, coaching is still fun for me and as long as it is I won't retire. The biggest thing I get out of it is to see a little pine knot [a young football player] get developed and do well and then graduate and do well in the business world. . . ." A pro moves on when he's fading; a col-

legian graduates when he's blooming. In basketball and football particularly, the big-time coaches in the big-time college athletic programs (institutions within institutions) raised marvelous flowers for the pros to pluck and strew along the primrose path of American sport.

12   Pro Tennis: A Net Gain

Tennis in the seventies is the triumph of professionalism. It has proved to be an international, year-around sport capable of sustained tournament play and therefore worthy of investment by promoters, as well as marketable on television and thus a magnet for sponsors' dollars. It has shed its peculiarly corrupt and tortured pretense of amateurism—one of the blatant shams of American sports history—and taken its place with golf, football, baseball, basketball, and hockey.

Like their counterparts in other sports, the tennis pros now have an infinitely wider range of opportunities for play and for earnings beyond the handsome but inevitably limited under-the-table payoffs of the amateur circuit.

The establishment that had controlled tennis almost since its inception, and saddled it with a reputation for snobbism, pettiness, and hypocrisy, fought the assaults of the entrepreneurs on its primacy and privilege. And it managed by the weight of tradition and of its displeasure to stall the takeover. But clearly it was outgunned. Its monopoly could not stand up to the challenge and appeal of personal independence and big money. As departures from the amateur ranks became a stampede, the establishment had to come to terms with "open" tennis—a mingling of amateurs and pros in tournament play—or lose its influence entirely.

The turning points were several, but of major importance was Rod Laver's decision to turn pro in 1963, when the game desperately needed a new superstar gate attraction, and the surprising decision of a Boston bank in 1964 to underwrite a pro tournament at Longwood, Massachu-

setts, which suddenly gave a ground anchor to a small but respectable professional circuit. The viability of the pro game was quickly demonstrated, and by 1967 Wimbledon bowed gracefully and admitted pros to its precincts for the first time. In an entertaining and successful all-pro finals, Laver won from Rosewall. The following year the British Hard Court Championships became the world's first open tournament and the breach was healed. Tennis has never been the same since.

It had all happened in a mere forty years. There had been touring pros since the mid-twenties, and most of the big names of the game—Tilden, Vines, Budge, Perry, Kramer, Gonzales, Trabert, Rosewall, Hoad—had given it a try, hoping to capitalize on Wimbledon, Forest Hills, or Davis Cup victories before time or younger players defeated them. Unfortunately, in those pioneer times, the big payday was a gamble and the road of the professional a hard one. Amateur tennis punished him as a deserter, excluding him rigorously not only from its tournaments and from Davis Cup play, but from its courts. Fred Perry was even forced to resign from tennis clubs to which he had brought honor and glory on the petty grounds that only amateurs could be welcomed as members.

Actually, the best pros became formidable players, as every hot-shot amateur champion who signed up soon learned. For a year or two—or until he sharpened his own skills—the new boy took a humiliating succession of beatings, night after night, in city after city. But since the pros had no one to play but themselves, their matches were regarded as exhibitions and sportswriters paid little attention to them. Only one or two amateurs were lured away each year. New blood was needed, but there was not enough money in the game to support a crowd. As a result, the pros became isolated, never numerous or brilliant enough to grab the headlines, a somewhat tarnished crew of money-grubbing barnstormers, playing wherever they were welcomed and even venturing into such unlikely places as Africa, South America, and Japan. Mean-

while, the golden children of amateur tennis danced in the sunshine of the best tournaments at the best clubs and upheld the honor of their countries in the Davis Cup.

This state of affairs was in effect, as noted, until the sixties. Rod Laver's defection from the great Australian tennis factory was only the latest in a succession that began with Frank Sedgman, but it came at a time when the dominant pro was a fellow Aussie, Ken Rosewall, a marvelous and remarkable player whose color and crowd appeal hovered near zero. Laver was quite the opposite. A small, quiet, freckled, left-handed, hawk-nosed redhead who, for all his modest demeanor, was a tiger on the court, he played superlative tennis and would get better in the years to come. Like most modern players he was a power hitter, a master of accurate, lightning-fast groundstrokes, yet a strategist as canny as he was efficient. Furthermore, in 1963 he was that rare bird, a Grand Slammer, winner the previous year of the world's four top singles championships—Wimbledon, Forest Hills, Australian, and French. If anyone could put the pro game on its feet, he would.

Rod Laver did. He had his ears pinned back for a year or so playing with Rosewall and Lew Hoad, but gradually he came into his own. By the time open tennis was in operation he was the premier professional in the world.

This was saying a lot. There were a large number of extremely good players around, and they had excited the interest of two go-get-'em American promoters. George MacCall founded a National Tennis League designed to play a series of pro tournaments, rather than one-nighters. His purses were reasonable if not huge and he quickly signed up the best pros: Laver, Rosewall, Pancho Gonzales, Fred Stolle, Roy Emerson, as well as four outstanding women, Billie Jean King, Rosemary Casals, Ann Haydon Jones, and Françoise Durr.

At almost the same time, World Championship Tennis entered the field. Bankrolled by the immensely wealthy Dallas oil heir, Lamar Hunt, it made a massive raid on the amateurs, snaring among others Tony Roche, Cliff

273

America's most prestigious tennis courts are located at Forest Hills in Queens, New York. The world's finest tennis players gather there in September to battle for the United States championship.

Drysdale, Dennis Ralston, Nikki Pilić, and the catch of 1967, Wimbledon winner John Newcombe.

This clean sweep of tennis's top seeds—Arthur Ashe was about the only holdout of note—forced the various so-called amateur associations to see the light. It was the better part of wisdom to open their gates and welcome the prodigals, which they did.

There was a bit of unseemly scuffling as the old guard made final, feeble efforts to reassert its power, but it no longer had the horses. Where the players were, there was tennis.

WCT and NTL lost bags of money getting under way. This pleased the amateurs, who hoped the pro ventures would collapse under a load of debt or in a fog bank of apathy as fans were tennised out by the unending matches and tournaments required to pay the freight. It didn't work out that way. Hunt shored up the levee with a few more moneybags and bought out the NTL, thereby placing virtually every player of importance under WCT contract. Meanwhile, fan interest, whetted by a national tennis boom, proved to be keen and undiminished.

WCT cut the NTL women adrift (and the men did not seem sorry to see them go, which caused some hard feelings), but fortune's wheel turned up Virginia Slims, the self-styled feminist cigarette, as a sponsor, and the women's game was assured stability, even as Longwood and the bank had backstopped the men. In the mid-seventies tournaments, prizes, and television coverage were at satisfactorily high levels, and an impressive youngster named Chris Evert was sweeping all before her as the assured successor to the high-spirited Billie Jean King.

For 1971 WCT announced a schedule of twenty tournaments, each presenting a flight of thirty-two top men players competing for $50,000 in prizes. At season's end the top eight would meet in a $100,000 tournament with a $50,000 first prize. The final, played at Dallas in November, saw Rosewall defeat Laver in four sets.

The 1972 championship pitted the same old antagonists

against each other. Laver, now thirty-four, with a second Slam added to his laurels, was still the powerhouse server and attacker at the net. Rosewall, who had been winning big-time tennis titles for twenty of his thirty-seven years, was still the baseline counterpuncher.

Their match, again in Dallas, developed into one of the great confrontations of tennis history. It went five sets, consuming nearly four hours, before Rosewall triumphed. Some twenty-one million people watched on television, and everyone got the message: Pro tennis was here to stay.

A working professional can now play virtually around the calendar: the old amateur circuit with its prestigious international championships, WCT, World Team Tennis (a league of American cities offering men's and women's team competitions), one-on-one knockout specials on television, and even Davis Cup. These days pros are welcome everywhere.

The money is so good that everyone, even a Rosewall in his forties, wants to play forever. But a younger generation is crowding the old boys: Ilie Nastase, Bjorn Borg, Roscoe Tanner, Manuel Orantes, Raul Ramirez, Vitas Gerulaitis, Guillermo Vilas, and Jimmy Connors, who on his best days suggests that he will dominate them all. He can earn more than six hundred thousand dollars in one year while people watch him try.

13   The Greatest

The original Cassius Marcellus Clay, a cousin of Henry Clay and a vehement Southern abolitionist, was once warned that he would be killed if he showed up at Stanford, Kentucky, to address an abolitionist rally. Clay, who was six feet four inches and well over two hundred pounds, strode down the aisle and shouted, "For those who respect the laws of God I have brought a Bible. For those who respect the laws of man I have a copy of the state constitution. For those who believe in neither I have

these." He drew two pistols out and waved them in the air.

William H. Townsend, a lawyer and historian from Lexington, Kentucky, says that Muhammad Ali, nee Cassius Marcellus Clay, is a descendant of this man; he is certainly his spiritual heir. Ali fought with religion, with law, and with his fists, and he won against great odds with all three. He joined the Black Muslims and convinced whites that he was not a racist. He declared himself a conscientious objector to the Vietnam War and beat the government in court when it called him a draft dodger. He proclaimed himself the best boxer in the world, and, even after five years' exile from the ring, he proved it by winning the heavyweight title.

"I am the greatest," he crowed incessantly, and eventually people saw the man behind the loudmouth and began to believe him.

In his early days he was a handsome, bumptious young man whose cheek was silly and appealing. In Rome, at the 1960 Olympics, where he won the gold medal for heavyweights, he told a Russian who needled him about race problems in the United States, "Look here, Rooshin, we got qualified people working on that trouble right this moment." It was said with such light-hearted innocence that one didn't have to be a cold warrior to enjoy it. Perhaps even the Russian laughed. Ali had a genius for the postured, playful confrontation.

It took a little while before the public realized he could be serious. Then, suddenly, the confrontation seemed threatening, when in fact he was just posturing again. Just because he joined a religious group whose leader called white men devils was no reason to believe that he, Ali, had anything personal against them. Or so he tried to explain. "The main focus of the movement is toward self-discipline and self-reliance," he said. "That is something you hear all the time in Sunday lectures at Muslim mosques. They don't talk about white devils and all that sort of thing. That's just to get somebody's attention. You gotta get people inside the doors before

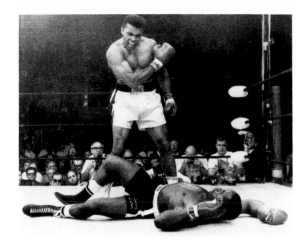

you can preach at them. They talk about moral, material, and cultural advancement. What's wrong with that? Isn't that what a whole lot of white people say we should be doing? Well, that's what the Nation of Islam is trying to do. How can white folks argue with that?"

On the morning Muhammad Ali further confused and infuriated white America by refusing induction into the armed services, he paced back and forth in a Houston apartment he had rented. He pushed four soft-boiled eggs around a plate and drank a glass of orange juice. He sipped a cup of coffee. Then he walked around. The clock was pushing him toward a fateful encounter. His career could easily be ruined. His reputation might be a shambles. He wasn't quite sure what he was doing, yet he seemed to know that it was right. While he walked and talked, a number of newsmen listened.

"I've left the sports pages," he said. "I've gone onto the front pages. I want to know what is right, what'll look good in history. I'm being tested by Allah. I'm giving up the heavyweight title, all my wealth and fame, maybe my future. Many great men have been tested for their religious beliefs. If I pass this test, I'll come out stronger than ever. I've got no jails, no power, no government, but six hundred million Muslims in the world. They'll give me strength."

Posturing? This time he himself didn't seem to know just where the hype ended and reality began. Was he a hero or a fool, he asked himself. "Will they make me a leader of a country? Will they give me gold? Will the Supreme Being knock down the jails with an earthquake, like He could if He wanted to? Am I a fool to give up my wealth and my title and go lay in a prison? Am I a fool to give up good beef steaks for what they feed you in jail? Do you fellas think I'm serious?" Did he? The answer would come quickly.

His lawyer asked him to get moving. If the champion were one minute late, he'd spend the evening in jail. They wouldn't waste an instant with him.

They walked out into the street—the champion, his lawyers, and his entourage. There were two black limousines waiting, both of them chauffeured by white men, a wry touch of humor on Ali's part. He had originally planned to stop at the Americana Hotel, about ten blocks away from the United States Customs House at San Jacinto Street, and walk the rest of the way, picking up followers as he moved. But the champion had been up most of the night, pacing the carpet and shouting at his handler, Bundini Brown. He was so tired that it was decided to drive straight up to the corner in front of the Customs House and emerge in full view of the television cameras.

There were dark, festering clouds above the glass and concrete towers of Houston when the limousines arrived. Perhaps three hundred people had gathered under the portico of a low stucco building across the street. A few dozen more were on the steps of the Customs House. As soon as Ali stuck his head outside, the camera lights went on. Ali pushed through the crowd, smiling and nodding, but making no jokes. The crush was so intense that many people could not get on the elevator, causing the examination schedule to start a half hour late. The other twenty-six potential inductees were carrying canvas overnight bags. Ali carried nothing.

They finally brought everybody together behind closed doors for a physical examination while the press waited outside. "You guys all taking this too hard," said Ali. "You taking this way, way, wa-a-a-ay too hard. I'm gonna tell a few jokes and loosen you guys up."

There it was again. Just when the confrontation seemed unavoidably real, the would-be warrior (and would-be martyr) turned comedian. That was a pose, too, of course. Keeping up with Muhammad Ali was as difficult in life as it was in the ring. He floated like a butterfly and stung like a bee, and his adversaries didn't know when to squash him, when to swat at him, and when just to ignore him.

This time, of course, he was dead serious.

"I didn't want to give up my championship and I sure

Soon after the second Liston fight, Clay disclosed that he had accepted the Islamic faith and had changed his name to Muhammad Ali. Stripped of his title because of his refusal to enter the army, Ali became a special symbol, as shown here by photographer Carl Fischer. In 1968, George Foreman won the heavyweight gold medal at the Mexico City Olympics and in a gesture both to the deposed Ali and to two American trackmen, Tommie Smith and John Carlos, who had made gestures of protest earlier in the Games, waved a small American flag in the ring.

didn't want to go to jail," he said years later when the Supreme Court ruled in his favor. "You had to make people aware that the Muslims were serious about what they was doing. Folks thought we were nothing but a bunch of cranks and nuts. Wasn't true. It was up to me to do something. I knew what was gonna happen to me and I didn't like it. I was undefeated. I was in my prime. I'll never forget that date. It was April 28, 1967. They can put that date on my gravestone."

The exile from the ring was harsh and cruel. One by one, state boxing commissions removed their recognition of Ali as heavyweight boxing champion of the world. He had been undefeated in the ring and unconvicted in the courts. Still, they stripped him of his championship as if he were a criminal.

By the time the Constitution upheld him, he had been away from the ring for five years. That is longer than most champions reign, much less lay off. To regain the championship—no, to reclaim it—he needed more than his stature as a newly prominent civil rights leader, more even than the faith that had sustained him through the exile. He did not have it.

On March 8, 1971, he received the first beating of his life, from Joe Frazier, then the heavyweight champion. He went down in the fifteenth round of the fight, and lost the decision.

This canniest of all teases was at last exposed, or was he? Many chose to see nothing but a silenced loudmouth, though of course he wasn't silent and he certainly wasn't repentant. Others thought they saw a humbled braggart. No, no such simple Christian morality play roles for Muhammad Ali. The vulnerable man defeat was supposed to expose turned out to be—surprise!—almost invulnerable after all.

"All over the world people know who Muhammad Ali is," he said the next morning. "But they don't know Joe Frazier. I am the champion. I should still be champion and I will be recognized as champion again. You'll see. I am *the greatest*. I been saying that right along. This is

just a setback. I am champion. No man is ever gonna beat me twice. You bet everything you got on that. Go home and sell your house and car and bet the money you get on that. A great leader has his followers. When the leader falls, his followers cry. I don't cry, so maybe they won't cry. Oh, I have to rejoice in defeat like I rejoiced in victory so my followers can conquer their defeats, the tragedies every day—the ones they face all the time: someone in your family dies, you lose your job, you lose your house. Those are real defeats and I must show them how they must be handled. Losing a boxing match is tough. I mean, I hate it. But I can't cry. Not Muhammad Ali!"

Three years later Muhammad Ali, then thirty-two, was ready to battle the heavyweight champion of the world, George Foreman, in the city of Kinshasa in the emerging republic of Zaire, formerly the Belgian Congo. Each fighter had received five million dollars because satellites were carrying it everywhere in this, the Electronic Age.

Despite the pale brown tone of his skin, Ali had somehow managed to portray the deep ebony Foreman as an "honorary Belgian." The fact deeply distressed Foreman, a man whose wholly African ancestors had slowly worked their way up the river from Galveston, where Jack Johnson's folks had lived. "I don't know why that half-breed is trying to do that to me," said Foreman. "I'm more black than he ever thought of being."

There were sixty thousand people near the ring and an estimated three hundred eighty million more around the world watching on television. Foreman was late, which upset Ali, a man always anxious to upstage his opponent. He grimaced for a while. Then he stood, eyes closed, offering a prayer to Allah. From that point on it was a classic Ali performance, a flaunting of the fleetness, flamboyance, and the Muslim faith that he predicted would take him to the "most spectacular wonder human eyes have ever witnessed."

Well, not quite. The champ was not a champ that night. (Actually, morning—the bout began at 4 A.M. Zaire time

in order to have it seen in the States in prime time.) He stumbled around the ring like a blind man, and not just because Ali was leading him. With snare drums booming in the background and the crowds shouting, "Ali, bu-ma-ye!" which means, "Ali, kill him!" the match seemed more a ritualistic slaughter. In the ring the executioner was baiting the victim with a vicious stream of insults. The saint had turned sadist.

In the eighth round two jolting lefts to the head and a right cross toppled Foreman. As he fell to his hands and knees, Ali cocked his right hand to fire again. There was no need for it. Foreman made it to his feet, but within a few seconds, he was down and out. Ali was heavyweight champ officially again.

Cold-blooded warrior and warm-hearted minister. The sport kingdom's wise man, its jester, and its king. Muhammad Ali is, on his own bizarre terms, indeed the greatest.

14   Goodbye Babe, Hello Hank

In the twilight of Atlanta Stadium in April, 1974, Henry Aaron found himself confronted by wall-to-wall newspapermen in the Atlanta Braves' dugout. It was not a new experience. He had been the object of attention, if not pure adoration, since he began closing in on Babe Ruth's record of 714 home runs in a career. Cameramen had been after him since the opening of spring training. Newsmen were asking the same questions. The pressure was enormous. It was not unlike 1961, when Roger Maris broke Ruth's single-season record by hitting 61 home runs. A sizable minority of baseball fans perceived in Aaron, as they had in Maris, a threat to the inviolate memory of Ruth. But this time there was an additional sociological factor: Henry Aaron was a black man.

"I thought that people would be pleased that a man of their own times was going to break the record," he said that evening in Atlanta Stadium. "When I tied the

On April 8, 1974, Henry Aaron of the Atlanta Braves hit the seven hundred fifteenth home run of his twenty-one-year major league career. The historic homer came before a national television audience of thirty-five million people and made Aaron the leading home run hitter of all time. The record he broke had belonged to Babe Ruth, and while most of the nation celebrated the event, many people felt that something of their past was being wrenched from them.

record in Cincinnati it only got worse. Folks who used to think I was a fine ball player started calling me 'nigger' just because I was going to push Babe Ruth out of the record book. They didn't think I was worthy.''

Henry Louis Aaron was not a man of flamboyance; he was not an angry man. He was merely the perfect model of consistency. In more than two decades in the major leagues he just kept hitting baseballs over outfield fences. His face was clean and pleasant. Nothing he did in his forty years, not even his home run quest, which now brought him to the brink of baseball immortality, made him more than an easy, decent, comfortable citizen. He was a man who did his best for the Braves in Milwaukee and later Atlanta, and he was paid very well for it.

Aaron began the 1974 season with 713 home runs. There was pressure on the Braves to open the year in Atlanta, but the schedule makers said no and commissioner Bowie Kuhn said he could do nothing. So Aaron tied Ruth's record in Cincinnati. "I wanted to hit the tying home run in Atlanta," he said. "God just saw fit for me to do it someplace else. I'd like to hit the one that puts me ahead in the Braves' home park. I hope it works out that way." And so it did.

At exactly 9:07 P.M. Eastern Standard Time, lefthander Al Downing of the Los Angeles Dodgers threw a fastball over the outside part of the plate, higher than Downing wanted. Aaron unleashed his first swing of the night and the ball sailed off toward the stands in left-centerfield. As he reached first base, he saw Bill Buckner of the Dodgers retreat to the 385-foot sign as if he had a chance to catch the ball. A light mist was drifting across the ball park, and Aaron couldn't see exactly what happened next. No matter; he'd seen it 714 times already. The ball cleared the fence and Tom House, a relief pitcher for Atlanta, caught it in the bullpen.

Later, Aaron made a last attempt to set the record straight: "Ruth held the record for thirty-nine years and I love him for what he did. He was a great player and deserved to hold that record. But now it's mine. I con-

sider myself one of the best players who have ever hit a baseball. I don't think I'm better than Babe Ruth. I think he did some wonderful things and it appears that I have equaled and surpassed at least one of them.

"I don't wish to be compared to him because we are different types of players. I don't think he'd want to be compared to me. There is only one Henry Aaron and he's not Babe Ruth. If Babe Ruth were alive, he'd say that there was only one Babe Ruth and it wasn't Henry Aaron. I think that's fair. You can't say somebody is the best baseball player who ever lived.''

It was all so simple and reasonable. Surely the racists and reactionaries, those self-proclaimed guardians of the sainted memory of Ruth, could see that Aaron and his feat only honored their hero. For those who proposed to screen home-run kings for humility, rectitude, worthiness, it should have been clear that Aaron passed with flying colors (whereas Ruth would have flunked).

So much for initiation rites. When Aaron broke the record it all became a moot point anyway. After all, it was the seven hundred fifteenth homer, not the consensus of tradition-bound fans, that made the man home-run king. Baseball gave its new ruler the traditional inauguration—champagne, more publicity, more money. The President called to congratulate him. A television manufacturer, Magnavox, paid him $250,000 a year for five years to promote its product, making him the first black to earn top dollar in endorsements. The grumbling of the malcontents had been swept away. Then, rather quickly, the fuss subsided. And Henry Aaron went on hitting more home runs.

15   Daytona Beach Madness

T he beach at Daytona, Florida, is broad and flat and stretches for miles. Its ash gray sand is so fine and so tightly packed that a car can be driven on it. This unique characteristic was discovered early in this century by the

More than a sport, automobile racing became a proving ground for innovations in auto design and safety. Qualifying speeds at the Indianapolis 500 approached an average of two hundred miles per hour, testing not only the machines and their various parts, but, most important, the skill and courage of the drivers. Motocross, a European sport, caught on in the United States in the late sixties, when the motorcycle gained new popularity. In many areas, any hill became a challenge and weekends were filled with the loud sounds of racing engines.

first automotive daredevils. It took a long time for the world's roads to catch up with the capabilities of its cars, and the Oldfields, Campbells, Railtons, Segraves, and Stanleys couldn't wait. They found that this swath of sand in bucolic Florida suited their purposes perfectly. Then the speeds increased, and the seemingly smooth surface of the beach became a treacherous washboard. It was soon abandoned by the record setters for the wide expanse of the Bonneville Salt Flats.

Even though the world's land speed record crowd had left, Daytona was still a magnet for men with more conventional cars who wanted to see how fast they could go. Each winter hundreds of them would venture to the beach and race. In 1947, a tall, slow-talking but fast-thinking entrepreneur formed an organization in a Daytona hotel room to further and promote the racing of these "stock" automobiles. He was William Henry Getty France, and the organization he founded was called the National Association for Stock Car Racing (NASCAR).

Its first sanctioned races were held in the South, where there was a long tradition of back-road racing between moonshiners in their souped-up whiskey runners and those hated tax collectors, the "revenooers." Some of the early heroes of stock car racing learned their trade fleeing the law, giving the sport a flavor and mystique (the romantic outlaw always having been a popular figure in American folklore) that it has capitalized on ever since.

Stock car racing grew and prospered, attracting a wide, if regional, following. Special tracks were built to accommodate the cars, replacing many of the dirt ovals that had sprung up at abandoned baseball fields and horse tracks. In 1959, the epitome of these new tracks was opened for racing, France's dream track, the Daytona International Speedway. It was several miles inland from the famous sands of Daytona, which by then were closed to racing. But it preserved and perpetuated the tradition of speed.

The track is shaped roughly like a giant "D." A thirty-four hundred foot long straightaway in the backstretch culminates at both ends in two, giant, sweeping turns. These are banked at such a steep angle (thirty-one degrees) that walking up them is like climbing a hill. On the grandstand side of the course, two short straightaways, with a gradual, less steeply banked turn separating them, complete the course. It is two and a half miles of asphalt laid out in a seemingly simple pattern but cunningly designed for breakneck speed.

The first Daytona 500 was held there in 1959 and won by a man from the tiny hamlet of Leval Cross, North Carolina, Lee Petty. Each year after that, the race grew in stature and more and more people trekked to Florida each February to see it.

In 1976, the biggest crowd yet descended on Daytona Beach. The people filled the little mom-and-pop motels that abound in the city, collecting the overflow from the big new hotels. Those people with tighter budgets—the kids and college students—pitched their tents at campgrounds for miles around. The track's vast infield became a sea of campers and motor homes; they had begun to dribble in a full two weeks before the race. Daytona Beach's bars and restaurants stayed open until the early hours of the morning. Liquor stores laid in great stocks of beer, stacking it by the cubic yard in every available space.

By Sunday, the day of the 500, the assembled masses had already had a week of speed. Every day there was a qualifying race, or an event for other classes of race cars, building toward the 500.

By the time the Race Marshall, Alabama Governor George Wallace, intoned the traditional, "Gentlemen start your engines," there were more than one hundred thirty thousand spectators jamming the stands and the infield. Hard-core fans of Pearson, Allison, Foyt, and others, painted the names of their heroes on their cars and wore T-shirts advertising their loyalties. If an accurate indication of popularity was the yells that greeted the announcements of his name over the public address system, the favorite by a large margin was Richard Petty.

Petty is the son of the man who won the first Daytona 500, and in fifteen years of racing he has won the prestigious race five times himself—an astounding record considering that no other man has won it more than once. Tall (six feet four inches) and rail thin, the thirty-eight year old Petty sported a full beard he had grown for a bicentennial celebration in his home town. Heads turned when he walked through the crowded garage and pit area at the track: "Howdy, Reechard;" "Win another one, King;" "Can I have your autograph?" The attention was polite but constant. And Petty loved it. His movie-star smile split his face constantly as he signed his name with a rococo flourish for anyone who asked. He joked with friends and other drivers, needling himself as readily as others. Although he acted like and is one of the boys (the "good ol' boys," as the cliché goes), his mien is such that it sets him apart. This man is special, and he knows it.

Richard Petty is, if nothing else, the most successful man to compete on the NASCAR circuit. The only other American driver to boast similar success is A. J. Foyt, who races everything from stock cars to midgets. His fame, of course, was established at the Indianapolis 500. Though this race is the richest and most famous in the world, it does not compare with the Daytona 500. Indy stands by itself, whereas Daytona is the capstone of a whole series of races at many tracks all over the country. Daytona is the showcase of a healthy, popular, and profitable league, if you will, for racers, whereas Indy survives by dint of hoary tradition and because it has become part of the fiber of American sports.

Unlike Foyt, Petty races only stock cars. And also unlike the great Texan (who is a driver first and a team member second), Petty sits at the hub of a finely honed family effort. Father Lee manages Petty Enterprises, Inc.; brother Maurice is the crew chief at the track; cousin Dale Inman is the chief mechanic. A dozen relatives, neighbors, and close friends contribute to the team. It is axiomatic in racing that preparation is half the battle. (The driver's skill and luck comprise the other half.) The

Petty conglomerate is one of the best at preparation.

The pace car brought the field around for a warmup lap. When the green flag fell to start the race, forty-two feet mashed their respective throttles to the floor, and the pack roared into the first turn.

This was a long race and Petty chose to hang back, staying in third or fourth place as the race sorted itself into segregated skirmishes among groups of cars. He stayed within striking distance, allowing the rabbits and the impatient ones to overextend their equipment. As he came off the first turn, banking at more than 170, he "drafted" the car in front of him—one of the more spectacular and daring maneuvers of stock car racing. The trick is to get your machine within inches of another and position yourself in the low pressure area that aerodynamics create when a vehicle is traveling at better than three miles a minute. The trailing car is in part towed by the leading one and can therefore run at the same speed with the engine less than fully extended.

The noise from the engine, the wind, and the vibration of highly stressed metal is unnerving, but Petty's concentration shut it out as he and his tow car swung into the next, high-banked turn. Centrifugal force riveted Petty into his seat and forced his car higher and higher up the banking, closer and closer to the unforgiving steel guard rail that rings the track. He controlled his car with minute twitches of the wheel and delicate corrections on the throttle. If he decided to pass, coming off the turn would be the place to do it. He dropped into the short chute in front of the grandstands, and using the power that drafting had enabled him to hold in reserve, he shot past the car he'd been following. Then, it was through the gradual turn at the start-finish line and straight into the banking again.

This was the routine for 200 laps. All the while, he passed slower cars, avoided the inevitable crashes and spilled oil from blown engines, sparred constantly with the leaders, and, above all, paced himself and his car, observing the truism that you can't win if you don't finish.

By lap 180, half the contestants had dropped out and only three were in contention for the checkered flag: Petty, David Pearson, and the 1975 Daytona winner, Benny Parsons. Only inches separated them; they seemed coupled together. The crowd sensed a dramatic finish and, as if on cue, rose to its feet, its roaring crescendo rising above the straining whine of unmuffled engines.

Parsons's engine started to miss and he dropped off the pace; it came down to the King and the Silver Fox, as the graying forty-one-year-old Pearson has been affectionately dubbed. With less than one lap to go, Pearson took a sliver of a lead. As they shot into the final turn before the finish, Petty made his move, a dangerous one: he pulled out to pass while both cars were still in the banking. Petty had just a tiny bit more horsepower and, keeping the car in hand, seemed to have Pearson in jeopardy. But the Silver Fox was not to be dealt with that easily; he stayed hard on the throttle, giving Petty little room.

Then, just as they came into the short chute before the finish line, Petty couldn't hold it anymore. His blue and red Dodge just grazed Pearson's maroon and white Mercury. Both cars instantly lost traction and careened madly into the wall, bending metal and crunching fenders, as they slid and spun wildly for a thousand feet. The crowd went berserk, as if grateful for this disaster that shattered the tension of an unbearably close finish.

Both cars, nearly destroyed, ground slowly to a stop. Neither driver knew exactly where he was or what had happened. But Pearson kept his composure better this day. He asked his crew chief over the intercom radio, "Has Richard crossed the line?" "No," came the hurried answer, and Pearson—who'd kept his engine running—forced his car back into gear and nursed it slowly, maddeningly, over the finish line, finally prevailing in one of the closest finishes in the history of auto racing. Petty, stalled not more than fifty feet from the finish, was forced to wait for his crew to run out and push-start his car. He managed to get it running but it was too late. He salvaged only second.

16   Air-conditioned Unreality

The building rose like a great plastic blister from the flat, depressing plains—its geometric ceiling catching the smothering heat of the Texas sun—an end product of one man's prophecy and another man's colossal drive. Back in 1939, when technology was becoming the new religion of the land, the inventor of air-conditioning, Willis Carrier, said that the day would come when man would live under geodesic domes of transparent material, taking the first step toward a futuristic, totally controlled environment.

Judge Roy Hofheinz was one of the visionaries of the Electronic Age of sport. He understood that the nation was drunk on sport. He was the son of an Alsatian immigrant, a Lutheran lay reader who drove a laundry truck and never made enough money. Roy Hofheinz was a true Texas hustler, a shrewd operator who naturally was attracted to Lyndon B. Johnson, whose campaign for the United States Senate he managed. At twenty-four, Hofheinz was the youngest man ever to be elected county judge. Later he became a highly successful lawyer and the owner of a profitable radio station. He made his fortune out of industrial sludge.

He wanted to be ruler of something, so for thirty-seven million dollars he built a stadium nobody thought could be built. Officially, the place was named the Harris County Domed Stadium, but Hofheinz found the name too prosaic, so he called it the Astrodome and nicknamed it "the Eighth Wonder of the Modern World." In 1965, the first year it opened, Hofheinz ran tours, charging a dollar a head, and made over a million dollars. Behind the palace walls were yards of gold carpet. The board of directors' room was a copy of a chamber at the palace of Versailles, with a raised platform supporting the chair belonging to the chairman of the board of the Houston Sports Assocation. There were gold fixtures in the bathrooms with the ultimate in sitdown comfort—gold velvet

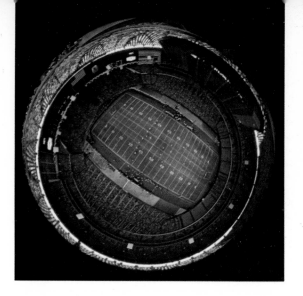

linings on the toilet seats. Oppulence was everywhere.

"Got to impress those fat cats from New York who come down here and expect Texans to act like Texans," Hofheinz said.

"Those Madison Avenue friends of mine think wild Indians are loose whenever they go west of the Jersey Palisades. Why, you know I got twenty-six thousand pounds of art that I bought in the Orient. Bought it all on a six-day tour through Hong Kong, Thailand, and the Middle East. Now I deal in intangibles. And the sooner people see something like this and realize you have some ideas, the easier it is to sell your product. That is what I'm doing, selling baseball and all other sorts of sports as a product. I've got a ten-thousand-dollar-a-day overhead here and to treat sport like sport is to fail to understand the seriousness of your business."

The Astrodome showed technology at its finest, or at least most adaptable. When the glare from the ceiling, with 4,596 lucite panels, made catching a fly ball an impossibility, the ceiling was painted over. With that, the natural grass ceased to grow. So Hofheinz substituted artificial turf—AstroTurf, if you please.

Some people complained about the extravagance of the entire venture, but Hofheinz said the fan was getting better treatment for his tax dollar than he ever dreamed of. He could sit in the bleachers in air-conditioned comfort, paying roughly the same price as he would for an eight-inch board in the blazing sun or biting cold some place else. The customer could park his car for half a dollar and take a tram to the Astrodome door. Naturally, there were advertisements on the tram, but any red-blooded American should be glad to listen to a few commercials in return for a free ride. When the fan reached the stadium, he could spend his beer money in a Bavarian garden beneath the bleachers. Perhaps the prices were a bit high and the food less than delectable, but a ballpark paradise, even one with plastic trees and synthetic leaves, can't have everything.

Or could it? Tired of imitation Bavaria, a patron could visit the Countdown Cafeteria with its uniformed Blastoff Girls, the Trailblazer Restaurant with its full-course meals, the Skydome Club, or the Astrodome Club, all of which were carefully planned to massage away a customer's resistance to spending money. When visitors returned home, they had the feeling of leisure time and money well spent.

"I made a long study of color psychology," said Hofheinz. "I know what crowd psychology means. Everything is colored to please. And the crowd wants to get away as soon as it has had a good time. They want to get back home and talk about how much fun it was. The Astrodome can be cleared in nine minutes. That's the fastest egress in stadium history. You get people in here in a happy mood. You give them sensual pleasure and you color things to make them content. Then you get them home in record time so they can talk about it with their friends."

American sport had become grandiose. Big money, big attendance, big attractions, big television audiences. From 1959 to 1976, $5.3 billion was spent on athletic facilities; nearly every major city constructed either a multipurpose stadium or an arena or both. In Kansas City two stadiums were built, one for baseball and one for football, in the same complex. New Orleans spent over $285 million for a bronze-topped Superdome, complete with a gigantic screen to show instant replays. Contractors put an air-supported fiber glass roof over the new football stadium in Pontiac, Michigan. The roof was not a true dome, the contractors explained, but it kept out the snow because the top of the stadium was filled with hot air.

Middle class Americans had achieved the thirty-five hour work week. They were prosperous and itchy. They were on a binge, demanding spectator sport with more flash and glitter than the world had ever known. "The opiate of the American masses," as Stan Isaacs called it, was no longer just the game; it was the arena that made the American sports fantasy complete.

In 1965 in Houston, Texas, the Astrodome—the "eighth wonder of the world"—was introduced by its overseer, Judge Roy Hofheinz. A new concept in multiple-purpose stadium design, the fully enclosed arena kept its audiences comfortable with a continuous seventy-two degree temperature. Nine years later, the city of New Orleans unveiled the ultimate domed stadium. The Louisiana Superdome, large enough to hold more than one Astrodome, was completed at an awesome cost of more than $160 million, raising the inevitable question: was this only the beginning . . . or was it the end?